The Cult of Nothingness

The Cult *of* Nothingness

The Philosophers and the Buddha

BY ROGER-POL DROIT

Translated by

David Streight *and*

Pamela Vohnson

The University of North Carolina Press

CHAPEL HILL AND LONDON

Originally published in French with the title *Le Culte du néant: Les Philosophes et le Bouddha*, © Editions de Seuil, 1997, Librairie du XXè siècle collection dirigée par Maurice Olender.

Manufactured in the United States of America

Designed by Gary Gore
Set in Garamond
by Keystone Typesetting, Inc.

The paper in this book meets the guidelines for permanence and durability of the Committee on Production Guidelines for Book Longevity of the Council on Library Resources.

This book has been published with the support of the French Ministry of Culture, National Center for the Book, and with the assistance of the William Rand Kenan Jr. Fund of the University of North Carolina Press.

Title page illustration courtesy of Zendōji; photograph by Richard M. Jaffe.

Library of Congress Cataloging-in-Publication Data
Droit, Roger-Pol.
   [Culte du néant. English]
   The cult of nothingness : the philosophers and the Buddha / by
Roger-Pol Droit ; translated by David Streight and Pamela Vohnson.
      p. cm.
Translated from French.
"Originally published in French with the title: Le culte du néant :
Les Philosophes et le Bouddha."
Includes bibliographical references and index.
   ISBN 0-8078-2776-2 (cloth : alk. paper)
   ISBN 0-8078-5449-2 (pbk. : alk. paper)
   1. Buddhism—Study and teaching—Europe—History—19th century.
2. Nothing (Philosophy). 3. Buddhism—Doctrines. I. Streight, David.
II. Vohnson, Pamela. III. Title.
BQ709.E85 D7513   2003
181'.043—dc21

2002015689

cloth 07 06 05 04 03   5 4 3 2 1
paper 07 06 05 04 03   5 4 3 2 1

In memory of my mother

Buddhism worships nothingness.
"What a religion!" one might say. Yes,
without a doubt, it is strange;
but it is an established fact.

—Victor Cousin

Contents

Acknowledgments

The present work is but one product of research begun in the 1980s. *L'Oubli de l'Inde* (Forgetting India), in 1989, was a first step in the same process.

My research later continued at CNRS (National Center for Research in Science, in Paris), within the framework of the Center for Research and Documentation on Hegel and Marx (Poitiers), directed by Professor Jean-Louis Vieillard-Baron, to whom I am indebted for the attention and support he has unfailingly given to my work.

Michel Hulin, professor of Indian and comparative philosophy at the University of Paris-IV, the Sorbonne, and director of the thesis project to which this book is directly connected, was better aware than anyone of the tentativeness of my research and the myriad difficulties in its development. As it evolved, he followed it with unfailingly watchful erudition and a friendly patience for which I am most grateful.

André Bareau, professor at the Collège de France, a great specialist in Buddhist studies, both followed and greatly encouraged the first steps in my work, with the extreme and sincere amiability so characteristic of him. He is no longer with us, and I am moved by just this mention of him.

I am likewise indebted for the comments and suggestions that have been offered from time to time by philosophers Guy Bugault, Pierre Hadot, Michel Henry, Lakshmi Kapani, Jean Pépin, and Francis Zimmerman.

My thanks also to those who, throughout the years, have invited me to present pieces of this research in their colloquia or seminars. Here, I refer especially to Fernando Gil of the Gabinete de Filosofia do Conhencimento in Lisbon, who invited me to speak at the Biblioteca Nacional of Portugal; to Ulrich Johannes Schneider, of the Institute of Philosophy at the Technical University of Berlin, who included me as a participant in a meeting at the Herzog August Bibliothek in Worfenbütteol; to Tony Andréani and the UER of philosophy of Paris-X, who invited me to the "Philosophical Encounters of Nanterre"; to Monique Morazé and the Association France–

xii Union Indienne, who were so kind as to invite me to the Maison des Sciences de l'Homme; and to Jean-Marie Paul and the Department of Germanic and Scandinavian Studies at the University of Nancy-II. I also extend my gratitude to the Associazione Italiana di Sociologia and the Istituto Gramsci in Bologna, to the University of Paris-VIII, to Jacques Poulain, and to the research group on "European Philosophical Identity" for the warm welcomes they have given me, and to the philosophy departments of the universities of Bombay, New Delhi, and Benares, and the Institute of Tibetology in Gangtok (Sikkim).

My gratitude goes especially to the researchers who have invited me to share time in reflection with them regarding common concerns. In this regard I refer specifically to Christine Maillard, who leads the research group "Images de l'étranger" in the Department of German Studies at the University of Strasbourg; to Michel Hulin and Denise Leduc-Fayette, of the philosophy department at the University of Paris-IV, for the research meeting focusing on nineteenth-century philosophers and India; to Pierre-François Moreau and his seminar at the École Normale Supérieure in Fontenay; and to my friend Maurice Olender and his seminar at the École des hautes études en sciences sociales.

At one moment or another in its development, this book was similarly enriched by the cordial conversations I had with Henri Atlan, Catherine Clément, Dominique-Antoine Grisoni, Roland Jacard, Béla Kohn-Atlan, Danielle Nees, François Rachline, and Patrice Vermeren.

I also extend my sincere thanks, for their assistance and their great patience, to Chantal Duhuy and the librarians at the Institut de Civilisation Indienne at the Collège de France, at the Asiatic Society, and at Centre Sèvres.

I am also indebted to Murielle Ohnona-Weizmann, who was of priceless assistance during the final preparation of the text, when she checked a number of references with both speed and precision.

This book would undoubtedly not have come into existence without Yvette Gogue, who was so kind as to take a great part of the responsibility for typing successive versions of the manuscript. Her efficient and faithful collaboration and her numerous suggestions have been decisive, and I am thus most grateful.

And finally, my thanks to the "shepherdesses" for their tenderness and, of course, for more than can be expressed, to N.F.

The Cult of Nothingness

Introduction

The Meaning of a Mistake

The true discovery of Buddhism is a quite recent event in Western history. At a time when the Orientalists were just beginning to translate texts and piece together doctrines, philosophers thought they understood who the Buddha was. This destroyer, in their eyes, denied existence and recommended annihilation. Why return to this error of antiquity?

Orientalist: a man who is well traveled.

—Flaubert, *Dictionnaire des idées reçues*, 1913

L et us say it straight out: Buddhism is not a religion that worships nothingness.

To our Western eyes, Buddhism does not appear—no longer appears, today—to entail either a desire for annihilation or a fascination for destruction. Quite the contrary: we are sensitive to its gentleness, to its compassion toward all forms of life, to its tolerance, to its nonviolence.

At present, Buddhism is first and foremost, for us, a kind of therapy. It cures suffering; it has nothing to do with annihilation. More than a religion or a philosophy, it is a combination of medicine and spiritual teaching. The treatment it recommends leads to a kind of deliverance that is very different from the salvation promised by other religions. It is possible to describe the ultimate goal of the Buddhist path with words like serenity, beatitude, calmness, or felicity, but this would be misleading: the terms used to describe

2   such a "beyond" are still being borrowed from our "here." All that one can really say about nirvana, after all, is this: when you reach it, suffering has forever ceased. On the other hand, none of the words used really fits: the opposition of beyond and here does not really pertain, nor does one *enter* nirvana as one would a place or a period in time. . . . Nirvana is the healing of all those torments that are caused by desire. There is no need to make a distinction, as the Western philosophical tradition has done, between desires of the flesh, on the one hand, which arouse passions that lead us astray, and desires of thought, on the other hand, which help construct conceptual systems like metaphysics and the sciences.

Buddhism thus appears to be both therapeutic and pragmatic: everything in it is subordinate to the cessation of suffering. If the exercise of metaphysics contributed to this cessation, it would be recommended. But such exercise is useless. Thus, it is detrimental. It is not bad absolutely (the idea of absolute evil has no place in Buddhism); it is just bad relatively. In a text from the Pali Canon,[1] the Buddha lists those cases where he remains silent and those where he speaks, as a function of combinations of what is true, what is pleasant, and what is useful. What is false, or useless, or disagreeable, he does not say. Nor does he say what is true and agreeable, but useless. On the other hand, he does speak, at the opportune time, about what is true and useful, whether it is pleasant or not for his listener. What is important here is not that truth takes precedence over pleasure, as is the case for Socrates, but that utility takes precedence even over truth—the sign of a pragmatic stance.

This explicit eschewing of metaphysical speculation undoubtedly does have some limited function in time: only the very earliest form of Buddhism held effectively to it. The scholastic treatises in Pali quite quickly developed analyses that are among the subtlest ever produced by the human intellect, and such was the case even moreso in the Mahayana schools of logic. Nevertheless, such refinements in abstraction have the specific characteristic of doing nothing for building a system or constructing affirmative propositions. Suspending metaphysics altogether remains their primary motivation, even if this task requires indefinitely prolonged labor that must forever be recommenced. The taste of pure theory can never entirely take the place of the ultimate goal, which continues to be deliverance.

Turtle Fur and Detachment

To stick to what is essential, it is perhaps enough to say, in the words ascribed to the Buddha, that deliverance is cessation. It is the result of the extinction of "thirst," that is, of desire, which itself is brought into being by ignorance. Because one does not know, one attaches, waits, hopes, fears. Thus, one suffers. If one were capable of seeing things as they truly are—disconnected, composed, conditioned, impermanent, devoid of their own nature—wanting would cease, and suffering with it. This grasp of reality "as it is" is not knowledge that results solely from theoretical constructs. Clear and discriminate vision is not obtained only via means that are purely intellectual. In general, it is not reached by the process of reason at all. Without excluding rational discernment, Buddhist deliverance remains inseparable from asceticism, from gradual and continuous training in detachment. Wisdom (*prajna*) and intellectual activity are not disconnected from meditation and recollection (*dhyana*).

Things such as they really are, if we could manage to see them, would turn out not to be things, and simply not to be. They have no continuity in themselves; they have no identity, no permanence, no stable nature. Buddhist doctors have attempted to brush aside (rather than to deny) any existence of a fixed, permanent, and organizing principle, in both objects and individuals. Nothing—neither "subject" nor "object"—has a "self." Everything is devoid of its own nature. The Buddhist universe is an ordered succession of disconnected and instantaneous phenomena that have neither support nor basis, that are in perpetual appearance and disappearance. The crudeness of our senses, the illusions brought on by our desire, and those aroused by our language, make us believe in the existence of objects and in our own being. In this sense, there is no thought that is more antisubstantialist, nor any system that is more analytically dissolutionist, than Buddhism. Atman (the soul, or the Self) is a word that has no referent. There is no question that can be asked about it that has an answer other than silence, for there is, in fact, no question. For example, asking if the soul is mortal or immortal, to the extent that "soul" does not have a reality to denote, is like asking if the son of a sterile woman is ill or in good health, or if a turtle's fur is soft or hard.[2] There is really no sense in getting tangled up in these stories that people call objects, subjects, substances, form, matter, and so forth. There is nothing but emptiness. Without being aware of it, we consider the world to be full, opaque, resistant, or lasting, while this real, scintillating vacuum never ceases to extinguish itself and come instantly back again. This emptiness is not nothing. And confusing it with nothingness is a serious mistake.

This vacuity is more easily understood via the idea of the middle path. This middle path, which is something specific to Buddhism, is found in the domain of practical behavior (neither the quest for pleasure nor painful

4 mortification), in the psychological domain (neither mental dispersion nor obsessiveness, neither desire to live nor desire to become nonexistent), as well as in the domain of "metaphysics" (neither life eternal nor annihilation; neither being nor nonbeing). It is not a question of reaching some "centrist" position equidistant from opposing excesses and whose only characteristic is moderation. Vacuity is movement: a path must be cleared between affirmation and negation. One must find one's way between opposing theses; "space" must be made in the midst of their antagonism. It is this act of clearing away opposites that gives access to emptiness.[3]

Buddhism also comes into our awareness today via images. Here and there we see silently smiling statues, the Dalai Lama getting off an airplane surrounded by famous people and meeting with scholars, the entrances to Tibetan temples in California or southwestern France, zen monks residing just about everywhere in the world. And more than anything we see countless dialogues between religions, appeals for peace, humanitarian projects, struggles for nonviolence, and so forth, led by the monks, the followers, or the "sympathizers" of Buddhism. The list could go on, but the conclusion would remain the same: we have almost completely lost the idea of a nihilist Buddhism whose goal was supposed to deny the existence of the world and undermine the foundation of any action or any real morality. We think about Buddhism as beneficent or inoffensive, but never as inhumane or dangerous. Westerners see it today as a curiosity, or perhaps as a remedy, but no longer as a threat.

A Bad Dream

And yet, there was a time when people were afraid of Buddhism. In the nineteenth century, while Europe was discovering Buddhism's teachings and wondering if it was a religion or a philosophy, a number of thinkers thought they saw in this great and ancient law of all of Asia, as they used to say, a nameless danger. The Buddha became the symbol of a nightmare. His basic teaching, they said, contained something impossible: the human spirit could not really desire its own loss. And yet Buddhism was real: its antiquity rivaled at least that of the Greeks, and the number of its adherents was greater than what Christianity could claim. It was difficult not to admire its moral teachings. Nevertheless, it was not possible to consider it a theological system. In the beginning, the existence of Buddhism, a quite late discovery, was like a bad dream for Europe. It was seen as a paradoxical and horrible religion of nothingness. The horror went something like this: an impossible reality which should not even be able to exist happens not only to be followed, but also to be widely established, and of a longevity that 5 defies both reason and nature. The fright raised by the Buddha in the minds of some philosophers was not unlike what happens with specters. Fear of ghosts, fright caused by recurrent apparitions, seemed to creep here and there into, and perhaps undermine, the very core of their well-formulated statements.

We have completely forgotten this old fear, or so it appears. And yet, in numerous but quite different trappings, there are traces of it in German philosophy—Hegel, Schopenhauer, Nietzsche, among others. Similarly, its mark has been left strongly on French philosophers, from Cousin to Renouvier, after passing through Taine or Renan. What they all have in common is that, to a greater or lesser extent, they equate nirvana with annihilation; they consider Buddhism to be like a nihilism that needs to be feared, or one that is all the more attractive because it is frightening. They tie Buddhism and pessimism together in a deadly, negative thought that is totally contrary to the "normal" order of the Western, Christian, living, affirmative world. They erroneously interpret the information. But what does it mean? The purpose of this book is to offer an analysis of this error.

Why study an old mistake in the first place? Is it not enough that it has vanished? After all, have whatever meanderings from the truth there were, when all is said and done, not led to verifiable and verified information? Have the early phantasmagorias not been replaced by numerous critical editions and canonical texts? Have distrust and disdain not been replaced in public opinion by an elementary but generally correct idea of what Buddhism is? Revisiting this specter that haunted nineteenth-century Europe is not only due to intellectual curiosity, even though this in itself would be a legitimate excuse. There are a number of lessons to be learned from the error. Analyzing it will not help us understand the Buddha's doctrines, but it will shed light on the attitudes of Western philosophers, on the way their imaginations worked, and on their relationship to others. My analysis is of a certain point in time: the texts in question here were published between 1820 and 1890. In their reference to Asia, to the Buddha's confrontation with the traditional Brahmanic hierarchy, to the place of nothingness in his teaching, or to his atheism, Europeans were really talking about themselves, about the old power structure that was now on shaky ground, about the breaking up of metaphysical systems, about the death of God—about the nihilism that was to come.

This event also teaches us—for errors are infallible guides—how a new mode of thinking gives rise to new delirium, for the works of the Orientalists, as they gradually began to construct a positive way of thinking about

6   Buddhist doctrines and their history, did not manage to wash away previous illusions in the same way that a new scientific idea might shatter an older one that has suddenly become useless and confusing. Quite the contrary. In a strange way, those facts that had the deepest roots fed the most improbable nightmares. The emergence and development of scholarly knowledge about Buddhism paradoxically aroused, nourished, and went hand in hand with a rich, hallucinatory kind of education. While the philosophers set out line by line the possible meanings of texts, and reconstructed—from the moment that Buddhist texts started making their way to the West—the history of Buddhism and the specific characteristics of its doctrines, another picture began to form in their minds: the disconcerting and troubling image of "worshiping nothingness." This picture was not pure fabrication; it was painted from material provided by the Orientalists themselves. But just as images in dreams rearrange elements furnished by reality in such a way that their ultimate composition is a grotesque and threatening assemblage, so too did these developments select, mold, and distribute Orientalist information in such a way that the resulting doctrine was frightening.

The meaning of this story is best understood by reconstructing the meanderings of the process involved in the European Orientalist discovery of the Buddha's teachings. It entails untangling that part of a particular philosopher's analysis that came from his own background from the part that came via older sources, and by searching step by step for the coherence of the whole of this now long-disappeared configuration that for so long tied philosophical interpretations of Buddhism to the theme of negation, of self-destruction, of nihilism.

Why Buddhism? The inquiry that I began with my *L'Oubli de l'Inde*[4] led me to think that Buddhism's discovery by Orientalists and its interpretation by philosophers marked a turning point, and probably a decisive one, in the process of the disappearance of Indian religious teachings from the scene of European philosophy, when they had just barely made their appearance with the generation of the romantics. In the primary studies dealing with the "reception" of Indian doctrines by European philosophers, on the other hand, no clear distinction was made between the reception of Brahmanism and that of Buddhism, although the two belong neither to the same chronology nor to the same context.[5]

The history of India, and that of Asia in general, here meets Western history to explain the contrast that Europeans saw between these two neighboring—yet quite different—events: the discovery of Brahmanism, and that of Buddhism. It was more than just a difference in teachings, such as this difference appears to us today: the omnipresent substantialism in the

Brahmanic schools, and the critique of any idea of substance in Buddhism. Two other basic facts must be borne in mind. First, Buddhism, born in India where it developed and spread during at least a period of 1500 years, from the fifth century B.C. to the tenth century A.D., disappeared from India toward the eleventh or twelfth century, for reasons that still today are somewhat enigmatic. The French, the Dutch, and the English, who moved progressively into India in the seventeenth and eighteenth centuries and reported no encounters with Buddhism, and found only ruined or deserted temples.

The second fact is that the texts themselves have disappeared from Indian soil, and the Brahmans appear to have almost completely lost any recollection of their long argument with Buddhism. It is in the foothills of the Himalayas, particularly in Nepal, that the Buddhist treatises composed in Sanskrit have been preserved. A number of others, the originals of which have been lost, can be found in Tibetan or Chinese translations. The first Europeans to know Sanskrit were thus able to go directly to the earliest texts of Brahmanism. Buddhism, on the other hand, had to be pieced together gradually, from information that was disparate, widely scattered, and haphazardly presented.

The reason for this, of course, is that Buddhism, which over the centuries spread throughout almost all of Asia, was never either uniform or unified. Even within the major division between the "Small Vehicle" and the "Large Vehicle," a number of schools and sects—and nothing pejorative is intended by the use of that word—existed quite early on, each having its own interpretation on some point of doctrine. This diversity was further enhanced by the influence of religious and other beliefs already in existence in the regions where Buddhism was taking root: Theravadan Buddhism in Ceylon, Burma, and Laos, and Mahayana Buddhism in China (toward the first century), Japan (sixth century), Tibet (eighth century), and Mongolia (twelfth century).

From Hope to Fear

Starting in the final years of the eighteenth century, Indian studies and Sanskrit philology began to form a discipline that was confident of both itself and its methodology. In the early years of the nineteenth century the English school of Calcutta, then the school in Paris at Collège de France and the Société Asiatique, and the German schools in Bonn and Berlin all began work on a huge area of study that up to that time had remained almost unknown. Progressively, and actually rather quickly, etymological

8   fantasies and exotic dreams gave way to precise information and high caliber translations.

At first, the number of works translated was not great. But the echoes that these works produced were resounding. Europe during the age of Romanticism, and Germany in particular, found in Brahmanism, or so it was believed, the reflection of its own preoccupations. India's great epics, her theater, her poetry, as well as the works of the "philosophers of the Ganges," created expectations of a new renaissance. Analogous in its repercussions to that of the fifteenth and sixteenth centuries, it was thought that this "Oriental renaissance"[6] would be even broader and deeper than its predecessor. After all, the past to which it gave access even preceded Greek sources. The thought was, then, that it was via a return to what was of greatest antiquity that a new future could be invented. The most distant, the most archaic past was thus thought of as the reservoir, or the resource, from which a future that would be very different from the present could be drawn. This concept, which was to enjoy considerable longevity, apparently did not recommend a return to times of old. But it did lay the foundation for the belief according to which contemporary disorders were seen as the last moments in a long parenthetical expression soon to be closed. On both sides of this maleficent sequence, the past and the future corresponded with each other without necessarily being similar.

Once the parenthesis was closed on modern strayings from the path, what was hoped from India—which Herder thought of as the "cradle of humanity"—was nothing less than the salvation of times to come. Rather than surprise, thus, the discovery of Brahmanism via the earliest works translated from Sanskrit produced curiosity, and even admiration. The India that was discovered, about which almost nothing was really known, was immediately dreamed of as an original homeland, inextricably poetic and reflective, whose perfection, order, and power, despite its history and subsequent degradation, remained like a great living force capable of reinvigorating the mind, and even the body, of Europe. On 18 December 1806, Schelling wrote to Windischmann: "To my mind, restoration of the East-West union is the greatest problem on whose solution the Spirit of the world is in the process of working. What is Europe, if not the sterile trunk itself that owes everything to Eastern grafts, and could only become perfected through them?" Much later, in Paris, Edgar Quinet, to name but one, expressed the same hope: "While Asia is creeping into the poetry and politics of the Western world, it is also working its way into the West's teachings; metaphysics is sealing the union of two worlds."[7]

This union, so hoped for, so expected, so announced, this renaissance 9 based on rediscovery and reinvigoration never took place. The reason why was not just that it was a dream with its naturally vulgar dissimilarity to reality. Something other than a common disenchantment took place; it was not a case of one of those silent disappointments where illusions are shattered. Hope was replaced by fright; the dream turned into a nightmare. The Indian Paradise was replaced by an Asian Hell. Buddhism came along and sundered a union already thought to be sealed. Long unknown, barely present even in the margins, existing only in a peripheral field of vision, the Buddha's teaching was swept aside during the first wave of Indian studies, like some of the dreams of which they were the object. When, beginning in 1820, people started to put together the puzzle whose widely scattered pieces were coming in from Nepal and China, from Ceylon and Tibet, from Siam as well as Japan; when the convergence of this information from such diverse places of origin made it possible to piece them together, in turn, and compare them; and when finally the characteristics of a doctrine with a style, history, and goals that were significantly different from those of Brahmanism could be discovered, then everything was thrown into disorder. The attraction toward an original kind of life became a repulsion provoked by a kind of death. Buddhism looked hideous, threatening, corrupted, and corrupting.

It was not looked upon as the primary point of contention within Brahmanism's social and spiritual order, nor even as a singular "logical revolt" against revelation or metaphysics of any kind. Rather than an internal, persistent challenge to the Brahmanic idea, rather than a rebellion whose existence actually entailed the theoretical exposition of all Indian thought, Buddhism was judged to be inconceivable, thus impossible, by a good number of Europeans. To their mind, Buddhism's primary goal was the annihilation of any thinking principle. That it was presented in a number of manners as a daze where consciousness is dissolved, as a negation of the will, as a desire for a death without return, Buddhism's distinctive characteristic was considered to be that it was an impossible doctrine where the human's only aim is to be no longer anything. The fact that the highest goal of a religion that was at the same time as old, as alive, and as widespread as Buddhism managed to be nothingness pure and simple, that hundreds of millions of individuals had vowed to seek their irreversible disappearance, that they were dedicating their most sacred and most constant efforts to that disappearance, and that they managed to see an unimaginable felicity in their annihilation—that is what was so completely unthinkable. How could

10 a human being possibly desire nothingness? That was the question. Such a monstrosity was contrary to the very essence of desire, as it was to the essence of man himself, as it was to the nature of any religion.

These horrors were believed, even if scholars were saying something entirely different. It was not a question of wondering via what mysterious process people of considerable intelligence could read a sentence and then formulate statements about it that were completely contradictory to what they had just read. So what did these countless speeches about the "religion of nothingness," the "Great Christ of the void," and the "Church of Annihilation" have to do with? What was behind these variations on the theme of negation, the void, and nothing? How did the chart of nothingness get filled in? What is needed first is a better definition of what these questions are dealing with.

A Fictitious Encounter

In order to ascertain who discovered what, and when, we must first understand what we mean by, in this case, "discovery" and "Buddhism." The authors who dealt with the subject felt no obligation to consider these questions. They appear to have not wondered how, at a certain point in time and under certain particular circumstances, something called "Buddhism" even got constructed in the Western mind. To them, the answer seemed so clear and simple that there was no need to ask the question: Buddhism had existed since the time of the Buddha's teaching, and the West became aware of it gradually; that is all. The Western perspective had undoubtedly seen the teachings of Buddhism in a way that was more or less complete, more or less exact, and extremely variable, depending on the time, the source of information, the linguistic capabilities, and the mindset of the observer. Nevertheless, from the time of the first references to India[8] in the Greek classics up to the erudite works of modern philology, there would be no solution to the problem of Buddhism's continuity. Buddhism, identical to itself, would not cease to be the object of attention. This attention would be acute or relaxed, depending on the time, and it would be armed with more or less critical tools and means of understanding, but it would not be of a fundamentally different nature from one century to the next, as it addressed issues that were different, perhaps even issues that were comparable only with difficulty.

This uniformity of "encounter" was pure fiction. Strabon, Diodorus of Sicily, or Clement of Alexandria, when they mention the "Samaneans," were not referring to the same phenomenon as were the first Jesuit mission-

aries who asked about the religion of Fo in China, or of Xaca in Japan.[9] The
Catholic and Protestant preachers did not have the same things in mind as
the nineteenth-century Sanskrit and Tibetan scholars. Megasthenes' index
was apparently not read, when it was published in 1846,[10] in the same way
that it might have been read by the scholars of the library in Alexandria or
the members of the learned societies of the Grand Siècle. It is thus wrong to
survey the field and stake out boundaries and landmarks as if there were
one, and only one, set of facts gradually making its way from antiquity to the
present day. It is not the same body of knowledge that has gone through,
depending on the authors and the vicissitudes of history, all the variations
from the void to the full, from nothing to everything, from zero to one.
Instead of thinking about it as a continuum, it is necessary to understand
where the breaks are. Instead of a smooth beach where gnostics and medieval wayfarers, explorers and missionaries of the Classical Age, the com-
pilers from the Age of Enlightenment and the stiff-collared scholars of the
learned societies of the Industrial Age are supposed to lay their towels
down side by side, it is necessary to consider the different ways of drawing
up the chart. A number of different configurations can be seen.

Thus, if we are not going to confuse one time or one speech with
another with which it has little in common, the line must be drawn. We
must specify to what the very idea of a discovery of Buddhism refers. And
this is fairly easy to circumscribe. There is a "discovery of Buddhism" from
the moment that questions like the following are explicitly asked. Who is it
that is referred to as the Buddha? What does his name mean? When did he
live? What did he teach? How did his teaching differ from that of the
Brahman priests? Was the Buddha a god? A philosopher? A moral teacher?
Why did his followers leave India? How did Buddhism spread in Asia?
During what period of time? How did it historically take place? What
modifications did it undergo? What are its canonical texts, their main commentaries, their original languages, their translations? What are the main
schools of Buddhism, and what are their main points of contention? And so
forth. . . . These questions, all of which come back to the very definition
of Buddhism, must be asked. It matters little whether the answer comes
sooner or later. It may even be that some of them will long remain inade-
quately answered. The fact that they are raised as questions to be resolved is
all that counts.

When were such questions first put into words, with the hope of finding
effective ways of answering them with as much specificity as possible? Not
from very early times, it appears. It is possible to date, with a certain amount
of precision, the turning point at which the object "Buddhism" took form

12   among the learned disciplines. But naming a specific year would enter too far into the realm of the arbitrary. On the other hand, the relatively short time period during which this took place can be stated quite easily; it was around 1820. It was at that time that a series of basic research projects was begun; it was then that our views left the realm of myth and entered into the domain of history; and, simultaneously, it was then that the first shadow of the "worship of nothingness" raised its head. The present work begins its enquiry, then, at this period. Those remarks about earlier periods that are presented here and there as background information are included only to make it easier to understand how the "new story" of Buddhism was constructed over the older one.

The Birth of a Word, and of a Thing

One simple way of marking the turning point is with the appearance of the word "Buddhism." Until about 1800 the word was not current in any of the European languages. Its birth marked the constitution of a new object of knowledge that, up to then, was nonexistent. Before it received a name, "Buddhism" did not exist. There were descriptions of cults here and there, of interrelated forms of idolatry, of discrete sects; but no systematic unity in doctrine or practice that might constitute a religion per se was seen. Thus, the Greeks, the Franciscans, the Jesuits, British administrators, and a few others had all observed and described a number of the behavioral traits and beliefs of Buddhist monks or "Talapoins." However, and for a long period of time in the eyes of Europe, "Buddhism" did not exist. It was only about 1820 that the word began to be attached to the idea, and to be spread. First incidences are always debatable, but all opinions revolve around this pivotal date. In French, Michel-Jean-François Ozeray wrote "bouddisme" (without the "h" of the present-day spelling) as early as 1817.[11] While Benjamin Constant was using "bouddhaisme" in 1827,[12] Burnouf and Lassen were writing "bouddhisme" in 1826 in their *Essai sur le Pali*.[13] The first occurrence of "Buddhism" in English-language works (Brian Houghton Hodgson, *Sketch of Buddhism*, 1828; Edward Upham, *The History and Doctrine of Buddhism*, 1829)[14] dates from this same period. In German, in 1819, Schopenhauer was writing "Buddhaismus," a word that survived for a considerable period of time (it can be seen in works up until at least the middle of the century) before giving way to "Buddhismus," which Hegel also used in 1827. These notes are only meant to illustrate the fact that there was information, in the languages themselves, of this transformation in knowledge that took place.

Until about 1820, the absence of the word corresponded to the absence of the object. No one was in the least aware of coining a new word, especially in the sense that what the word was referring to at that time—a specific body of religious teachings, half-way between a religion and a philosophy, with its own history and organized system of thought—was still unknown. The research that led to this book was limited, voluntarily, to a close examination of the process of discovery begun and pursued during the nineteenth century. Earlier layers of work were deliberately left out of the main body of our research, whether they be from antiquity, from the Middle Ages, or from more modern times. This body of works fills in the chart in a number of different ways, ways which have only a few characteristics in common: a weak and indecisive description of the specific doctrines of Buddhist beliefs, brutal assimilation of superficial data into Greek or Christian realities, and a preference for qualitative judgments over study and analysis.

Tenacious Misinformation

Should the little that is mentioned in Greek sources be included in such a collection? It would not be easy to justify doing so, since the information they contain is of little help. The great Orientalist Sylvain Lévi had pointed out as early as 1891: "Despite the Hellenistic world's uninterrupted relations with India, and Alexander's expedition toward the end of the Roman Empire, Buddhism was very poorly known, and indeed almost unknown, to the Greeks."[15] The "Samaneans" or the "Sarmanes" who were mentioned by the Greek texts at the same time as the Brahmans have been mentioned frequently throughout the centuries. But to what does the name refer? To whom is this name ascribed? Buddhists? The question of exactly who the Samaneans and Sarmanes were would not be cleared up until the arrival of nineteenth-century philology.[16] The answer was controversial: some affirmed that they were Buddhists, while others denied it.[17] In order for this debate to be waged, the opinion of Greek texts needed to have already changed under the influence of Buddhist studies; the records of antiquity were themselves already becoming the objects of analysis and critical study. The turning point came in German philology. In 1830, Peter von Bohlen, who taught Sanskrit at the University of Königsberg, maintained that the Sarmanes were indeed Buddhists.[18] In 1833, Christian Lassen, who was teaching in Bonn under Wilhelm Schlegel (whom he would succeed in the Sanskrit and Indian Studies chair), replied that the word referred only to the wisest of the Brahman priests, and not to the Buddhists

14 as such.[19] A reading of the Greek texts, even taking into account the supplementary information available to us today, leaves the question unanswered. Actually, the data furnished by Strabon and Clément, both of whom used Megasthenes' *Indica* as their source, were both too abundant and too vague—especially in the latter case—to allow a clear definition. In the Greek *sarmanai*, it certainly is not difficult to recognize the Sanskrit *sramana*, which refers to the ascetics. But this generic term was evidently not applied exclusively to the Buddhists, and the other characteristics ascribed to them by Megasthenes were so general that no firm conclusion can be drawn. Moreover, the Pali expression *samana-brahmana*[20] does not denote any particular denomination of Buddhists, but rather, more generally, all kinds of monks.[21] Thus, there is no sure way of knowing whether the Sarmanes, or the Samaneans, were Buddhist monks.

Even though we have the tendency to consider discussions of this issue as leading down a blind alley, the debate continued throughout the nineteenth century. While Henry Thomas Colebrooke, Christian Lassen, and the Reverend Samuel Beal tended to believe that the Sarmanes were orthodox Brahmans,[22] Childers, Cunningham, and Barthélemy Saint-Hilaire believed them to be Buddhist monks. Barthélemy Saint-Hilaire relied upon "three sources of information": "The Greek historians informed by Alexander's expedition, Indian inscriptions discovered recently, and the Chinese annals."[23] This cursory look at the vague and indeterminate nature of the information transmitted by the authors of antiquity, on the one hand, and the fact that critical examination of their incertitude did not begin until the time of the "discovery," on the other, is hopefully sufficient. This is why the Greek sources, from the point of view taken here, cannot be considered, in themselves, as the premises for a science that would later develop gradually. They really should be looked at from the perspective of the indirect influence they later had on the philologically assured discovery, the support they gave, or the disturbances they caused.

Other collections of Western texts related to what has been called "Buddhism"—a name given after the fact and which is, in a way, anachronistic—might be mentioned in the same vein. A first group concerns the sources at the end of the thirteenth and into the fourteenth century. There are, as it happens, a number of interesting observations in the accounts of Jean de Plano-Carpini and Guillaume de Rubrouck, in Haiton l'Arménien's *L'Histoire des pays orientaux* (History of the Oriental Countries)—which circulated in French starting about 1307, thanks to a version dictated in Poitiers by the author to Nicolas Forlani (who would later compose a Latin version, retranslated into French by Jean le Long d'Ypres)—in Marco Polo's book, in the *Itinerarium* by Brother Odoric de Pordenone (1330), and in the accounts of Jean de Cora and Jean Marignolli.[24] These texts really ought to be placed in their context as "mental tools" for travelers in the Middle Ages, but doing so would go beyond the scope of the present work. However, their contents have been more or less erased, blurred, and rediscovered over the course of the centuries. Even if some of these accounts were reedited from time to time, even if they accompanied, at a distance, the years of discovery that took place later, they did not play a role in the process. But this was always the case in the relationship of the West to Buddhist teachings: taken in the long scope of things, the information was never cumulative. Time after time, it appears, writers either started from almost zero, without being aware of previous knowledge, or they worked without being able to articulate correctly the previous data with new knowledge.

Such was not the case for Muslim and Arabic sources. Although the Orientalists at the end of the eighteenth and the beginning of the nineteenth centuries did not appear to know Al-Bîrûnî's *Tahqîq mâ li-l-Hind*, which was composed in 1032—but not translated into English by Edward Sachau until 1888[25]—they were familiar with Abul Faziz's *Aîn-i Akbarî*. It was frequently cited at the end of the eighteenth century in the early issues of *Asiatick Researches*,[26] notably by William Jones, the first president of the Royal Asiatic Society of Bengal, who had been proficient in Persian for a long time before learning Sanskrit.[27] It would be shortsighted to overlook the fact that part of the information available to the first scholars to study India, besides their own observations on India or their work with manuscripts, came from Arabic sources.

Another source of information, and one that is even more voluminous, came from the relationships that resulted from the missionary discovery of Buddhist countries, starting in the middle of the sixteenth century. The Society of Jesus was especially prominent in this regard.[28] Thus, in 1552, Guillaume Postel, who was one of the first readers in the "Collège" founded by Francis the First, inserted in chapters 6 and 8 of his *Des merveilles du monde* a "copy of M. François Schiabier's letter on noble things from the Island of Giapan," saying, "I wish to admonish the reader to be wary of things that are Oriental."[29] Postel's conviction was, namely, that the inhabitants of Japan received word of the existence of Jesus Christ, and thus of the Redemption, via astrology. In his opinion, it was not by Revelation or preaching that they were apprised of Christ's advent, but via the high quality of their astral knowledge. Only the result of his hypotheses is relevant here: Postel ascribes no particular importance to the religion of Xaca (the Japa-

16 nese name of the Buddha), nor does he see the need for any further investigation of the religion. "Xaca is no more than a dark cloud, taken from Evangelical history,"[30] he says in his commentaries. The assimilation of this still unknown religion into Christianity is decreed, rather than concluded. Thus, in fact, in the text that he reproduces, that there exists in Japan a prince who wears a cross as an insignia, and he alone has the right to this insignia, Postel sees "true confirmation that Xaca is there worshipped as Jesus Christ crucified."[31]

That varieties of hidden Christianity exist "out there" is only one example among many of convictions that inhabited people's minds from the end of the Middle Ages to the dawn of modern times. Lost and isolated brethren at the farthest corner of the world, as far East as it is possible to travel, have done their best to maintain the religion and to perpetuate the rituals they received long ago by a Christian preacher. The passage of centuries has undoubtedly corrupted the texts and damaged the symbols, but observation of the Buddhists shows signs that confirm this common identity buried under the weight of history. Monasteries, tonsure, bells, a frugal life, a regulated schedule, psalms and prayers *recto tono*: all these apparent resemblances were seen as so many signs of a Christianity still there, that would perhaps need to be restored to itself by washing away its amnesia. This goal set into motion the great religious missions, the traversing of oceans and the crossing of the Himalayas.[32] There were actually two hypotheses, whose differences and similarities have raised questions, doubts, and confusion: one was that the Buddhists were transformed, "undone," forgotten Christians who had thus become, gradually, forgetful of themselves. The other was that they were pagans who one day borrowed the motions and signs of a Christian faith they had never shared in order to counterfeit them—but without really understanding them. In the latter case it was no longer a question of lost brethren, but rather of false brethren: impostors, and perhaps even brigands.

Take, for example, what Saint Francis Xavier wrote from Japan to Saint Ignatius Loyola in 1552, the same year that Guillaume Postel's work was published. These famous letters are of a rare violence. Buddhist monks are vilipended in the most vitriolic of terms:

> If their crazy and arrogant pretention is convinced of untruth, the principal reason for their profit will cease to exist. If their shameful crimes, if the heinous disorders that are of no real seriousness in their eyes—rather almost a reason for glory—are bent by lively and just reprobation, then we shall see these wild boars—as they feel the

piercing of the spear in the mud wherein they wallow—rush with rage and wanting to rip to shreds those who tossed them their pearls.[33] The plan to confuse the monks solely via exposing them to Revelation, to make them blush [!] by exposing their errors, and to lead them to the true faith is the sole goal of the missionary: "I am filled with confidence," he said, "that, through the cares of our Society, the Chinese and the Japanese will soon give up their idolatrous superstitions and worship Jesus Christ, the savior of all peoples.[34]

It was undoubtedly of great importance to the history of Christian thought that Guillaume Postel saw disciples of Christ in these followers of Xaca's sect, while Francis Xavier saw only boars—a savage kind of pig—in need of transformation through evangelical truth. Nevertheless, this long-lived quarrel, which would persist, in a number of different forms, into the middle of the nineteenth century, does not belong to the history of the knowledge of Buddhism per se. Both possibilities (corrupted Christians or pagans in Christian disguise) had in common, despite their apparent opposition, their prejudices against Buddhist monks. Here, Christians, there, charlatans: no mystery, no question about it.

There are a number of texts that present a historical overview of Western representations of the Buddha. In some cases these are relatively well disseminated, as can be seen, after the letters of Saint Francis Xavier and those of Father Cosme de Torres (1551), in the existence of a number of collections published in Louvain, such as *Epistolae Indicae* (1566), the *Epistolae Japonicae* (1569), and then the *Epistolae Indicae et Japonicae* (1570). Long before the Jesuit Father Athanase Kircher's[35] *China Illustrata* (1667), several volumes had appeared—some of which, like Nicolas Trigaut's *De christiana expeditione apud Sinas* (Anvers, 1615), had been translated into German, French, Spanish, and Italian. These texts, which had occasionally been widely disseminated, tended to be apologetic in nature. They sought less to understand and study than to judge and convert, and consequently were relatively lacking in information that might help advance an effective study of Buddhism. The exact contents of Buddhist doctrines, their founding texts, and their later evolution were not, for these authors, problems that needed a solution involving rigorous research. That is why they have not been considered.

There are, however, a certain number of internal reports, not written for public dissemination or for the propagation of the faith, that contain information of a different nature. It happens that some accounts sent by

18 missionaries back to whatever congregation had dispatched them contained specific information, and occasionally even fragments of Buddhist texts with fairly accurate translations.[36] In any case, if these documents were neither disseminated nor available for public use, they are of little use to our purposes here. Of course, it is interesting to note that "people" knew such and such prayer, or such and such argument long before they were discovered by university philology. Nevertheless, as soon as these "people" are reduced to a single missionary, to a manuscript filed away in the library of some religious order, or to uncirculated papers, what it really boils down to is no one. From God's point of view, or from that of a historian unconcerned with the social fabric, it could be said that such and such a thing "has been known"—at least once, at least by someone—but this does not constitute the discovery of Buddhism as a social process of Western knowledge.

Space should be set aside for a group of texts from the century of the Enlightenment, for it is possible, through them, to follow the spread of recognition of the link, already established during the seventeenth century, between an Indian origin of Buddhism and its forms as they had been discovered in China, Japan, Tibet, and Siam. This is seen, for example, in Father Pons's letter of 23 November 1740 to Father Du Halde, published in 1743.[37] Likewise, an idea of the Buddha's place in Indian history can be seen in a collection of diverse "pre-Indian" works published by Dow,[38] Holwell,[39] and Anquetil-Duperron,[40] as well as in a number of other publications.[41] This picture is full of holes and uncertainties, it is fragmentary and incomplete, and yet it makes an attempt to gather disparate information from a variety of sources into an understandable whole. Thus, the French traveler Le Gentil, who crisscrossed the seas of India from 1761 to 1769 and published an account of his trip in 1780, writes for example: "There was once on the coast of Coromandel and in Ceylon a religion whose teachings are completely unknown; the god Baouth, whose name is only known today in India, was the object of this religion."[42] Some of these works will be examined in the following pages, to the extent that they help us understand how we have progressed from a general characterization of the Buddha to the scholarly study of his teachings.

Languages Learned, Writings Deciphered

It was thus out of concern for a methodology that a general panorama, "Buddhism and the West," was carved. It seemed hardly possible, upon reflection, to place on the same scale the snippets of ancient information about the Samaneans, the amazement of the medievals, the apologetic ardor of the missionaries, the studies of modern travelers filled with curiosities, the speculation of the Age of Enlightenment, and the painstaking attentions of positivist philologists. Those diverse speeches that come from quite dissimilar configurations cannot be placed on a continuum where they represent, each in its own way, the successive and cumulative modalities of the same discovery process. One would have to be a magician to place these very different periods of time into the same framework. One would be better off positing that there never was a discovery of Buddhism, strictly speaking, until such time as the languages in which its canonical writings were composed were deciphered, and Buddhism's fundamental texts were systematically translated. Even though Sanskrit was known as early as 1780, the Buddhist treatises in Sanskrit were not discovered in Nepal, by Brian Houghton Hodgson, until the decade beginning in 1820. Pali was not deciphered by Eugene Burnouf and Christian Lassen until about the same time, and the Chinese Buddhist texts were being studied at that time only by Jean-Pierre Abel-Rémusat. The Hungarian Alexandre Csoma de Körös would begin learning Tibetan shortly thereafter.[43] In short, this was the time of a breakthrough that would lead the Western world from ignorance to knowledge.

What was needed was a change in perspective. For this to happen, it was first necessary to consider the discovery of Buddhism as taking place—the name conjointly with the phenomenon, in the scholarly mind—in about 1820, and not with Clement of Alexandria, Marco Polo, or Francis Xavier. But at the same time, the existence of this body of works that had come down over the centuries should not be denied, nor should they be thought of as either irrelevant or unimportant. It was absolutely essential to find a way, in light of the discovery, to think about these scattered works and these tenacious myths, this multiple tradition so evocative of a somewhat muffled but persistent, occasionally stifled rumor, but one that consistently managed to reappear here or there and from time to time. I have chosen to consider these texts not as early foundations upon which new knowledge was based, but rather, to a certain extent, as "confounding variables," as noises that from time to time stood in the way of new information, as a background whose order could be upset and course could be changed by the somewhat strong interference of more recent data. When taken this way, "Buddhism" is carved out of a mass of ancient knowledge that certainly did not produce it, but did help it to take shape.

First of all, it is undoubtedly this kind of interference that helped to explain, at least in part, why nihilism came to mind every time the Buddha and his teachings were mentioned by nineteenth-century philosophers and essayists. This is the primary fact: when they spoke of the Buddha, nineteenth-century philosophers were dealing with nothingness: regularly, explicitly. "Buddhism" and "worshiping nothingness" became synonymous, or equivalent, in their writings. "Nothingness" was taken in a number of ways, as shall be seen, but the word was ever so present, ever so tightly tied to Buddhism, its teachings, its practices, and its practicers. In paragraph 87 of the 1827 and 1830 versions of the *Encyclopedia*, Hegel states: "Nothingness, which the Buddhists make the principle of everything, the final goal, and the ultimage aim of everything."[44] In his *Lessons on the Philosophy of Religion*, he explains that in Buddhism "man should become nothingness"; he should attempt to reach the "eternal peace of nothingness."[45] Following suit, philosophers have long seen a "fanaticism of nothingness"[46] in the doctrine preached by the "Great Christ of the Void."[47] This unthinkable religion, "which gives life the supreme goal of nothingness," this "machine for emptying souls" was, for Renan, the sign that a "Nihilist Church" existed.[48] While Schopenhauer did not hesitate to celebrate the "admirable agreement"[49] that, to his mind, existed between Buddhism and his own pessimism, Nietzsche decried the "nothingness nostalgia" that was the "negation of tragic wisdom," the "asthenia of the will" that led to a flight from suffering, and thus no longer either to loving or enduring life. Nietzsche particularly denounced nirvana, the "Oriental nothingness" he found at the heart of a way of thinking that, in his opinion, was essentially more pessimistic than Schopenhauer's.[50] So proper and so sweet in some ways, Buddhism, in Nietzsche's eyes, was nothing more than a vast "negation of the world."[51] It is quite fitting to "give it the *coup de grâce*" if we want to rediscover the tragic meaning of life. "Tragedy," says Nietzsche, "should save us from Buddhism."[52] A number of other texts should also be mentioned. The writings of Mainländer and von Hartmann follow in Schopenhauer's footsteps. And then there are those of Schelling, in *Philosophie de la mythologie*, and those of the French writers Cousin, Quinet, Barthélemy Saint-Hilaire, Taine, Comte, Gobineau, Amiel, and Charles Renouvier, most notably in his *La Philosophie analytique de l'histoire*.

This thread of nihilism worked its way into the maze of discussions

Buddhism raised in Europe. What actually happened was that a great fiction with Buddhism at its center took shape around the question of nothingness and its different meanings. As the writings of nineteenth-century thinkers were gathered together and compared to one another, it became evident that the discovery of Buddhism, and especially its new interpretation in the form of this impossible religion of nothingness, had been part and parcel to the developing concept of nihilism and the differences between its many meanings in recent Western philosophical thinking. This was not a cause-and-effect relationship: it is pointless to think that any kind of Buddhist influence on Europe was responsible for contemporary nihilism. The question lies elsewhere. Let us eschew any thought of Buddhist nothingness—in any form, regardless of whether it is seen as either a philosophical concept or a morbid fascination—influencing the Western mind, spreading through Western thought, and changing it via contamination. Such an idea was already incorporated into the religion of nothingness, as shall be explained below.

Better, let us look at the process as "precipitation" in the chemical sense of the word. The elements that would combine to form this nebulous so-called "nihilism" were already present. Some of them were quite old, even ancient. Others dated from the still recent time when, among other breaks with the past, consciousness of the limits of metaphysics was spreading, the death of God was proclaimed, and the end of absolute monarchies was in progress. Within this post-Kantian, post-Revolutionary framework the discovery of Buddhism in itself appeared to cause no particular new difficulty. But, when the questions raised by Buddhism began—a religion with no need of God, a road to salvation without immortality, beatitude devoid of content, a law unattached to the divine word, morality with no connection to transcendence, and so forth—especially within the context of the enduring plasticity, for European thinkers, of teachings that were for a long time poorly known, that were discovered by bits and pieces only, that were understood via elements that were haphazardly presented, that were more imagined than closely examined, and that were reconstructed or reconstituted by the imagination rather than by scientific methodology, a kind of catalytic element appeared. Thus, the principal characteristics of nihilism took shape and were refined in increasing detail within the framework of Buddhism and the paradoxes it presented. Thinking they were talking about the Buddha, Westerners were talking about themselves. They attributed their own preoccupations to Asia; they projected upon Asia their own fears, their own confusion.

Three Nihilisms, At Least

All these reflections revolve around three principal ways of thinking about nihilism that filigree through the pages that follow. In the first place, "nihilism" can be understood in a purely metaphysical sense, in which case it means that no fundamental distinction can be seen between being and nothingness. In this case, which might be referred to as "ontological," nihilism consists in maintaining that, from a certain point of view, nothingness "equals" being, that it is not opposed to it in any irreducible or insurmountable manner. Such a perspective allows two statements, which at first appear contradictory, to be used interchangeably: (1) there is only nothingness behind appearances and the sheen of the images that make up the world; and (2) beyond the individual and finite events that we are given to experience, there is only Absolute, pure Being, the infinite with no determinate characteristics.

According to a second meaning, nihilism can be an active refusal in opposition to life, a "no" hurled out in the face of everything that perpetuates existence, that proliferates existence, that allows existence to cling so tightly to its own presence. This choice of nothingness proclaims its superiority over being. It is better that life deny itself, be snuffed out, erased, obliterated, and forever dissolved, for it could never manage to be either happy or lastingly peaceful. Existence is nothing more than a painful decoy. Finding how, definitively, to put an end to it is the only justification for intelligence. This pessimistic nihilism appears to absorb everything. Despite everything, it has its limits. As a matter of fact, it recognizes optimism as its opposite. The affirmation of a "yes" to life is the pole that stands in contradiction to its lucidity. Blind aspiration to happiness and its repetition is only an illusion, in the eyes of the pessimist, but it does have its own internal consistency. This nihilism thus allows the opposition between true and false to remain in existence.

One last possible meaning manages to annul this antagonism. Nihilism, in this final case, no longer denotes a refusal of life, nor does it deny what positive values may be attributed to the world. It is, in fact, the existence of a world of values that, after all, constitutes nihilism. Any afterworld is an artificial paradise, and the very idea of truth is a harmful phantasmagoria. It is no longer a question of maintaining that life is worth nothing, or that everything is worthwhile, but rather of maintaining that nothing could have any determined value, for reasons that are outside the world or independent of it. From this point of view, nihilism exists from the moment that one places on cruel and felicitous reality a judgment that is attempting to impose an external law, from the moment that one sets the world such as it is in opposition to the preferable order of what ought to be.

These three primary meanings of nihilism can be found in the nine-teenth-century descriptions of Buddhism that provide the material for this book. The texts have even dictated their own sequence. I have found it in-dispensable to cite them, sometimes at length, not only because they are generally unknown and sometimes rather difficult to find, but also, and especially, because they are extraordinarily explicit. That Buddhism was the worship of nothingness, a hideous system of thought, a grass-roots revolt, a sleeping danger, an invitation to weakness, or a lassitude for life, is all there in the texts, in black and white. These statements need to be neither de-duced nor reconstructed. They are not hidden away, crouching in the cor-ner of the painting like a message hidden beneath the visible contents of the picture. There is no need to put the pieces together from scattered elements or fragile signs. They are all there, offered with insistence and clarity. All that is needed is to step into their unfolding, to take the trouble to follow the occasionally winding course that they set out, to listen to their turns of phrase, not to be satisfied with a word that shows up just here or there.

As the research for this book was taking place in archives, one impres-sion became clearer and clearer. It had been left on the periphery for a long time, out of necessity, since it could not be trusted. It was a strange thought, not very rational at first. I actually had the feeling that, under the pretext of speaking about the Buddha, these texts were not only talking about the Western world of their time, about a nineteenth century upset by distur-bances of all kinds, but that they were also talking about our time, about the twentieth century and its "worship of nothingness," about its unprece-dented wars and massacres, about its negation of all that is human, about its destructive nihilism. How could that be? And why? By what kind of magic, in a discussion of others, of places far away, of Asia, of the Buddha, could one become upset about what was going to be happening later, in the West? My impression has not gone away. On the contrary, it is stronger than ever. It has ended up being a sort of conviction, one that cannot be anything other than a hypothesis in need of an interpretation. This question will be revisited at the conclusion of the book.

Between here and there, there is nothing to do but follow the tracks.

The Birth (1784–1831)

1784. In Calcutta, William Jones presides over the first session of the Royal Asiatick [*sic*] Society of Bengal. The study of Sanskrit and Indian culture becomes a rigorous discipline. Despite everything, the teachings tied to the Buddha's name, which disappeared from India in the eleventh century, remain unknown in this first phase of Indian studies.

1831. Hegel dies in Berlin. "Man should become nothing," he writes in his last years, to characterize this religion called by a new name, "Buddhism." The term spreads throughout the European languages with the work of pioneers.

I

The Faceless Idol

*In the works of the eighteenth century, the Buddha is
frequently considered to be one of the elements of the
"primitive world." Nearly devoid of identity, he continued,
for the most part, not to have a strong connection with the
theme of nothingness.*

Buddha, just as
the Egyptian Thot,
the Greek Hermes, the
European Mercury, and
Woden of the Gothic
nations, etc., is a
lawgiver older than
Brahman.

—Langlès's note in the
French translation of the
Recherches asiatiques, 1805

Before the beginning of the nineteenth
century, there was no clearly defined system attached to the Buddha's name. This
founder with many names was not seen as a single individual in either the accounts of travelers
or letters from missionaries. Long after it was
recognized that the Chinese Fo, the Japanese
Xaca, the Sammonacodom of the Talapoin
monks in Siam were the same person as the Indian Budda, he was still generally credited with
no more than fathering an obscure idolatry ex-
iled on the perimeter of Asia. Bodh, Budh, or
Bouddou were the starting points for an archaic
idolatry. His vague religion of poorly defined
outlines scarcely attracted either interest or concern. The idol incarnated, so it was believed, an
ancient and general representation of knowledge and wisdom. It had no existence of its own,
it corresponded to no human reality, it held no

28 definite place in history. The status of its reality—legendary or historical?—the detailed contents of its doctrine, and the points upon which it differed from the Brahmanic schools, the paths and circumstances of its spread in Asia, were not of great concern.

Such questions were not even noticed to be missing. They did not even need to be formulated. All kinds of answers, ready made and judged with confidence, were already cluttering the space in which they could have been formulated. The answers available related to requests that had no relationship to anything that differentiated, defined, or specified. On the contrary, they tended to satisfy a need for equivalence and comparison. Authors worked out models with elements regrouped or superimposed one over the other. They forever established new coincidences among images, figures, signs, or names that were initially disparate. Before the development of philology gave birth to positive, ordered knowledge, the question of the Buddha was in a sense no more than a matter of rhetoric. It was a question of inserting the name into a series, not of determining what it stood for.

Current in the seventeenth and eighteenth centuries, these constructions were still found in a work as late as George Stanley Faber's *The Origin of Pagan Idolatry* (1816). In his own way, he summarized a form of discourse that was already old. "The primeval Buddha," Faber wrote, "is the same as Vishnu, or Shiva, or Osiris."[1] Why? What documents, what arguments permit this assertion? Such questions do not really appear to be pertinent. All that mattered was the affirmation of a single identity with different names. Other passages from the same work confirm this; we learn that "Thoth and Bouddha were the same person as Idris," or that the Buddha, Vishnu, and Noah were one and the same person. George Stanley Faber was nevertheless not someone with a deranged mind. Dozens of works compared the Buddha to Hermes, to the planet Mercury, to Noah, to Moses, to Thoth, to Odin, or to Wotan. These series of identifications first signaled the Buddha's belonging to the "primitive world." The formula designated the great primordial layer in which, it was believed, the common origin of myths, gods, rites, and words belonging to different places, times, peoples, and languages could be arranged. This idol of indistinct traits thus had no origin; it was original. Essentially, almost organically, it incarnated the very origin from which the "primitive" was inextricable.

What Is the "Primitive World"?

Perhaps we have forgotten what "primitive" meant for a long time. The word's meaning changed with the disappearance of the intellectual construct to which it belonged. "Primitive world," "primitive people," "primitive language and beliefs" did not refer to a state that was immature, prelogical, or even little developed by humanity, as we might have a tendency to think based on Lévy-Bruhl. What was primitive was not a "mentality" or a stage of intellectual, psychological, or social development. It was not a way of being relative to the world that could be placed at such and such a degree on the scale of evolution where we would be placed at a higher level. Nor was it something rudimentary, some yet-to-be-displayed ability waiting for its actualization.

It was, on the other hand, a uniform space-time continuum that constituted the substrate of history—a first, ageless, self-sufficient world where unity supposedly reigned. The same gods were worshiped everywhere, under different names. Despite the disparity in customs and the diversity in appearances, the same beliefs were present everywhere. Given the differences between languages, the same names still referred to the same gods. Jean-Sylvain Bailly wrote, for example: "A crowd of ancient practices claims both an earlier people and a common source."[2]

The constituent formula in this closed world might be worded as follows: X is the same as Y. The primitive was, above all, a function. It intervened like an operator in such a way that it might unify the multiple, reduce the diverse, or make cultures interchangeable. One would be wrong to see in it, after the event, a degree zero of evolution, an initial period of history. Its role was to constitute the original smooth, consistent, and flawless platform whence history one day departed. Historical time lifted itself off this foundation, it rose up from it, but it did not belong to it—just as this original plain escaped from the course of time.

The purpose of this book is not to be the study of such notions. Born in the classical age and developing in the century of the Enlightenment—in works like those of Court de Gébelin[3] and de Bailly—and extending into the nineteenth century, with George Stanley Faber and Frédéric de Rougemont,[4] the primitive world had, we might dare to say, a long history. This expansive network, in which figures that for us are totally dissimilar become identical through some game of permutations producing the undefined equivalence of forms of idolatry, is very much contemporaneous, from its emergence to its decline, with the opening of Europe to the world as a whole and to the premises of the society that has become ours.

In this long expanse of time, which stretches from the epoch of the great discoveries to the rise of industry, the European conscience tried to conjure up the multiplicity of others, to neutralize the diversity of elsewheres by working to consider them all as a single thing—primitive, idol-

30   atrous, pagan. For nearly three centuries, as the world expanded and divided, as space tiered itself into new distances, as the time of history gained depth, efforts to preserve the bearable aspect of a common, homogeneous, compact archaism—in this diffusion and division—intensified. Before and after the Greeks, a multitude of polytheisms, myths aplenty, unsuspected pantheons, new writings, enigmatic monuments were out there to be discovered . . . the principle of a primitive world brought all this multiplicity back into unity. This principle countered a proliferation of differences with the reduction to a single system, where singularities, all with permutations, were all annulled the minute the key that allowed their translation indefinitely into one another was in hand.

    Curtailing the proliferation of worlds, the principle of the primitive seems to have had an even greater role in imaginarily compensating for the acceleration of movement specific to the West. Actually, just as—from the Renaissance to the Reformation to the French Revolution—the rhythm and the intensity of European transformation was increasing, the traits attributed to the primitive world as an immobile background, beyond age, so subject to history that it was unable to sense to its own course, hardened. Little did it matter if it was compared, here to a subterranean shadow out of which we proceeded, or there to a milky dawn from which the events of the day were uncoupled. In all cases, the primitive, in both essence and function, was anti-modern. Predating history, it was in opposition to the future and its mobilities, just as much as it was opposed to diversity.

The Buddha's Name Is Mercury

    The existence of a single, solitary "primitive world" implied the early communication of the beliefs, the languages, and the myths of Egypt and Persia, of the Greeks and the Scandinavians, of the Chinese and the Etruscans. So it is not surprising to see "the Buddha," with no other identity than an uncertain name, likened to a real diversity of divinities. Among these identifications, one of the most lasting associated Buddha and Mercury. La Loubère, in his famous account from 1691, *Du Royaume de Siam* (On the Kingdom of Siam), a work crammed with exact notations and precise observations, gives a sense of this similarity. He explains it as follows: "Mercury, who was the God of the sciences, seems to have been adored by the whole earth: because knowledge is undoubtedly one of the attributes of the true God."[5] The idea of likening the Buddha to Mercury comes only from the fact that the name of the day Wednesday in the Romance languages (*mercredi*, in French), Mercury's day, is *budha* in Pali and in the lan-

guages derived from Sanskrit. This similarity is pointed out by a number of 31
authors.[6] As a matter of fact, the two words have nothing to do with one
another, but their resemblance was enough to assure longevity.

The same equivalence is found in Antoine Augustin Giorgi's *Alpha-*
betum Tibetanum (Rome, 1762), a work that was frequently cited and mentioned for the half-century that followed its publication.[7] It also showed up
in Bailly's text, mentioned earlier, which was written about the "primitive
people": "It is with these people that the famous Mercury Trismegistus of
the Greeks lived, the Thaut or Thoth of the Egyptians, the Butta of the
Indians, who is one and the same individual placed at the common source
of these peoples, and whom these peoples appropriated for themselves."[8]
This identification of the Buddha with Mercury comes up again a number
of times, and for a number of years after the beginning of the nineteenth
century, as is shown, in addition to G. S. Faber's book mentioned above,
in Friedrich Creuzer's great work *Symbolik und Mythologie der alten Völker*
(Leipzig-Darmstadt, 1819–23).[9] Most of the time, the Buddha-Mercury
similarity was mentioned only in passing, almost as evidence, an accepted
fact, a milestone about which there was really not much to say. It was not a
question of an opinion that might have been the object of a debate, held or
attacked with vehemence. There was one exception to this: the Carmelite
Paulin de Saint Barthélemy, who in 1793, in his capacity as *répétiteur* at the
College des Missionnaires, dedicated a significant portion of a work[10] composed in Latin, in Rome, entirely to the defense and illustration of this
thesis. With rare vehemence, this former missionary from the coast of
Malabar fought to defend an astrological and symbolic interpretation: Buddha or Gautama, in India, and Fo, in China, were not men, but the unique
sign of the planet Mercury.[11] For all peoples, the genius of Mercury would
have been considered as the creator of moral laws, and the institutor of the
arts and sciences.[12]

One name and one religion, the same, thus met in forms that were more
or less corrupted through their pilgrimages, in India with Buddha, in Egypt
and Ethiopia with Thot, in China with Fo, as well as in Tibet and among the
Scythians, not to mention Scandinavia and Sweden.[13] These different faces
of the same idol, about whom, it might be added, little is known besides his
omnipresence, were multiplied one by one. Paulin de Saint Barthélemy
wondered if Buddha was not the Manichean Jesus, or perhaps Mithra.[14] In
order to have so many faces, the Buddha evidently had to have none himself. An element caught in the play of substitutions and equivalencies,
something malleable, susceptible to having the same value attributed to him
as that of all sorts of mythological "powers," the number of which was

32 practically indefinite: this too general equivalent had no identity, really. Buddha-Mercury had a particularly long career. Mentioned by Loubère in 1691, he was seen again in 1742 in the great *History of Philosophy* by Brucker,[15] in the *Siaka* article from Diderot's *Encyclopédie*,[16] and several times in the notes composed by Langlès for the French edition (in 1805) of the first two volumes of *Recherches asiatiques*.[17] He also held an important place, in 1829, in Edward Upham's work entitled *The History and Doctrine of Buddhism*,[18] where the reader learned, for example, that "the followers of Brahma honored the planet Mercury as the star of Buddha."[19] As we have seen, identification of the Buddha was not limited to just equivalence with Mercury. He was generally mentioned in a chain associating a number of "other" mystical figures. Langlès, for example, wrote that Buddha was "the same as the Egyptian Thot, the Greek Hermes, the European Mercury, and the Woden of the Gothic nations."[20] In one of the last works that developed such speculations at length, Colonel William Francklin declared that "the ancient Bood'h of India is none other than the ancient Hermes Trismegistus of Egypt," before specifying that "this original personnage is from an antediluvian race."[21]

This quite stereotyped list was thereafter used on a number of occasions, with few variations. Despite everything, it far from exhausted the possibilities of the Buddha's identification. One might even say that there is no spiritual tradition or geographic region (with the exception, unless we are mistaken, of the Americas) where his presence has not been spotted and eruditely justified.[22]

Bonzes Deep in the Fjords

Among these strange relationships and identifications that, in hindsight, seemed to disappear almost from one day to the next, particular mention should be made of the identification of the Buddha as "Odinn-Wotanaz-Woden," which was first picked up by the Orientalist William Jones. The point of departure is always Wednesday, the day to which Woden gave his name among the Scandinavians, as Mercury had done among the Latin peoples and, so it was believed, Buddha among the Indians. That Woden is for us the master of knowledge who confuses but does not instruct—the manipulator of dialectical ruses and casuistic tricks—or that he is missing one eye, ugly, deceitful, cruel, cynical, and a misogynist is not of direct concern here. The only thing to be remembered is that the supposed identity of the Buddha with Woden points to the dream of a secret identity of the peoples of Asia and those of the North. This fantasy would not disappear with the advent of assured Orientalist knowledge. Connecting the Scandinavian fog to the Ganges sun is in effect a tenacious illusion from the generation of the Romantics. They would imagine all kinds of migrations in the days of old turning the Germans into the descendants of the Brahmans who set up residence along the Rhine, the Vistula, or the Oder.[23] Similarly, they would work to establish, again quite late, a proximity between the Buddha and the Nordic god. Petrus Benjamin Sköldberg, for example, was the editor of a collective publication on this theme in Uppsala (1822), which was taken over the following year by August Wilhelm Schlegel, in his attentive *Indische Bibliothek*.[24] But what is most surprising is undoubtedly still to find a trace of their rantings a number of decades later, in scholarly publications, at a time when the field of comparative religions was already well established. Thus, the serious Norwegian linguist Holmboe published in Paris, in 1857, a dizzying thesis entitled *Traces du Buddhisme en Norvège avant l'introduction du Christianisme*.[25] The following year, this text would be the subject of an article titled "Buddhism and Odinism, their Similitude," published by the serious *Journal of the Asiatic Society of Bengal*.[26] Holmboe explained in particular the lapses in time between the relative datings of Odin according to the specialists of the period and the chronology of the life of the Buddha by the quantity of time necessary for the migration of Buddhist colonies from India to the shores of the Baltic.

A Distant Christ with Kinky Hair

The Buddha was also, albeit more rarely, identified as Christ, most notably by Guillaume Postel, during the Renaissance,[27] and by de Guignes, in the age of Classicism. For the latter, the doctrinal content of the religion of Fo, which reigned among the Chinese, was identical to that of Christianity. Thus, he wrote in his *Histoire générale des Huns, des Turcs, des Mongols et des autres Tartares occidentaux. Avant et depuis Jésus Christ jusqu'à présent, etc.* (1756–1758): "In the year 65 the Fo Religion was introduced into China. This religion was established in the part of India where the Mogul is today. I think it is Christianity."[28] This is why Buddhist teachings, in his opinion, contained nothing that was fundamentally puzzling, even though they might have been, over the course of history, debased and altered. "Those who take a look will see only a Christianity such as the Heresiarch Christians of the 1st century were teaching it, after they mixed into it the ideas of Pythagorus on metempsychosis & a few other principles drawn from India. This book might even be one of the false gospels that were current at the time; all the precepts that Fo gives, with the exception of a few specific

34   ideas, seem to be taken from the Gospel."[29] Identifications of the Buddha
with Christ were certainly not numerous. Moreover, they were never presented as anything other than possibilities, hypotheses, or inner convictions. They were not arguments supported by long lines of proof. When the
question of the relationship between followers of the Buddha and Christian
revelation arose, what emerged victorious—an example was seen in the
letters sent from Japan by Saint Francis Xavier[30]—was, on the other hand,
the urgent need to convert idolaters. Despite everything, in the blur hanging over what the Buddha's religion actually was, given the plethora of iden-
tities that were proposed for him, given the juxtaposition of origins and
filiations, what people were really searching for was Christian brethren on
the other side of the world. The question of rivalry would not be raised in
any pressing or conflictual way until the time that "Buddhism" began to be
understood. Prior to that, the question of judgment, of battle, of praise or
scorn, existed only rhetorically. The figure of Hermes, to the extent that it
symbolized the foundation of knowledge and especially the possession of
the most powerful and subtle kind of "sapience," was undoubtedly the
mark of a respect. The comparison with Christ was undoubtedly a sign of
esteem, even though the loss of the original message and corruption in the
worship aspect of the religion would have made the followers of the Buddha both pitiful and grotesque. Nevertheless, in this vast game of per-
mutable and substitutable signs, there was no real understanding of a history, a belief, or a representation of the world by which it could have been
measured. This primitive exterior had nothing more than relatively undif-
ferentiated and barely distinguishable aspects that could be agreed upon.

Even more than Christ, it was believed, the Buddha might have been an
"Ethiopian," with dark skin, thick lips, and kinky hair. This idea was seen as
an attractive one by a number of authors. The first remark concerned his
hair, and the others followed. On 2 February 1786, in the speech given for
the third anniversary of the foundation of the Royal Asiatic Society of
Bengal, its president—the poet, Orientalist, and Sanskrit scholar William
Jones—pointed out that the name "Ethiopians," in certain texts of antiquity, included the peoples of India, adding: "We frequently see representations of the Buddha with kinky hair, which were apparently aiming at
depicting him in his natural state."[31] In the third publication of *Asiatick
Researches*, in 1792, Lieutenant Wilford, in a long article aimed at showing
that the Indians had specific knowledge about the course of the Nile,
maintained that the physical appearance of the Buddha was of "Ethiopian

type," rather than Indian: "Whether the Buddha was a sage or a hero, the   35
head of a colony, or even an entire colony personified, whether he was black
or white, that his hair was kinky or straight, or if he even had hair at all . . . if
he appeared ten, two hundred, or a thousand years after Krishna, it is
completely certain that he was not of truly Indian descent: in all the images
and all the statues of Buddhas, both male and female, which can be seen in a
number of places in these provinces and these two peninsulas, there is
something Egyptian or Ethiopian in their appearance; and in physical characteristics as well as in dress, he differs greatly from the figures of the
ancient heroes and demigods of the Hindus."[32] This assertion was subsequently used on a number of occasions. For example, Captain Robert Percival, in 1803, remarked that "Buddou is always shown with thick, black,
curly hair, like an African black man."[33]

In 1819, in the *Journal des Savants*, the French Sinologue Jean-Pierre Abel-
Rémusat refuted this hypothesis, which he judged to be contrary not only to
plausibility, but also to the epithets traditionally attributed to the Buddha,
and particularly to his hair, by the traditional Sanskrit vocabulary.[34] In any
case, the idea of a "Black Buddha" continued to spread for at least a
decade.[35] It was still sufficiently present in memories in 1850 that Eugène
Burnouf, whose work was foundational to the scientific analysis of the
Buddhist phenomenon, went to the trouble of specifying, in his study "On
the Thirty Two Characteristic Signs of a Great Man," that analysis of the
Sanskrit and Tibetan terms describing the Buddha's hair, his tightly ringed
locks, and the darkness of his complexion, do not allow us "to conclude so
quickly that the founder of Buddhism belonged to the Negro race."[36] Not
without irony, he concluded his analysis a few pages later: "We are presently
in a position to appreciate the correctness of the inductions that a few
scholars early in this century reached from the appearance of the hair on the
statues of Buddhas. These statues, no more than the written authorities that
describe them, do not tell us of kinky hair, but rather of curly hair, two
things that are sufficiently dissimilar that they should not be confused."[37]
    Nothing seemed to stand in the way of the many combinations of these
myriad possibilities. It would have been possible, for example, to envision
that the Buddha was an Ethiopian who went to Egypt to read the Penta-
teuch, who left there to go to Japan, passing through India on his way,
where the earliest Greeks had gone to seek the first seeds of their knowledge from him. This combination is not a whimsical invention. We find
under Diderot's pen, in the many articles from his *Encyclopédie* where

36 the teachings of the Buddha are referred to, a quite similar melange of elements that not only erudition, but also simple good sense show to be irreconcilable.

A Quite Discreet Nothingness

Let it be said again: in the gray continuity of that "primitive world," where divinities ended up replacing one another, where mythologies reciprocally answered and translated one another, the unity of the world was intact. There was not a multiplicity of histories with no necessary connection to one another; there were not disperse mythologies; nor were there separate systems, each of which was unique. In the place of disparate, heterogeneous, irreducibly diverse worlds—difficult to grasp since each was singular, and difficult to understand given their dissimilarity—there quite reassuringly reigned a single grand, smooth shore where all the differences ended up being canceled out and melted together through the magical interexpression of symbols, of figures, and of powers.

In this drab unity, the Buddha was still no more than an idol without a face. It was only very slightly a question of nothingness in this literature on primitive religions. There undoubtedly existed, limited solely to an anecdote transmitted by the Jesuits, a portrait of the Buddha depicted as a master deceiver who on his deathbed revealed to his followers that all was nothingness, that that was the only truth, that he had been fooling them all along.[38] But this was no more than an incidental element in a corner of the picture. The total picture would be modified. At the beginning of the nineteenth century, the Buddha began to be an indistinct idol no longer. He became—and abruptly enough to make one wary—a "distinguished philosopher." This transformation remains to be described.

2

Bouddou, Distinguished Philosopher

In 1817, a small work—today forgotten—is published
in Paris. The author is obscure; its text, rarely mentioned.
However, it marks radical changes in the way the Buddha
is regarded.

Descended from the altar upon which blindness and superstition placed him, Buddou is a distinguished philosopher, a wise man born for the happiness of his fellow creatures and the good of humanity.

—Michel-Jean-François Ozeray, *Recherches sur Buddou ou Bouddou, Instituteur religieux de l'Asie orientale*, 1817

"This god was a man." The statement marks a break: the move from myth to history. Better: if "Bouddha" was not the name of a divine power, then it was possible that Buddhism was not a "religion" in the accepted meaning of the term. The above quotation appears in a little book published in 1817: *Recherches sur Buddou ou Bouddou . . .* , by Michel-Jean-François Ozeray.[1] This was one of the very first works in the French language in which the term "bouddisme" [*sic*] appears, to denote the "religion of Bouddou," which the author contrasted with "the principal religious aberrations of polytheism."[2] Aside from this distinctive feature, these pages seem to have only very few reasons to hold a reader's attention. They contained neither any Orientalist discovery nor any purely philosophical analysis. The author did not reveal any new information con-

38 cerning the Buddha. The authors he quoted were not the most current: La Loubère, de Guignes, Sonnerat, Kaempfer, Pallas, Paulin de Saint Barthélemy, and so on. His sources dated from before the development of Indianism that occurred during the years preceding the publication of his opuscule. The tone of the first pages, the ambitious works whose arrival these pages proclaimed, suggested an author who, in spite of his mature years,[3] still confused projects and their completion.

However, in its insignificant way, this short text signaled profound changes of perspective. Its author obviously did not "produce" such modifications. But the hundred or so pages he devoted to "Buddou" or "Bouddou," in their apparent banality—even up to the hesitation regarding the appropriate name for this new object of current curiosity and of future studies—drew the first traits of a face of the Buddha that has not stopped preoccupying Europe. The opuscule brought together elements that would furnish the substance of new common ground in the years to come. It should thus be thought of as an example, or a symptom, for remembering the primary transformations of which it is evidence.

Nothing but a Man

The first indication concerned the human and therefore historical nature of the personage whose name was still hard to pinpoint. He was a "deified man,"[4] not a divinity. "One must not confuse deified Bouddou with all those gods that are products of immorality. . . . In the fable of Bouddou is something of his history."[5] This initial affirmation led to the rejection of all of the preceding comparisons to mythological figures. Believing—like La Loubère and, even more so, Paulin de Saint Barthélemy—that the Buddha was "the spirit of the sky, Mercury, the god of the sciences and the arts," amounted to "a rash judgment,"[6] in matters that did not allow one. Although M.-J.-F. Ozeray decidedly mentioned not a single new fact and could hardly produce proof to support his peremptory declarations, he audaciously wrote: "One cannot raise the slightest doubt as to the identity of the personage."[7]

The only proof mentioned concerned the statues of Buddha, all identical in the various temples, from Ceylon to Tibet. These same statues were referred to by Paulin de Saint Barthélemy to uphold the exact opposite affirmation: the identity of Buddha and of Mercury. Thus, it was not the state of available information that changed, but rather the way it was considered and the meaning it was given. The same accounts, the same evidence that some years earlier supported the Buddha-Mercury thesis, served here to proclaim that the Buddha was a man. Buddha was still a "religious teacher of Asia." But he no longer had a divine essence.

This allowed for a new consequence: the revealed religion could be preserved. To state only the human existence of Buddha, to lead thus to the study of his Asian nature, was to break with what was linking the themes of the "primitive world" and the "original revelation." In a move that broke with the attitudes of the classical age, Ozeray swept aside from the outset all discussions that would focus on the Buddha's supposed participation in knowledge of the Scriptures, by means of some primary revelation or through some kind of transmission. "Buddha," he wrote, "is not the guardian of the most ancient and most authentic traditions; he did not step into the light of this torch with which Moses led us to the cradle of the world and made us contemplate the admirable work of the creation."[8] This in no way prevented the "legislator," by means of "beautiful and imposing maxims," from combating and subduing superstition.

Another indication was that this "famous personage," neither god nor prophet, was not simply, or vulgarly, a man. He was a philosopher. The form of this Buddha-philosopher would occupy the century. Ozeray's brochure was in some way one of his births. For, throughout the chapters, the hero was not judged to be wise, or saintly, but rather, most often, a philosopher—in a sense that at once evokes the use of reason against dogmatism, the practice of the mastery of self, and the primacy accorded to morality. It was thus advisable to abandon the esoteric representations of a Buddha-idol whose form was uncertain and whose absurdity suddenly became obvious. "Descended from the altar where blindness and superstition placed him, Buddou was a distinguished philosopher, a wise man born for the happiness of his fellow creatures and the good of humanity."[9] This is why Buddhism, in the eyes of Ozeray, "enjoys a kind of universality."[10] The planet Mercury seemed decidedly far away.

The Life of a Moralist

What remained to be known was which system was connected with this philosopher, or at the very least what main idea oriented his thought. A great vagueness prevailed. The activity of the Buddha-reformer seemed to have been restricted to diminishing obscurantism and savagery, to reforming morals, and, in so doing, even attenuating them. This was certainly not insignificant. But it was in no way the distinctive trait that allowed recog-

40 nition of a system of thought like no other. The invention of metempsychosis, which M.-J.-F. Ozeray attributed to his personage, hardly made the
description more precise, as might be seen from the following:

> On the first level of error, where altars were raised to the noblest
> aspects of nature as to so many divinities, everyone built to his
> liking. In the middle of this deluge of false opinions, a man born in
> east Asia presented a less crude polytheism to the people there; he
> freed the religion of its most monstrous superstitions, and he gave it
> a religious morality and a system of punishments and rewards—a
> very singular and especially new system—metempsychosis. These
> are the merits of this dogmatic enthusiast and this austere philoso-
> pher; these are the degrees by which he reached his apotheosis.[11]

The historical intervention of the "philosopher" was described—at the
very least—in broad strokes. But the attitude was favorable. This Buddha
was nice. Progressive, one might say. His actions changed the course of
things, broke with the *status quo* of an archaic tradition, reformed the spiritual world. These traits would likewise remain stated in a variety of ways,
judged in differing manners, almost always negatively. Consistent with the
idea that Buddha was a philosopher, Ozeray stated as an implicit rule of
method that it was always possible to recognize the rational core of his
undertaking behind the fable: "Let us consider as certain that mythological
aberrations take nothing away from the heart of the Buddha's teachings
[when they are] reduced to their fundamental points."[12]

This is a major point. Although it is here only a *petitio principii* directly
linked to the preceding ones (Buddha is a man, this man is a philosopher), it
marks a new intention: that of teasing out a veritable system of thought
from the Buddhist texts, even when it is a question of works overloaded
with mythical accounts and fabulous episodes, encumbered by myriads of
fantastic "embellishments." In the second half of the century, commentators would be split on this matter. By affirming the existence of a "content"
of Buddhist rationality independent of the aberrant "forms" with which
history has clothed it, Ozeray once again broke with earlier points of view.

It is true that the "fundamental point" of this "basic teaching" remained hazy. What remained was the primordial place accorded to morality
in the analysis of Buddhism, a major trait that would subsequently be seen
in the works of many later authors. This morality was called "grand and
sublime."[13] Outlining the details of its contents and explicating all the details of its maxims remained difficult: specific information was still lacking.
Such a situation did not prevent the author from attributing to the one he

called "our philosopher" the curtailing of human sacrifices and the prohibition against abandoning the elderly and leaving children out to die, before repeating, following the ranks of already old and known glossarists (La Loubère, de Guignes, Kaempfer), the five points that constitute what is considered to be Buddhist morality: "Kill no animal, do not steal, commit no impure act, never lie, and drink no intoxicating spirit."[14]

These similarities are not of the same type as those relating to the primitive world. In the closed system of recognition and identification, any new element (X), even imperfectly defined, was already comparable to (Y) or (Z). "Knowing better" only meant having at one's disposal supplementary arguments to support and reinforce an already imposed equality. Here, the possibility of effective historical research opened up. It was not simply a question of knowing this supposed philosophical doctrine better. It might have been a question of finding, next to the mass of legendary tales, clues to the life of the "real" man-Buddha. They were few and far between. "In truth, our biographical literature only offers brief glimpses."[15] But nothing, in fact, keeps us from thinking that new research will bring still unknown elements and brand new details. On this point also, the perspective totally broke with that of the primitive world.

The bare necessities of any possible biography: knowing where and at what date the Buddha lived. Ozeray vacillated among several regions: Siam, following Sonnerat; Kashmir, after Jones; Bengal, with Chambers. He decided on Ceylon. So Bouddou was born in Ceylon, "in about 1029 B.C."[16] The story of his life was extremely perfunctory: "Son of a king (of Ceylon, according to Japanese tradition), he left the paternal palace at the age of nineteen, abandoned his wife and son to be the disciple of a hermit who had a great reputation of austerity."[17] That was all. There was not even any question of the other rupture, by which the Buddha abandoned austerity and mortification. This second break, symmetrical and the inverse of the separation from the luxury of the paternal palace, was nonetheless inseparable from the constitution of the middle way, and was an integral part of the "dual refusal" that characterized the Buddha's attitude.

What did it matter? Even fragmentary and disappointing, or even impossible, what was needed was the biography of a real man. These were no longer the conventional attributes of an imaginary being that people invent or repeat. This will to separate truth from legend continued, without the solution of continuity, up to the present time. After centuries and centuries of interpolations, of additions to imaginary episodes, of willingness to magnify the noble achievements attributed to the Blessed One, of customs taken from the marvelous and from hyperbole, it was undoubtedly difficult

42 to make a clear distinction between what was historically certain, what was doubtful, and what was clearly invented in the Buddha's biography. Perhaps this was a task where it was even impossible to succeed. It was, however, worth pursuing, and the monumental work of André Bareau has shown that new advances remained possible.[18]

There is more. Before the multiform study of the schools that claimed to represent his teaching began, before the specter of "Buddhism" that would haunt Europe took shape, what was presented was a silhouette of the Buddha. The shape of the founder, his personality, his character traits, and the characteristics of his spiritual path would continue to raise questions, to such an extent that the "life of Buddha" could be considered a Western literary genre in the nineteenth century that still remained to be studied—to such an extent, especially, that comparing him with Christ would seem inevitable. The "lives of the Buddha" would rival the "lives of Jesus"—with all the possible characteristics of such a dialogue. The comparison would conclude in favor of one or the other, or proclaim the absence of difference, or even the affirmation of some hypothetical historical relationship.

Ozeray was undoubtedly still far from the "Jesus-Buddha" literature that would develop in the second half of the century and become abundant in its final decades. But the changing outlook indicated by this book opened the way to this kind of speculation at the same time. Indeed, from the time when a man supplants the idol, the question of the relationship between this philosopher deified by his disciples and God-made-man arises. How is it not obvious, especially, that such a "personalization"[19] strongly distinguishes the Buddha's doctrine from the rest of the Indian heritage? Brahmanism, which romantic Europe was in the process of discovering through the work of Sanskrit scholars, considered the text of the Vedas to be revealed. The traditional thought and works of India were not "signed." Their "authors" were gods, or mythical names, that transmitted "truths" that they neither invented nor discovered.

On the contrary, the Buddha's sermons, the stories of his life, and the dogmatic treatises attributed to his disciples all carried the mark of a link with a human reality. It mattered little, from this point of view, that this reality was reconstructed by the imagination and made to measure afterward. What distinguished radically the place of the Buddha in India was that he did not fit into the scheme of an immemorial and self-justified tradition. The Buddha was not content with transmitting or reviving a native truth. Breaking with what came before, proclaiming his autonomy simply, his preaching was legitimized by his experience and nothing more. The founding theme of the Awakening (the *bodhi*, whence came Gautama's sobriquet, the "Buddha," that is, the "Awakened One") had no other meaning.

European opinion would be increasingly sensitive to this singularity of the Buddha in Indian history. In his own way, Ozeray referred to the premises of this long fascination. Once again, even if no other purely philological discovery proved the worth of these *Recherches sur Buddou ou Bouddou*, the work indicated the profound change taking place in the representation of the Buddha. Admittedly, in more than one way, this 1817 book still belonged to the eighteenth century. For example, it continued to affirm the anteriority of Buddhism over Brahmanism, an idea that irreparably distorted any understanding of the relationship between the Buddha and India. But, as has been seen before, his purpose took shape around theses that had nothing to do with those that the representation of the "primitive world" assumed.

How Many Are There?

One last sign confirms it: the attention paid to the number of Buddhists. The issue was never dealt with in the works of the authors comparing Buddha to Mercury, Thot, or Odin. The mythological identification seemed to screen the demographic reality. Hermes' twin remained a god of immaterial existence, an idol without flesh-and-blood followers. No one inquired about the number of his actual followers. Knowing of their present existence, and their dissemination throughout Asia, no one dreamed of the crowd thus formed. The nineteenth century was acquainted with this concern for numbers up to the torments of an obsession: it counted Buddhists by tens, by hundreds, by millions. They were said to be more numerous than Christians, their swarming struck a note of fear, as with Ozanam, or else their multitudes elicited joy, as was the case with Schopenhauer.

Ozeray, for his part, put the number of those who "follow the . . . opinions uttered" by "Bouddou" at "more than a hundred million individuals."[20] He justified his calculations in some ten pages at the end of his opuscule, in which he attempted to proceed, region by region, to estimate the general population and the proportion of Buddhists in the whole picture. It is of secondary importance that the numbers are figments of the imagination. What is important is that, in their desire to measure and apprehend reality, they lined up from page to page by inaugurating a long series of additional peoples.

44 *The Specter's Sketch*

Doubtless the cult of nothingness was still far from arriving. Between this distinguished Buddha philosopher, who fought superstition and bloody sacrifices as an informed moralist and, on the other hand, the incoherent, destructive, stupid, or perverse preacher who emerged in the works of subsequent commentators, the difference was obviously more than marginal. But even though the theme of nothingness was still not in the picture, even though nothing about this "Bouddou" seemed to be frightening, it might nevertheless still be noted that some of the new traits could easily become grounds for concern. Might it not be threatening for Europe that the Buddhists were so numerous? That their belief was a purely human way to salvation, without revelation or transcendence? That their nihilism was creating new followers? That the Buddha was in competition with Christ as a real historical figure, with his paradoxes, his harshness, his disconcerting density, rather than a malleable idol with uncertain and changing attributes?

Nothing yet created real dread. But it was not far away. The essential background was ready. Only a few characters were missing. They were coming.

3
A World Emerges

In thirty or so years (1800–1830), the universe of Buddhism appears in its diversity and its unity. Orientalists establish that the Buddha's religion postdates Brahmanism. They outline the history of its spread in China, in Japan, or in Tibet, and begin to decipher texts. . . . A doctrine of nothingness? "Not at all," say the scholars.

Questions regarding Buddha's religion are neither idle nor in pure curiosity.

—*Le Globe*, 25 November 1829

Francis Buchanan's study, "On the Religion and Literature of Burma," was published in 1799, in volume 6 of *Asiatick Researches*.[1] The text was read, some years later, by both Hegel and Schopenhauer. This long article was one of the first to insist strongly on the differences between the Brahmans and the Buddhists, to be inspired by Burmese texts that themselves came from Pali originals. More than anything, it offered the first coherent approach to the singularity of the concept of nirvana, neither total collapse nor fusion in the divine essence. On the other hand, the circumstances of its composition were exemplary of the situation existing in this field of studies that was barely beginning its existence just at the point of transition from the eighteenth to the nineteenth century. Indeed, Buchanan spent only very little time in Burma, and he did not speak the language. While he was

46   on this trip, Captain Symes gave him a manuscript in Latin, written by an Italian missionary, Vincentius Sangermano. Sangermano had translated two Buddhist treatises from Pali. He had also translated from Burmese into Latin—probably so that the work of the missionaries could be based on a better knowledge of the adverse arguments—a text written by Buddhist doctors in reaction to the arrival of these Christian missionaries; its aim was to convert the Christians to Buddhism. Buchanan wrote only one text based on the three, and translated it from Latin to English, slipping in his own observations and remarks. The filters of successive translations and the diverse judgments of an observer who does not hesitate to label Buddhist doctrines as absurd or crazy therefore intervene between the original texts and the Western reader.

Thirty years later, in 1829, the French newspaper *Le Globe*, in its Wednesday, 25 November, edition, published an article covering its entire front page titled "About Buddhism." It began with the sentence: "For some time now Oriental studies have made great progress among Europeans." The fundamental reference points were thenceforth established. The respective positions of Brahmanism and Buddhism were set in their broad lines: "Buddhism, according to what we know up to now about its history and its teachings, was in India, in relation to the dominant religion of this vast land, approximately what the Reformation was in Europe in relation to the Catholic religion." The author then qualified this judgment, trying to clear up confusion that the analogy might engender, but the original and primitive nature of Buddhism, its anteriority over Brahmanism, already belonged to past knowledge. Likewise, unreliable identifications were set aside in the name of a growing convergence of scholarly judgments in favor of the Indian nature of Buddhism:

> The opinion of Kaempfer, who thought that Buddha was the priest from Memphis, that of W. Jones, and of other writers who consider him the same character as the Woden, or Odin, of the Scandinavians, cannot reasonably be admitted, in spite of the great authority of these writers. Nor can the countless images of the Buddha that represent him with frizzy hair support the belief that he was a native of Ethiopia. The new paleographic discoveries concerning the Orient confirm incontestably the most commonly held opinion of his Indian origin.

The very idea of a "common opinion" supposes a plurality of specialists. The anonymous author[2] of this article relied notably on a series of works that began to explain Buddhism from several distinct domains of Oriental-

ism: the studies of the French Sinologue Jean-Pierre Abel-Rémusat, those
of the specialist of Mongolian culture, Julius von Klaproth, a German living
in Paris, and those of the British Brian Houghton Hodgson, resident of
Nepal, who brought to light the existence of a good number of Sanskrit
sources conserved in the Himalayan regions.

Between Buchanan's article and the one published by *Le Globe*—just
thirty years separated them, as we have seen—a body of knowledge began
to form. "Buddhism" was born, and with it the "cult of nothingness."
Indeed, we see forming at the same time, then growing together hand in
hand, both the scholarly study of the doctrines, and their interpretations,
centered around the different registers of nihilism. Until the end of the
century, one was not seen without the other. It is false to think that the
positive work of the Oriental scholars dissipated, as it advanced, tenacious
errors and alarming ideas. The example was completely different: their
most objective works aroused phantasmagorias, invited dreaming, nourished delirium. If a profound sharing existed, it was not, in the end, between
the hard patience of the linguists and historians and the fabrication of the
philosophers. For several decades, the latter would feed on the former.

New Questions

The only true rupture brings up previously nonexistent questions. The
identity of the Buddha was sought, as was the significance of his name, the
dates of his birth and death, the details of his education. People wondered
for what reasons Buddhism disappeared in India, by what means it was
spread over the Asian continent. When these questions became explicit,
"Buddhism" came into being as one element in a body of knowledge that
was possible for Western consciousness. It was understood that it did not
matter that these questions could not all be immediately answered. The
essential here was obviously the drafting of the questions themselves. They
were what defined the field of research and made it exist by marking its
boundaries. These questions, one of which resulted from the other, were
not really a multiplicity of questions. They were only variations of the single,
same query: what is Buddhism?

Once this question was formulated, the answer could remain outstand-
ing, perplexity could be declared, ignorance could be confessed. The question of Buddhism was nonetheless asked. Even if its specificity remained
unknown, it was henceforth to be known. Its identity remained problematic, but at least it was actually a problem to be solved. Thus, in 1833, August
Wilhelm Schlegel, one of the great German figures in Sanskrit philology,

48   could write in his review *Indische Bibliothek*: "I could not manage to form a clear idea of Buddha's doctrine, either in itself or in its relationship or its opposition to Brahmanism."[3] Again in 1839, in the very Catholic review *Annales de philosophie chrétienne*, Abbot de Valroger spoke of the Buddha as "this truly mysterious character [who] seems to get lost in the night of the ages and to be linked by some secret tie with all that is most ancient, most obscure, either in the Orient or the Occident."[4] These two sentences, one scholarly, the other naïve, remind us, if need there be to remind, that everything does not change from one day to the next in the history of ideas. This is why attempting to set dates and to fix reference points can become deceptive. One would be deluded indeed in thinking that one knew the exact date when everything would change radically. But it is possible to proceed by approximation, almost to seize the moment when an affirmation, until then accepted, seems outdated and begins to become difficult to maintain.

The Right Chronology

The most significant example is undoubtedly the chronological place of Buddhism in relation to Brahmanism. The entire eighteenth century was convinced of the anteriority of Buddhism over Brahmanism. This judgment was not absurd: it corresponded, in a pertinent way, to what was ascertained. The idea of an original Indian religion, later driven out of the subcontinent by new arrivals—a false idea with regard to historical reality—was coherent with direct observations. It could evoke the physics of Aristotle, explaining why wood floats (it contains air and tends to seek height) and why a stone sinks (it is "earthy" and moves to the bottom). Indeed, what did Europeans observe in India at that time? They could note that the temples of the Buddha were abandoned, that no religion remained, that no disciple visited the ruins of these monuments anymore. The faithful were in China or Tibet, in Mongolia or Siam. How could one not believe, given the model of the arrival of Christians in pagan lands, that the Brahmans evicted this primitive religion, fought some more or less bloody war with it, and finally drove these idolatrous rituals into the surrounding areas where they survived with other, perhaps less sophisticated, peoples?

Numerous texts were built on this framework. In 1777, Father Coeurdoux, a Jesuit, wrote an important manuscript on the *Moeurs et Coutumes des Indiens* (Habits and Customs of the Indians). The authorship of this text was attributed to him definitively thanks to the perspicacity of Sylvia Murr.[5] The following passage is a good example of the most common

state of knowledge and lack thereof relative to the history of Buddhism, 49
among those knowledgeable on Indian matters at the end of the eighteenth
century:

> However ancient I believe the Brahmans of India to be, I do not
> think they were the first to spread Idolatry there. They were pre-
> ceded by other sectarians who, although they shared a common ori-
> gin with them, and the same language, were very different from the
> Brahmans. These are the worshipers of Boud. Their sect spreads
> from the depths of Turkestan to Cape Comorin in the south, on the
> north side into both Tibets. To the East, it goes into Pegu, the
> kingdoms of Siam, Laos, Cambodia and perhaps many other coun-
> tries. I except China for these distant times. It was only shortly after
> the birth of Jesus Christ that this idolatry passed through the king-
> dom of Siam, following the history of China. This worship of Boud
> still survives wholly in Tibet, in the kingdom of Siam, and in many
> other countries, even in some cantons of India, and especially in the
> island of Ceylon. It was almost exterminated by the Brahmans in
> India beyond the Ganges.

The spread of Buddhism throughout diverse regions of Asia was thus
perceived, but its effective temporal relationship with the religious ideas
and the rites of the Brahmans was reversed. This belief in the anteriority of
Buddhism over Brahmanism endured for a considerable time. Omnipresent in the works of the eighteenth century, it persisted some time after the
beginning of the nineteenth. Buchanan's study of the religion of Burma—
cited above, published in Calcutta by the *Asiatick Researches* in 1799, but
principally diffused in London, Paris, and Bonn between 1803 and 1810—
supposed the adoption by the Brahmans of the reigning religion, that of the
"sect of Buddha," at the time of their arrival in Hindustan, as they say. This
conversion contributed to damaging even more, according to him, beliefs
that were already somewhat incoherent: "However pointless and ridiculous
the legends and ideas of the followers of Buddha may have been, they were
in large part adopted by the Brahmans, but horrendously increased in all
their defects."[6]

In the first years of the nineteenth century, doubts were born. People
began to ask questions about the respective positions of Brahmanism and
Buddhism, albeit without being yet in a position to come to a decision in
any soundly argued way. In 1805, Langlès, curator of Oriental manuscripts
for the Imperial Library, annotated the French translation by Labaume of
the first two volumes of *Asiatick Researches*, an edition to which Cuvier and

50 Lamarck, especially, contributed, for the exact sciences. While remaining true to the theory of original Buddhism, the Orientalist became prudent: "The history of the religion of Buddha, and that of Tibet, are too little known for us to seek to discover the era of the establishment of this priesthood, which I believe, moreover, to be well before Brahmanism."[7] Even though the old opinion of the anteriority of Buddhism remains, its justification changes. This evidence becomes problematic: why exactly do we think that Buddhism came first? In Joinville's opinion, in 1801, the preposterousness of Buddhist beliefs was a guarantee of their primitive nature: "An uncreated world and moral souls, these are ideas that one can have only in an infantile state of society, and as society progresses such ideas must vanish—*a fortiori*, they cannot be established in opposition to a religion already dominant in the country whose fundamental articles of faith are the creation of the world and the immortality of the soul."[8] On the contrary, in 1817, Tytler expressed the view in his *Enquête sur l'origine et les principes du bouddhisme sabique*, that it was the virtuous simplicity of Buddhism that proved its ancient character: "The simplicity that one can discern in Buddhism, and the authentically disinterested principles of humanity and piety that impregnate the whole system, demonstrate clearly the early nature of this admirable and unadorned system in relation to the complicated structure [of Brahmanism]."[9]

The anteriority of Buddhism was no longer a *petitio principii*, an unquestionable piece of evidence, but rather a supposition that had henceforth to be justified. But these justifications began to become confused and proved to be uncertain; they lost their categorical evidence. On 3 February 1827, Henry Thomas Colebrooke[10] read the Royal Asiatic Society his dissertation on the sects of the Jains and the Buddhists, in which he proved how these two philosophico-religious doctrines were dissents against Brahmanism and in some way were heresies stemming from Vedic dogma. The first European monograph based on Sanskrit texts, Colebrooke's detailed work affirmed from the outset that the Buddhists belong to the same cultural background as Brahmanism: "The Jainas and the Bauddhas," he said, "I consider to have been originally Hindus."[11] However, his study was supported, as he informed his listeners and readers from the outset, only by the criticisms addressed by the Brahmans to the Buddhists, not on Buddhist texts themselves, to which he was unable to have access. Although the very detailed "accusation" of the Brahmans—in the case of the *Vedantins*—offers a relatively precise idea of the accused, it is never more than the prosecutor's file to which one begins to have access.

That said, it is fair to think that scholarly opinion began to change markedly in the early 1830s. One needs no more proof than the discussion devoted to this question by August Wilhelm Schlegel in 1832. In a booklet written in French, *Réflexions sur l'étude des langues asiatiques* (Reflections on the Study of Asiatic Languages),[12] he eloquently described the different, more or less sectarian groups engendered by the expansion of Indian studies. Among them, one sect "had only too much success: these are the *Bouddhomanes*." Under this term, A. W. Schlegel regrouped those who swore only by Buddha, who still held to the myth of his absolute ancientness, and who continued to maintain, against evidence acquired from then on, that Brahmanism was a latecomer.

> They maintain that Buddhism is more ancient than Brahmanism; that the first was formerly the general religion of India and that the Brahmans are intruders and modern usurpers. It is just as reasonable as if one said that the Jews are the apostates of Islam, and that their rabbis substituted the law of Moses for the Koran. Buddhists themselves, having a rather well established chronology, do not claim this priority, and the borrowing they have made from the doctrine and the religion of the Brahmans is obvious. They have not even supplanted the Brahmanic gods, they have merely placed their prophets above all of them. In vain Mr. Colebrooke has the condescendence to refute the Bouddhomanes with invincible arguments: they continue to bring up the charge without ever entering into the discussion. What was able to give some appearance to this hypothesis for superficial observers is that Buddhism indeed spread through India during a number of centuries. In some provinces it seems to have entirely obliterated the religion of the Brahmans, in such a way that the latter were only able to reestablish their authority after the expulsion of the Buddhists, in a relatively recent era. In these provinces there are thus many monuments to Buddhism, the existence of which proves that the priests of this religion, while renouncing the privilege of birth, were able to take what was due to them, and that they acquired great riches by pious donations. But the Bouddhomanes leave absolutely nothing to the Brahmans: as soon as a sculpted figure is seated with legs crossed, it is infallibly a Buddha in their eyes. I invite them to read the excellent treatise by Mr. Erskine on the distinctive marks that characterize the temples of one religion and the other.[13]

The first turn being taken, in an obviously irreversible way, was that of historicity. The term can be understood in two ways. The change in the

52 knowledge about Buddhism indeed had two aspects. On the one hand, the chronological succession of Brahmanism-Buddhism was recognized. Buddhism now seemed to be younger or, in any case, second. It was no longer antediluvian, archaic, or original. It came after Brahmanism, forming a heresy, a reformation, or a challenge. What it lost in romantic attractiveness and in the power of dreams, it gained in reality. Moreover, it was more like the West, which was, in a sense, also a late-arriving, ratiocinating world opposed to truths that were passively inherited from tradition. It becomes possible to identify with this Buddha who comes over the horizon of history, stands out against the motionless background of immemorial revelations, and seems already to break away from beliefs received as if from established orders. As a result his dissent was not unlike that of Socrates, or Christ, or Luther, understood as emblematic of the Western spirit.

On the other hand, conquered historicity signifies as well, in a way obviously indissociable from the concern for chronological exactness, that Buddha is henceforth considered a real individual, having existed in a given place and at a given time, and whose deeds and gestures must be learned. This acknowledgment, as was seen regarding the little work by Ozeray,[14] gave rise to the demand to know specifically when the Buddha lived, to establish what he thought and preached, to translate the texts that bear witness to his teaching and to the interpretations of commentators. This accession to historicity is accompanied by a will to situate the Buddha, to place him within a culture, on a spiritual, social, and linguistic horizon. The second turning point thus begun, we can anticipate as well the recognition of the "Indian-ness" of Buddhism, of its belonging to a common background of Indian civilization, in spite of both its heterodox nature and its pan-Asiatic destiny. In Europe at that time, people did not know the subtle distinction in modern Anglo-Indian vocabulary between what is *Indian* (an entity geographically present in the Indian territory—without necessarily coming from it, however; such as, for example, Islam), what is Hindu (any element connected to Hinduism, to its myths, its rites, and its history) and—a category untranslatable in French—what is *Indic* (a creation which by its very nature remains Indian, even if it has left the territory and broken away from Hinduism). We cannot therefore say, around 1839, that Buddhism is *Indic*. But it is certainly toward this idea that we are moving.

Two Buddhas or Only One?

Among the signs of the change in course, the theory of the two Buddhas is worthy of note. We begin to see the existence of a historical individ-

ual next to the primitive idol. But one does not preclude the other. During   53
the first quarter of the nineteenth century the original sign of Mercury
coexisted with both the ancient Buddha and—"not to be confused" with
this founding figure, as the commentators state—a historically datable,
recent, and human Buddha. The hypothesis was outlined for the first time
by Antoine Augustin Giorgi, in 1762, in his *Alphabetum Tibetanum*. It was
repeated, expanded, and spread by William Jones in a text written in January
1788, devoted to the study of the chronology of the Hindus, and published
two years later in the second volume of the *Asiatick Researches*.[15] The principal difficulty from the outset for Jones was the contradiction that can be
seen in the discourse of the Brahmans relative to the Buddha: on the one
hand they are very hostile to him; on the other, they recognize in him an
incarnation of Vishnu. "The Brahmans constantly speak of the Buddhas
with all the malevolence of an intolerant spirit; yet the most orthodox
among them consider Buddha himself as an incarnation of Vishnu. This is a
contradiction that is hard to reconcile; unless we cut the knot, instead of
untying it, by supposing with Giorgi, that there were two Buddhas, the
younger of whom established the new religion that caused such trouble in
India, and was introduced into China in the first century of our era."[16]

In 1827, Benjamin Constant, who followed the Orientalist publications
of his time with great attention and devoted long passages to them in *De la
religion*,[17] indicated clearly what the perplexity of his time was toward Buddhism, and why the theory of the "two Buddhas" seemed to offer a way out
of these difficulties:

> The scholars are divided on the person and the era of Buddha.
> Some consider his religion a deviation, a reformation or a heresy
> that got into the religion of Brahma, and Buddha consequently as
> later than the Buddha himself. Others have adopted the opposite
> opinion. They confuse Baouth—an ancient idol of whom one still
> finds here and there rough images and temples falling in ruins—
> with Buddha. They suppose that his religion, anterior to *Bramaïsme*
> [*sic*], was supplanted and proscribed by the Brames, and took refuge
> in Tibet, in Ceylon, in Tartary, in Japan, and in China, while remain-
> ing in some Indian tribes.
>
> This question is very difficult to shed light on: on the one hand
> the religion of Baouth would seem to be older than *Bramaïsme*. The
> traditions attached to it and the crude exterior of the figures indi-
> cate fetishism. On the other hand, the Buddha who pondered the
> abolition of the castes certainly came after Brama. The castes must

54 have been established without contradiction, or they would never have been established. Buddha could attack them, after they were dedicated, as modern philosophers have attacked existing institutions; but these institutions preceded the philosophers.

The difficulty would resolve itself by admitting to two Buddhas: the first would be the same as the former Baouth, and the second the author of the religion that produced the schism in India and was introduced into China with the substitution of the name Fo for that of Buddha. Then there would be nothing in common between the second Buddha and the ancient Baouth.[18]

This Baouth, inherited from the night of time, soon ceased to be in competition with Buddha. After 1830, the theory of the two Buddhas faded. Undoubtedly it survived for a long period, and the moment of its extinction would be set at one time or the other, depending on whether scholarly publications or popular works are used. In the works of the Orientalists, not more than one Buddha is recognized from the beginning of the fourth decade of the century. In a good number of encyclopedias, on the other hand, for still another ten years, two articles on "Buddha" were frequently found—one devoted to the original idol, Mercury-*mercredi*, the symbol of the primitive world, and the other centered on the historical reformer of Brahmanism, Gautama the Buddha, and his preaching in opposition to the traditional hierarchical order.

Moreover, a time lag of the same sort is discernible everywhere. Whether it is a question of the anteriority of Brahmanism over Buddhism, of the Indian origin of this pan-Asiatic religion or philosophy, of the presumed date of the birth of the Buddha, or of the salient points of his teachings (the four truths, the theory of the twelve causes, compassion), the average opinion of the cultivated public—as we might think it is shaped by journals and dictionaries—is considerably later than the consensus of the Orientalists.

The Mastery of Languages

One thing, at least, is certain: the emergence of the Buddhist world in European eyes came primarily through deciphering languages and translating texts. There again, the situation was radically different from the discovery of Brahmanism. In order to have access to the fundamental sources of Brahmanism, the mastery of Sanskrit alone sufficed. It was undoubtedly a

long time coming. Even once mastery was reached, the language of the 55
Vedas and its archaic expressions, distinct from those of classical Sanskrit,
undoubtedly gave scholars a hard time. But a unity of language, of culture,
and, if we dare say, of "spiritual place" seems given from the outset. It
was not the same for Buddhism, subjected to a kind of linguistic and
cultural diaspora where Westerners had long had difficulty getting their
bearings.

The first glimmers came from the Chinese domain. Thanks to the
methodical efforts of the Frenchman Jean-Pierre Abel-Rémusat, reformed
Sinology contributed to the foundation of Buddhist studies. After 1815,
Abel-Rémusat studied the adjectives describing the Buddha, opened up the
Manchu domain, tried to untangle the chronology of the Buddhist patriarchs and the lamas, recalled that Buddha was not black, and studied the
"cosmos" of the Buddhists from Chinese sources.[19] Hegel encountered
him in Paris at the committee of the *Journal des Savants*, and Schopenhauer
read him attentively.

The philosopher of pessimism also studied the works of the Russian
Isaac Jacob Schmidt,[20] who was one of the first to make known a few
fragments of the traditions of the Great Vehicle according to Mongolian
sources. He revealed, in sometimes wild interpretations, possible parallels
between Buddhism and gnosis.[21] It was Schmidt, as well, who was somewhat
later responsible for the first work on the *Prajnâparamita* (1836).[22] The Mongolian manuscripts were deciphered also by Julius von Klaproth, who published, among other works, a *Vie de Bouddha d'après les livres mongols* (The Life
of Buddha in Mongol Books).[23] This first textual knowledge of Buddhism
begins, therefore, with the end. It follows the inverse order of the effective
evolution of the doctrines. The latest schools and texts are tackled before
those that gave rise to them. The Mongolian texts were actually translations
from the Tibetan dating for the most part from the fourteenth century; the
Chinese works were from well after the Indian corpora. The same is true of
the Tibetan *Tanjur* and *Kanjur*, which Alexandre Csoma de Körös began to
introduce.[24] Therefore, people read the glossaries before they had access to
the treatises they concerned. They knew both the names of schools of logic
and some fragments of their lines of argument—culminations of a long and
complex history—before clearly seeing the points of departure.

Next to a new exploration of domains already formerly known, like the
Chinese or Mongol corpora, a major role was played by the deciphering of
new languages, yielding the key to entire regions of the Buddhist world.
Young men threw themselves into this adventure with as much enthusiasm

56 as genius. When he deciphered the Pali alphabet, Eugène Burnouf was not even twenty-five years old.[25] The first lines of the *Essai sur le Pali*, which Burnouf published in 1826 with the Dane Christian Lassen, clarified wonderfully the moment when an essential instrument of discovery was grasped, knowing all along that Buddhism still remained unknown, but that it would not remain so for long.

> Among the numerous special languages that are spoken, or at least are cultivated, on the peninsula beyond the Ganges, Pali or Bali is in several respects one of the most curious. Little known by Europeans, it offers the kind of interest that any new study offers; and furthermore, when one thinks, on the one hand, about its intimate relationship with one famous language, Sanskrit, and on the other hand, about the high position it holds in the nations where it is dominant, one cannot keep from hoping that it will soon become an important branch of the studies presently occupied by European curiosity regarding Asia. Nations whose common languages offer great differences all recognize Pali as their sacred language. From the powerful and vast empire of the Burmese, to the kingdoms of Siam, and perhaps of Tchiampa, it reigns with the venerable title of language of religion and of science; and it tightens the powerful link that, in the philosopher's eyes, brings back under a kind of unity peoples of civilizations as diverse as the heavy and crude mountain dweller of Arakan, and the more civilized inhabitant of Siam. That link is the religion of Buddha, the common divinity of all these peoples. From Tchittagong to China, his religion prevails totally, with its hierarchy, its monasteries, and its succession of philosophical ideas, and it has erased the former popular beliefs so much that it is difficult to find their traces today.
>
> This religion that, in its inner constitution, undoubtedly answers to the needs of Asiatic minds, since nearly all of oriental Asia has adopted it and still speaks it today, can thus, thanks to Pali, which serves as its interpreter, be studied at a new place on the globe . . . and it is perhaps not too audacious to hope that the knowledge of Pali must help, in large part, to lift the veil that still hides the mysteries of Buddhism from our eyes. We can actually believe that closer to India, the place of its origin, this religion must have protected itself, on this peninsula, more easily from all innovation, and kept itself pure from any blending.

From these first works, an assertion is drawn concerning the relationship of Buddhism to nothingness: the relationship does not exist. As soon as the witnesses are heard and the texts deciphered, nirvana and nothingness could not be confused. In substance, this is what the principal authors who participated, along with the Orientalists, in this first stage of discovery maintained. Buchanan was categorical on this point: nirvana has no connection with nothingness, and the translation and commentaries leaning in this direction are inappropriate. " 'Annihilation' used in the text by my friend, and in general by the missionaries when treating on this subject, is a very inaccurate term. 'Nieban' implies being exempted from all the miseries incident to humanity, but by no means annihilation."[26]

The one who was, as we have seen, one of the best Sanskrit scholars of the Calcutta school, Henry Thomas Colebrooke, strongly insisted on this point in the dissertation he devoted to the Buddhists in 1827. Speaking of deliverance (*moshka*) as a happy state from which one does not return, he pointed out that the term that the Buddhists are particularly fond of is nirvana, "profound calm." "The idea attached to this word, in the meaning we are presently examining, is that of perfect apathy. It is a situation of tranquil happiness, unadulterated and without ecstasy."[27] The Buddhists, Colebrooke insists, "do not consider the unending rest attributed to their saints as linked to a discontinuity of individuality. It is not annihilation, but an incessant apathy that they understand by the extinction [*nirvâna*] of their saints."[28] In 1828, in volume 16 of *Asiatic Researches*, the first text sent from Nepal by Brian Houghton Hodgson is in the same vein. Buddhists are not devoted to nonbeing nor are they sectarians of disappearance: "By their doubtful *Sunyata* [vacuity], I do not mean, in general, annihilation, nothingness, but the infinite weakening that they assign to their material strengths and powers in the state of *Nirvritti*."[29]

This serene nirvana, profound calm and incessant apathy, would soon give way to a bottomless abyss where existence vanishes forever. Buddhist emptiness would be considered a universal and radical void, ultimately threatening what humanity holds most precious. In the meantime, in the works of the Orientalists, the first descriptions of Buddhism denied nothingness. Even if they otherwise affirmed that the doctrine was obscure, that its coherence was uncertain, even that its absurdity was obvious, these studies took care to point out that annihilation was not the supreme purpose of the disconcerting religion. But why did this detail seem necessary to

58 them? How was it that these various authors insisted on this point? Might the Buddha, first considered an indistinct idol of the primitive world, then an enlightened founding philosopher of morality in Asia, have still another face? There must have existed some rumor tying together the life of the Buddha and the desire for death. It was undoubtedly already repeated somewhere, even very softly, that this doctrine was a religion of worshiping nothingness. If not, the first "Buddhologists" would not have felt obligated to point out that this was not the case. Where was this said? Who made such comments? How were they passed on?

4

The Nothingness of the Buddhists

Finally, Hegel arrives. With him, in the late 1820s, the myth of the cult of nothingness becomes established. Where did he get this idea? What meaning does the philosopher attribute to the idea?

Nothingness, which the Buddhists have made the beginning principle for everything and the final goal and the ultimate end of everything, is this same abstraction.[1]

—Hegel, *Encyclopédie des sciences philosophiques en abrégé*, 1827

Hegel was extremely attentive to the progress of Orientalism. As scholarly works appeared, he acquainted himself with those that dealt with Persian, Sanskrit, and Chinese. His courses relative to the Orient, whether they were on art, religion, or world history, were founded on first-hand documentation.[2] The philosopher undoubtedly altered the information available, sometimes markedly, to be able to make it fit into his system. But the accuracy of his information was generally remarkable. Concerning Buddhism, Hegel clearly discerned in 1827 that, at least in India, Buddha was a historical figure.[3] He was not unaware of the Indian origin of the doctrine, its subsequent diffusion outside of India, or the fact that the disciples of Buddha were probably more numerous than Muslims and Christians.

However, his awareness of the principles ac-

60 quired from the emerging Buddhist studies did not keep Hegel from emphasizing the "nothingness of the Buddhists." Nothingness (*Nichts*) was
indeed the main characteristic, in his eyes, of both their doctrine and their
religious practices. In the philosophical imagination, Hegel established the
link between Buddha and nothingness that endured for several decades. He
thus paved the way for a long and diverse connection between Buddha and
nihilism, setting up a kind of obligatory link between the supposed doctrine
of Buddha and the themes of annihilation. How did this relationship get
established? In what way, apart from the incomplete but positive details
furnished by the philologists of his day, did Hegel give the initial impetus to
the assertion that there was a cult of nothingness?

No one seems to have noticed the existence of this question. The reason for
this is undoubtedly that the pages Hegel wrote about Buddhism remained
even more neglected than his analyses of Brahmanism and of the "religion
of flowers." What was most striking to those who did comment on them[4]
was the differing roles accorded to Buddhism within Hegel's system of
thought. It was in 1822–23, in his courses on the philosophy of history, that
Hegel first dealt with Buddhism. In this first version, he tackled Buddhism
by associating it with India. In 1824–25, a "Mongolian principle" appeared
in the same courses; this time Buddhism was linked to it in the form of
Lamaism. However, *das mongolische Prinzip* had but a brief life. It disappeared when lessons resumed in 1830–31. These variations did not simplify
his editors' work, and their indecision does not simplify the reader's work.
In 1840, Hegel's son returned to his father's 1824–25 framework, which the
editor Georg Lasson also followed. Lasson restored an "appendix on Buddhism" to the place it occupied in the 1822–23 course.

Foot in the Mouth

The same variability of the place occupied by Buddhism is found in the
Leçons sur la philosophie de la religion. The content of the analyses changed
little, on the whole. However, in the *Leçons* of 1824 and 1827, Buddhism
appeared as a form of "nature religion" (*Naturreligion*) older than the religion of India, whereas in 1831 Buddhism, considered as a "religion of
being-in-itself," appeared after Brahmanism as a third "religion of substance."[5] Buddhism's mobility in the system rather than a real plasticity of
material was therefore noted. The relative thematic continuity of the different versions, principally formed by the question of nothingness, did not

prevent some curious notations. Thus the Buddha, who marked a relative 61
progress in the interiority of the spirit, was represented in an exemplary
manner, for Hegel, by the "pensive attitude" in which "the feet and arms
are placed upon one another in such a way that one toe enters the mouth,"
which represented perfectly "the return to oneself, the suction of oneself."[6]

Let us get to the main point of the different texts. Buddhism, according
to Hegel, was a religion in which "man must make himself nothing." This
wording appeared in the 1827 text of *Leçons sur la philosophie de la religion*,
which is a major reference.[7] The fundamental determination in both the
thought and the behavior of the Buddhists was their conviction, so to
speak, that "from nothing everything comes, to nothing everything returns."[8] In accord with the principle thus attributed to Buddhists, Hegel
considered their religious practice to be a return to this inherent and immutable "nothing," supposed to form the only and ultimate reality in their
eyes. Their spiritual discipline tended therefore toward the systematic destruction of the self, toward the obliteration of consciousness, toward the
annihilation of thought itself. The most constant action of Buddhism, its
ultimate purpose, according to Hegel, was destruction (*Vernichtung*). This
total destruction passed through a series of negations and refusals that were
just so many attempts at desubjectification and depersonalization. By
means of these diverse attempts at self-destruction, consciousness set for
itself the goal of effacing its reflexivity. This *Vernichtung* might therefore
look like a dissolution of the soul. Indeed, in order to attain "*nirvana*,"
according to Hegel, man

> must continually take great care to want nothing, to desire nothing,
> to do nothing; he must be without passion, without inclination,
> without activity. . . . Saintliness consists in man uniting himself with
> God, with nothingness, with the absolute in this destruction, in this
> silence. The supreme end, happiness, consists in the cessation of all
> movement of the body and soul. . . . Man must make himself
> nothing. In his being, he must act in a negative way, defend himself
> not against the outside but against himself.[9]

As we have seen, Hegel could not have read anywhere, in the latest of
sources available to him, that Buddhism had destruction as its purpose.
None of the works in existence during his time that he examined carefully
and scrupulously indicated that Buddhist deliverance, the nirvana that began to be intriguing, was the equivalent of nothingness. The question to
be asked was therefore what other sources did he have at his disposal, and

62 for what reason—if it is even possible to know—did he follow them rather than the works of contemporary Orientalists? Hegel carefully read Buchanan and Rémusat, Turner and Colebrooke, among others. It was not in their writings that he encountered the affirmation of a Buddhist nihilism. Better: the recent research he learned about denied explicitly the thesis which he himself placed at the center of his analyses.[10] By what means did the relationship between Buddhism and destruction come to be formed in Hegel's eyes?

The Deceptive Master

The link was already present in certain sources consulted by the philosopher. They were works that one would consider ancient, that preceded, in any case, the drafting of the Orientalist philology. De Guignes, for example, in his *Histoire générale des Huns* (1756–58), wrote: "He who abandons his father, his mother and all his family in order to concern himself only with learning about himself & in order to embrace the religion of destruction is called Samanean."[11] This name was generally supposed to designate Buddhists in Greek doxography, in particular in the works of Clement of Alexandria.[12] According to de Guignes, what did the follower of Buddhism want? His own destruction. This passage shows it: "The Samanean, always busy meditating on this great God, only seeks to destroy himself in order to go back to him & to lose himself in the bosom of the Divinity who has drawn all things from nothingness, & who is not at all material himself. That is what they understood by voidness & nothingness."[13]

The ambiguity in de Guignes's wording is noticeable. He did not believe that either nihilism or atheism existed in Buddhism; they were incompatible with his conviction of a probable similarity between the religion of Fo and Christianity.[14] De Guignes concluded the account of the legendary biography of Fo-Buddha with this final assertion, presented as the master's last word, that only nothingness is at the same time inherent and ultimate. This thesis, which in Hegel's work is found to be the principal determinant of Buddhism, is held at a distance by de Guignes. This is how he presents the end of Fo's life:

> He died at seventy-nine years of age, after having told his dearest disciples that everything he had taught them up to that point was only parables, that he had hidden the truth from them with figurative & metaphorical expressions; but that his real feeling was that there was no other principle than void and nothingness, that every-

thing came from it & everything returned to it: expressions that must not be taken either literally or in a rigorous sense, as will be seen in what follows.[15]

By relativizing the last words attributed to Fo in such a manner, de Guignes saved the possibility of a link between his teaching and Christianity. He thus stood in the way of condemning Fo-Buddha for either skepticism or atheism. But, based on the same legendary scene, reported by the Jesuits in 1687, such charges had been retained throughout the preceding decades. Let us note in passing that this scene of the ultimate revelation of nothingness is obviously apocryphal. It does not correspond to any other known episode in the life of the Buddha, as legendary as his biography might be.

But it was successful. The same episode was repeated. For example, in 1725, Louis Moreri's *Grand Dictionnaire historique*[16] stated in the article "*Fê* (or *Fo*, or *Foê*, idol of China)":

At the age of seventy-nine years, sensing he was close to death, he declared to his disciples that, during the forty years he had preached to the world, he had not told them the truth at all, he had theretofore hidden it under the veil of metaphors & figures, but that it was then time to tell it to them; there is nothing to seek, he said, nor anything to hope for other than void and nothingness, the first principle of all things. His method caused his disciples to divide his doctrine into two parts, the exterior one, which is the one that is preached publicly & which is taught to the people; the other one interior, which is carefully hidden from the common people, & which is only revealed to followers.

Buddha was thus the master of double truth: one for the crowd or the simple followers, the other for the truly initiated. This master was deceptive: he did not cease to teach a doctrine that he himself admitted was error and falseness. He was perverted: it was only in the throes of death, at the last breath, that he told his followers, his own disciples, that he had always deceived them. He had only taught them conventional truths, that good and bad are really distinguishable, that good deeds and bad deeds are respectively rewarded and punished in another life. As for the ultimate truth, the one from the "interior doctrine," according to Moreri's *Dictionnaire*, it consists in

establishing as a principle and as an end of all things, a certain void and a real nothingness. They say that our first parents came out of this void, & they return to it after death, that it is the same for all

64 men, who dissolve back into this principle through death; that we and all elements and all creatures are part of this void, that there is thus only a single same substance that is in all individual beings through shapes alone, and through qualities, or exterior configuration, somewhat like water that is always essentially water, whether it has the form of snow, or rain, or ice.[17]

In addition to the materialistic monism of the Enlightenment, this article may bring to mind, for the contemporary reader, the distinction introduced by the teachers of the Greater Vehicle between conventional truth and ultimate truth. But, in the course of repeated retellings, this same anecdote about the Buddha's last sermon changed meaning: this supreme ruse, more than a brazen act of deception, was the mark of a devious and partisan atheism. It was also the cause of the differences between the sects claiming to follow the Buddha. Thus, Abbot Banier wrote in his *Histoire générale des cérémonies de tous les peuples du monde* (General History of the Ceremonies of all the Peoples of the World [Paris, 1741]):

> In an act of supreme impiety, seeing that he was close to death, he wanted to inspire atheism in his followers. He declared that until that time he had spoken to them in enigmas: but do not be mistaken, he told them, by seeking the first principle of things outside of Nothingness. Everything has come from nothingness and everything must return to it. It is the abyss of our hopes. . . . by this retraction, he divided his followers into two branches; one followed what Fo had taught during his life to the letter, that is to say Idolatry, the others received the last words of their master as an article of faith & declared themselves for Atheism.[18]

Hegel's text was not lost. The central concept of Buddhist nothingness (the "beginning and end" of all that exists), the possibility of likening this nothingness to a purely abstract substance, the equivalence of sainthood according to this religion and the destruction resulting from fusion with the indeterminate principle of things—after a long evolution!—actually ends up back under the scrutiny of the philosopher in Abbot Grosier's *Description générale de la Chine*.[19] The passage is worth citing in its entirety, because several of its phrases are found word for word in Hegel's text:

> Let us finish reporting what the bonzes tell about their so-called god. He had reached his seventy-ninth year when he realized, in the deterioration of his strength, that his borrowed divinity would not prevent him from paying tribute to nature like other men. He did

not want to leave his followers without revealing to them the secret and all the hidden depths of his doctrine. After bringing them together, he declared to them that until that moment he had always believed that he could use only parables in his speeches; that for forty years, he had disguised the truth from them with figurative and metaphorical expressions; but being on the verge of disappearing before their eyes, he wanted to show them his true feelings and finally reveal to them the mystery of his wisdom. "*Learn*," he told them, "*that there is no other principle of all things than emptiness and nothingness, that it is from nothingness that everything has come, it is to nothingness that everything must return; it is there that all our hopes end up.*"[20]

Thus, rather than his most recent Orientalist sources, Hegel favored a conception of Buddhism/religion of nothingness that came from prior interpretations. Repeating the remarks of the Jesuits, and their posterity with Abbot Banier or Louis Moreri, Abbot Grosier characterized the nothingness of the Buddhists in terms that, later, Hegel's text would recall in detail:

Nothingness, according to this doctrine, is the beginning and the end of all that exists; it is from nothingness that our first parents drew their origin, and it is to nothingness that they returned after their death. All beings differ from one another only in their shapes and their qualities. From the same metal a sculptor can fashion a man, a lion, or any other animal: if one then melts these different pieces, they will immediately lose their shape and their respective qualities, and will form only one and the same substance. It is the same with all animate or inanimate beings: however varied in their shape and their qualities, they are all only one same thing, coming from the same principle, which is nothingness.

This universal principle is very pure, exempt from any alteration, very subtle, very simple; it is at continual rest; it has no virtue, nor power, nor intelligence; much more, its essence consists in being with action, without intelligence, without desire. In order to be happy, one must, by continual meditations, by frequent victories over oneself, endeavor to become identical to this principle, and, in order to reach this point, [one must] become accustomed to doing nothing, wanting nothing, feeling nothing, desiring nothing.

As soon as one reaches that happy state of insensitivity, it is no longer a question of vices or of virtues, of pains or rewards, of providence, of immortality for souls. All saintliness consists in ceas-

66   ing to be, in merging with nothingness; the nearer man gets to the nature of the rock or a tree trunk, the more perfect he becomes; finally it is in indolence and immobility, in the ceasing of all desire and of all bodily movement, in the destruction and the suspension of all the faculties of the soul and the spirit, that virtue and happiness exist. From the moment that man is raised to this degree of perfection, there are no more trials and tribulations for him, no more future, no more transmigrations to fear, because he has ceased to be, and because he has become perfectly identical to the god Fo.[21]

Several elements of this text are found scattered through Hegel's analysis: the nothingness of the Buddhists as a point of departure and as a goal; as a simple, ethereal, subtle substance of which everything is made (even the strange image of "metal" as universal material making up man and animals is found in the Hegelian text); finally, like saintly apathy, the ceasing of desire and the end of the subject. All these nothingnesses, it could be said, are found in the 1827 *Leçons*. Why did Hegel adopt the interpretation suggested by these "ancient" sources as opposed to the indications furnished by his "recent" sources? The answer is of a philosophical nature. It is the mutation introduced into the conception of the opposition of being and nothingness through Hegel's *Logique* that must serve as a guide in understanding that statements that are formally very close do not have the same impact.

Pure Being, Nothing

Indeed, in the same pages, Buddhism was also presented by Hegel as the moment when the "immortality[22] of the soul in its real determination" begins. This "religion of being-in-itself" is thus not destructive. It also constitutes the moment when man, as thinking subject, becomes aware of his interiority unaffected by becoming. In Buddhism, for Hegel, God gives himself in the form of pure, infinite, unique Being. How can one combine these different statements? How does one reconcile the nullification of the soul and the constitution of its immortality, the worship of nothingness and infinite Being? How does one bring together the destruction of oneself and of Being—destined, one and the other, to rejoin a nothingness that they disturb only in an illusory way—and the immortality of the soul, the immutable interiority, the development of an idea of God? This opposition, as any reader of Hegel is already well aware, is only an illusion. The second part of the logic of Being is actually characterized by equating pure Being (*das Reine Sein*) with nothingness. This is confirmed in §87 of the *Encyclopedia*, where Hegel writes: "This pure being is *pure abstraction*; [it is] consequently what is *absolutely negative*, that is, if one takes it in an immediate fashion, *nothingness*."[23]

So this apparent difficulty is resolved, from the Hegelian point of view. Buddhism, like "religion of being-in-itself," is awareness of the infinite nature of substance in its simplicity and its immediacy. It can be considered as a "religion of nothingness" to the extent that nothing makes a distinction, from the speculative point of view, between pure Being and nothingness. Buddhism can thus be seen as according the first and the last place to nothingness, to the extent that its Absolute is indeterminate. At the same time it can be characterized as an important original conception of the immortality of the soul, since this representation of the domain of the Absolute as an abstraction signals the advent of a spiritual interiority in man.

Thus nothingness in Hegel's thinking, the very nothingness that he attributes to the Buddhists, is to be understood not as the absolute opposite of Being, but as its indetermination. Nothingness is the Absolute considered in its generality, its pure abstraction, its lack of determination. So Buddhism is not atheistic; it considers God in his pure infinity, in the impossibility of his receiving any concrete determination. Which finally comes back to nothingness. This equivalence undoubtedly has something shocking about it, and Hegel was aware of it:

> From the outset, it must seem surprising that man thinks of God as nothingness; that must seem like the strangest thing in the world; and upon closer examination it means nothing more than that there is nothing determinate about God, he is indeterminate; there is no concrete determination that is appropriate for God, he is infinity. . . . When we say: "We can know nothing of God, no representation can be made of him," it is a toned-down way of saying that God is nothingness for us.[24]

Hegel picked up the old rumor according to which Buddha left his disciples under the sarcastic threat of nothingness and the disquieting sign of emptiness, but he did so in order to change its meaning completely. As he reinvented it, the religion of nothingness became an ascetic practice of negative theology, a moment in the voyage of the Spirit toward free interiority, a kind of birth, still indistinct and too vague, of the immortality of the soul. This religion of nothingness was another name for the religion of God. So nothing atheistic will be found in this will to destruction attributed

68 by Hegel to the disciples of the Buddha. This reduction of self to nothing in order to melt into the Absolute seems closer, in a sense, to the approach of the Rhineland mystics than to the destructive forms of nihilism of modern times.

Hegel's singularity was thus, regarding the question of "nothingness of the Buddhists," in drawing primarily from relatively obsolete sources that were generally hostile to the Eastern religion and transforming the data by giving them a new meaning. If one is unaware of this meaning, if one takes Hegel's sentences out of their context, one can make them say that Buddhism is a destructive, atheistic religion given to challenging the human as well as God. And some of his successors would not hesitate to state such a view. But that is not what Hegel said. He remained as if suspended between two kinds of remarks hostile to the Buddha: those that draw their information from the Jesuit missionaries and those unleashed in the aftermath of scholarly discovery. On the crest, his remarks are subject to all kinds of misunderstandings.

From Contempt to Recognition

This point should have been clarified, for it is usually thought that the judgments passed by Hegel on the doctrines of India were systematically hostile. But such is not the case. A large number of his statements, it is true, lack nuances. Dozens of pages show his strong antipathy toward this "stupor" that he presents as the supreme goal of the meditation of the yogis. Hegel does not hesitate to say that India shows an "unbalanced imagination," a "confused spirit," a "happiness that is the happiness of folly." In that land, "children have no respect for their parents." There reigns at the heart of that monstrous society a veritable chaos: there is "neither morality nor human dignity" in it. In addition, one can have confidence in no one: "Cunning and cleverness, that is the fundamental nature of the Indian; deceit, theft, murder are part of his ways."[25] These statements are neither isolated nor extremely rare. They cannot be encountered without comment. It is difficult to consider them as negligible, to judge them as insignificant, strictly speaking, to classify them among those curious "prejudices of the old days," which would appear for no apparent reason and would manage to disappear without a trace. Those are truly embarrassing sentences. The diverse tactics aimed at reducing the embarrassment they arouse always leave an aftertaste.

Hegel differentiates between the East Indies, of the Ganges and the Indus, and the West Indies, of the Amazon and the Mississippi. The two

Indias are obviously peopled by Indians: *Indier*. Hegel's language made no distinction between *indisch* and *indianisch*, words that allow the distinction to be made between the Indian from India (*indisch*) and the American Indian (*indianisch*) in modern German. These two Indias, the ancient and the new, the eastern and the western, from the Hegelian point of view, have some large features in common: proximity to nature, the fact that the spirit does not yet know interiority or objectivity or universality, that it remains outside of history, in a stupor that does not allow it access to either conceptual thinking or ethical thought (*Sittlichkeit*). This state of dependence and immaturity destined the India of Asia, like the one on the other side of the Atlantic, to be conquered by Europe.

In spite of everything, it would be wrong to draw the conclusion that there was some kind of fundamental "xenophobia" in Hegel's thought. With Hegel, it is never sure that the most apparent, and often the most outrageous, side of some analysis or other could be enough to disqualify the entire body of thought. If it is true that Greece, and only Greece, constitutes, according to him, a "native land" (*Heimat*) for the heart "of the cultured man from Europe, and for our German hearts in particular,"[26] it is equally true that a number of things help to moderate strongly the commonly held belief of an "Indophobia," or an "Asiophobia" in Hegel. It is better to abandon the widespread idea of Hegel's massive and almost monolithic hostility toward India and its teachings.[27] The philosopher of the objective Mind shared neither the convictions nor the enthusiasm of the romantics. He led the polemic with them, both directly and indirectly. It might thus be wise to reread his judgments about India, and about Greece, keeping in mind this opposition of Hegelian reason to the displays of "Indomania" that had dwelled in so many German minds during the early years of the nineteenth century. Another cause for his reserve was due to the fact that the Sanskrit treatises that we can legitimately call philosophical were completely lacking in the first discoveries. Sanskrit ceased to be an enigma or a subject of fables, and became the object of studies with the constitution of Calcutta, on 15 January 1784, under the presidency of William Jones of the Royal Asiatic Society of Bengal and especially with its first publications under the title *Asiatick Researches*. It was henceforth planned to support the analysis of multiple aspects of Indian civilization by deciphering its texts. Instead of being imperfectly summarized, works were translated: in 1785, Charles Wilkins published an English translation of the *Bhagavad-Gita*, and soon thereafter William Jones translated the *Laws of Manu*, *Shakuntala*, and the *Hitopadesa*—to mention only the main titles.

German adaptations of these English translations followed one an-

70   other at a steady pace. Soon the first original works of the German Sanskritists followed, notably those by Friedrich Schlegel, then by his brother August Wilhelm. From Herder to Schelling, from Goethe to Humboldt, from
Hölderlin to Görres, these first volumes raised a passionate interest. But the
absence in these publications—for over forty years!—of argued, demon-
strative, and refutative texts must be underscored. Among these volumes, it
was rare to find a systematic argument that used logical consistency alone in
its attempt to be rationally convincing. Among the more or less certain
means of access that Europe began to have at its disposal, not one yet led to
the *sutra* of the Brahmanic schools of thought or to their many didactic and
dialectical commentaries.

For more than three decades, from about 1790 to about 1820, the
existence of "philosophy" in India was thus affirmed, or supposed, without
access to the kinds of works that could ask the question precisely and with
good reason regarding "in what sense and to what extent" this was philosophy or not. From Herder to Friedrich Schlegel, the dream of an India that
would be the homeland of pure thought, of a Sanskrit that would be the
perfect language, where sentiment and perception would not be dissociated
from one another—that dream was based exclusively on mystical poems
(the *Bhagavad-Gita*), on a few epic passages (*Ramayana*), on a lyrical drama
(*Shakuntala* by Kalidasa), and on a collection of fables (the *Hitopadesa*). They
were not aware of places where rationality was used in India, where a
speculative "technicity" comparable to our own could be seen, whether it
was a question of the logical analyses of the *Nyaya* or the speculations of the
Brahma-Sutra.

This situation changed during the course of the 1820s. Hegel modified
his verdict then as well. From 1823 to 1827, with the publication of the
studies of Henry Thomas Colebrooke on the Brahmanic systems, Europe
began to discover the Indian philosophical systems. Colebrooke's five
monographs on the *darsana*, and the "heterodoxies" of the Buddhists and
the Jains, furnished the first reliable elements that Europe could use. These
scrupulously composed memoirs, remarkable in all regards, were the work
of a philologist who had read the treatises in their original language and had
made inquiries among the *pandits*, the literate Brahmans. Their publication
marked an important change in the history of the representations of philosophical India in Europe. Before Colebrooke, what could be called "Indian
philosophy" was pieced together out of necessity—not without a large dose
of arbitrariness, of artifice, and of inaccuracy—from what it was believed
could be pulled from texts that were, in fact, mainly poetic and mystical.
The situation became altogether different from the time that some well-

established reference points relative to the theses and the principal lines of argumentation of the Brahmanic schools were obtained. From then on it became possible to discern their differences, even their antagonisms. We began to leave behind the time of mythical images that developed out of signs perceived only in filagree. The demands for patient work became apparent, work that would need to be conducted on coherent and subtle conceptual research material. The systematic rigor of these as yet unheard of thoughts still needed testing; the specific ways they were developed had to be understood; and the ways they deviated from, or converged with, what our history has called "philosophy" was in need of measuring. Such were the tasks that Colebrooke's work gave a glimpse of, and began to demand.

Hegel was hardly wrong about it. Insufficient attention was probably paid to his real philosophical vigilance in this domain. Reading the memoirs published by Colebrooke actually led this denigrator of things Indian to go back on his previous judgments in the course of the last years of his education in Berlin, from 1827 to 1831. After reading Colebrooke, he did not hesitate to say, in the course of his *Lessons on the History of Philosophy*, that one could not talk about "real Indian philosophical systems"![28] And it was Hegel himself who recognized it! If we noticed the extent to which Hegel's courses, and especially this one, dealt with delicate issues, the authenticity of the text frequently remaining unconfirmed, one would notice that several identical judgments appear under his pen in the *Berliner Schriften*. For example, he wrote that speculative Indian thought, such as Colebrooke made known, "completely deserves to be called philosophy"![29] And, once again, these are Hegel's words! If one is accustomed to reading, in his written words, only about the horrors of India, there is something to be disconcerted about.

Thus the conclusion is unexpected. While for a number of nineteenth century thinkers, the charm of India was suspended or broken as they thought they had discovered the nihilism of the Buddha, Hegel followed a different path in the later years of his life. He recognized in India the existence of true philosophical systems at the same time as he described the path of pure abstraction to which Buddhism was committed. Hegel did not condemn the Buddha and his followers for their boundless Quietism. The incoherence or the absurdity of their beliefs was not emphasized. On the contrary, the meaning of the central concept, "man must become nothingness," meant that man, in Buddhism, endeavors to become God. For Hegel, it was probably an illusory path, tied to a too general and indeterminate degree to an idea of the Absolute. Probably this pure abstraction was

72 tantamount to the very idea of nothing. But the religion of nothingness remained a path to God. It was an error, not malice. By setting up Buddhism as a religion of nothingness in European philosophy, Hegel did not give it the features of a threatening, destructive doctrine. He did not see in it the incarnation of an enemy to be fought. The Buddha, a toe in his mouth, was a figure of the necessary distraction of the mind.

The Threat (1832–1863)

1832. Eugène Burnouf is elected to the Collège de France. With him the scientific study of the "Buddhist question" begins; facts are gathered from a number of different fields of Eastern studies.

1863. The polemic about the cult of nothingness reaches its peak in France, England, and Germany.

5
French Terror

It is in Paris that terror first develops. At the Collège de France, with Eugène Burnouf, Buddhist studies enter the scientific age. But the Catholic Party and the spiritualists discern the "principle of evil" that threatens Europe in this doctrine of annihilation.

> The unhappiness of the time wishes that the doctrines that are the basis of Buddhism find singular favor among us again.
>
> —Jules Barthélemy Saint-Hilaire, *Le Bouddha et sa religion*, 1860

Let us imagine a man, still young—about thirty years old—with fine features, straight hair (a bit long), pale skin, with an intelligent look in his eyes. He talks about "the growing interest that has been raised since the beginning of the century by questions relating to the language, philosophy and religion of ancient and modern India."[1] He would teach this language and master its various rules, from Vedic Sanskrit to the quite different Sanskrit of Buddhist treatises. In 1832 at the Collège de France in Paris, this thirty-one-year-old genius succeeded Léonard de Chézy in the first chair of Sanskrit that was established in Europe. His name was Eugène Burnouf. His was one of the greatest minds in a century that had many. In a few years, with an exceptionally powerful capacity for work, and in the midst of still completing other tasks, he founded the scientific branch of

76 Buddhist studies. In 1826, he set about decoding Pali with Christian Lassen.[2] This work opened a path of prime importance to the understanding of Buddhism, since it made possible the reading of the Canon of the *Theravâdin*. The scholar would later return to the Sanskrit manuscripts sent from Nepal in 1836 by Brian Houghton Hodgson. He thus tied the threads already woven by Schmidt[3] for the Mongolian sources, Rémusat for the Chinese texts,[4] Hodgson for the Buddhism of Nepal, and Csoma de Körös for the Tibetan domain, back to their Indian sources.[5]

In publishing, in 1844, the collection modestly titled *Introduction à l'histoire du Buddhisme* [*sic*] *indien*,[6] Burnouf offered the first rigorous account of the Buddha's teaching, as it was possible to reconstruct it in his time. "It is a torrent of light that falls on the chaos of the Buddhist doctrines and reestablishes order," noted Jules Mohl in the *Journal asiatique*, after the Orientalist's death.[7] This foundational work would have Schelling as one of its noteworthy readers. He indicated, in his preface to Victor Cousin's book on French and German philosophies: "It is truly unfortunate that the tone and the manners of political discord also pass into literature; but even this cannot destroy the true scientific genius of France, where, in the midst of all the upheavals, the most profound and most solid studies still maintain their quality and where, to take an example in an area foreign to philosophy albeit not without importance for philosophical research, there appear men like Eugène Burnouf."[8] In Germany in the following decades, Eugène Burnouf's foundational book was read by Schopenhauer as well as by Wagner and Nietzsche. In France, it influenced Taine, Renan, and before them Victor Cousin and Jules Barthélemy Saint-Hilaire. Because of Burnouf and thanks to him, Buddhist studies were, during a decisive period, an area where France excelled and Paris became an essential place of education, of reflection, and often of publication for the Orientalists.

Let us return to the Collège de France. For Eugène Burnouf, the first years of the 1830s were particularly fruitful. From 1829 to 1833, he taught a course, General and Comparative Grammar, at the Ecole Normale Supérieure, attended notably by his former fellow student Jules Barthélemy Saint-Hilaire, who was soon to offer a new translation of Aristotle. Eugène Burnouf, born in 1801, was barely thirty years old. Grammar for the Burnoufs was a family affair: Jean-Louis, Eugène's father, a professor at the Collège de France and translator of Tacitus, was the author of a book of Latin grammar and a book of Greek grammar, both authoritative. The son, from the early days of his youth, was a prodigy noticed by all. At thirty, he already had an impressive past: Louis-le-Grand, l'Ecole des Chartes, a degree in humanities and one in law, publications that were authoritative, including

the *Essai sur le Pali* in 1826, and in 1829 the first fascicle of a monumental 77
edition of the *Vendidad Sadé*.[9] Burnouf, in addition to being a scholar of
both Pali and Sanskrit, was also one of the European experts in Zend. In
1831, he received the Volney Prize for Oriental languages and became
secretary of the Asiatic Society of Paris. In 1832 he entered the Académie
des Inscriptions et Belles-Lettres. The same year he was elected to the
Collège de France.

Cautious Nothingness

The scrupulous honesty of Burnouf's analyses was as obvious to the
reader as the extraordinary extent of the scholar's erudition. There is absolutely no doubt that his *Introduction à l'histoire du Buddhisme indien* marked a
turning point in the history of Orientalism. Likewise, it marked a stage in
the development of a Buddhism imagined to be the "cult of nothingness."
For, in spite of his rigor and the precaution of his methods, Burnouf came
to reinforce, with his immense authority, the position of those who would
transform the Buddha into a nihilist specter. After teaching the law, said
Burnouf, the Buddha "enters into *Nirvana*, that is to say into complete
destruction, where, according to the most ancient school, the definitive
destruction of both the body and the soul takes place."[10] It could not be
clearer. The Buddhist nirvana, for Burnouf, was indeed total annihilation.
The adversaries of the Orient, the defenders of Christianity, of the person,
and of the immortality of the soul, would not fail to wrap their arms around
this prestigious expert and hold him up a thousand times.

However, as soon as one looks at his text, it is easy to note that Burnouf
was extremely cautious. Even though he clearly took the side of an "anni-
hilationist" interpretation of nirvana, he punctuated his conclusion with
several indications of uncertainty. These indications are highlighted in the
following passage,[11] which is often quoted, although without any mention
of the precautions with which he cushioned his remarks:

> *Whatever danger there is in precisely stating opinions so difficult to understand*
> *through texts still as incompletely known* as those from Nepal, *I imagine*
> that Shakyamuni, by entering religious life, had as a starting point
> the facts given to him by the atheistic doctrines of the *Samkhya*,
> which were ontologically the absence of a God, the multiplicity and
> eternity of human souls, and physically, the existence of an eternal
> nature, endowed with qualities, able to transform itself, and pos-
> sessing the elements of the forms the human soul assumes in the

78 course of its journey through the world. Shakyamuni took from this doctrine both the idea that there is no God and the theories of the multiplicity of human souls, of transmigration, and of *Nirvana*, or deliverance, which belonged to all the Brahmanic schools in general. Only, *it is not easy to see* today what he meant by *Nirvana*, because he did not define it anywhere. But since he never speaks of God, *Nirvana* for him cannot be the absorption of the individual soul into a universal God, as the orthodox Brahmans believed; and as he spoke hardly more of matter, his *Nirvana* is not the dissolution of the human soul within physical elements either. The word "empty," which already appears on the monuments proven to us to be the most ancient, *leads me to think* that Shakya saw the supreme good in the destruction of the thinking principle. He imagined it, as an often repeated comparison *makes one assume*, as the disappearance of the light from a lamp that has been extinguished.[12]

The elements pointed out by this text were seen again, some fifteen years later, expanded and intensified, in a quarrel that continued from Paris to Oxford and from Bonn to Madrid,[13] and which formed one of the significant moments of the "cult of nothingness." Eugène Burnouf's interpretation of nirvana constituted an anchoring point for this myth in Orientalist knowledge. His statement concerning the Buddha—he "saw the supreme good in the destruction of the thinking principle"—served as a clever warning to artisans of the diabolical specter of a religion of nothing. Burnouf's scholarly analysis was but a first step in this area. Indeed he declared the Buddha's nihilism, but in a hushed, scientific, and level-headed manner. It was far from the anathemas, the imprecations, or even the insults that were already in the offing in the shadow of seminaries and the agitation of salons and journals. Burnouf's interpretation unquestionably drew Buddhism toward the religion where nothingness was worshiped. But it was still a soft version of it. There were others.

Despicable Nothingness

While Eugène Burnouf's studious brow huddled over the little curlicues of Pali and the sutra of the School of the South, or over the Devanagari characters in the treatises of the *Prajnâparamita* coming from Nepal, minds outside the libraries began to heat up greatly. Theretofore unknown, Buddhism had suddenly become a threat. And then it embodied, in a far-reaching way, a principle of evil refusing to be struck down. Asia was considered the last refuge of an ancient revolting beast, the beast of barbarian idolatry, of the Evil One, and of the dreadful things it engenders. The treatise was not forced. Let us read—preferably aloud—what the Catholic preacher Ozanam wrote in 1842:

> There is in the world a religion that rules over one hundred seventy million men, and it is not Catholicism; it is professed in five empires, four kingdoms, and numerous provinces, and it extends from the borders of the Volga to the South Seas, entrenched, so to say, as far as the extreme edges of the Orient. Idolatry, driven successively out of Europe, western Asia, northern Africa, and the American coastline, forced to hide everywhere else among barbaric tribes and nameless people, seems to have amassed the last of its forces for the last of its fights. . . . For more than three hundred years this religion has been resisting all the efforts of the apostolate. The feats of Saint François-Xavier, the blood of the martyrs of Yedo, the science of the missionaries of Peking, the voices of several thousand preachers, the wishes of the Universal Church, did no more than rattle its secular tyranny. Through terror and torture, it defends itself with the energy of despair. It was this religion which, at the entrance to the ports of Japan, placed the crucifix under the feet of the merchants, which published its persecution edicts in the cities of Tonkin and of China, which, in three years, made three bishops and more than twenty priests from our world perish, and which led chained-up neophytes in iron cages to death every day.—The religion calls itself Buddhism.[14]

Diabolical, bestial, cruel, murderous, Buddhism was also, in the eyes of Ozanam, licentious and debauched, exceeding "all the madness of Nero, of Commodus, and Heliogabalus."[15] What then were its terrible perversions? A talisman made from a pellet of dried excrement: "The revolting relics of the grand Lama are going to adorn the necks of kings."[16] And also, and especially, the existence of several husbands for only one wife, a practice commonly admitted in Tibet. Indeed, the mores of the most Buddhist of lands "sanction polyandry, the most shameful disorder of earthly societies, because it assumes the complete absence of the last feeling that is extinguished in the last moral refuge of humanity, a sense of decency in the hearts of women.[17] Other times and other skies have known vices before which Christian knowledge covers its face. Only Buddhism sanctioned this ignominy under the protection of laws."[18] What was the secret reason for so much dissoluteness, the hidden motive of these countless and revolting

80 troubles? Nothingness, of course, always nothingness . . . and the fanatical, insane, and obscene religion that these dangerous, devout people dedicated to it. Ozanam imagined what the old bonzes said "when, far from the common people, in the solitude of the pagodas, they initiate the young Lamas into the secret of their obscure doctrines."[19] What must a disciple do to be perfect? "He must make himself like a man deprived of his four limbs, he must think without seeming to think, and he must identify with the doctrine of destruction."[20] What is the sovereign good? "Eternal inertia through the suspension of the personality."[21] This is finally the goal: "After the successive destruction of all attributes, of all acts, of all forms, there is only one thing left in the empty space, rest (*Nirvana*). And yet, since that which has no attribute could not be defined, one can say that rest is nothingness; and the wise, seeking to understand from this last term where their thoughts get lost, are divided among themselves, and distinguish four ways of understanding nothingness and eighteen kinds of emptiness."[22]

The Buddha, behind a serene masque, is Satan himself. The preacher made that clearly understood. The doctrine of the Orient did no more than pursue the fundamental error of pantheism; it was "the soul of paganism of all times and all places," it prolonged a "tradition of error"; it was part of a "steady design, which, from the beginning, opposed divine councils." What did the diversity of the times or the apparent dissimilarity of the myths matter: "There are several attacks, but only one war, and the former enemy has not changed."[23] For Ozanam, those were "the same opinions" that were found from India to the mysteries of Thebes, from Alexandria to the Gnostics, from John Scotus Erigena to Spinoza. "They have reappeared to the favor of the metaphysicians of Germany; for a time, they threatened to invade science, art, and behavior. They were stopped again by what is left of common sense and morality in European society. But eloquent voices labeled them the greatest religious danger of our times."[24]

This diabolical nothingness doubtless was exaggerated, as one would have said at the time. But it was far from being an isolated phenomenon. Christian apologetics began regularly to denounce the absurdity of Buddhism and the threat that the "fantasy of nothingness" left hanging over Europe from that time on. The words of the Catholics, as shown by the example of Ozanam, showed a particular virulence. But he was not the only one to vituperate against the pernicious character of this "absurd and contradictory" "religious system," to repeat the words used in 1843 by Abbot Bigandet, of the Society of Foreign Missions of Paris, who had barely begun to discover the beliefs of the Burmese.[25] In the *Annales de philosophie chrétienne*, he wrote, for example: "A trunk without a head or feet. Such is

Buddhism. It is without principles, without fundamental cause. It is also without end since it cannot give any clear or exact idea about the end of man. After making man turn in an almost infinite circle of various existences, it transports him out of the circle of what exists in order to throw him into the void, into an unending abyss, where he gets lost, disappears, and destroys himself."[26] For, once again, nirvana is a complete annihilation[27] and Buddhism a religion where "one reaches the complete renunciation of oneself only by the destruction of one's being."

By "discovering" the nature of Buddhism, the extent of its influence, the ancientness of its ravages, Catholics were also convinced of the renewed necessity of an evangelization of this East Asian Orient whose religion of nothingness threatened both common sense and the Church. "But from where will this great and generous help for the peoples of Asia come, help that would suddenly raise the rank of slaves to the quality of friends and brothers?" exclaimed Félix Nève, professor at the Catholic University of Louvain, in a dissertation published in 1846.[28] This opuscule had as its objective inciting missionaries to study the most recent Orientalist works, insofar as they could find new information there, useful to their vocation. For example, Félix Nève wrote: "Mr. Burnouf's book could be of help to our missionaries from several points of view, either in order to be acquainted with the spirit of the ancient institutions of Buddhism, or to probe the depths of the aberrations of its modern followers."[29] Thus the scholarly discovery of Buddhism led to planning a renewal of missionary activity, which it furnished with both the renewed feeling of its necessity and the arms, recently sharpened, for the conquest of souls. The author went further. After references, throughout his dissertation, to the principal studies devoted to Buddhism between 1820 and 1846, after a lengthy emphasis on the decisive nature of Burnouf's summa, published in 1844, he did not hesitate to interpret this proliferation of new knowledge as a divine sign, pointing to a task to be accomplished: "The regeneration of the Orient seems visibly to enter into the designs of Providence."[30] So, the more the philologists disseminated information about Buddhism, the more demands were imposed to convert the followers, like a Christian duty. The last lines of the text could not say it more clearly:

God, who for two centuries has again closed the greatest part of Asia to the profession of Christianity, opens the main doors one by one: once He has opened them, no one can close them. As we see happening in our time, He calls His ministers to a new and more complete liberation of those nations that are captive under the yoke of idealistic illusions or of idolatrous superstitions; He seems to be naming the immense group of Buddhist peoples as a new portion of the heritage He has destined to His Church over the centuries.[31]

What counted here was not principally the proclamation of the supposed designs of Providence or the analysis of the duties of a proselytism specifically destined to the peoples of the Orient, whose errors would henceforth be better known. It is the fact that this missionary enthusiasm was based on the fear engendered by the nihilism that Félix Nève also attributed to the Buddhists: "As a theory of salvation they teach the annihilation of all individuality, which takes place by their complete annihilation in the absolute void."[32] We also find here the previously seen images of the error, of the prayer confusedly addressed to nothingness, of the leap, with no return, into the void: "Eternity, like time, horrifies this lost intelligence that sees everything change, but does not believe in itself; it takes off beyond the transmigrations that the idea of existence portrays; it invokes nothingness, and, in the grip of this drunkenness of extinction that it forms in the ideal goal of *Nirvana*, it rushes with a single leap into the abyss."[33]

For Félix Nève, the "cult of nothingness" went hand in hand with other considerations. Closely linked to this central theme, these remarks led to the question of racial groupings. The "Buddhist world" was actually defined as a world where *error* was developed and strengthened secularly: "The errors that were short lived in other parts of the world seem to have taken root in the soil there, and all of them seem to have absorbed the actions of several racial groups for a considerable number of generations."[34] This ancient, untouched, tenacious error was both *local* and *racial* at the same time. The text speaks for itself:

Far from being universal, far from answering from a humanitarian perspective, its doctrine was not even made for the peoples of Western Asia, people of action and movement that the philosophical quietism of Buddhism could not have lulled into quietude. What would happen if we compared the peaceful tendencies and instincts of the races that stayed seated in immobility beyond the Ganges or the Himalayas to the natural and enthusiastic activity of the colonists from European soil, for whom Homeric Greece begins their history? Can it remain doubtful that the contemplative idolatry that was able to subjugate millions of men at the far end of Asia would have been incompatible, in the time of paganism, with the male character and the logical mind of the peoples of Europe? Buddhism could not cross certain boundaries drawn by nature and especially by the genius of nations.[35]

The conversion of the Buddhist peoples would not only be an extension of Christianity, but obviously, by the same token, the victory of truth over error, of movement over immobility, of a strong nature (male and logical) over a weak nature (female and absurd), of construction over destruction, of Europe over Asia. These last two traits are explicit in the following passage:

> European societies have effectively become the mistresses and the arbiters of the rest of the world, and they have, in a way, made themselves everywhere present, and even necessary, through their industry and their navy: would they not judge that it would be cowardice on their part to leave the immense populations of Buddhists subject to so many horrible troubles, to such long and poignant anguish? Will they not proclaim that it would be inhumane to see in these populations only dependents and slaves, to whom one owes no more than the beneficial effects of the administrative regime? But the thought of proselytism must go further than the preoccupations of commerce or bureaucracy: Europe must win the souls that renounce all the gifts of human intelligence in order to invoke destruction.[36]

The elements of this crusade juxtaposing nations and racial groups, and dreaming of rescuing the crowds of barely responsible, perhaps barely human, wandering souls from the powerful charm of nothingness would soon be seen again, differently emphasized and in other contexts.[37] It already appears that at this point Buddhist nothingness no longer had the serenity of a scientific hypothesis. Burnouf's calm was replaced by apologetic ardor, or even missionary violence. The cult of nothingness was not just an object of curiosity or perplexity for the scientific observer. It showed itself to be dangerous to the utmost degree. It was an ancient enemy, identified, but still the same. It was the new incarnation of an ageless evil, and of an endless fight. In new clothes, and yellow skin, Satan had returned.

Deplorable Nothingness

What have we seen so far? The establishment of a new science for the Orientalists, the predecessor to a philosophical interpretation in Hegel, and

84   a first consequence, in French Catholic apologetics, of the fear aroused by the discovery of Buddhism. What was happening in France in the same period in philosophy? One figure dominated the second quarter of the nineteenth century: Victor Cousin.[38] Let us bear in mind that it was he who coined the expression "cult of nothingness" to refer to Buddhism.[39] The impact of the discovery of Buddhism on the idea of India as a "philosophical land" can be seen in an exemplary way in his works. In order to understand this, the main steps in the development of his opinions regarding the doctrines must be succinctly reviewed.

"So, gentlemen, was there or was there not, philosophy in the Orient?" On 24 April 1824, Victor Cousin's answer to that question was cumbrous. Philosophy, he was saying, is necessarily present in the Oriental world, in the sense that it is a "special, certain, inalterable need of the human mind."[40] However, whether it be in Egypt, in Persia, in China, or in India, the presence of philosophy still remained indistinct, "enveloped," too dependent on the religious element to be itself yet. Cousin still judged Indian civilization to be devoid of chronology, of history, as well as of—probably borrowed from Hegel—"true morality."[41] This philosophy was actually not a philosophy: "All Indian philosophy appears to me to be hardly more than a more or less free interpretation of the religious books of India."[42] It was "a beginning of philosophy";[43] it was not yet the free form of philosophy. Such a form only develops when "the world takes a step,"[44] passing from immobility to movement, from despotism to liberty—from the Orient to Greece. This was nothing more than a very classical view.

From the following year on, Victor Cousin answered very differently: "One can literally say that the history of philosophy in India is an abridged version of the entire history of philosophy."[45] "Indian philosophy is so vast that all philosophical systems meet within it, that it forms a philosophical world."[46] The rhetoric concerning the Orient in general thus left room, in an interval of a few months, for analysis of Brahmanism's diverse speculative systems. Most of them were considered from then on as independent from the Vedic revelation. The intellectual Indian world, engendering opposing systems that had developed rationally and without being subjected to belief, could legitimately be qualified, according to Cousin, as philosophical. What so profoundly changed Cousin's judgment about India from one year to the next, as was the case for Hegel at the same time, was reading the works of Henry Thomas Colebrooke.[47] More than thirty years later, in 1863, his *Histoire générale de la philosophie depuis les temps les plus anciens jusqu'au XIXe siècle* (General History of Philosophy from Ancient Times to the Nineteenth Century),[48] which had some ten successive editions, returned to

these lessons of 1829 devoted to Indian philosophies in a nearly unaltered 85
form. Cousin then formulated his conclusion in these terms:

> You must have convinced yourself that there is unquestionably a
> philosophy in India different from her mythology, and that it is
> henceforth impossible not to include it in the general context of the
> history of philosophy.[49]

He who was the great legislator of philosophical teaching in France, the
organizer of its programs, the founder of its institution in the contemporary
state form, was also the first university philosopher to proclaim, loud and
clear, that the speculative doctrines of the Sanskrit domain were as worthy
of the attention of philosophers as those of the Greeks. He was not the only
one by far to affirm it in his time. But he remains, in the history of French
university philosophy, at the same time the earliest, the most constant, and
the most politically powerful of the thinkers convinced of the existence of
strictly philosophical texts in India, and of the necessity of both making
them known and interpreting them. However, under the influence of the
discovery of the so-called "annihilation" desired by Buddhism, his opinion
about India was to be modified. Without eliminating the positive opinions
he had first formulated, he would juxtapose them with the firm refusal of
the "deplorable idea" that "forms the basis of Buddhism." In this sense, the
case of Victor Cousin reminds us of the extent to which, in the disaffection
of philosophers for the Sanskrit domain, the crisis unleashed by the emergence of this late-arriving, nihilist Buddha cannot be underestimated.

Actually, in 1829 Cousin specified: "Not one of the Buddhist books is
translated; Colebrooke did not even have at his disposition any of the
original writings that may have survived in Sanskrit and in the dialects of
Prakrit and Pali."[50] The little that Cousin knew about it[51] led him to think
that the sect of Buddhists "cannot be disassociated from the history of
philosophy, since, next to a mythology put there as if by design, is a system
of regular metaphysics, founded on rational and purely human methods."[52]
So nothing could have predicted the worst. Moreover, at that time Victor
Cousin preferred to distance Buddhism from systems subject to examination, thus following both common sense and the advice of the Sinologue
Jean-Pierre Abel-Rémusat: "A wise criticism advises using reserve with
notions that have such an origin, and not making statements regarding
ideas that are only known through the words of those who have an interest
in distorting them."[53]

Therefore, Buddhism was not, at that early date in 1829, a domain
where it was possible to give an opinion with full knowledge of the facts.

86 But the fact remains that the history of spiritual matters, in the opinion of Cousin, from that time on possessed an Indian side, which rightfully belonged to the realm of philosophy properly speaking. Such an integration was justified for Cousin by the fact that he discerned, in the systems described by Colebrooke, the four models by which the cyclical history of philosophy in psychological terms was explained: sensualism, idealism, skepticism, mysticism. Philosophy existed in India, according to Cousin, for the following reason: he found in India explanatory models that had already allowed him to understand Greek thought, from the classical age to the Enlightenment. Eclecticism could therefore encompass the Indian systems, and include them in the history of philosophy. And it should do so. For, with its advent, in a sense, this history concluded. Eclecticism is actually founded on a supposedly complete and balanced understanding of the nature of the human mind. Therefore, he was able to consider all the historical incarnations of the four model systems. Each time, eclecticism would see a doctrine from an angle where it was true. In his opinion, error was born of a belief in a unilateral truth. It was of seemingly little importance that the philosophy under consideration be Greek or "barbarian."

In fact, Cousin's position was ambiguous. On the one hand, he was legitimizing India as a "philosophical land." On the other, he was comparing Indian systems to Greek systems too dramatically and without sufficient reflection. The first of these approaches, legitimization, opened the possibility for philosophers to refer to India's speculative doctrines and it strongly emphasized the philosophical pertinence of such readings. On this point, Cousin's importance did not reside in his personal constructs, which were actually rather inconsistent, but in his decision to proclaim that India was philosophical. Once again, he would never explicitly go back on that decision. Although he had not actually worked over these questions, the statements of 1829 would be kept in the revised editions of this *Cours* and distributed up to the 1870s. This choice had its own specific character. It could not be confused with that of the German Romantics, who, in an India still very poorly known, were looking for the elements of a new mythology that conformed to their aesthetic and political aspirations much more than to the articulations of philosophical systems comparable to our own. In spite of the strangeness of certain pages, Cousin's text therefore had the specific merit of affirming the existence of a diverse philosophical corpus in the Sanskrit language, worthy of being explored and compared to Europe's. Reading Colebrooke allowed him to understand that a myth of original unity, in being shattered, had just opened a new field of research to philosophy. It is worth emphasizing that he proclaimed this without being carried

away by the search for the origin, or by the cloudy desire to magnify a 87
political-social model whose immobile hierarchy had so stirred imaginations on the other side of the Rhine.

The philosophical legitimization of India by Cousin also had a negative
side. In order to make Indian thought worthy of philosophical study, Cousin
actually brought about its direct, even brutal, integration into the framework of our traditional reference points. He did so from the outset, without
caution or critical concern. This assimilation of philosophical propositions
quite unwisely erased in the Sanskrit treatises all that constituted the specific
forms of their difference: their issues, their notions, their natural forms of
coherence. Wanting to include the Indian "systems" in the philosophical
field, Cousin postulated that, of necessity and with no confusion, all the
categories and preoccupations of our history must be found there. Insensi-
tive to the fertile distances created by the multiplicity of languages,[54] he did
not seem able to conceive that philosophy could be other than familiar,
without necessarily ceasing to be philosophical. His legitimization of India,
seen from this point of view, had all the elements of a naturalization. Cousin
could not imagine that any history of philosophy existed other than the one
known to us, that it could include other objects, other aims, other concepts.
His psychologizing universalism, founded on the unity of the human mind,
kept him from it. By proceeding, too quickly and too massively, to a pure
and simple identification, he missed, and incited others to miss, that to
which the philosophical study of the speculative Sanskrit corpus should
have led: testing our identity. In order for such a test to become effective and
have meaning, a sufficient proximity of intellectual steps was obviously
required, whether it be question of the consistency of the uses of rationality,
of the schema of the problems, or of the systematicity of the views. But in
order for such a test to be possible, it was necessary that this proximity not
be a total resemblance.

Victor Cousin's Indophile position focused Jules Barthélemy Saint-
Hilaire's attention on an examination of the Sanskrit texts of philosophical
import. After being installed by Cousin in the chair of Greek philosophy at
the Collège de France, Barthélemy Saint-Hilaire became, in a way, his delegate to Indian affairs. This Hellenist who had studied Sanskrit in the company of his colleague Eugène Burnouf[55] read, in 1839, at the meeting of the
Journal des Savants, a "Dissertation on Sanskrit Philosophy, the *Nyâya*."[56] In
it, he attempted a comparison of the techniques of inference in Indian logic
and those of the Aristotelian syllogism. He devoted a new work to the
Sâmkhya, in particular, before publishing *Du Bouddhisme*, reedited later under the title *Le Bouddha et sa religion*.[57] The most faithful of Victor Cousin's

88 faithful followers,[58] Jules Barthélemy Saint-Hilaire conscientiously carried out the duty of studying the texts. But he constantly ran into difficulties comparing them. All that he could ascertain, in patiently deciphering the *Nyâya* or the *Sâmkhya* sutras, were the differences that separated them from Greek philosophy. Instead of wondering about a different philosophy, he could only conclude, in being careful not to repudiate Cousin's work, that this was not philosophy. From his double conviction in 1839 that a philosophical India existed and that it was identical to our philosophical world, that of the Greeks, Barthélemy Saint-Hilaire reached the point, because his studies failed to find a strict identity, where he succeeded in erasing all of India's philosophical legitimacy after the death of his master: "Indian wisdom, he wrote in 1887, is reduced . . . to a poetic and religious genius."[59] This opening, then closing, could not, however, suffice to explain why philosophy was eliminated from Indian studies and why the institution came to be almost unaware of their existence. One could have actually imagined a reexamination of the direct comparison of the Indian systems, a work to measure the distances separating them from the Greeks, a questioning of the integration of these "barbarian" issues into philosophy. The path that was taken, going from legitimization to indifference, then to contempt, was not at all inevitable.

It was really with Buddhism that the situation became radically different. By discovering an unexpected and disturbing religion in this philosophical land that had so quickly filled him with enthusiasm, Cousin would see his representation of India break apart. Listening to Barthélemy Saint-Hilaire report on Burnouf's work, he noticed "that deplorable idea of annihilation that forms the basis of Buddhism." Philosophical concern gave way little by little to fear, assimilation to stupor, vigilance to condemnation. From then on, India also had the face of nihilism. Moreover, Cousin's first public stand against Buddhism was not motivated by purely philosophical concerns. In 1847, at the Academy of Moral and Political Sciences, after Barthélemy Saint-Hilaire reported on Burnouf's work, he intervened as a defender of Christianity: "I reject the analogies claimed to be established between Christianity and Buddhism; the doctrines of each have not the least resemblance to one another, or rather they are in absolute opposition. If there is in the world anything contrary to Christian doctrine, it is this deplorable idea of annihilation that forms the basis of Buddhism."[60] Cousin's attitude, which directly determined that of Jules Barthélemy Saint-Hilaire, consisted in attempting to defend Christianity against this eminently pernicious religion, which supposedly set annihilation both as its ultimate goal and its enigmatic salvation.

Cousin rid himself of the caution Burnouf held to by affirming that   89
nirvana was the annihilation of the thinking principle: "Such is, without a
doubt, the meaning of the Buddhist *Nirvana*," wrote Cousin, after citing
the Orientalist in the "Addition sur le Bouddhisme,"[61] published in 1863 in
his *Histoire de la philosophie depuis les temps les plus reculés jusqu'au XIXe siècle* (an
appendix to the minimally revised text of the lessons of 1829). A look at
this "addition" shows how the presence of Buddhism blurs the earlier
statements.

A Negative Religion

Buddhism was, certainly, "essentially a philosophy,"[62] according to
Cousin. He followed Burnouf in judging that the philosophy of the Buddha
came from the Brahmanic *Sâmkhya*—always considered as sensualism by
Cousin. Buddhist philosophy was thus first characterized as the extreme
deviation, atheistic and nihilistic, of the original sensualist attitude—which
can be seen everywhere—of the human mind. However, two major pecu-
liarities converged to make Buddhism a disturbing oddity whose existence,
an observable fact, was not rightly possible. On the one hand, this philosophy had become a religion, while the natural movement of the human mind
follows the inverse order. It proceeds by acquiring the autonomy of reason
in relation to faith. On the other hand, this philosophy that had degenerated into a religion appeared to be a religion contrary to the very nature of
any religion, since it was not the adoration of being, but a "worship of
nothingness."[63] This worship had something inconceivable about it, and yet
it still existed. For French spiritualism, the idea that hundreds of millions of
humans aspire, with fervor and constancy, only to their destruction was
going to play the frightening role of an impossible phenomenon that would
be real in spite of everything. Impossible, because from the point of view of
Cousin and his colleagues, the human mind cannot aspire to nothingness.
Such a desire is, like a square circle, contradictory. One could only want
something. One can only wish for a new continuity of the will. In no case
would desire know how to covet its own suppression. Such an impossibility
should impede any manifestation of a desire for annihilation. Yet, this
was attested to in Buddhism. In an ancient, continuous, massive way, the
Buddha's religion wanted annihilation. It crossed over centuries; it subju-
gated peoples. It extended throughout Asia and endured uneroded, even
when it seemed logically excluded from all reality. This was clearly the face
of a nightmare.

The appearance of this ghost shook the very foundations on which the

90   initial attempt to legitimize philosophical India rested. With regard to Buddhism, it was no longer a question of classifying, of inciting to study, or even of granting a place in history to what was "essentially a philosophy." It was time for invective: it was only a "sad philosophy."[64] According to Cousin, atheism led the Buddha to nihilism. Since the teachings of the *Sâmkhya* had "eliminated God," in the opinion of the Buddha "pure and simple annihilation remained the only true and effective deliverance."[65] One could wonder how it so happened that this atheistic, materialistic, nihilistic Buddha did not simply leave any religious universe. A curious idea was born in Cousin's mind with the very idea of worshiping nothingness: that of a negative religion. It had all the usual characteristics of religion—a clergy, rituals, a body of belief, an eschatology—but it inverted the signs. Instead of adoring being, it prostrated itself before nothingness. It did not want eternity but extinction. It did not aspire to the immortality of the soul, but to its definitive disappearance. The religiosity remained; the religion disappeared. Buddhism was an anti-religion.

Upon what was its success founded? How did it manage to get millions and millions of human beings to overcome the "instinctive horror of nothingness"?[66] The answer was both social and political. The existence of this religion, according to Cousin, "can be explained by the abyss of misery into which humanity had sunk."[67] This misery was not just the distress common to any human condition. It was also an economic misery, a social disfavor, a suffering of the dominated. "Shakyamuni spoke mainly to the inferior castes of Indian society who must have felt more specifically the misfortunes of existence and more willingly embraced the both terrible and beneficial remedy proposed to them. Whence, so to speak, the democratic character of Buddhism."[68] What is the relationship between nothingness and democracy? Between this negative religion and the rebellion of the poor? The cult of nothingness was not simply an anti-religion; it was a counterworld, a threat to order.

Cousin wrote those lines in 1863. The workers' movements were organized. The commune was not far away. The struggle of the classes obviously was aroused. When one reads this "Addition about Buddhism," it is hard to believe that the text was talking only about India, in the past, and about very ancient conflicts. The hypothesis comes back to mind: maybe it was about the twentieth century, in advance and without knowing it, that the worship of nothingness was speaking. And Cousin ends: "This is how a philosophical struggle became a political and social struggle that gave birth to wars of extermination, and how the vanquished had to leave their country."[69]

6

Frankfurt and Tibet

*Schopenhauer, at the age of sixty-eight, purchases a
Buddha and has it gilded. Only at the end of his work is the
connection between Buddhism, pessimism, and the negation
of existence made.*

Henceforth, nothing
more lies before us but
nothingness.

—Arthur Schopenhauer,
*The World as Will and
Representation*, 1819

Schopenhauer was generally thought to be a Buddhist. Contrary to his contemporaries, the Frankfurt philosopher spoke in laudatory terms about the teachings of the Buddha. He emphasized the "excellence" of the religion; he wrote that it was "perfect."[1] The high priest of pessimism opined that the Buddhists' idea of the world should be placed "above all others,"[2] and considered that, on the honor roll of spiritual beliefs, it could rise to the "top of the list."[3] In short, he was not sparing in his positive evaluation. Such assertions do not mean that Schopenhauer completely shared Buddhist beliefs, or even less so that he worshiped as Buddhists did. It was not a question of affiliation, but rather of declared agreement. Late in his life, and not without surprise, Schopenhauer thought he recognized some of his favorite themes in the fundamental positions he attributed to Bud-

92 dhism: renunciation, compassion, negation of the will to live. And the choice of nothingness.

Since life is essentially suffering, in his opinion, and since negation of the will to live is what the will can do best, there remains—at the end of this annihilation of will and the idea that is its correlative—nothing other than nothingness, a nothingness which is impossible to imagine. In contrast to his contemporaries, here, too, Schopenhauer refused to be frightened by nothingness. On the contrary, he saw in it the culmination of true philosophy: his. "The last word of wisdom no longer consists, for us, in anything other than losing ourselves in nothingness,"[4] he wrote at the end of *The World as Will and Representation*. Thus, the philosopher who ended up at negation as the final point in his path[5] and who looked upon existence as unhappiness—and the fact of its not being anything like a preferable situation—was likewise the philosopher who praised the Buddha. It was not enough that the defenders of Christianity and the social order condemn a supposedly atheistic, nihilistic, and subversive doctrine. What was necessary was that an atheistic, nihilistic, and provocative philosopher claim the Buddha as an ancestor, if not as a precursor.

A turning point came for Schopenhauer toward the middle of the century. Buddhism was no longer a cult of nothingness that was discovered to be an impossible strangeness in the depths of faraway Asia. It was no longer just the religion of others, the absurdity and dire consequences of which were denounced. The will to nothingness was claimed in the heart of the West, in the name of philosophy, after Kant, as the last word in a wisdom for the ages to come. For those who denounced the cult of nothingness, it was thenceforth in the European mind of the nineteenth century that it should, thenceforth, be located and combated. Those faraway peoples needing conversion had been replaced by an enemy within that would have to be eradicated. Nothingness, on the other hand, no longer referred to the same idea. Far from Hegel, where it was the equivalent of pure Being, far, also, from the Catholic preachers, for whom nothingness referred to the absence of God and of everything beyond this world, the new meaning of the word attacked life itself. It was life that was to be extinguished. The desire to prolong existence should disappear; the will, itself, should be denied. The cult of nothingness would thus no longer be able to refer only to an erroneous piety, a kind of paradoxical adoration of the void. It henceforth meant, in the furrow that Schopenhauer was plowing, that annihilation was becoming the highest of activities. Suppressing, extinguishing, and abolishing are repetitive actions of the same quite negative sovereign. And it was from the inside that this annihilation was acting.

It is not important here that such nihilism be, in fact, totally foreign 93 to the Buddha, or that—for us, today—it be based on a series of misunderstandings.[6] The last half of the nineteenth century believed, with increasing firmness, that Schopenhauer and the Buddha were saying the same thing. Pessimism and nihilism were lastingly associated with Buddhism in the European imagination, beginning with the decade of the 1850s. As Schopenhauer's work became more popular—after his death, in 1860, it became extraordinarily widespread—the connection became even stronger. It was, however, only in the last few years of his life that Schopenhauer discovered this alleged "concordance"[7] between Buddhism and his thought, and that he made it a curious personal matter in both his works and his life.

Veneration and Gilding

"I look roughly just as old as in the lithograph: *Diable*,[8] I am in my sixty-ninth year,"[9] the philosopher wrote to one of the best of the expositors of his doctrine, his "archevangelist," Frauenstädt. In the same letter, 7 April 1856, he explained how "the private counsel to the Prussian government" had just brought him from Paris, at his request,

> a bronze Buddha covered with black lacquer, a foot tall, with pedestal. . . . It is completely authentic and shown in a quite orthodox fashion: I suppose it came from the great foundry in Tibet; it is already quite old. It shall rest on a console in the corner of my living room: visitors, who usually already enter with considerable fright and some flap, will now understand immediately where they are: in a holy place. Perhaps Herr Pastor Kalb of Sachsenhausen, who from his pulpit was vituperating "that these days even Buddhism is being brought onto Christian soil,"[10] will come.

This statue's arrival deserved to have people stopping to look at it. A few weeks earlier, to the same Frauenstädt, the philosopher was announcing another present: "The government's private counsel Crüger,[11] a Prussian, made me the sacrosanct promise that after his next move he would give me a copy of the *Critique of Practical Reason* with Kant's own notes in it, duly authenticated."[12] It is known that finding original texts by Kant was one of Schopenhauer's fixations. He long insisted that the first version of the *Critique of Pure Reason* should be reedited, since, according to him, it had been disfigured by omissions and modifications in the second edition. One may wonder about the strange juxtaposition of a supposedly Tibetan

94 Buddha—one that was authentic, "completely authentic"—sitting next to an autographed, "certified" book by Kant. The statue was clearly an object of fantasy, given, for example, that Schopenhauer does not appear to have had any special competence for judging either its authenticity or its orthodoxy, and that "the great foundry in Tibet" existed only in his imagination. The latent idea seems to have been that of a secret among initiates, of an esoteric complicity,[13] with a touch of provocation aimed at visitors, and more generally at Christian orderliness.

This statue seems to have given Schopenhauer deep satisfaction. The following month, he wrote to Carl Grimm:

> The same [man] came across a little statue of the Buddha for me in Paris—in bronze, apparently from the big foundry in Tibet; it is approximately a foot tall: with its black ancestral coating taken off, it shines like gold, on a console in my room: I've been wanting one of these for a long time. It shows all the canonical signs: it shall remain here—for domestic worship.[14]

Domestic worship? In his bedroom, and no longer in the living room? With this shining, so desired statue, stripped of its blackness? Schopenhauer kept Frauenstädt up to date on 13 May, repeating nearly the same information.[15] On 6 June, he returned in a different way to the small joys inspired by the statue, which seemed to have been made just for the purpose of encouraging childishness:

> My Buddha is going to be gold plated, and it will shine in all its splendor on the console in the corner. According to the *Times*, the Burmese have just gilded an entire pagoda: I don't want to be outdone. There's another Buddha belonging to a rich Englishman here. I made a pilgrimage over to it, to recite my *sutra*. It is life size, but unlike mine, it is not made of bronze, but rather papier maché, so it was cast in a mold, probably in China, gilded all over, and looking like mine in all the details, down to the last hair. I like mine better: it is authentic; it is Tibetan! The other is only different from mine in that its nose is flatter and the proportions of the limbs are finer: it is Chinese! Mine is thin, with long arms: otherwise, they are identical. Both have that famous, orthodox sweetness in the smile on their lips, exactly the same! The postures, the clothing, the hair, the lotus: just the same. Look here, Professor Kalb! Om, Mani, Padme, Hum![16]

Such was the end of the 11 July episode: "The Buddha, newly gilded, stands   95
shining on the console, blessing us,"[17] wrote Schopenhauer to Frauenstädt. He no longer discussed the statue, at least with that privileged
correspondent. To Edward Crüger, to whom he was indebted for the object, the philosopher wrote on 29 November 1856: "The Buddha is ges-
turing to you from his console, giving you his blessing; for you have saved
him from an imprisonment of over a hundred years, freed him from the
hands of unbelievers, bringing him to where veneration and gilding awaited
him."[18] In March 1857, Schopenhauer sent the Buddha's blessings to
his follower Adam von Doss[19] and to his childhood friend Christian
Karl Josias Bunsen: "You are no less a man of God: I, on the other hand,
am a bad case: there the thing sits, beautifully regilded, in the corner
of my bedroom, on the console—the idol—which has come from Tibet,
alas!"[20]

A number of threads undoubtedly come together in this story. It appears as though Schopenhauer had a positive view of the Buddha relatively
precociously. In his travel journal dated 11 May 1803 (he was but fifteen at
the time), he noted his encounter, in an Amsterdam porcelain store, with
those figurines of the Buddha that "make you laugh even if you are in a bad
mood, their smile is so friendly."[21] It is, on the other hand, probable that the
philosopher felt a kinship with the Buddha before he took a public position
in favor of Buddhism. In the posthumous manuscript known by the name
Cholerabuch (Cholerabook), composed in 1832, he wrote: "At seventeen
years, without a university education, I was seized by life's distress, as was
the Buddha in his youth when he discovered the existence of illness, of old
age, of suffering, and of death."[22] In any case, the arrival of the Tibetan
Buddha in his living room, and then in his bedroom, only resulted in the
insertion of a series of positive comments and various other additions by
Schopenhauer, primarily during the decade of the 1850s, into the reeditions
of his philosophical works.[23] These revisions show Schopenhauer's position in favor of Buddhism.

A Concordance Proclaimed

Schopenhauer was alone in Europe, during the mid-nineteenth century,
in affirming his affinity for the Buddha. He paid homage to the compassion
of the "Enlightened One," to his understanding of suffering, to his sense of
ascetic renunciation. At a time when Buddhism was arousing Catholic irri-
tation and spiritualist fears, Schopenhauer took malicious pleasure in seeing
a convergence, even a similarity, between the teachings of Shakyamuni and

96　his own. At any rate, one could never overly emphasize the fact that this was a question of a belated—and in part even abusive—annexation.

The annexation was belated: it is certain that Buddhism did not influence Schopenhauer. An 1856 letter to von Doss regarding Spence Hardy's *Manual of Buddhism* (1853) underscores this: "I wrote the first volume[24] in 1814–1818, and I did not yet know anything about all that, nor was I able to know anything."[25] The text of chapter 17 of the *Supplements*, in the 1859 edition of his *World as Will and as Representation*, repeats the following part of this letter almost word for word: "I find this concordance [*Übereinstimmung*] all the more pleasant because my philosophical thinking has certainly been free of all Buddhist influence."[26] Between the poles of Buddhist and Schopenhauerian thought there would be a meeting, a "concordance," that seems admirable, after all, when the discovery of Buddhism gives it something to be measured by. There was hardly need to wonder about Schopenhauer's sincerity: when his work and his definitive thought were constructed, between 1814 and 1818, what Europe knew of Buddhism was, after all, less than substantial.

Schopenhauer followed every step of the progress of the Orientalists' discovery of Buddhism. Arthur Hübscher made a list of the works that the philosopher owned, and noted his many annotations in the margins of his scholarly readings. The references Schopenhauer made to Buddhism increased in the later years of his life. The number of references grew in the Supplements to *The World as Will and as Representation* (1844), in the *Parerga and Paralipomena* (1851), in the second edition of *On Will in Nature*[27] (1854), and in the many additions to the last edition of *The World as Will and as Representation* (1859). Nevertheless, in this case we are dealing with Schopenhauer's annexation of Buddhism, and not with philosophical truth's affiliation with a previous, and in a sense inferior, myth. None of the positive comments regarding Buddhism made by Schopenhauer over the course of the years failed to make it clear that philosophical truth, and not religious or mythical intuition, constituted the unit of reference. For example: "[This religion], because of its excellence and its inner truths, should be considered as the first among all."[28] Or: "Myth has never come closer, nor will myth ever come closer, to that truth that is accessible to a small number of the elite, to philosophical truth, than this ancient doctrine of the noblest and the oldest of peoples."[29] And: "If I wanted to see the measure of truth in the results of my philosophy, I should place Buddhism above all the other religions."[30]

There is nevertheless a striking disproportion between Schopenhauer's comments on the importance of the Buddha's teachings and the relatively less detailed contents of the passages that refer to them explicitly in his publications. In fact, the general nature of his affirmations stands in contrast to the abundant and specific documentation at his disposal. Most of the time, Brahmanism and Buddhism are found together in the same statements, to which Schopenhauer occasionally adds "true Christianity." What they have in common can be summed up for him in the ascetic negation of the will to live, universal compassion toward all forms of life, and the mythical expression of a common intuition—that of surpassing individuation—which only Schopenhauer's philosophy manages to think through fully.

If we set aside the sentences in which Buddhism is considered as an element in a series, there remain only three characteristics in Schopenhauer's writings that can be attributed to it. Buddhist doctrine is credited with elaborating "the most subtle expression of the truth, and the one that is closest to it"[31] regarding the doctrine of metempsychosis, since Buddhism conceived of the idea of a transmigration without transmigrating individuality. It also had the merit of referring to deliverance only in a purely negative way: nirvana, in being located beyond representation, cannot be described without falling into the error of borrowing from our representations to denote what escapes them.[32] It ends up constituting an atheistic mysticism, or rather a kind of spirituality and ascetic negation of the will to live that formed and developed outside all reference to the idea of God. "Monotheism is . . . foreign to Buddhism."[33]

This "atheistic religion"[34] was, to Schopenhauer's mind, a negative path to salvation, in the sense that one speaks of negative theology when the accent is placed on the unspeakable, unimaginable, and unknowable nature of God. In the case of Buddhism, nirvana as "the other side," or as "transfiguration," cannot be described. Thus, in saying that nirvana is nothing, that it is nothingness, we are actually only saying: there is nothing we can say about it. The Buddhists' nirvana, from Schopenhauer's point of view, is not a nothingness "in itself." It comes down to a nothingness, but only "for us," because of the fact that we are incapable of saying anything about it without falling into an illusion: "Defining *Nirvana*, nothingness comes back only to saying that *Samsara* does not contain a single element that could be helpful to the definition or the construction of *Nirvana*."[35] Thus, one should understand the term nothingness (*Nichts*) as the sign of an ignorance that is impossible to take away, of an insurmountable limit to our speech, and not as the affirmation of the absolute inexistence of anything. This would be only the very edge of the utterable.

The Last Word

"Nothingness" is the last word of the book that contains all of Schopenhauer, and the only one that counted for him, *The World as Will and as Representation*. The last word, in all senses. It is not going too far to say that, for the Frankfurt philosopher, the "last word" in the world—its ending point, at the end of the movement through which the Will affirms, and then denies, itself—is its abolition, its definitive extinction. From this point of view, what immediately distinguishes Schopenhauer from his contemporaries is the fact of having turned nothingness into a positive word, of having considered it as the absolute to which holiness leads. This must not be forgotten if one wishes to understand why Schopenhauer's readers were so impressed by his references to nothingness. "Absolute nothingness," as such, is undoubtedly unspeakable. We are undoubtedly incapable of truly conceiving it. The nothingnesses that we have in mind are only . . . something, relative disappearances. We cannot conjure an idea of absolute nothingness. But we are in a position to understand that there is nothing more to which, supremely, we can aspire. The final pages of Schopenhauer's book, the goal of his path, were devoted to this final consequence:

> Having reached this point, we will not remove ourselves from the consequences of our doctrine; at the same time that one denies and sacrifices the Will, all phenomena should likewise be abolished; abolished also, should be any limitless, goal-less impulses and evolution that used to constitute the world in all degrees of objectivity; abolished likewise should be those diverse forms that progressively followed one after the other; along with the will, the totality of its phenomenon should also be abolished; and, finally, the general forms of that phenomenon, time and space, should also be abolished; the supreme, fundamental form of representation, that of the subject and the object, should also be abolished. There is no longer will, or representation, or universe.
>
> Henceforth, there remains nothing before us but nothingness.[36]

What surges forth within us when we face this abyss, what trembles and becomes frightened, Schopenhauer underscores, is nothing other than the will to live, which should, rightly, be extinguished. The solutions are meager. Meditating on the lives and deeds of the saints, contemplating what history and art teach us about those who have passed beyond that attachment which, for Schopenhauer, engenders nothing more than misery and pain: those were, to his mind, the most comforting options available. Spiritual meditation sustained by aesthetics was "the best way to dissipate the somber impression that nothingness produces in us, that nothingness which we dread in just the same way that children fear the darkness."[37] The sentences that follow, the last ones in the work, speak twice of the Buddhists, but from quite different perspectives. Dissipating the fear of nothingness through meditation on works of art or on the example of the mystics "is better than tricking our terror, like the Hindus, with myths and words that are devoid of meaning, like resorption in Brahma, or the nirvana of the Buddhists."[38]

Nirvana, the word that André Lalande's *Vocabulaire technique et critique de la philosophie (Technical and Critical Vocabulary of Philosophy)* considered to be a "Sanskrit term popularized by Schopenhauer,"[39] is explicitly judged by the philosopher, at a decisive moment in his work, to be a word devoid of meaning. "*Nirvana*" is classed among the words that are devoid of meaning, the "*bedeutungsleere Worte.*" It should undoubtedly not be forgotten that this phrase was published in 1819, in the first edition of *The World as Will and as Representation*. The term *nirvana*, which was still not widely known, called to mind the calmness and the definitive serenity of deliverance. But in the 1844 and 1859 editions Schopenhauer chose to leave the wording just as it was. In order to understand this, one undoubtedly needs to remember the superiority that philosophy had in his eyes over all myth, even venerable and concordant myth. This is why, at the conclusion of "his" philosophy, Schopenhauer set apart what could be understood as positive beatitude in nirvana; he was avoiding, in view of nothingness, any recourse to myth or mysticism. The last sentences of the book could thus be understood as follows: we who are philosophers, we who cannot afford the luxury of hollow words, we who have no illusions, we who are not Buddhists. . . . "The rest of us are proceeding hardily to the end; for those whom the will still animates, what remains after the total annihilation of the will is, effectively, nothing. But, inversely, for those who have converted and annihilated the Will, it is our current world, this world that is so real, with all these suns and all its Milky Ways, which is nothingness."[40] Such is the end of the text, which is, in a sense, an end of the world.

There is, however, still a note. Beginning with the second edition, the 1844 edition, there is a detail attached to this final nothingness: "That is precisely what the *Prajna-Paramita* of the Buddhists is, the point 'beyond all knowledge,' that is, the point where the subject and the object cease to be. Cf. I. J. Schmidt, *Über das Mahajana und Pradschna-Paramita.*"[41] Schopenhauer thus returned once again to the Buddhists, but this time he cites an authority. He no longer rejected nirvana, but compared his own point of view to the "perfection of wisdom,"[42] the point where any subject-object distinc-

100   tion would disappear. On the last line of this final note, Schopenhauer refers to an Orientalist work[43] that was one of the first to make known in Europe, with any degree of specificity, the turns of thought of the Great Vehicle. What was it about this that Schopenhauer felt to be important? Might it have been the opposition between two elements, or two moments, in Buddhism: one, a *nirvana*-beatitude devoid of meaning, and the other, something that goes further than the principle of individuation, a "pure" knowledge beyond the vanished Will? There is little probability in that. He merely wished to place the accent on the reign, beyond the Will and individuation, of an "eternal subject of pure knowledge" to which section 39 of *The World as Will and as Representation* had already referred: "Against the illusion of our nothingness, against that impossible lie, there rises up in us the immediate consciousness that reveals to us that all those worlds exist only in our minds; they are nothing other than modifications of the eternal subject of pure knowledge; they are only what we feel within ourselves at the moment we forget individuality; in short, it is in us that that which constitutes the necessary and indispensable support of all worlds and all times resides."[44] It is evident that such a conception, which is not far from that of the Vedantins, remains quite foreign to the majority of Buddhist schools of thought.

But Schopenhauer was interested neither in the possible internal tensions of Buddhism, which he nearly always considered to be a unified whole, nor even in the oppositions between Brahmanism and Buddhism. The differences had nevertheless been quite well delineated by Orientalists by the time Schopenhauer underscored his intellectual affiliation with the Buddha. But he was apparently more sensitive to the unity of the Indian background than to the ruptures and dissensions of its history. This is why, until the time of his death, the philosopher referred to the Vedas just as willingly as to the Buddha. Posterity, for its part, would retain only the image of a Schopenhauer who was a Buddhist and a nihilist at the same time. The reputation began early on.

Icy Breeze

In 1859, Paul Challemel-Lacour paid a visit to Schopenhauer. "I shall never forget the evening that meeting took place," he wrote shortly thereafter in a text that would not be published until much later.[45] "Every time his words come to mind, a shiver, which I know well, runs down my spine from the top of my head to the tips of my toes, as if an icy breeze were slipping through the door to nothingness."[46] What did the "German philosopher," stroking the head of a black spaniel with a disdainful tenderness for all humanity, say to him that night? That love is an illusion, that only the blind mechanics of perpetuation of the species is at work in it, that compassion barely tosses but a few dim rays of light into an ocean of suffering that nothing can redeem. "We are here in full Buddhism," noted Challemel-Lacour in another account of the same meeting. "These ideas are an emanation of the desperate doctrines that have been flourishing in India since the dawn of time."[47] The Buddha was advocating "voluntary annihilation in which one finds salvation."[48] Schopenhauer did as much: "This is the same result our philosopher proposed for the efforts of humanity."[49] This is why the text published by *Revue des Deux Mondes* in 1870 could be titled "A Contemporary Buddhist in Germany."

In 1862, Alexandre Foucher de Careil published *Hegel et Schopenhauer*, the first French work devoted to the Frankfurt philosopher. The author did not fail to point out the connection between Schopenhauer and the Buddha: "Ancestors had to be found for this radical pessimist. [Schopenhauer] chose the Buddha."[50] A few lines later, the text specified that the Buddha's teaching constituted "oriental nihilism."[51] Adopting this nihilist doctrine, or joining with it, in Foucher de Careil's opinion, did not show an imbalance solely in Schopenhauer, the individual. This arrival of Buddhism in Germany was a sign of the failure of the speculative efforts displayed on the other side of the Rhine, as well: "Seeing all this work accomplished as a complete waste, this avalanche of systems falling in upon one another, this incomparable mental effort that ends up with Foé's nihilism—that is, with an error the likes of which speech has trouble describing, given how vague, negative, and indecisive what it offers is—one reaches the point of wondering whether this Germany, which an almost universally disseminated commonplace describes to us as the veritable birthplace of philosophy, might not be, rather, its tomb, and one begins to doubt, despite the prejudice to the contrary, the philosophical qualities of a people who push all ideas to the point of the most notorious exaggeration, who are no longer frightened by the absurd, and in whom all errors are found."[52] Had Paris simply begun to go from the fear aroused by Buddhist nothingness to the fear that would be caused by the birth of a Buddhist-nihilist Germany in perdition?

The situation was more complicated than that. To Foucher de Careil's mind, the Oriental renaissance raised, in Germany, a questionable mixture of nihilism, of Jewish—thus anti-Christian—influence of racial superiority and of Kantian rationalism. It is true that this combination had something surprising about it. It was nonetheless described at length by the diplomat, and it is informative to read a substantial excerpt from it, in the sense that

102 it allows us to see, in the new light of the early 1860s, a few of the individuals we have already met.

> The Oriental renaissance, slowly prepared in the offices of the doctors on the other side of the Rhine, has made progress despite Goethe, who could not tolerate the Schlegels. While France, initiated into the Sanskrit language by her Burnouf, was protesting against Oriental nihilism through M. Barthélemy Saint-Hilaire, Germany thought it had found in India the culmination of the ancient wisdom and an entire philosophical and religious renaissance. India has become like a second fatherland for the Germany of universities. The center of studies today is as much in Berlin as it is in Calcutta. We see the rapid formation of a sect of Indianists—one that is flourishing today—that sees in Christianity nothing more than a product of India that was spoiled on the way, in Palestine.[53]

Foucher de Careil then underscores that a recent stay in Berlin had allowed him to check the new progress of Orientalist influence on German intellectual life: "It appeared to me as though the philologists had dethroned the philosophers. The Buddha was holding school, he had his initiates and his catechumens; it is by these latter that I was welcomed. Sanskritists and Semites were meeting evenings around Albrecht Weber's or Kuhn's tea table to talk about Nirvana or Dyana."[54] Sanskritists and Semites—the comment is not followed up, for the time being. So what were the two doing together? We shall soon see. For his part, the author pursued a fairly common theme—the Germans were the Indians of Europe[55]—here renewed by the inhabitual presence of the Buddha: "Scratch a German and underneath you will see an old follower of the Buddha come back into view. They believed sincerely in the doctrine of transmigration and previous existences, and—since a common cradle appears to have contained the Germans from the banks of the Ganges and the Hindus from the shores of the Spree—they founded, on this distant parentage, claims that, among our *literati*, ring of caste pride. The Indo-Germanic race of which they claimed to be the only direct inheritors represented, if we are to believe them, high speculation, great art, and great poetry. One needs very little knowledge of this race that pushes everything to the point of greatest exaggeration, that delves into thought to the point of nothingness, that is restrained by no scruple, that is no longer frightened by the absurd, to understand what infatuation with themselves and their brothers in pantheism, the Hindus, had taken control of them; they saw, in Kant's alliance with the Buddha, the seeds of the world's progress."[56]

Schopenhauer was perhaps not as far astray as he thought. He scarcely believed in the progress of the world, and he certainly was not a racist. He was even a thinker in a truly cosmopolitan sense, more European than German. On the other hand, his love of India does not seem to have ever caused him to pour Indo-Germanism into certain works. "Nothing revolts me more than the expression 'Indo-Germanic languages'—meaning the language of the Vedas tossed into the same basket with the rough jargon of the above-mentioned good-for-nothings."[57] In any case, as soon as the question of divine creation arose, of a God looking at His world and "seeing that it was good," of optimism, of "rationalist Judaism," Schopenhauer spoke of "Jewish stink" (*Foetor judaïcus*).[58] And then, there are those times when Schopenhauer was prophesying, for example, that the return of Buddhism announced a purification of Europe, or about the reconciliation of the Aryan peoples with their original beliefs: "We can thus hope that one day Europe will be purified of all Judaic mythology. We are perhaps approaching the century where people of Asiatic origin from the linguistic branch of Japhet will take back the sacred religions of the homeland: for, after a long period of being on the wrong track, [these peoples] have again become ripe for them."[59] Readings done in hindsight are of course not to be trusted. Schopenhauer certainly was not using these terms in the same way or with the same intentions as the anti-Semites who came after him. But the latter might well have been mistaken.

7
Black Classes and Lost Peoples

Gobineau believes he knows who the Buddhists were: some subhumans trying to overthrow the order of the castes previously established by the Aryan Brahmans. But their revolt failed. Is there a connection between Gobineau and Friedrich Schlegel's theory of languages?

Brahmanism represented, in India, the just supremacy, although greatly altered, of the white principle; the Buddhists, on the other hand, were attempting a protest from inferior ranks.

—Arthur de Gobineau,
Essai sur l'intégralité des races humaines

Arthur de Gobineau spoke little about nirvana, but much about nothingness. He—like so many others—considered the term nirvana to be a synonym of annihilation. A diligent reader of Eugène Burnouf's *Introduction à l'histoire du Buddhism indien*,[1] Gobineau kept on his bedside table Christian Lassen's *Indische Altertumskunde* (published beginning in 1847),[2] in which the essential part of the knowledge scholars had about India at the time was published. From these readings, he drew the simplistic, albeit quite common, conclusion that "nirwana" was "complete and eternal nothingness,"[3] and that Buddhism was following the path of Brahmanism "up to the point of the abyss of negation."[4]

Throughout his work, and particularly in his *Essai sur l'inégalité des races humaines* (1853), he continued to repeat that we are doomed to nothingness: the human species is rushing to its perdition, history is rolling toward a silent, icy void. Soon, nothing more will exist. The causes of this annihilation are the intermingling of the races and the ensuing consequences: the loss of original purity, the degradation engendered by miscegenation, and finally death through a series of successive degenerations.

Was there a relationship between these two nothingnesses—that to which the Buddhists aspired and the one toward which humanity is aiming? For Gobineau, Buddhism was very much a cult of nothingness, but in a sense that differed clearly from what we have seen up to now. He envisioned the question of Buddhist annihilation from the point of view of a social and racial affront. The Buddhists wanted not only to annihilate the castes from the Brahmanic system, but any hierarchical structure from society itself. Besides a threat of social nothingness, Buddhism was also, for Gobineau, a threat of racial nothingness.

Gobineau, the ancestor of contemporary racism, did not really fit with the image of ordinary racism. He did, of course, staunchly affirm the existence of a radical biological heterogeneity of human groups. He never failed to attack the "Unitarians," those who held there to be a unity to the human race. He was, thus, a racist. And there is no lack of evidence to show it. In the first place, he affirmed the existence of human racial groupings in the "zoological" sense of the word. The human groups that are most distant from one another (according to type, clearly, not according to space or time) have, among themselves, only a "vague resemblance in form."[5] Even more clearly: "Man *does not exist.*"[6] There are only "Blacks," "Yellows," and "Whites," and this enumerative order was, for Gobineau, a hierarchical order going from worst to best. In the second place, he thus added to his affirmation of the existence of distinct biological races that of their inequality.

Languages as Races

This inequality shows up on five different registers, according to him. (1) It is an aesthetic inequality: "Of all the human groups, those that belong to European nations and their descendants are the best looking."[7] (2) It is an inequality of strength and physical resistance: "The Negroes also have less muscular strength."[8] The "savages of America" or the "Australians" "are infinitely less tolerant of fatigue" than the white race. Here, it is appropriate to distinguish between "strength that is purely muscular" and the "strength of resistance," which relates to duration and should be measured statistically. "The weight of the fist, if one wished to take it as the sole criterion of strength, finds a few individuals—among the highly stupefied Ne-

106 gro peoples, among some weakly constitutioned New Zealanders, among the Lascars, among the Malaisians—who are able to exercise it in such a way that it counterbalances the exploits of the English populace; while when we take the nations as groups, judging them according to the sum of the travails they endure without bending, the laurels go to our peoples from the white race."[9] (3) It is an intellectual inequality. The quality of the blood and the capacity for abstract thinking are in a direct and hierarchical relationship. Black blood will never allow a white thought; it constitutively rejects it: "Since the European cannot hope to civilize the Negro, and manages to transmit to the mulatto only a fragment of his aptitudes; and since this Mulatto, in turn joined to the blood of the Whites, will not yet create individuals who are perfectly capable of understanding something better than a cultural crossbreed at a more advanced degree relative to the ideas of the white race, I am authorized to conclude the inequality of intelligence among the different races."[10] (4) It is a linguistic inequality: "All the facts that have just been reviewed establish that there was originally a complete identity between the intellectual worth of a race and that of its own, natural, maternal language; that languages are consequently unequal in value and in scope, dissimilar in both form and content, as races; that changes in them occur only through mixing with other languages, like modifications among races; that their qualities and their merits are absorbed and disappear, absolutely like the blood of the races, in an overly considerable immersion of heterogeneous elements; and finally that, when a language of a superior caste is found in a human group unworthy of it, it does not fail to degenerate and become mutilated."[11] (5) It is, finally, a political and historical inequality. The Aryan race is destined to command and to create. It has natural aptitudes for this, by virtue of its intellectual and cultural superiority. In the history of the world, the only civilizations worthy of this name are its works, and bear its mark. This is the central thesis of the book.

If we remain there, Gobineau is not truly embarrassing. One can clearly wonder how such a speech could have appeared, for a while, legitimate to some people. One can look into how it was constructed, and under what conditions it becomes evident that it cannot be held. Gobineau was making what was in some ways the archetype of the racist speech. Despite everything, it is difficult to include Gobineau's essay among the racist speeches that produced the horrors of the twentieth century. For his affirmation of the existence of human racial groupings and their inequality was constantly coupled with a historical pessimism that tried to be radical. In effect, Gobineau's vision prophesied the irrevocable decline of all humanity. It was based on a theory of a generalized, irremediable human degeneration. The history of humanity was driven, to his mind, by a movement of entropy ineluctably leading to uniformity and death. Gobineau affirmed less the present existence of human racial groupings than he did their past existence or their disappearance. What we still call the white race is nothing more than a "mestizo agglomeration." It has "henceforth disappeared from the face of the earth."[12] Whether in Europe or in India, the Aryan family had degenerated. Mixtures, crossings, hybridizations of all kinds had turned humanity into a "multitude of multicolored mestizo races."[13] The Aryans, like the others, had almost faded. Their blood had been diluted, their civilizing powers dissolved. Today there reigns the most horrid disorder, "a frightening spectacle of ethnic anarchy"[14] from which humanity will die.

Human racial groups, for Gobineau, can thus be considered as intellectual constructions, as reconstitutions of a time now past, destined to explain how history leads to the ineluctable disappearance of humanity. They constitute early types reconstituted by deduction, and their progressive fading, presently in progress, was bringing to an end the suppression of both historical movement and, finally, the human race in all its forms. Just as races no longer exist, inequalities have today been reduced, at the end of this "infinite series of melanges" where we presently find ourselves. We have reached "the final end of mediocrity of all kinds: mediocrity in physical strength, mediocrity in beauty, mediocrity in intellectual aptitudes; one might almost say nothingness."[15] Soon "men will all look alike. Their size, their features, their bodily habits will be similar. They will have the same amount of physical strength, the same directions in their instincts, analogous measures in their faculties, and this general level will once again be of the most revolting humility."[16]

Gobineau continued to insist that this evolution toward nothingness was "hopeless."[17] Our time is that of the "last sigh" of humanity. Henceforth, we experience "through a secret horror, that the rapacious hands of destiny are already lain upon us."[18] Death was near, it was total, and it was definitive. Another six or eight thousand years of an agony caused by uniformity, apathy, and stupor, and "the globe, become mute, will continue—albeit without us—to follow its impassive orbs in space."[19]

Saved by Defeat

The *Essai sur l'inégalité des races humaines* (Essay on the Inequality of the Human Racial Groupings) should thus be read as a meditation on the end of human racial groupings, and on the mortal annihilation of inequalities. This step, which goes from the original order to our present chaos, leading

108 toward a future nothingness, is the determining element in Gobineau's thought. It was within this framework, and to justify it, that his speech on the human races took shape. His historical pessimism can thus not be overly emphasized. There is apparently no place for relief from decline. No restoration of the faded early unity will come about. The Aryan myth, here, melds into the past. It serves to explain humanity's march toward its disappearance; it cannot help to avoid it. This singular coupling of a racial biological unit and a hopeless concept of the end of history is awkward, since it does not correspond to what we normally call "racism." One would not be able to get an action project to devolve from this essay. If we remain faithful to the radical pessimism that constitutes the main thread of his reasoning process, it would appear as though we cannot draw the slightest racial politics or the least activism from Gobineau. No selective eugenics, no practice of discrimination, of exclusion, or of liquidation can be founded upon his concept of history. Gobineau thus leads us to dissociate two elements of racism that we habitually tend to believe are necessarily conjoined: a biological inegalitarianism and a politics of race. What is a racist without politics? What is a racist who has lost hope? Is he still a racist?

Just when one might be tempted to recognize that Gobineau's historical pessimism keeps him from being an "active" racist, at the very moment where one might almost be inclined to wonder if one should really hold to the customary judgment in his regard, one does well to read chapter 3 of book 3, in his *Essai sur l'inégalité des races humaines*, titled "Le bouddhisme, sa défaite; l'Inde actuelle" (Buddhism, Its Defeat, and Present-Day India).[20] One realizes that the case of Buddhism changes the situation. It actually constitutes a unique example: for Gobineau, it is a rebellion of inferiors, of mixed-bloods, of everything that constitutes the subhuman dregs of Aryan society. Now this revolt, in the very long term, was finally overcome in a definitive fashion by the purity of the blood of the highest caste. The emergence of Buddhism in India marked the stirring up of the low people whose resentment was like a fermentation of vile blood. Buddhism's growing influence, its persistence in India throughout the centuries, for him, confirmed the degeneration noticed by him in every place. But the fact that both the teachings and the disciples of Buddhism disappeared totally from Indian soil, the fact that the final victory was handed to Brahmanism, which saved the permanence of castes and the "just supremacy of the white principle,"[21] signaled for Gobineau an exception to general decline. In India, the triumph of the Aryan Brahmans over "lost peoples"—whom Buddhism had so long stirred up and raised up against the immutable order of the society founded "in nature"—is proof that the power of blood persists, that it is not totally corrupted, that the best race is far from becoming extinct. This victory of the Brahmans contraindicates pessimism. The defeat of Buddhism pointed out that entropy is not certain. In short, it effectively changed all that previously could be concluded. It was, certainly, a turning point. Let us take another look at it, in order better to grasp both elements and scope.

Here is the starting point: Buddhism was a transgressor. It upset the hierarchic organization of Indian society. For the Buddha, there was something leveling about it; for his followers, there was something almost socialistic about it. The subversive master was rounding up all the enemies of the true masters: "It was among the lower classes, especially, that it made its greatest number of converts."[22] In a note, Gobineau explained how the Buddha undid the established order, first of all, by turning the speech of Brahmanism against himself: "One of his principal arguments in addressing men of lower castes was to tell them that, in their previous lives, they had been among the highest, and that, by virtue of the very fact that they were listening to him, they were worthy of returning to them."[23] Attracting the rancor of the weak, Buddhism met with immediate popular success: "To the call of a doctrine which—claiming to take into account only the moral value of men—he told them: 'By the very fact that you receive me, I take you out of your debasement in this world,' everything that did not want or was not able to obtain a social rank naturally[24] was necessarily tempted to come running."[25] It was in the name of moral egalitarianism and the sovereignty of reason alone that this "political and religious" doctrine pushed the "rabble" to equate themselves with the Aryans. Gobineau was stating an interpretation of Buddhism marked by the perspective of the social affronts of which he was the contemporary and of which he felt himself to be the victim. In the ancient Brahmans, scorned by the Buddhist populace in the name of reason, the viscount saw brothers in aristocracy. They seemed to him to have endured this iniquitous negation of their natural superiority to which the European nobility was likewise being subjected. But with this main difference: the Brahmans finally won. The Buddhist "peat" lost its usurped haughtiness. With time, everything returned to what it had been: "Today Buddhism is as much a non-entity in India as if it had never existed."[26] After so many centuries, this triumph of a "natural" hierarchical order over the advocates of inequality constituted, for Gobineau, if one dare say it, a "divine surprise": "What is there to say about the power, the patience, and the skill of a school which, after a campaign of nearly two thousand years, if not more, won such a victory? I must confess that I have seen nothing more extraordinary in history."[27]

Unusable Whiteness

For the author of the *Essai sur l'inégalité des races humaines*, this was a case of a racial victory. Buddhism was not white. Its blackness was not only moral. Actually, it was overloading the Indian pantheon "with all the Buddhas, with all the bodhisattvas, and other inventions of an imagination that was all the more fecund because of its plunge into the black classes."[28] Buddhism, which maintained itself in India for a long period "by recruiting all the lost souls,"[29] was banished, finally, because of its ethnic inferiority, and today "the immense multitudes whose consciences it guides belong to the vilest of the classes of China and its neighboring states."[30] As for the principle that explains the millenarian survival of Brahmanism and its final victory, this is found in the quality of a superior, better-preserved blood: "The excellence of Aryan blood was also much more on its side than on that of its adversaries who, recruited primarily from the lower castes—those less strictly attached to the laws of separation whose religious value they denied—offered, from the ethnic point of view, quite inferior qualities. Brahmanism represented, in India, the just supremacy of the white principle, albeit quite altered, and the Buddhists were attempting, on the other hand, a protest from the lower ranks."[31] This "excellence of Aryan blood," which maintained itself sufficiently under the alterations of the millennium to allow an unexpected triumph, refuted the pessimism displayed by Gobineau on other pages, we must state again. The "white principle, albeit quite altered," still survives enough to emerge victorious. The defeat of Buddhism suggests that hope is not in vain, that nature is still holding strong, that a restoration is possible. In India, among the Brahmans, "the Aryan nature was sufficiently strong, and is so still, to keep its organization standing in the midst of the most terrible trials that a people has ever undergone."[32] It is really no longer possible to speak of a decline without recourse. Most of Gobineau's affirmations are thus called into question by him, himself, from his analysis of Buddhism.

It is even possible that the victory of the Aryan blood of the Brahmans constituted the transition point between the apparently "inactive" racism of Gobineau and the racial politics of the Nazis who claimed to follow him. It is actually hard to understand, when one holds to the elements normally available, how an author who repeats that history is ineluctably proceeding toward the death of humanity, and that the white racial group disappeared so long ago that, at the dawn of history, it can only be found in the mind's eye, managed to become one of the essential references of the *völkish* speeches of the 1920s and 1930s.

The history of the spread of Gobineau's thought beyond the Rhine is not irrelevant. A series of events won him notoriety as a German thinker before he was recognized as a French prose writer. His friendship with Wagner, the foundation in Strasbourg in 1894 of a *Gobineau-Vereinigung* aimed at making his work better known, might serve as points of reference here. This association was led by Ludwig Schemann. The author of an essay on Schopenhauer, and a Wagnerian from very early on, Ludwig Schemann devoted a good part of his life to translating, editing, and commenting on the works of Count Gobineau for the benefit of his compatriots and for a long period corresponded with the French racist theoretician Vacher de Lapouge. The Cercle de Beyrouth greatly contributed to Gobineau's popularity in Germany. The idea of an almost mystical union between the king and his people was especially borrowed from his writings. The posthumous tribulations of Gobineau's work, a detailed history of which remains to be written, are clearly not without consequence. These particularities alone, nevertheless, do not provide an explanation for how one managed to go, in less than a century, from the schema that seemed to be his ("Yesterday the Aryans, tomorrow the death of humanity") to the schema that has been considered to have appropriated it ("Today the death of the Jews, tomorrow the Aryan Reich"). If one thought about characterizing Gobineau's thought process given this background, it would be necessary to look at the two things happening in it. On the one hand, he was making biological a theme that had up to that point remained purely linguistic. While for Friedrich Schlegel, Sanskrit was presented as the "mother language" from which, via "linguistic intermingling,"[33] the European languages were derived, for Gobineau the Aryans became the "mother race" from which, via successive degenerations, the present day white peoples would stem. On the other hand, and at the same time, Gobineau was breaking with the German romantics' system of thought, for whom the degradation of early perfection could, and should, be compensated by a return to the sources allowing modernity to regenerate itself. His concept of history, on the other hand, supposed a growing degradation leading humanity from perfection to death.

The way the Nazis and their epigones refer to Gobineau can then appear in a clearer light. One might, by oversimplification, say that they preserved the biologization of the Aryan myth constructed by Gobineau, by combining this biologization with a final figure of "Indo-Germanism," where Germanity got the lion's share. One should, above all, underscore that the Nazi speeches, to the extent that they intended to promote a revolution connected with a racial politics, necessarily needed to find, and

112 restore, the idea that a distant past is the guarantee of a better future, or that an early stock constitutes the reserves for a harmonious future. It was precisely with these themes that Gobineau (closer to Schopenhauer than to the German romantics, in this regard) seemed to have explicitly broken.

Dawn without Schism

In order to understand what was at stake, it is probably best to return to the early nineteenth century, and to the wild hopes that India, before the discovery of Buddhism, raised among certain German romantics.[34] Their dream was that of finding—preserved from the alterations of history and free from the upheavals of all kinds of revolution (scientific, spiritual, technical, and political) that might either blur it or degrade it—the earliest source of the West, and, through this, a possible resource for their future. From it, they hoped to draw strength, always in reserve, for a new life. With the cradle of humanity finally knowable, they felt they had gained access to a perfection prior to that of Greece, a perfection more fundamental and more all-encompassing. This colossal dawn, sprung from the depths of time, was to have held the power of our future in reserve. Learning Sanskrit, thus, did not simply mean the extension of Western knowledge to new domains that had theretofore remained opaque and practically impenetrable. It was not enough to point out, or even to celebrate, the possibility of new studies, and the gradual progression of scholarly disciplines on the ruins of earlier fables. On the contrary, the myth of a new renaissance was forged, one that was more decisive than the renaissance brought about by the Greek studies of the humanists. Just as Europe's rediscovery of its Hellenic roots had allowed us, it was believed, to bring the Middle Ages to an end, to see the classical age and modern times begin, with their parade of theoretical, aesthetic, and social changes, so also did we expect from this second Renaissance—this time "Eastern"—the return of a groundswell capable of closing off modernity and getting back in touch with the most buried, the most vibrant, of spirits. Discovering a past that was earlier than that of the Greek thinkers and Greek gods, confronting the mind with one of its own faces that was so forgotten and so archaic that it looked at first like something foreign and distant, this Renaissance was judged to be the bearer of changes that were more basic than the preceding one.

This ancient, present, and future paradise was that of reconciliation. The India dreamed of by the romantics knew nothing of rifts or clefts, of the oppositions that have been so much a part of our history. This coales-

cent Eden remained foreign to any process establishing conventions, in-
stituting codes, or making up human rules for lack of being able to decipher
in the silence of reality the signs that God or nature had engraved therein.
India referred to a universe from which our separations were absent, where
our antagonisms were unknown. This unsundered dawn was supposed, for
example, not to know any distinction between God and world, any more
than between concepts and intuition, between science and poetry, between
religion and philosophy, or between thought and expression, or subject and
object, or the collective and the individual.

Once this first perfection was glimpsed, another future seemed to an-
nounce itself. In this dream, the crises and convulsions that presaged modern times found themselves canceled or suspended. The first generation
of romantics, contemporary with the learning of Sanskrit, saw physics,
chemistry, astronomy, and the natural sciences become emancipated—all
together—from supervision by philosophers; they saw Christianity decline,
divine right monarchies end up on the gallows, the republic make wide use
of the guillotine, history give birth to Napoleonic wars, factories increase,
other civilizations emerge from the past, and philosophy explore its own
limits and set the boundaries for the domain of the validity of reason.
India's mythical horizon could provide an answer for the troubles brought
about by the birth of a world. Immobile and integral, India was first constructed like an anti-modern paradise. People thought India brought together and preserved some harmonious, living whole—some early connection that had to be reinvented—everything we had separated, opposed,
isolated, and undone artificially, mechanically, and finally mortiferously.

These themes were at work in the writings of Friedrich Schlegel.[35] At
first glance, his purpose seemed very much in line with speeches on the
early world. The first lines of his introduction explicitly placed India in this
perspective: "The friends of Antiquity were awaiting, from this country, the
lamp that would shed light on that history so long obscured from the
primitive world."[36] Schlegel's procedure nevertheless followed other paths,
and got laid out in completely unprecedented ways. In the first place, he
split the primitive world into a noble, living, fertile part and a mechanical,
artificial, and sterile part. India and Greece fell into the first of these categories, soon to be joined by Germany. China, Arabia, and Mexico fell into the
second, to which Judea would later be added, after a few delays.[37] The unity
of a universal system of equivalencies wherein every element of the primitive was virtually correlative to every other thus found itself broken. With
Schlegel, who on this point disagreed with William Jones, the idea of a

114 common source for all of humanity was found explicitly challenged. Humanity had cradles, if they can be called that, but not just one. And they were not of equal value.

Strong Languages, Weak Languages

Languages are evidence of this. It was actually starting with a criterion of linguistic classification that, in Schlegel's writings, both this schism in the primitive world and, eventually, the one in mythologies and literatures managed to take place, before it was applied, in turn, to peoples. Now this division of languages is strangely worded. Historians of linguistic theories recognize Schlegel for having first made a distinction between inflected languages and agglutinative languages. Inflected languages, like Sanskrit and Greek, are those in which words are created by means of some alteration within the root: where from the same root, internal modifications allowing new words to be engendered. Agglutinative languages, like Chinese and Arabic, essentially create words through the addition of suffixes and prefixes: they juxtapose and combine set elements around roots that remain unchanged. If we remain there, it is not really clear what such an opposition was leading to, nor is it clear what there is about it that is specifically romantic, or why it had such a long tenure in German history.

Nevertheless, it was all said quite explicitly by Schlegel. The Indian language and Greek (as well as the "naturally noble" German language) were bearers of the "inner strength" of a "living tissue."[38] This family of noble languages developed its "sprouts of life," its "fertile seeds," in a manner that was lasting, powerful, and harmonious."[39] Moreover, those languages that are in affinity and mutually connected possess "original meanings" that are also called "natural" or "primitive."[40] In a way, these are like the true names of things or, if preferred, what things mean in themselves. For many of us, this may be an idea that is quite difficult to comprehend. Let us underscore this, so that this vision of language, and its relationship to the world, can at least be seen to exist. As shall be seen, it entails more than just a distant image of India or a few points of erudition for the historian of ideas.

What is at issue here? What is at issue is the assertion that meaning exists by itself, independent of our arbitrary constructions, our fleeting conventions, and the ways in which we believe we create it. It is perhaps ultimately of little import that such early meanings can be read in nature, or that they offer themselves within the depths of a vision in which God, in the dawn of time, showed Himself to humans, or that they are available to a perception that is finer than ours, one capable of grasping in an immediate and intuitive manner what sounds, by themselves, "mean," or that they emerge even for no reason, showing themselves as absolute, early evidence. These variants are not at the heart of the concept, though. What is characteristic of it is believing that it is possible that meaning is not humanly instituted, that it is not necessarily created by social life or by history, that in certain privileged cases it escapes the fragile status of a symbolic network thrown upon a silent, insane world. Somewhere, some day, for some people, God-Nature spoke with "his" words and not by means of ours. Things were said in their very being, prior to any convention, to any distinction between words and things, between sounds and meanings, prior to any separation between thought and reality, nullifying in advance any distance in the future between the spoken word and being.

This is undoubtedly not a new idea. Cratylus and Hermogenes had already debated the natural or arbitrary nature of signs. The long fights about Adam's language in Paradise were crisscrossed by these questions.[41] More simply, there is probably no religious thought, properly speaking, that has not in one way or another posited the existence of an original language. What Schlegel changed in this ancient outline was the division of languages by family, and their respective destinies. At the beginnings of Sanskrit, or Greek, or German, there were "seeds of life": original and natural meanings, like meaning-substances, like an organic fabric capable of indefinitely engendering myths, poems, or works in which thought does not get dissociated from feeling.

The Buddha-Monkey

On the other hand, the languages that do belong to this group, soon to be referred to as Indo-German or Indo-European, were considered by Schlegel to be devoid of living, internal strength. Because they are arbitrary, guileful, and mechanical, these languages that combine elements from outside, instead of letting them grow from inside, say nothing. It is as if they were tacked onto the world, instead of the world itself coming to speak within them. They speak of life, but life does not speak in them. This is why they go astray, and get lost by themselves. Their development, without an internal regulating framework, leads to bizarre results, or to monstrosities. When these languages grow, their lack of harmony explodes. In fact, such "weak" languages, "a simple cry of sensation,"[42] only get larger at the cost of disorder and ugliness.

Without the addition of strength, intelligence, and the beauty brought

116 together by this early living language, the others would not have been able
to grow, and one cannot even imagine what would have become of them.
"We would have been taken too far," Friedrich Schlegel said, "if we wanted
to research in what state the other languages bearing the traces of poorer,
cruder origin would be, had they not had recourse to intermingling with
these originally beautiful languages."[43] According to Schlegel, only two
directions were available after this earliest moment in which man was "en-
dowed with a look of certainty for discovering the natural meaning of
things, with a delicate feeling for grasping the original expression of all the
sounds."[44] On the one hand, when he had the chance to belong to the
domain of noble language, "man, in the light of this intelligence, led a
simple, wandering, yet nevertheless happy, life."[45] When this was not the
case, he remained "in a state quite near the imbecility of beasts."[46]

Those men who spoke the first, authentic, original language, despite
their peregrinations, preserved their heritage intact, since a "firm stabil-
ity distinguishes all the noble languages, that is, those born and formed organically."[47] It is difficult to "subject them by forced mixtures."[48] On the
other hand, the noble languages more easily imposed their domination
upon those that had only "weak beginnings." This allows us to see why,
to Friedrich Schlegel's mind, German—so close to the Indian "mother
language"—is found practically everywhere: "It would be difficult to name
a language, regardless how distant its constitution or its geographical lo-
cation from German might be, in which a few German roots are not
found. . . . This is explained by the time spent by Germanic peoples in,
and their passage through, those countries of Northern and Western Asia
which have forever been the meeting place of peoples and the theater of
their migrations."[49]

In any case, it would be wrong to believe that a simply linguistic model
of the superiority of the Indo-Germans—or of the Aryans—could later be
transformed into a biological superiority, into a racism in the proper sense
of the term. Friedrich Schlegel, apparently, was in no way a racist. The
idea of founding a hierarchy of physical, intellectual, or spiritual abilities
did not cross his mind, nor did that of the privilege of noble languages
over weak languages and the consequences that ensued therefrom. It was
Gobineau, as we have seen, who began to "biologize" Schlegel's linguistic
model, leading to an undeniably racist theory. It would be better to say that
Gobineau transposed to human racial groups what Schlegel was saying only
about languages, since Gobineau did not "biologize": Schlegel's linguistic
model was, deep down, already overtly biological, since it set a living, fertile,

naturally and originally noble and harmonious fabric in opposition to a mechanical, sterile amalgam destined to imbalances and the production of dangerous disorders.

Was it purely coincidental that, from the time of this work's publication in 1808, and thus quite precociously, Friedrich Schlegel, in opposition to the dominant indifference of his time, vowed explicit hatred for Buddhism despite how little known it was? For him, Buddhism represented the very exemplar of pantheism. "[Pantheism's] spirit is manifest in the teachings of the Buddhists."[50] Now it is a "frightening teaching which, by its negative and abstract—and thus erroneous—idea of the infinite is necessarily converted into a vague indifference of being and nonbeing."[51] We thus find, in 1808— under the pen of the fervent defender of both all things Sanskrit and the poetic and intellectual grandeur of India, Friedrich Schlegel—pronouncements about Buddhism presaging those that would come from Hegel some twenty years later:[52] "When all is destroyed and disappears before a simple abstract and negative idea of the infinite, this very idea vanishes in turn; it— which was originally only empty and devoid of substance—is converted into the idea of nothingness."[53]

And so Buddhism began to dry India up. "The human mind has not gone lower in Oriental philosophy than pantheism, a system, moreover, that is as pernicious to morality as is materialism, and which is no less destructive to the imagination than the latter."[54] The primordial dawn, without age, without conflict, was obscured by this latter thought, "the youngest of all the Eastern philosophies."[55] Sterile, negative, rationalistic, this Buddhist corruption immediately said farewell to the Orient: "Pantheism alone is the system of pure understanding, and this is why it is already making the transition from Eastern philosophy to that of Europe."[56] Finally, Schlegel underscored that Buddhism was a troublemaker. India had certainly known "foreign conquerers" and "changes of dynasty," but it was ignorant of the "modern revolutions" and "notable changes of constitution."[57] Not completely: "Only the Buddhists are an exception: the latter have been pursued and banished, not because of their teachings, but because they attacked the constitution and the division of states with their hereditary distinctions."[58]

The existence of the Buddhists made warfare against them a necessity. The battle had to be waged "when these sectarians' innovations attacked the constitution such that war could be nothing other than an inevitable consequence."[59] In fighting against this frightful sect, however, it was not absolutely certain that it was men that were being massacred. Is it ill-willed

118 to think, in the context that has just been outlined, that this final sentence sounds strange? "The religion of Fo possesses, in a number of points of doctrine, and even in exterior organization, a quite striking—albeit false . . . —similarity to the religion of Christ; it is the similarity of the monkey to man."[60]

8

The End of the Human Race

Is their ultimate goal thus nothingness? "Yes," some
clearly say, and therein lies the error, and the horror, of the
Buddhists. "No, surely not," say the others, "for no one can
desire nothingness." The polemic spreads in Europe.

The human spirit has scarcely been observed except in the racial groups to which we, ourselves, belong.

—Jules Barthélemy Saint-Hilaire, "Le *Nirvana* bouddhique," 1862

It is a page from an anthology. On it, everything is said, condensed once and for all. The text speaks for itself; all one need do is let its rosary beads of juxtaposed paradoxes slip by, one by one. It is undoubtedly one of the passages where the "cult of nothingness" reaches its culmination, the totality of the speeches that, for a while in Europe, turned Buddhism into a nihilistic scarecrow. Here it is:

> A doctrine which assigns life's highest goal to be nothingness, or—if preferred—a paradise in which man finds himself reduced to the state of a dried up cadaver; a doctrine which proclaims that the annihilation of the succession of lives is the height of perfection—where man is presented as the highest goal of creation—where the idea of a supreme being appears only at a later period in time—is such an extraordinary phenome-

non that our minds have great difficulty admitting its possibility. And yet such a doctrine does exist. To complete the paradox, this doctrine, apparently the most desperate that has ever been professed, has inspired marvels of devotion in the most diverse races; the Church of Nihilism has, to our day and without a notable schism, remained the most compact religious edifice of the Orient. This is a singular feat in the history of the human spirit. Strange in its destiny, Buddhism is even stranger in its philosophy, its teaching, the legend of its founder, and the bizarre style of its sacred books. Combining the abuses of the most abstract scholasticism with the dreams of the wildest imagination, this religion, first of all without a god and nearly without worship, ends up with the extravagances of an unbridled mythology. The religion that was the most philosophical at its beginning, and where certain modern schools claim to have found the last word in wisdom, has become the coarsest of popular forms of worship. In contradiction to all our instincts, Buddhism inspires who knows what unhealthy appeal, like those frightful monstrosities where the secret abysses of nature unveil themselves in fits and starts.[1]

When he received young Ernest Renan's article, in 1851, which began with the above paragraph, Bulloz, the director of *Revue des Deux Mondes*, was astonished. He even doubted the existence of Buddhists. People "as stupid as that," he supposedly said, are not possible. With the idea of worshiping nothingness, the unity of man appeared to be again in question: so contrary were Buddhism's aspects to what was believed to be normal. Three solutions then presented themselves: the Buddhists did not exist; they existed but were not men; or the very definition of human nature was in need of rethinking. Few could consider another possibility, that of reconsidering the supposed horrors of these partisans of the void, of taking another look at their teachings and rituals, of attempting to understand, patiently, of refusing to want to understand. . . . This was not the case for Renan. On the contrary, he accentuated the exclusion of the Buddha's disciples from the field of normality, he pushed for their being included in nihilism. The Buddha was the "atheistic Christ of India." His doctrine was the "Gospel of Nihilism."[2] "Such nihilism we find revolting," Renan added, "for, in our eyes, life is good. But for the Hindu life is an evil; rest, non-being, is the primary good."[3]

This is why, in that nihilistic Renanian India, supreme happiness was reached only in destroying both oneself and all beliefs: "One is a buddha when one has thus reached the point of proclaiming that nothing exists, of abdicating one's own personality, of seeking nothing more than rest, of seeing that all is vanity, even the law of the Buddha."[4] Materialism, skepticism, and atheism were, to use the term, the teats of that monstrous Buddhism. As a result, its moral elevation may look surprising. On the other hand, we would scarcely be surprised that "the revolution to which Shakya's name was attached . . . was a revolution of equality."[5] Renan was another one to emphasize Buddhism's political significance. "So the Brahmans' objections to Buddhism are neither theological nor philosophical; they are all political. . . . Either Buddhism had to be conquered or the old society would crumble. . . . The castes offered invincible resistance."[6]

Once this show of force succeeded and society was saved, signs were curiously reversed. Out of the worst came the best there was; and peace out of horror. Buddhism, here, was a negation that turned into positive reality. Its paradoxical nihilism was only temporary; it was finally fecund. Instead of condemning the Buddha for definitive absurdity and incurable malignancy, Renan observed the extent to which the consequences of his teachings differed from his premises: "The negation of all morality has produced the height of devotion; atheism, a legend full of an ineffable feeling of benevolence and sweetness; and nihilism, little paradises of sweet, happy life."[7] This is a strange fact, which the historian is limited to describing without being able to realize what it is. How does one get from one pole to the other? Why has the less become the more? It is an enigma of climates and a mystery of racial groups. The roads of cultural contamination are obscure: "Buddhism," says Renan, "has become contagious among those racial groups that seemed as though they ought to have been the least accessible to it."[8]

Look at the Chinese, "that race with no metaphysics, with no mythology, almost without poetry."[9] Who would have thought? They caught fire, after all, with the most extravagant of what India has produced. That bizarre religion, offering man nothingness as its highest goal, offering him, as the height of perfection, the moment where, having managed to shake off the bad dream of existence, he reaches a state where there is no longer any thought, any absence of thought, nor desire or absence of desire; this exaggeration of the Indian genius, too strong for India herself, since she had no rest until after she had banished it from her confines, has stirred up bouts of ardent mysticism among thousands of Chinese."[10] The fact can be observed, although it is difficult to understand. One must conclude, according to Renan, that the very definition of what is human must be reconsidered: "These encounters between the most contrasting geniuses open to

122 the thinker singular perspectives on human nature, its expanse, and its diverse combinations."[11] Nothing is offered in this study regarding what these "singular perspectives" might be. It is nevertheless sure that Buddhism, its nihilism, and the paradoxical successes that it brings about lead to the question of human nature, even to that of the unity of the human species. The very strangeness of such nothingness worship forces us to suspect that, perhaps, human nature does not have the unity that has been attributed to it. Its universality seemed acquired; it was challenged by the supposed strangeness of Buddhism.

Jules Barthélemy Saint-Hilaire went farther than Renan in this direction. In *Le Bouddha et sa religion* (The Buddha and His Religion),[12] he challenged the unity of the human species quite clearly: "In the presence of a phenomenon so curious and so deplorable, which is, moreover, confirmed by a whole religion, one might ask if the intelligence of these peoples is constructed in the same way ours is; and if, in those climates where life is so horrific and where nothingness is worshiped instead of God, human nature is still that same nature we feel within ourselves."[13]

Regrettable Politeness

In 1862, Barthélemy Saint-Hilaire had still not budged. Fifteen years after getting Victor Cousin to say that Buddhism was a religion where nothingness was worshiped, ten years after the death of Eugène Burnouf, two years after his work on *The Buddha and His Religion* incited a variety of attacks, as had his preceding publications on the same subject, he confirmed to his academic colleagues that his analysis had not changed. "The interpretation I gave of Buddhist nirvana, based on E. Burnouf, has been strongly contested. I am not surprised. The belief that nothingness has become a religion professed, still today, by a quarter, or perhaps a third of humanity, with a variety of modifications, is a fact so extraordinary that it must have provoked, first surprise, and then denial. Worshiping nothingness! That is scarcely comprehensible. . . . After long reflection and an in-depth examination of the arguments that have been raised against this idea, I persist, and I still believe that I am in no way mistaken."[14]

Jules Barthélemy Saint-Hilaire, born in Paris in 1805, would undoubtedly have pursued an obscure career in the Ministry of Finances if he had not met Victor Cousin, through his editing of the *Globe*, a newspaper on which he began collaborating in 1826. In the course of his long life he went from opposition to power by passing through the Collège de France. Elected to the Collège's chair of Greek and Latin Philosophy in 1838,

thanks to Cousin, by 1848 he was head of the secretariat of the provisional
government, refused to pledge allegiance to the Empire, and, after a time as
secretary general of Thiers in 1870, ended up as Jules Ferry's minister of
foreign affairs in 1880. His faithfulness to Victor Cousin was faultless: it
was he who was there at the philosopher's bedside when he died in Cannes
in 1867, and who decided to have himself buried in a tomb nearby, in
the Parisian cemetery of Père-Lachaise. Georges Picot saw in Barthélemy
Saint-Hilaire "a soul of antiquity lost in time."[15]

Schopenhauer's opinion was clearly different: "a venal, abject obscurantist."[16] In 1857, the Frankfurt master reminded his faithful "apostle,"[17]
Adam von Foss, that he had already had occasion to lay into him in the
preface to *On the Will in Nature*, where Schopenhauer was accusing the
author of having spoken of Kant "in the most undignified of terms." A
note mentioned: "These gentlemen, be they French or German, must learn
to understand that philosophy was not made for carrying water for the
clergy's mill."[18] This time, Schopenhauer had just received Jean-Baptiste-
François Obry's *Du Nirvâna Indien*,[19] where the analyses of Buddhism and
its "fanaticism for nothingness" developed by Barthélemy Saint-Hilaire
were criticized. "I see that this piece is directed against him," Schopenhauer
continued in his letter to von Doss, "but in a much more peaceful fashion,
because of that regrettable French politeness."[20]

Barthélemy Saint-Hilaire did not display that politeness in regard to the
Buddha, to say the least. He did grant him true moral grandeur, here and
there, perhaps even a form of sanctity. But, more than any other author, he
piled on the disparaging epithets. The reader has an embarrassment of
choices. The Buddha's teachings are "deplorable and absurd," his system is
"hideous," founded on "sad principles," stuffed with "monstrous errors,"
full of "gloomy meaning" and leading to a "moral suicide." In short, it was
the "most revolting of religions." In view of his "noxious doctrines," there
was no half-measure: "A general condemnation is the only thing that is
fair."[21] The main motive for the condemnation levied against Buddhism
here was that of being a "religion of nihilism."[22]

Barthélemy Saint-Hilaire's argument centered around his interpretation
of nirvana. It developed and expanded Burnouf's,[23] while caricaturistically
hardening it. Given what was said in the Academy session, which condensed and summed up the essential part of the polemic,[24] the primary
affirmations basically hold. For the Buddha, in the eyes of Barthélemy
Saint-Hilaire, "the only sanctuary, and the only reality, was nothingness; for
one does not return from it; and once it has taken its rest in nirvana, the soul
has nothing more to fear, nor to hope for."[25] Since it is useless to object, the

124 exegete is sure of himself: "I do not hesitate to affirm that this is the true meaning of all the Buddhist sutras; and one would be quite at a loss to discover a single passage on nirvana that means something else. Nirvana is never offered with any meaning other than that of eternal deliverance, the infallible cessation of all pain and all rebirths through annihilation of all the principles of which man is formed."[26]

The Buddhists are nothing more than nihilists. Barthélemy Saint-Hilaire said it over and over in terms that, if Schopenhauer were still alive, would go straight to his heart. Actually, the "obscurantist" attacked the Buddhists on points that are found at the very end of *The World as Will and as Representation*:[27] "They have so weakly denied believing in nothingness that their most famous and most complete book of metaphysics is nothing more than a long theory of nihilism. I refer, of course, to the *Prajnaparamita*. Composed long before the first century of our era, the *Prajnaparamita* is certainly the highest expression of Buddhist philosophy. As its name less than modestly suggests, it offers itself as the Perfection of Wisdom, transcendental Wisdom, and it is nothing more than the development of seeds scattered throughout the sutras and speeches of the *Tathagata*. Now what does the *Prajnaparamita* teach as the highest degree and the only truth of human knowledge: It is the negation of the object that is known and of the subject that knows."[28] Conclusion: "There is no doctrine in all of Buddhism's metaphysics other than that of nihilism."[29]

A Question of Principle

The discussion provoked by Barthélemy Saint-Hilaire in the Academy that day is particularly meaningful in this quarrel as a whole, the terms of which vary little from one episode to the next. In the course of the debate following the speech, the philosopher Adolphe Franck rejected the analysis presented, because it seemed impossible to him that human desire could have self-destruction as an objective in any lasting, common fashion. "I cannot allow that three hundred million men live in the hope of their future annihilation, and know no other religion than that. No nation, no human race can be reduced to that horrible condition; otherwise, there would be not varieties of the human species, but a number of humanities, with different faculties, intelligences, and natures."[30] Adolphe Garnier went one step further: "Human nature is instinctively repulsed by nothingness."[31] One holds to that which is essential. The curious nature of this discussion comes from the fact that it was not supported by the study of texts, the comparison of sources, or the critique of ideas. The polemics were not directly related, as could be expected, to the interpretation of Buddhist sutras translated by Burnouf or Foucaux.[32] On the contrary, their two primary themes were the *a priori* possibility of a desire for nothingness and the unity of human nature. At each point in the controversy, the adversaries of the thesis of nirvana-nothingness first had recourse, as was the case here, to the argument of a fundamental incompatibility between, on the one hand, the universal desire for deliverance, for salvation, for unending beatitude, for a pacified happiness residing—in a variety of fashions—within the adepts of all the religions of the world and, on the other, the horror of a disappearance from which there is no return, the undesirable terror of self-destruction that ultimate annihilation would incur. One always desires something; one cannot desire nothingness itself. One always wants some form of existence; one cannot want the absence of any form and of any existence. In short, there would be a fundamental contradiction between desire and nothingness. Desiring nothingness would be every bit as impossible as thinking "I do not exist."

Since, according to the holders of this argument, this would be a case of impossibility of principle, relative to the very nature of human desire, he who holds that the Buddhists escape this general norm—by perpetuating a "religion of nothingness" in which they make their disappearance in an eternal abyss their highest aspiration—should also agree that human nature is thenceforth in question. If we allow the existence of this religion so contrary to the very essence of human desire, either the Buddhists are not humans, or the human race no longer has unity and should henceforth be split into a diversity of dissimilar, scarcely related species. . . . Now, in the face of this objection (formulated by J.-B.-F. Obry in his first dissertation),[33] it might be said that Barthélemy Saint-Hilaire preferred to sacrifice the unity of the human race rather than let go of nothingness. In fact, he admitted no longer wanting to "attach too much importance to an objection that he had initially found quite striking, and that would be repeated again more than once: "Buddhism, it has been said, understood as the worship and the search for nothingness, is in clear opposition to the very nature of the human mind."[34] In view of this observation, those who do not believe in the possibility of a religion of nothingness are going to conclude that it is appropriate to interpret the doctrine in another fashion, and to see a special theology in this so-called nihilism. This is how the speaker summed up their point of view: "Buddhism is not what one might think; when it is better understood, it does not emerge from the immutable laws

126 of the human mind. It understands God in a different way than we do but it is always to God that it returns; it is God and not nothingness that is hidden beneath these bizarre words."[35]

Indeed, Jean-Baptiste-François Obry, one of Barthélemy Saint-Hilaire's primary adversaries, supported this point of view. After an initial attack against the analyses of Victor Cousin's disciple and friend, in his 1856 work titled *Du Nirvâna indien*—which Schopenhauer considered to be an excellent work—Obry returned to the question in 1863, taking as his point of departure the discussion that ensued in the Academy.[36] His interpretation of nirvana should be placed concisely back into the procedure in which he engaged to defend the Buddha, his teachings, and his influence. On the contrary, far from condemning a "hideous system," he placed great emphasis on Buddhism:

> Buddhism occupies a grand and beautiful place in the general history of the human spirit. In the two score years that it has been better known among the learned of Europe, it owes its high standing not to its obscure and subtle metaphysics, of course, nor even to its way of worshiping, which was quite simple at first, and then quite pompous, but rather to the purity, the holiness, the subtlety of its morality, to its tolerance and its gentleness, to its beneficial influence on the barbarous or ferocious populations that have embraced it.[37]

This soothing religion played an essential role in the development of Asia. One should, nevertheless, not speak about it in past tense: it is today that the Buddha "reigns flourishingly over a multitude of peoples."[38] This enlightened sovereign was vaguely reminiscent of some constitutional monarch remembering the Revolution. In effect, the Buddha, according to J.-B.-F. Obry, "carved a sect out of the ranks of the common people."[39] He was not unaware of the fact that he was sowing the seeds of trouble and leading a revolution, since "preaching the equality and brotherhood of all men in the presence of intolerant and haughty Brahmans who believed themselves to be human gods was undermining the hateful regime of the castes at their bases."[40] Contrary to Gobineau, who emphasized the defeat of Buddhism, Obry was advancing its ability to dominate. The Buddha took the risk of exposing himself, his disciples, and their successors to incessant struggles from which they nevertheless emerged victorious to such an extent that a couple of Chinese pilgrims, Fahien and Hiuen-Tsang, found them triumphant throughout India in the fifth and seventh centuries C.E.[41]

In this global tone, it does not seem surprising to see it affirmed that nirvana has nothing definitively destructive about it. Obry relied on the authority of the "wise and profound Colebrooke,"[42] an authority recognized, he stated, by Barthélemy Saint-Hilaire himself. Now Colebrooke asserted, Obry reminds us, "that the true nirvana, the great complete nirvana of he Buddhists and the Jains, their inheritors in India, was not the annihilation of the soul at all, as one might be tempted to believe from sticking to the letter of the word 'nirvana,' but rather its deep calm, its perfect apathy, its incessant impassability, its imperturbable quietude, in other words, the state of rest, of unending beatitude or ecstasy acquired by the soul through its definitive emancipation from the bonds of the material world."[43] Buddhism is thus not worshiping nothingness, or rather this nothingness is not an abolition, but only another name for God. This is what Barthélemy Saint-Hilaire, in Obry's opinion, did not manage to grasp:

> Just one more step, and he would have better understood that it was not in the least nothingness that was hidden beneath their bizarre sayings, but rather absolute being, being in itself and through itself, without specific or definite attributes, that is, God, understood in a way that is different from ours, but in a way that had nothing either strange or unusual about it for the pantheists of India.[44]

Let us note the extent to which, on this point, the century's thought comes back around. What did Obry discover, in 1863, in the Academy of Amiens? He discovered what Hegel was expounding in Berlin in 1827.[45] It seems that the debate, regardless of its ramifications, devolved from one dilemma: either being and nothingness are opposites, one being desirable and the other incapable of being so, or they are equivalents and are no longer anything but two names for the same reality. Obry does not show any particular originality on this point. Where he is innovative, on the other hand, is in his explanation of the nihilistic aspects of Buddhism. They owe nothing to the Buddha, but come rather from "those oddballs of Indian Pyrrhonism"[46] who brought the teaching "to extreme consequences which the Buddha would certainly have disowned."[47] The Buddha thus needs to be saved from the fatal consequences of a later plot on the part of skeptics. They have worked to misappropriate his teachings, and in so doing to lessen consideration for him: "Is Buddhism to lose its high position of esteem in the learned world . . . because, six or seven centuries after the Buddha, a school of Nihilists has dared to mix into his teachings, under the pretext of complementing them, the most outrageous and absurd skepticism?"[48] Thus a new dilemma, just as general as the preceding one: either the Buddhists had to be split off, or the human race did. In the first hypothesis, the

128 worship of nothingness, which is actually an homage paid to God under a different name, has been perverted and disguised as nihilism by a later school motivated by an "unbelievable pyrrhonism."[49] With the second hypothesis, the worship of nothingness is a kind of nihilism, but in this case one is forced to wonder if all the Buddhists are truly men. This is Jules Barthélemy Saint-Hilaire's position.

"I am not eager," he said, "to place outside the constitutive laws of humanity a portion of humanity as sizable as the Buddhist populations, numbering three or four million."[50] It is assuredly difficult to cast such vast multitudes outside of all humanity. The problem, of course, is where to put them. What is one to do if one's goal is both that of safeguarding a relative unity of the species and that of maintaining that these "populations" have minds that work so differently from ours? How are we to understand that they are human, and yet so dissimilar to us in their most intimate, most constant, most fundamental desire? The solution:

> The human spirit has scarcely been observed except in those racial groupings to which we, ourselves, belong. These racial groups undoubtedly deserve an important place in our studies; but even though they are the most important, they are not the only ones. Should the others not also be observed, despite their supposed inferiority?[51]

Let us rest assured: "superior races" that we are, nothing has been taken from us. But let us be able to focus our attention, objectively, on those beings—inferior, but human—that the universal curiosity of science should know, even if reason disapproves of them and the heart takes offense. "Is Buddhism, because of this, placed outside the law of humanity? I do not believe so. It merely offers a side of the human spirit to our impartial study that we had not noticed, one which repulses us by its falsity, and by its ugliness, but which is still curious nevertheless, regardless of the surprise and the pain that it causes."[52] It is a question of races, once again. Races of life, races of death: "Just the idea of nothingness makes us shudder; but there are minds that, far from being frightened, are charmed by it. They love nothingness because they detest life; we, on the other hand, adore life and abhor nothingness."[53]

The question was not raised only in France. Max Müller, who was Eugène Burnouf's student and taught Sanskrit at Oxford, published a long report on Barthélemy Saint-Hilaire's book.[54] "To believe, as we are asked to believe, that half of humanity might desire nothingness is nearly tantamount to believing that there is a difference in kind between man and man."[55] A similar argument is found, later, in Madrid, in 1885. Taking inspiration from Barthélemy Saint-Hilaire, D. F. Garcia Ayuso published a brochure titled *Buddhist Nirvana in Its Relations with Other Philosophic Systems* (in this case, those of Schopenhauer and Eduard von Hartmann).[56] In the text, initially published the same year by the Catholic review *La Ciencia Cristiana* ("Christian Science"), one can read: "The morals and metaphysics of Shakyamuni are so poor and his theories so insipid and, in general, so devoid of foundation, that the enormous propagation of his doctrine cannot be understood other than by peoples who are already degenerate."[57] Between degeneration, pessimism, and the worship of nothingness there is a direct connection: "The Buddha's system, like that of Hartmann and Schopenhauer, gets its source in the most exaggerated pessimism, from which the principles of these philosophers emerge like the rings on a chain, and what emerges from it is nothingness."[58] As Phillippe Edouard Foucaux— the Collège de France professor who reviewed the work in *Revue d'Histoire des religions*—said, Ayuso "still seems to want to throw Buddhism back into the worship of nothingness."[59] The remark was made in 1885. The cult of nothingness, at that date, could begin to appear as a rut that was hard to get out of. Orientalist studies, and the spirit of the times, made Buddhism get out of it. The only ones who wanted to keep it inside were some already backward-looking exegetes and some late-comer interpreters. In short, at that moment, the decline of that episode had largely begun. What remained was to understand how it took place.

The Decline (1864–1893)

1864. Scholarly studies increase. The stir about nihilism persists, but diminishes.

1893. The Parliament of Religions takes place in Chicago. The age of ecumenism, eclecticism, and occultism—in the background of literary pessimism— becomes a dream. Buddhism has ceased to be frightening.

9
The Invention of Weakness

*Taine detects in Buddhism something other than the desire
to disappear: a revolution in the history of feelings. Nietzsche
announces the birth of a new Buddhism in Europe, and
declares war on it.*

Probability of a new
Buddhism. The greatest
danger.

—Nietzsche,
The Will for Power, 1901

Among the works dealing with Buddhism, one of the most widely read and commented upon, in 1860s and 1870s Europe, was the German work by Carl Friedrich Köppen, *The Religion of the Buddha*.[1] The author was a free-thinker, a disciple of Feuerbach's, a partisan of both a conception of history somewhat distantly inherited from Hegel and the struggle against religious institutions and their influence. His personal sympathies for Buddhism were founded on the traits he attributed to it: the affirmation of a purely human deliverance, and the proclamation of an equality of all men independent of their geographical and social positions. Köppen spoke of an "ethical revolution" supposedly unleashed by the Buddha. The work also attempted to synthesize the knowledge thus far acquired about Buddhism. Its two volumes contained no unpublished in-

134 formation: they borrowed their material from the works of the Orientalists, especially from Burnouf's summa published in 1844, *Introduction to the History of Indian Buddhism*.[2] This panorama of the knowledge available at the time, which did remain generally faithful to its sources, was a successful work for its genre. Köppen had truly read most of the research published during the preceding three decades, and his compilation managed to sum them up with considerable fidelity.

It was undoubtedly that fact, rather than the personal comments of the author, that explained the work's success at the time. In fact, even though the work has been forgotten today, such that it is not even mentioned by erudite authors like J. W. de Jong or Wilhelm Halbfass,[3] it was, in 1860s Germany, a reference work whose importance was recognized by readers like Schopenhauer, Wagner, and Nietzsche.

So Schopenhauer wrote (14 March 1858) to his "disciple" Adam von Doss: "Köppen's Buddhism is a truly complete compendium that shows great diligence, as well as knowledge [*Fleiss und Belesenheit*]. He knows everything."[4] In the third edition of *On Will in Nature*—which Schopenhauer was preparing when he died in 1860 (it would be published in 1867, thanks to Frauenstädt)—one is not surprised to see that the long note in the chapter on "Sinology" listing the works the philosopher would recommend to "those who wish to acquire a deeper knowledge of Buddhism" has a reference to Köppen's work added to it. The title, the twenty-sixth and last of the ones Schopenhauer recommended to his readers, was accompanied by commentaries that can be considered all the more laudatory for their not coming from the pen of a critic who was either flattering or indulgent: "a complete compendium of Buddhism . . . a work written after considerable reading, with great application and seriousness, as well as with intelligence and perspicacity, containing the essentials of Buddhism."[5]

Such was not Wagner's opinion. Reading Köppen clashed with everything he had imagined regarding Buddhism from the works of Burnouf, and he felt a strong repulsion toward *The Religion of the Buddha*, which he described in a letter to Mathilde Wesendonk on 5 October 1858. To him the image of the Buddha that emerged from the book seemed petty, caricaturistic, somewhat stunted: *eine "kleine Figure."*[6] It did not correspond to the great individual that, during those years, he was thinking about staging in *The Conquerors*, the opera about the Buddha that would never be completed. Nietzsche did borrow Köppen's work from the Basel library on 25 October 1870.[7] A number of his statements regarding Buddhism are directly dependent on that text. These details are sufficient to point out that the work published by Köppen managed to constitute, for more than a decade, one of the primary roads of access to Buddhism—or at least to what the Orientalism of the day had been able to find out—for a good number of educated Europeans.

Five or Six Thousand Dissertations

In 1865, in the *Nouveaux Essais de critique et d'histoire* (New Essays on Criticism and History), Taine devoted a study to Köppen titled "Le Bouddhisme." In the original edition, the article took up over sixty pages[8] and was presented as a summary. It was, rather, a quite free commentary. Taine effectively borrowed most of the details of his interpretation of Buddhism from Köppen's work but, on a number of occasions, he deviated from his model on fundamental points. From the very first sentence, he nevertheless affirmed that "this book is an excellent and complete résumé," adding: "It is moreover quite clear, stylistically rich, written by a competent, resolute, and in no way pedantic man, an excellent logician, quite well versed in philosophical matters."[9] Taine, moreover, proposed an overly generous estimate regarding the number of works Köppen had supposedly summarized: "five or six hundred monographs . . . five or six thousand special dissertations which have accumulated over a period of twenty years." For his part, Köppen only cited the titles to some forty works. If one wanted to calculate the total number of European philological works devoted to Buddhism during this period, it would be necessary to divide by about ten the numbers Taine proposed: fifty to sixty "monographs," if we wanted to use that term for complete works, and five to six hundred special dissertations, if we allow this term to denote magazine articles and communications to learned societies; these are orders of magnitude closer to the bibliographical realities than the numbers proposed in the text.[10] Their exaggerated nature is connected to the general feeling reigning in the 1860s: knowledge relative to Buddhism was increasing exponentially, and its growth demanded that the disconcerting singularities of this doctrine be explained.

It was from this perspective that Taine used details furnished by Köppen. It is appropriate to refer to it as a reelaboration rather than a repetition, so different was Taine's study from the German work in both its organization and its interpretations. The organization of the "summary" included four parts, whose respective functions were not extremely clear. First part: "Origins." Contrary to what the terms suggests, this did not deal strictly with the emergence of Buddhism, but rather with a fresco recalling what could have been the evolution of India from the arrival of the Aryans up to the appearance of the Buddha. Second part: "Buddhism," an exposé where

136   the accent was placed mainly on the feeling of compassion as opposed to an intellectual path to liberation. Third part: "Speculation," where the principal traits of the doctrine were recalled, in both its philosophical evolution and its mythical developments. The fourth and last part, titled "Practice," was not devoted to ritual or to Buddhist worship, but rather to an examination of the social and cultural consequences of the spread of Buddhism in Asia.

This summary does not give a sense of the unity of the text. Throughout, Taine spoke of only one thing: weakness. Looked at from a number of points of view, weakness was presented as the central characteristic of Buddhism. How should the word "weakness" be understood here? It is not a question of looking at Buddhism in its essence, as "insufficient," for example, because of a faulty logical framework, or some kind of fragile sensitivity, undoubtedly inherent in human nature, but which Buddhism might make manifest in an exacerbated or simply exemplary form. Weakness is here defined as being the "residual"—if that term can be used—use of a strength that has been broken. The weakness at issue is not native. It is, on the other hand, the last stage in a shattered energy that has thenceforth become incapable of exercising its old power. It is not a factor in, but the result of, a process of weakening, the final point in a progressive decline in power irremediably affecting the abilities of individuals and groups. This is what makes Taine's text original. He was the first to explain the development of Buddhism and its consequences in this manner.

This analysis of Buddhism as a sort of historical weakening of a "bio-socio-cultural" type has a singularity all its own. The worship of nothingness is not absent from Taine's analysis. But it is not central to it. It falls into the background, blurred by the theme of weakness, which is the guiding thread running through those pages.

To begin with, there was the arrival of the Aryans in India. No weakness, nothing but a healthy strength and autonomic individuals. Under Taine's pen, everything was set up such that weakness came only later. In the beginning, it was absent:

> Each family ruled by the father, each tribe led by a kind of king or war chief; no castes, no clerical bodies, each father of a family performed the sacrifice in his house; simple, free, and healthy morals, as is found at the origins of all peoples in our racial group; no sickly mystical reverie, on the contrary: honorable male feelings and prayers to the gods requesting strength, glory, victory and booty.[11]

This early group of conquerors had an imagination "of the rarest deli-
cacy and the most astounding fecundity."[12] Its sense of storytelling and the
creation of myths only infinitely increased the play of forces, placing the
forces of nature and divine forces in an incessant correspondence, like two
mirrors reflecting one another.

> The beverages offered to the gods, the prayers, the hymns, every
> aspect of worship ends up being transformed into a divine force,
> into a divine being that is invoked and revered. Wherever there is a
> power—and that is everywhere—the Aryan puts a god who is not at
> all an individual, but a power.[13]

The strength of imagination attributed to the Aryans would be dis-
turbed, according to Taine, by the conquest of India, through the settling
that ensued for these semi-nomads, under a climate that scarcely suited
them, and would begin to alter them in all senses of the word, thus already weakening them. "They progressed by degrees from the Indus to the
Ganges, subjugating the straight-haired black population living on the pen-
insula, a crude population, subject to horrible infirmities of the skin, which
worshiped serpents, the demons of the air, and which was treated like a herd
of ignoble animals. There were long wars there, a great settlement, and a
kind of medieval period, as after the invasion of Alaric's Goths, Alboin's
Lombards, and Clovis's Franks. The sedentary life replaced nomadic life;
the patriarchal regime gave way to the military monarchies. Classes began
to become distinguished from one another."[14]

The process of degradation among the Aryans had begun. Not only did
the theretofore unknown classes form, but the Brahmans and the Kshatri-
yas waged war against one another. With the Brahmans overcoming their
adversaries, the division into castes and priestly supremacy became intan-
gible. The noxiousness of the climate did the rest. It managed to upset the
great imaginative abilities of the Aryans, who were undergoing the mis-
deeds of a "terrible sun" to which they had adapted.

> Just imagine, under a stifling sun, a foreign race that had come from
> a temperate, even cold, land. Bodily exercise became intolerable; the
> taste for rest and sluggishness began; the stomach no longer had
> needs; muscles got weak, nerves became excitable, the intelligence
> turned dreamy and contemplative, and the formation of the strange
> people that travelers describe today took place; a quivering, femi-
> nine sensibility, an extraordinary keenness in perception, a soul

situated on the limits of folly capable of all kinds of fury, of all kinds of weakness, of all kinds of excesses, ready to get overturned at the slightest shock, close to hallucination, to ecstasy, to catalepsy, an imagination abounding, whose monstrous dreams twist and turn man like giant worms crush a worm; no human soil has offered a similar setting to religion.[15]

So the divine forces turned into so many constraints against those who had given them form. Those who, earlier, circulated in sovereign comfort in dealings among the gods and those of nature finally found themselves constrained, shackled, prisoners of a frightening ensemble of prescriptions and interdicts impossible to observe, crushed by an unending system of purificatory penances and mortifications that was devouring itself. "Sacrifice, the sacred word, prayer, for those exalted heads, are not simple solicitations, but rather constraining, sovereign forces."[16] Taine described a series of immobilizations, stiffenings, one movement after another stopped by dessication and tetanization: "There is no longer, in man, a single movement that is free. Ecclesiastical tyranny, much narrower than the tyranny of the laity, has left nothing in him that is not bound and muzzled."[17]

The rich tastes of both things and the gods, tastes that were thought to be inexhaustible, were followed by bitterness and despondency. All the early forces were paralyzed, seized up, turned back against themselves. Thought no longer seemed up to representing any positive issue:

> The world is rot, life is an evil, the earth is an abyss of misery. There is no perfection or happiness except in immobile, empty existence, and the sovereign good for every being lies in once again immersing itself in Brahma, whence it first emerged. Such a teaching indicates and maintains incurable despair, a universal distaste for life and the complete crushing of the entire human person.[18]

The time of Buddhist weakness had arrived.

What, in Taine, distinguished this specific weakness from the paralyzed force that, in his opinion, finally constituted Brahmanism, was not a fundamentally different theoretical conception. It was the unique expression of a theretofore impossible feeling: compassion as a perception of the suffering of others. Let us underscore this: Buddhism's novelty, the reason for its spread, was the appearance of a new feeling, not that of a new philosophy. Taine emphasized this strongly in the second part of his text. In any case, it is not certain that the arguments he used were the best to support his own thesis. In effect, he seemed to be advancing, in a way that could be considered extremely banal, the idea that the masses are not conquered by arguments, but by emotions. It would thus be appropriate to contrast, within Buddhism, an early, albeit minority, "philosophical path" with another path, completely for the masses, that is affective and compassionate.

In fact, the text's internal logic leads to affirmations that are more clearly cut: Buddhism was an event from the history of sentiment, not from the history of philosophy. If one actually compared the positions that Taine attributed to the Brahmans and those he attributed to the Buddhists on the philosophical scale, one would be at a loss to discern an irreducible and sufficiently marked difference between the ones and the others to make Buddhism into that "capital event in Asian history" that was at issue at the end of the study.[19] Taine thus attributed the following concept to the Brahmans:

> There is but a single being, Brahma, the indeterminate, pure being, without quality or form, whose particular creations are nothing more than metamorphoses and degradations; then, developing the dogma, they added that the world is an illusion, that deep down nothing exists outside of Brahma; that science consists in recognizing the nothingness of things, that the sage, at the end of his meditation, ceases believing in his distinct existence and perceives nothing more than empty being outside of which there is nothing.[20]

It is not easy, if one wishes, with Taine, to maintain the autonomic existence of a "philosophical path" specific to Buddhism, to draw a clear boundary between this self-dissolution that is characteristic of Brahmanism and the following description of Buddhist self-effacement:

> When he becomes aware of his nothingness, man escapes suffering; for suffering, like being, as it is only smoke, fades with being into that point where everything in the universe vanishes. He is thenceforth freed; events no longer have any hold on him; he rests eternally in the peaceful sensation of the void that is his deepest self and the deepest aspect of all things; he has touched Nirvana; he is the Buddha.[21]

Buddhist Compassion and Christian Charity

It is best to recognize Taine's inability to shed light on a specific split between Brahmanism and Buddhism from either an ontological or a soteriological point of view. This does not mean that no originality has been seen in Buddhist thought. On the contrary, after Burnouf and Köppen, Taine

140 saw clearly—and on a number of occasions quite strikingly and rightly put into words—some of its specific traits. Buddhist phenomenalism, which would hold Nietzsche's attention, did not escape him. He summed it up in words that, despite their simplicity, were nevertheless not false: "Every being, as it is composite, is perishable . . . as it is perishable, it is a simple appearance with neither solidity nor support, a phenomenon in the process of disappearing, like the foam that appears and disappears on the surface of water, like the image that dances in a mirror."[22] He understood that the conditional correlation of phenomena among the Buddhists was different from metaphysical causality: "Having suppressed fixed causes, nothing is left but the series of mobile effects."[23] The description of the double efface-ment through Buddhist practice—of affirmation and negation—is particu-lar evidence of his lucidity. Seeing the successive elimination, under the effect of its meditative practices, of object, space, and even consciousness itself, the Buddhist mystic "could affirm that there is nothing, and this affirmation would be something. And he abolishes it, too. At this level, there is no longer any thought, nor is there any negation of thought."[24]

These interesting traits nevertheless remained scattered, and Taine seemed incapable of pulling them together into a whole that would allow an explanation for how Buddhist thought was distinguished, fundamentally, from that of the Brahmans. The logic of his analysis was incapable of giving an advantage to intellectual or doctrinal changes. The forces—biological, climactic, or social—that lay behind these changes prevailed. What Taine was trying to set up was a story of a "bio-psychic" nature. The only thing really novel it left to Buddhism was its being the transmitter of a feeling that had no precedent—as well as that of being transmitted by it. What was peculiar to this feeling was that it made possible a new kind of movement, at the very place where the paralysis of forces seemed general and without recourse:

> In the deepest part of man, through a strange fermentation, on the
> debris of ancient shattered passions, when everything appeared to
> be inert and empty, we see, like an unexpected, ancestorless plant, a
> new power to act arise.[25]

This new power should be called a negative power. Actually, Buddhist compassion displays no action, properly speaking. It does not remobilize the old forces that were reduced to paralysis. On the other hand, according to Taine, it finds its potential and takes its roots in this immobility and in the crushing of old forces. In order to flourish in its paradoxical existence, what Buddhist weakness thus needed was first to maintain despondency, suffering, and servitude. It had to go to the limits of the absence of strength in order to be able to cross over to the other side. This crossing clearly could not consist of either a return to violence or a resumption of autonomous struggles. It was only a question of feeling that someone else, nearby, was also left powerless and suffering. If this is a "complete revolution of morals and morality," it lay in accepting powerlessness and in the strange and apparently truly new strength that was born from a lack of strength that is continued and endured.

"At the depths of extreme pain and in the abyss from which there is no escape, when energy and the bitterness of virile passions have been shattered, when the delicate soul and the nervous system, through being strained, have fallen into resignation and given up resistance, when tears have been stanched from so much flowing, when the hint of a sad smile is traced upon his pale lips, when, from so much suffering, man has ceased to think about his suffering, when he relaxes and frees himself from himself, then, like a murmur, there is a touching, sweet, small voice that often speaks in his heart, and his arms, no longer possessing the strength to fight, find a final shred of strength to stretch out toward the unhappy individuals who are weeping beside him. It is this gesture that melts hearts; it is this gesture that conquers and saves."[26]

A few difficulties arise here. Taine's analysis runs into obstacles that give rise to ambivalent judgments on his part. The first difficulty is that of knowing how such a feeling of shared unhappiness and common suffering, which characterizes Buddhist compassion, is different from the analogous feelings present in Christianity. The answer is twofold, and the two panels do not coincide. The affirmation on the one side is that there is, deep down, not a lot of distance between Buddhism and Christianity. Christian charity appears later among those whom Taine calls the "Western brothers" of India's conquerors, but it constitutes "a nearly similar renovation, and of all the events of history this concordance is the greatest."[27] There are undoubtedly a few differences that allow one to assert that Christian love is "more moderate, healthier than in India."[28] But these are only superficial nuances. Deep down, they are identical. Taine felt that in both Europe and India love, that "great feeling . . . , is the center of human development, and marks the point where man, like an animal tamed by force, abandons the worship of natural powers for the adoration of moral powers, goes beyond the ideas of caste, of class and privilege, and has a sense of the brotherhood of the human species."[29]

In the other panel of the diptych, the opposition has the advantage. Of Buddhism Taine wrote:

142   To conceive of such a teaching, we must overturn all our Western
        habits, efface all the dark colors with which we surround the idea of
        nothingness, no longer consider as equal miseries, with Pascal, "the
        horrible alternatives of being either eternally unhappy or eternally
        annihilated." Doing so is good for strong and active racial groups
        that are fiercely attached to their plans, incessantly picked up by the
        salubrity of the lastingness of their climates, and carried forward by
        a continuous breath of courage and hope. Here the point of depar-
        ture is the teaching that change causes suffering, that desire is a
        source of pain, that life is an evil; the idea of happiness is that of
        emancipation and rest; not being troubled, no longer feeling, re-
        maining eternally in a uniform quiet: that is the peaceful image that
        floats within man during his dreams.[30]

Two weaknesses should thus be distinguished: one being strong, and European, so to say, and the other weak, and Asian. These two degrees of
weakness would be relative to the historical future that is different from
Aryans in Europe and in India. In any case, the contradiction between the
similarity of Buddhism and Christianity, affirmed on the one side, and their
opposition, affirmed on the other, remains unresolved.

A more serious difficulty is raised by his opinion regarding the consequences of this Buddhist weakening for the history of humanity in Asia. Is
this a "new power for action"? Or is it rather a definitive paralysis of all
activity? Is it a constructive domestication of energies that might otherwise
be destructive? Or is it rather a question of a diminution of any form of
action possible and of all creation, of the crushing of all rebellion and all
conflict, even of any form of life before it is ever hatched? The end of this
long article shows that both these facets of weakness coexisted in Taine's
mind without his being able to opt for either one. To his thinking, in fact,
Buddhist weakness constituted a softening, thus an amelioration relative to
the brutality of a reign of force. On the other hand, it constituted a weakening, a deterioration or degradation relative to the power of this same reign.
This is why, depending on which face is lit, we find under Taine's pen terms
that are laudatory or pejorative. In suspending the use of violence and
domination, in keeping force alone from responding to force, Buddhism
establishes peace in society for the first time. Taine listed its victories over
barbarity: the end of sacrifice, prohibition of hunting, the disappearance of
wars. This weakness-softening had the positive result of establishing tolerance, of constructing cosmopolitanism, of protecting the family, of im-
proving the fate of women.

But there is another side to this face. Pacification has its price: "If they 143
have softened man, they have done so by deadening him."[31] Weakness-
deterioration is thus that which threatens societies impregnated with the
Buddhist mindset. Animal metaphors illustrate this fading of life itself and
this irrevocable loss of vitality and its conflicts: "If we imagine wild animals,
bulls and rams, that get turned into sheep and cows, and if we stick them in
an enclosure to have them live together fraternally, and if we get them to go
out to pasture at a monotonous pace: certainly they will do less harm than
before, but they will be quite mediocre creatures."[32] What is the mark
of mediocrity? The imagination dries up, the style of one's thought and
one's writing becomes languid, docility and subservience spread, obedience
grows along with superstition, and the weakness of the child combines with
that of the old man. In the Buddhist treaties there is an "extravagance of
childish exaggeration with a monotony of quaint drivel which quite quickly
one finds displeasing."[33] In the final lines of the study, Taine does not
hesitate to speak of the "thickening of the mind," and of the "decline into
which the intellect is falling" because of Buddhism, which "reduces man to
being a mannequin."[34]

Thus, the capital event represented by the birth of Buddhism has two
facets: a polishing that abrades human hardness; and a decrease in human
capacities and diminution of the power to believe. Conclusion: "If, in the
enormous, swaying jungle that has occupied the vastest part of the conti-
nents for twenty-five centuries, one sought to unravel, and then to define,
the fundamental trait of the work, it might be compared to a beneficent and
debilitating surgical operation. The human animal, like a stallion that is too
strong and terrible in himself, has been bled from all four limbs; weakened
and softened by this loss, he has become less active and more sociable, and
henceforth he has created less, and destroyed less."[35]

The Choice of Tragedy

Nietzsche, in 1870, read Köppen's work. He never hid his admiration
for Taine, and it is quite probable that he was not unaware of the French
philosopher's study devoted to Buddhism. Nietzsche's readings and knowledge regarding the Orient, and particularly regarding Brahmanism and
Buddhism, were undoubtedly less extensive and less detailed than one
might think based on his own assertions.[36] Nietzsche's proclamations regarding an "Oriental," "trans-European," or "supra-European" manner of
thinking becoming, because of him, both possible and necessary come
from the powers of the imagination more than from the patient work of

144 reality. "I can imagine," he wrote specifically in a passage in the summer of 1876, "thinkers of the future in whom the perpetual agitation of Europe and America will be combined with Asiatic contemplation, the heritage of hundreds of generations: such a combination will lead to the solution of the enigma of the world. Meanwhile, free contemplative minds have their mission: they abolish all the barriers that present obstacles to an interpenetration of men."[37]

When all is said and done, this dream of a Euro-Asiatic association—wherein we see the possible creation of a new generation of thinkers capable of displaying, beyond West and East, the acuity of an unprecedented intelligence—ends up being more an incantation than a research program. Such a situation undoubtedly contains nothing that is either surprising or really specific: it is common that the desire to unite East and West not go beyond a declaration of intention. It is more curious, on the other hand, for Buddhism to get a reaction from Nietzsche that is completely opposed to this fusion plan. Instead of considering it to be a possible resource, he sees in it a threat, a danger, a future that Western civilization ought to attempt to escape. Confronted by Buddhism, Nietzsche wished to raise a barrier, not abolish it. This is what we must attempt to clarify and understand.

"Tragedy should save us from Buddhism," wrote Nietzsche in a passage in 1871, contemporary with his first great work, *The Birth of Tragedy*.[38] It is not a note made in passing, destined to disappear from one day to the next. On the contrary. Even if Nietzsche's attitude toward the Buddha varied as a function of his development, his readings, or the context, the guiding line still remains this choice of tragedy which allows one to escape . . . exactly what? What, for Nietzsche, was the meaning of "Buddhism"? It was first of all, as the same passage tells us, "peaceful inactivity." Preferring tragedy to Buddhism was first and foremost opting for action as opposed to indolence. It was recognizing oneself as being strong enough for the conflict, and not so weak that one desired only calm. It was a desire for war, rather than an anesthetizing peace. It was choosing power, the play of forces in battle and the domination of conquerors, rather than nonviolence and renunciation. "Toward Rome, or India," Nietzsche noted on a number of occasions around the same time.[39] It was not an eternal, intemporal, ideal choice, but a situation that made a comeback, in Europe in the late nineteenth century: "We are reliving the phenomenon that pushes us either toward India or toward Greece."[40] Choosing Greece and not India was evidently, for Nietzsche in those particular years, tantamount to choosing Wagner rather than Schopenhauer. The two sides of the equation were thus:

Buddhism, Schopenhauer, India, peace, quietism, and weakness on the one side; and strength, conflict, Europe, Wagner, and tragedy on the other.

The list could go on, since the choice of tragedy is also one of pain. What the Buddha wanted to set aside, abolish, and definitively undo—the suffering connected with life—was on the other hand, to Nietzsche's mind, just what should be wanted, assumed, and even desired deep inside us. This suffering was clearly never coveted for itself: it was not a masochistic attitude that motivated Nietzsche's tragic wisdom. It was merely a question of desiring strongly enough to overcome the apprehension of suffering, to wish that pain as being a part of the totality of the life to which one says yes, no longer to consider even death as a major inconvenience. "We no longer take illness, unhappiness, old age, or death sufficiently seriously—and especially not with the seriousness of the Buddhists—to believe in the objections to life."[41]

Double Face

The choice that gets made against Buddhism clearly does not mean that Nietzsche condemned it *en bloc*, seeing in it only a bad weakness that preferred nothingness to existence. As always, it is a question of knowing if one's vantage point is the mountain or the valley, from above or below; it is a question of perspective. Buddhism incarnates not only that peace (to the point where Nietzsche could say that Jesus represented "a naïve beginning of a movement of Buddhist pacifism")[42] that one can always judge to be cautious, timid, plaintive. It incarnates lucidity; it is no longer caught in the trap of the illusion of the transcendence of moral values; it sees feelings from a rigorous psychological and physiological point of view—extremely complimentary, coming from that particular pen! The Antichrist underscored that superiority of Buddhism: "Buddhism is the only *positivist* religion that History has shown us, and even in its theory of knowledge (a strict phenomenalism) it no longer says 'War on *sin*,' but rather, rendering unto reality that which is its due, 'War on *suffering*.' It has left behind—and this is what distinguishes it radically from Christianity—the self-mystification of moral concepts; it finds itself, to use my own terms, beyond good and evil."[43]

The great advantage of Buddhism in Nietzsche's eyes is thus that of being deprived of transcendence and a world hereafter. This completely worldly "atheistic religion"[44] cannot postpone deliverance into a distant beyond. It is here and now that one can attain the sovereign good in it:

146   "One assigns oneself as one's highest goal serenity, peace, the extinction of all desire, and one *attains* this goal. Buddhism is not a religion in which one aspires only to perfection; perfection is there the norm."[45] To get to the point of describing Buddhism as a soft wisdom with very little asceticism, much like that of Epicurus, Nietzsche needed to transform the rules of the Buddha's monastic community into those of a kind of philosophical circle with neither obligations nor sanctions: "*Prayer* is excluded, just as is *asceticism*. There is no categorical imperative, no *constraint* of any kind, even within the conventual community (which one can leave)."[46]

Nietzsche went so far as to "divert," it might be said, some of the rules of Buddhist asceticism, changing them into simple hygienic prescriptions. As Michel Hulin notes, "The obligation the monks had, at least in the beginning, to live 'in the forests, at the foot of a tree, in an open space or in a place of cremation' became '*das Leben im Freien*' "[47]—life in liberty. A rule of ascetic discipline is transformed into life in the open air. This is how Nietzsche imagined the Buddha's community: a center in the fresh air, a vegetarian rest home, a sort of clinic for natural therapies for depression. Depression was actually a great evil to be cared for. It was the result of that pathology of exhaustion that philosophy attributes to the ruling classes of India. According to him, the human type the Buddha discovered was the product of an almost complete weakening of vital energy and resistance. The best Indians were victims of the extreme lassitude of a refined old population that had arrived at the end of the line. Regardless of whether it was the result of the digestive mechanism or of the brain, their viscera were all affected by a form of irritability or excitability—*Reizbarkeit*, the word Nietzsche used, is understood in both of these meanings.

This perpetually exposed psycho-physical sensibility is a cause of depression. "That is what the Buddha takes hygienic measures against. As a remedy, he applies life in the open air, the wandering life, moderation in everything, and a strict diet; prudence in regard to all 'spirits,' and prudence, likewise, toward all the emotions that cause the secretion of bile or that heat up the blood; the refusal to *worry* about oneself and others. He brings images to mind that either appease or cheer up, and he invents ways to disabuse oneself of others. He conceives of goodness, of 'being good,' as good for the health."[48] This hygienic way of thinking in Buddhism finally leads Nietzsche to curious misinterpretations: he ends up in favor of an increase in selfishness, regarding the teaching that, more than any other, endeavored to dissolve it at its very foundation. "In the teaching of the Buddha, selfishness becomes a duty . . . and the question 'How will *you* escape pain?' both rules and defines the entire regime imposed upon the mind."[49]

If the Buddha had been nothing more than a Pastor Kneipp or a Doctor Kellogg advocating cold baths and soothing gruel, we might consider him either boring or ludicrous, but certainly not threatening. His religion obviously had, to Nietzsche's mind, another face: he is one of the great figures of nihilism, the most powerful enterprise, with Christianity, of the "negation of the world."[50] The philosopher's tactical alliance with Buddhism, which cannot really be understood except from the perspective of his battle against Christianity, leaves room for a strategic confrontation. Buddhism then appears as one of the two great nihilistic religions in which "the will toward nothingness has the upper hand over the will toward life."[51] *The Genealogy of Morality* underscores "Buddhism's aspiration toward nothingness, toward nirvana,"[52] which Nietzsche describes in his notes as an "Oriental nothingness."[53] In Nietzsche, also, nirvana is thus seen as a complete annihilation, and Buddhism as a religion worshiping nothingness. The peculiarity of this philosopher's position would be that of considering Christianity, likewise, as a religion of nothingness. Buddhism's superiority over Christianity would thus—all nothingnesses being equal, of course—be that of the Aryans over the Semites. Nietzsche actually wrote that Christianity was "a Semitic religion of *not*, a creation of the *oppressed* classes," while Buddhism constituted "an Aryan religion of *not*, created among the *dominant* classes."[54] Might that be, in the countless treatises Nietzsche devoted to nihilism, the only thing that distinguishes Buddhism's place? No.

Tomorrow, Europe

Buddhism's singularity, as Nietzsche saw it, was that of being what Europe was waiting for. According to him, Buddhism was "silently making progress everywhere in Europe."[55] It was really not a question of Asia's Buddhism. It was not a conversion to the teachings of the Buddha that Nietzsche was announcing, but rather a "second Buddhism."[56] He imagined the possibility of "a kind of European China . . . with a soft Buddhist-Christian belief and, in practice, an Epicurean savoir-vivre"[57] soon to form. It was not from outside that an Asiatic doctrine was coming to Europe; it was from the very heart of its own weakening that this will to avoid pain, this crepuscular, gloomy sweetness of ruined energies was being born. "Our European culture is only today beginning once again to come back to that state of philosophical friability and belated culture from which the formation of a Buddhism becomes understandable."[58] At the same time, Buddhism, which was described by Nietzsche as being liberated from moral illusions, which was said to place itself "beyond good and evil," was becom-

148 ing a new instrument for nihilism: "Every purely moral judgment (like Buddhist judgment, for example) leads to nihilism: as far as Europe is concerned, one must consequently expect its arrival!"[59] In this "latent Buddhism,"[60] Nietzsche clearly saw the inverse of his own position: "Nostalgia for nothingness is the *negation* of tragic wisdom, its opposite!"[61]

The Messengers of Pain

Buddhism ended up being seen as responsible for the different meanings of the term "nihilism," which overlapped in an occasionally disconcerting manner in Nietzsche: saying no to life; the preference accorded to nothingness; a mixture of lassitude, indifference, and depression; the moral evaluation of existence, the construction of a world beyond this one. This last meaning is undoubtedly the most interesting, and the most specifically Nietzschean. Any system of values would be nihilistic when it confronts life, when its world of norms stands in opposition to the real world, when instinct, in this construction, turns back against itself and blocks its own progress. As soon as it exists, God says, "The world is dead." And even without God, even in his concern about a healthy physiology of resentment, the Buddha, in his own way, proclaimed the death of the world. It is in this sense that he is once again the inventor of a religion of nothingness, which Nietzsche was combating. But how? In opposing one nothingness to another, in taking negation to the extreme, in justifying destruction, without our knowing exactly what, in fact, that provocative rage was aiming for.

In any case, Nietzsche was declaring war:

> To the two most widespread present day conceptions of negation of the world, organized Christianity and Buddhism, I say welcome; and in order to strike the final blow to the degenerate races now in decline—the Indians and the Europeans of today, for example—I, myself, would gladly favor the invention of an even more severe, authentically nihilistic, religion or system of metaphysics.[62]

The tragedy that should save us from Buddhism passes unquestionably through war, specifically qualified: "Socratic men, we should rebecome tragic men—and for us Germans, it is a restitution of all things. Our Median wars have scarcely begun."[63] In order to fight the limited view of happiness, the time of "humanity's great *messengers of pain*"[64] is returning. We thus pass, perhaps, from one nothingness to another.

10

The Time of Pessimism

Some writers might wish no longer to exist, weary with the sadness of the world, sighing for the coming end. They carefully record the state of their souls and diligently sing of nothingness.

Etienne and Saturnin decide not to leave. "Do you not find that nothingness absorbs being?" said the latter to the former; he replied: "Does being not encompass nothingness?"

—Raymond Queneau, *Le Chiendent*, 1933

"I have perceived the great implacable abyss into which all these illusions which call themselves beings rush. I have seen that the living were nothing more than specters fluttering for an instant over an earth made from the ashes of the dead and quickly returning into the eternal night like will o' the wisps in the sun. The nothingness of our joys, the emptiness of existence, the futility of our ambitions filled me with a peaceful distaste. From regret to disenchantment, I have drifted to Buddhism, to universal disenchantment." This piece composed by Amiel in 1869 was published in the first edition of his private diary in Geneva in 1882.[1] In his meditations, Buddhism is always considered relative to nothingness, but the horror has subsided. The distaste is peaceful; Buddhism is only a lassitude. It appears as though distaste is henceforth cultivated as a lasting lifestyle and an assured comfort.

150   The philosopher Charles Renouvier noted, in regard to Amiel, that "Buddhist philosophy" was "a tendency of his,"[2] which the writer himself had
pointed out: "My instinct is in accord with the pessimism of both the
Buddha and Schopenhauer."[3]

This instinct seems more in accord with the spirit of the times than with
the forces of nature. Schopenhauerian and Buddhist pessimism in the final
decades of the nineteenth century had become fused to the point where
they were synonymous. This cautious, clear-sighted fatigue wherein Nietzsche thought he had discerned Buddhism's *raison d'être* is also found among
his contemporaries, once again attributed to some lack of physiological
strength, to a wearing down of organisms such that it was capable of
creating a time of sadness. This supposed asthenia was not uniform and
general. It left room for hesitations, for conflicts. Renouvier felt, for example, that nature was dual for Amiel, with two principles waging battle in it:
"More Oriental, more Buddhist, he would have given himself over to the
contemplative life, with no thought of action; better steeped in the Christian civilization of the West, he would have shaken off the intoxication of
the dream by plunging into the battle of life."[4] What is important is not the
actual accuracy of this diagnosis, nor even Amiel's case in itself, but rather
the sign of a change in the way Europe thought about Buddhism.

Some thenceforth thought about the Buddha as melancholy and satur-
nine. His image was like that of silhouettes familiar to Europe, those of the
sages of black humor, silently, somberly contemplating human vanity. The
Buddha was thus no longer terrifying. "Neo-Buddhism" made its appearance,[5] dreaming of integrating inspiration from Shakyamuni into the composition of new religions. It began wanting to fuse Buddhism and Christianity, and worked to compare them, to juxtapose them, or to pass them by.
Buddhism continued to be an imaginary doctrine, but it was no longer
conceived as an exterior element.

The elements of this new situation nearly all cropped up in Amiel.
The religion of nothingness lost its frightful nature to become one choice
among other possibilities: "The art of annihilating oneself, of escaping the
agony of rebirths and the spiral of miseries, the art of reaching nirvana
would be the supreme art, the method of deliverance. The Christian tells
God to 'deliver us from evil'; the Buddhist adds 'and in order to do so
deliver us from finite existence, return us to nothingness!' The former feels
that, freed from the body he can enter into eternal happiness; the latter
believes that individuality is the obstacle to all quietude, and he aspires to
the dissolution of his soul itself. The fear of the former is the paradise of
the latter."[6]

Reading the famous *Philosophie de l'inconscient* (Philosophy of Uncon-
sciousness) by Schopenhauer's disciple, Eduard von Hartmann,[7] Amiel
wrote: "This book posits the following dreary thesis: creation is a mistake;
being, such as it is, is not as valuable as nothingness is, and death is worth
more than life. . . . The black sadness of Buddhism has enveloped me in its
shadows."[8] But such humor is bearable, in addition to being temporary.
Amiel's seriousness and diligence in urging himself on to despair are almost
comical: "With the Buddha and Schopenhauer, we should work toward the
radical extirpation of the hope and desire that are the cause of life and its
resurrection. Not being reborn is the point, and that is the hard part. Death
is only a rebeginning, while annihilation is what matters."[9]

Very much in line with the simple statements characteristic of him,
Amiel summed up the superiority of nothingness, in 1879, in these terms:
"Nothingness is perfect; being is imperfect."[10] This literary fascination
with the worship of nothingness, which became the pretext for figures of
style and aesthetic complacency, was spread in the wake of Schopenhauer's
thought. In 1880, in a work titled *Le Pessimisme au XIXe siecle* (Nineteenth-
Century Pessimism), Elmé Caro declared that "the filiation of Schopenhauer's ideas with those of Buddhism has often been brought to light."[11]
Though it is well known, this relationship nevertheless remains enigmatic:
"That such a clear-sighted and learned man—and one so little prone to
either self-deception or being duped by others—as Schopenhauer should
imagine taking up the theory of nirvana, that he expects to destroy not only
life, but also being, and that he, with the seriousness of a Buddha, should
delve back into this senseless work, the theurgy of nothingness, that is what
is beyond belief."[12]

A Passion for Death

This obligatory connection between Schopenhauer, a pessimist, and
the Buddha, a nihilist, was present for a long period. To observe it, one
needs but read what H. Fierens-Gevaert wrote in *La Tristesse contemporaine*
(Contemporary Sadness), in 1908:

> Even though Schopenhauer might grant the existence of pity, he
> pays no heed to the feeling in the lives of men or societies; nature
> always and everywhere establishes the reign of strength and egoism.
> What remedy does he propose? Buddhist asceticism. Let us recog-
> nize the four supreme truths of Shakyamuni: "Pain is the inevitable
> consequence of life; desire, the cause of life, is the cause of pain; the

illusion of existence and the pain of desire can cease through the annihilation of illusory existence: nirvana; one reaches nirvana through absolute renunciation!" Let us then smother within ourselves the will to live, which is nothing more than suffering; let us resist with all our strength the genius of the species, let us cease to perpetuate human misery and torments.[13]

Later still, Freud was clearly a tributary on this link between Schopenhauer and the Buddha, when he borrowed from the English psychoanalyst Barbara Low the expression "the Nirvana Principle" (*Nirvanaprinzip*), to make a connection between the principle of constancy and the death impulse.[14]

Equating Buddhism and Schopenhauer's thought ultimately became so evident that Charles Renouvier, when he wanted to underscore that Eduard von Hartmann, the author of *Philosophie de l'inconscient*, was not a faithful follower of Schopenhauer, spoke about von Hartmann's "degraded Buddhism."[15] It is true that Eduard von Hartmann, while claiming to be representative of Schopenhauer's pessimism and his concept of the Will, remained reserved in regard to the Buddha, to whom he attributed a pure and simple atheism. In 1874, in *L'Autodestruction du christianisme et la Religion de l'avenir* (The Self-Destruction of Christianity and the Religion of the Future), von Hartmann wrote:

> The Buddha threw the baby out with the bath water; that is, along with the popular gods of polytheism, he rejected metaphysical divinity, the substance of the world, and the essence of its phenomena, and he taught pure atheism. The mistake he made in claiming the world to be nothing more than the simple appearance of nothingness would not have been possible without that subjective, dreamy idealism ever ubiquitous in India. . . . It was not actually possible to found an atheistic religion without recourse to such presuppositions of the theory of knowledge.[16]

What von Hartmann wished for was some kind of eclectic procedure that borrowed from philosophy, both Eastern and Western, as well as from the sciences, the elements of a new doctrine:

> The philosophy of religion was on the wrong track up to now, believing that it needed to consider a single religion to be the absolute religion, and to prove it (Hegel, for Christianity, Schopenhauer for "the venerable primitive religions of humanity in Asia"). The development of critical consciousness should necessarily reveal the inept-

ness of this effort and determine the sole task of the philosophy of
religion to be that of both designating those philosophically defen-
sible and useful elements in the creation of new religions which are
found in all existing religions—particularly in those that are the most
evolved—and pointing out the goals of the now-converging history
of the development of religion in the different civilized countries.[17]

The enterprise proposed seems as though it ought to transcend all
oppositions, those of Hegel and Schopenhauer, those of Christianity and
Buddhism, those of religion and science:

> One task still remains for German philosophy, that of melding the
> truths of the religious ideas of Asia only fragmentarily grasped by
> Hegel, Schopenhauer (Fichte, Schelling, Herbart, and others) to-
> gether, on the one hand, with the elements of Christianity worthy of
> being preserved, and on the other hand with the circle of ideas
> developed by modern culture (which most often finds its expres-
> sion in Hegel) into a general heterogeneous system, and thus ob-
> taining a metaphysical view of the world which, gradually infiltrat-
> ing the deeper layers of popular consciousness, will offer the most
> favorable conditions for the development of a religious life destined
> to replace that of Christianity, which is in the process of decline.[18]

Why was this a question of a task belonging specifically to *German*
philosophy? Was von Hartmann, a former officer in the Prussian army,
simply inclined, like anyone else, to favor his national culture? Something
else is at issue here—again, what Schopenhauer called "Jewish stink."[19] The
religion of the future, if it preserved elements of Christianity, would have
washed their Jewishness out of them. Thus, a German task for tomorrow:

> Despite all the Aryan tendencies aimed at transforming it, Chris-
> tianity has nonetheless to a great extent remained faithful to the
> Semitic source from which it sprang. But today, as in the second
> century, it is through the words of philosophy that the Aryan mind
> presents its demands to traditional Semitism.[20]

A Few Cups of Milk

Jean-Marie Guyau, the author of *Vers d'un Philosophe* (Verses from a
Philosopher) and *Esquisse d'une morale sans obligation ni sanction* (Sketch of a
Morality without Obligations or Sanctions), wrote the following in his last
work, *L'Irreligion de l'avenir* (The Irreligion of the Future):

154   We do not believe, with Schopenhauer and Mr. Von Hartmann, that pessimistic pantheism can be the religion of the future. One will not persuade life to want to live no longer, or speed acquired through movement itself suddenly to change into immobility.[21]

Two points should be borne in mind in the representation of Buddhism at issue in this work. One is already known: nirvana, understood once again as annihilation, was being criticized in the name of a vitalist spiritualism. This criticism of the concept of nirvana, which "today is attracting Westerners,"[22] was formulated in an uncustomary fashion. Guyau described nirvana as the fact of "practicing a kind of complete interior circumcision, of bending back over oneself and believing that one is penetrating the intimacy of the All."[23] For the rest, the philosopher affirmed he was finding in the nihilism of the Buddhists a fascination for the void that to our eyes is a constant temptation for humanity:

> Clipping all the ties that attach us to the exterior world, thinning out all the young shoots of new desires, and believing that clipping in such a manner is liberating; . . . opening an abyss deep within ourselves, feeling the dizziness of the void and believing, nevertheless, that this void is supreme plenitude, Pleroma—such has always been one of the great temptations of man, just as one comes from far away to the edge of great precipices for no other reason than to lean over, to feel that indefinable attraction.[24]

This Buddhist pessimism is to be set aside:

> Holding to this lassitude of being and acting, and believing that the deepest life is also that which is stripped the barest, the coldest, the most inert, that is a weakness which is equivalent to a defect in the struggle for life. Nirvana leads in fact to the annihilation of the individual and of the race; might those conquered in life be precisely those who are the conquerors of the miseries of life?[25]

One other development in the book was completely unexpected. Guyau appealed to a test of nirvana to be able to reject it on a scientific basis. The passage should be cited in its entirety, in order to understand his reasoning:

> It would be strange to experience nirvana practically. We are acquainted with an individual who has pushed this experience of the ancient religions as far as a scientifically inclined European mind could do so. Practicing asceticism to the point of giving up all varied

food, excluding meat from his diet (as Spencer did for a time), and even wine, any ragout, anything stimulating to the palate, he reached the point of diminishing as far as is humanly possible even that very last desire that remains in a being, the desire for food, that little ripple of awakening that any famished being experiences at the sight of an appetizing dish, the pleasant expectation of a meal—the moment that, so they say, constitutes for so many people the future of the day. Our observer had replaced long meals by the ingestion of a few cups of unseasoned milk. Having thus effaced in himself nearly all the pleasures of taste and the cruder senses, having renounced action, at least in its material aspects, he sought compensation in the joys of abstract meditation and aesthetic contemplation. He entered into a period that was not yet a dream, but nevertheless no longer real life, with clearly drawn and fixed lines. What actually gives its depth and richness to everyday life, what adds true excitement to our lives is the succession of our desires and our pleasures. We have no idea what cloud can be brought into life by the simple suppression of a few hundred meals. Through analogous breaks in all the other orders of pleasures and sensual desires, we reach the point of giving something ethereal—without flavor and color, although not without charm—to our entire lives. The whole universe steps back by degrees into a kind of distance, since it is composed of things that you no longer touch with a hand as strong, that you no longer feel as crudely, and which consequently touch you less, and leave you more indifferent; alive, you enter this cloud where the gods sometimes used to envelop themselves, and you no longer feel the earth beneath your feet as firmly. But you soon perceive that, even though your feet are not completely on the ground, you still are not any closer to the sky; if you have retained the power to observe yourself with exactitude, what you will find most striking is the weakening of your thought, specifically when you thought it to be more detached through its liberation from material concerns. No longer resting on any reality with solid contours, it becomes, because of that, more incapable of abstraction: thought lives through contrasts, like the rest of our being, and turning it away for moments from the objects that seemed to be the most natural to it—far from taking strength away—gives it strength. Wishing to purify one's thought too much, and to sublimate it, takes away its ability to be precise; meditation melts into a dream, and the dream can easily become that ecstasy in which the mystics lose themselves in *hen kai*

156   *pan*, but where a mind accustomed to being in possession of it-self cannot remain for long without feeling its emptiness. Then there comes a revolt; we begin to understand that the most abstract thought still needs to be whipped by desire in order to acquire its best moments of lucidity and attention. We suggest this practical experience of nirvana to those who speak about it from hearsay, without ever having extensively practiced complete, absolute re-nunciation. The only thing to be feared is that this renunciation might produce a certain mindlessness too quickly; that we might lose complete self-consciousness and we might be gripped by dizzi-ness before completely measuring it with our eyes or seeing clearly that, deep down, there is nothing in it.[26]

This is what announced the decline of the cult of nothingness. The nirvana that from one moment to the next was, in the Western imagination, a great lie or a great rest, an absolute or an abyss, an enigma or a haven, capable of becoming practical experience. A few glasses of milk, "unsea-soned," is all it took. Regression. . . .

The Time of Neo-Buddhism

We have probably not borne sufficiently in mind the fact that pessimism did not represent just a moment in the history of philosophy or literature. To a certain extent, it was also a spiritual movement marked by a kind of mystical aspiration toward a religious renewal, generally undefined but as-piring to be universal. Without the existence of this more or less confused experience of a new, and transconfessional, spirituality, it would not be possible to understand what Charles Renouvier was writing about Tolstoy in 1873:

> Whatever the case, this theory of life, which must be compared to the pessimistic theory regarding the conditions of existence, is in accord with the teaching of nirvana, provided we understand the word nirvana, as a number of interpreters do, not in the sense of a simple nothingness, but in that of a nothingness of phenomena, and of a certain state of extinction of feelings for temporal things, and of beatitude outside the conditions of time. Granted, the writer's affiliation was to Christianity rather than to either ancient or mod-ern Buddhism; but since his interpretation of Christian morality was rejected by all the Christian Churches, and since he allowed neither the divine personhood nor the life hereafter in the way that

it is taught throughout the Christian world, we believe we are justified in calling his religion nihilistic or Buddhist Christianity.[27]

A nirvana that is no longer a nothingness, a pessimist who is a Christian
nihilist, a Russian Buddhist who is attached in no way to Buddhism, these
statements, under the pen of a French neo-Kantian, suggest the extent to
which the situation had changed.

In 1879, Edwin Arnold published *The Light of Asia*, a long exposé in
verse crafted with Victorian fervor on the Buddhist doctrine, in which
Master Buddha was the savior of the world.[28] The book's international
success was extraordinary. The "dictum" of this "illustrious prince"—who
could only "appear to be the most noble, the sweetest, the holiest, the most
beneficent individual, with one exception, in the history of Thought"[29]—
had tens of thousands of readers, and gave rise to both imitations and
refutations.[30] The author was writing, he said, penetrated by a firm conviction: "One-third of humanity could never have been led to believe in such
hollow abstractions, or in Nothingness as an ending point and a crown to
existence."[31]

In the early 1890s, Buddhism was no longer considered to be a religion
of nothingness. "Buddhism properly understood is absolutely foreign to
the crude idea of annihilation that has wrongly been attributed to it," wrote
Léon de Rosny in *Le Bouddhisme éclectique*.[32] The very name of the teaching
was indicative: it was almost a question of understanding Buddhism in the
quite general sense of "wisdom," and stretching the connection between
this teaching and that of the Buddha.[33] "Neo-Buddhism, Christian Buddhism, seeks no more to turn people away from Suffering than the earliest
followers of Jesus attempted to keep from becoming martyrs."[34] There was
undoubtedly no more nothingness, but neither was there much doctrine:
"The teaching of Shakyamuni and that of Jesus, brought back to their early
natures and detached from all the dangerous accessories of which ignorance and petty ambitions made them partisans, have shown the world a
single, same path for the salvation of beings: the way of Knowledge acquired through Love of creatures and through the incessant work of inner
Rectification."[35]

When he heard the word "neo-Buddhism," Jules Barthélemy Saint-
Hilaire again took the floor. He was eighty-eight years old on 25 February
1893 when he read, in the philosophy section of the Académie des Sciences
Morales et Politiques, the thesis that began as follows:

By neo-Buddhism one should understand the craze that a few
minds, among us, have conceived for Indian Buddhism. These neo-

158 phytes undoubtedly know very little about the doctrine behind their admiration; and if they better understood what it was, they would not have the feelings they are displaying for it. Meanwhile, it is a kind of moral epidemic which, although it is not as dreadful as the material epidemics, is nonetheless just as deleterious to the intellects it corrupts and leads astray.[36]

Once again, he called for vigilance toward the "implacable pessimism" of this "deplorable," "hideous," "revolting," "gloomy" religion. This pessimism was taking over Europe. It was a plot:

Is the Buddha not, everywhere, a multitude of accomplices? Are the atheists and the materialists not of his opinion? Do they not, likewise, believe in annihilation? Do they not, likewise, think there is a need for a life hereafter? They are rushing into the same abyss.[37]

Nevertheless, there was no longer any real threat in that. Buddhism was

a belief that is not worthy of our time. Regardless the shortcomings for which our societies could justly be reproached, they would need to decline by a number of degrees to take refuge in the Buddhist nirvana; that is not where they are; and it can be asserted that they will never reach that point. Destined to perish, like everything that lived before them, it is not by this death that they deserve to finish. A rehabilitation of Buddhism is thus not seriously attempted; it is, at most, a literary fantasy, which in itself presents certain drawbacks. Souls are racked with enough pains without adding one more. Let the Buddha's character, his intentions, his entire life be admired as much as one wishes; but let us flee his deleterious teachings. Buddhism should take the place that is its due, in history; but let us keep it out of hearts.[38]

The man was quite advanced in age, certainly. And his speech, through repetition, had already become like something of another age. It was nevertheless he, one of the inventors of the cult of nothingness, who on that day put an end to the nightmare that he had so long upheld: "but," as someone has said, "one cannot address either prayers or homage to him. Also, it is not nothingness that the Buddhists adore; it is the Buddha; and his worship is just as sweet as he himself was. Perfumes, flowers, fruit, lamps, and music: these are what adorned the temples where the ceremonies and sermons that reproduce his teachings and revive the example of his life take place."[39]

The Parliament and the Aryans

The idea of a fundamental convergence of the different religious confessions had made a certain headway. The feeling of a relative decline in their institutional forms had increased. The need for new meetings, announcing dialogues that were still in embryonic form, seemed to be imposing itself. It was in this spirit that in Chicago, on 11 September 1893, the "Parliament of Religions" opened. Vivekananda, the disciple of Ramakrishna, attended out of his own interest, even without an invitation. He was a delegate of no religious group. On 31 May 1893, he left Bombay for Chicago, via Tokyo and Vancouver, according to Romain Rolland in *La Vie de Vivekânanda et l'Evangile universel* (The Life of Vivekenanda and the Universal Gospel).[40] The information Rolland offers is probably not all correct. It is doubtful, for example, that long ovations were unleashed solely by the proclamation of a stranger: "Sisters and brothers of America!" The hagiographer nevertheless noted: "Scarcely had he pronounced his first quite simple words when hundreds of individuals stood up at their seats and acclaimed him."[41] The American press reserved an enthusiastic welcome for the young Indian. His conviction that the diverse religions were saying the same thing, that they were not many but rather one, was attractive to the audience. "There is, among the world's religions, neither contradiction nor antagonism," he said. If religions did not contradict one another, it was because they were all one: "There have never been several religions."[42] The religion, the only one, the single one, is that of India, Vedanta. "We claim that only Vedanta can be the universal religion, that it is already the only universal religion that exists in the world, because it preaches principles and not individuals."[43]

The influence of Schopenhauer, through Paul Deussen,[44] worked on Vivekananda in such a way that he gave an ethical meaning to the *mahavakya* (the Great Word) of the *Chandogya Upanishad*: "*Tat tvam asi*" (You are that). In effect, it is quite probably from his reading of Schopenhauer, and from his conversations with Deussen—the Sanskrit scholar and editor of Schopenhauer who had gone to India in 1896—that Vivekananda gave an ethical slant to the phrase, which is not attributed to it in the Sanskrit corpus.[45] This German influence probably explains the use Vivekenanda made of the word "Aryan" (not in the normal Sanskrit meaning, but in the European, *indogermanisch* sense of the Aryan myth)[46] in pronouncements dealing with "race," or "type," or "blood." These characteristics were not without consequence for the idea Vivekenanda formed of Buddhism.[47] In fact, the passages where he spoke of Buddhism do not coincide with one another. In

160 a first group of statements, the Buddha is judged positively: "Buddha was a great Vedantist."[48] He was explicitly considered by Vivekananda to be an incarnation of God, with intentions that were identical to those of Krishna (of whom he was a new incarnation)[49] in the *Bhagavad-Gita*. Elsewhere, on the other hand, it is clear that the Buddha was an agnostic, was opposed to the Veda, rejected the existence of the soul, was the cause of religious sectarianism, and placed himself in diametric opposition to Vedanta. "Wishing to confuse [Buddhism] with Vedantism makes no sense."[50]

Why this juxtaposition of contrary affirmations that can be reconciled nowhere? On the one hand, Vivekananda wished to affirm the fundamental unity of Indian thought. He could not, therefore, recognize that the development of Buddhism caused a split. On the other, he had been influenced by Western thought. Vivekananda could get out of this double bind—saving Indian unity against European erudition, and inheriting from Europe the horror of a what was believed to be Buddhist nihilism—only with difficulty and without glory. He imagined a degeneration connected to the existence of Buddhism. It was not without racial connotations. "The Tartars, the Baluchis, and all the horrid racial groups of humanity poured into India and became Buddhists, and mixed in with us, bringing along their national customs."[51] This degeneration was referred to in the most disparaging of terms. Vivekananda wrote, for example, "The most repulsive of ceremonies, the most horrible and obscene books ever written by the hand of man or conceived by his brain, the greatest brutalities ever offered in the name of religion have all been the product of degenerated Buddhism."[52] Is this the same author who was saying in Chicago, in 1893, that "the divine is in all religions"? The same author who was asserting that there was only one religion? That no one should be excluded? That tolerance should be universal?

The cult of nothingness was ending. This circumscribed whole of European speeches about an imaginary Buddhism was coming to a close. At the end of the century, there was an increase in learned societies, and large publications on Orientalism were in progress; the rumor was extinguished. Occultism took hold of a few fragments of the Buddha's cadaver, but it left nothingness in its place. Amiel, with his sententious placidity, noted in his private diary: "Evolutionism, fatalism, pessimism, nihilism: is it not curious to see this terrible, desolate doctrine spread at the same time that the German nation is celebrating its grandeur and its triumphs?"[53] The remarks of alarm about the Buddha were quieted. The time of wars was soon to come. Another cult of nothingness was beginning.

11
A Secret Laboratory

How did we go from a religion without a god to the cult of nothingness? Might it have been the face of the twentieth century that was taking shape? At least in part. . . .

There is no nothing-ness. Zero does not exist. Everything is something. Nothing is nothing.

—Victor Hugo,
Les Misérables, 1862

Was it really about the Buddha? Clearly not. Europe alone, under a variety of names and masks, was at the center of the texts examined in this inquiry. In the many pages from the nineteenth century that dealt with Buddhism, Asia, and the cult of nothing-ness, the only thing at issue was really only European identity. Europe was already no longer eternal and triumphant, supposedly always identical to herself, unchanged since the time of the Greeks, sure of her balance and proud of her measure. On the contrary, she was an anxious Europe, a Europe uncertain of her identity, a Europe that invented, with the cult of nothing-ness, a mirror in which she still did not dare recognize herself. For nearly a century, this post–French Revolution Europe was caught between monarchies and republics, between capitalism and social rights, between colonialism and uni-

162 versality, between Christianity and free-thinking. These tensions ran through the speeches about Buddhism as a cult of nothingness. Let us, one last time, point out the essential results.

What kind of operation was it, after all, that allowed this Buddhism to be imagined as a cult of nothingness? Throughout the period where Buddhism was called nihilistic, silence got confused with negation, or, if we prefer, suspension with refusal, or abstention with destruction. Buddhism, thus, a religion "without" God, became "atheistic," denying God. The absence of God, his *de facto* inexistence, if we may put it that way, saw itself transformed either into something missing from which the Buddhists were supposed to suffer even without knowing it, or into a hostility, a destructive activity, an adoration of nothingness *in the place of* God. The worship of nothingness, evidently, was not freedom of thought, but rather a negative worship. Adoring nothingness meant not adoring anything. It was, at best, a case of fetishizing inexistence, of transforming inanity into an object of fantasy, of wishing to disappear. At worst, it was wanting evil, activating destruction, wanting the other, the world, and oneself to disappear.

It was the same with nirvana. Out of this salvation without qualities, someone tried to fashion annihilation. Nothing can be said about it? Then it is nothing at all! It cannot be imagined, or described? Then it must be destruction! It has no cause? That is an unending death! Everything happened as if, at each turn, the "negative path" were being confused with negation, with ineffability, with absolute nothingness. The same procedure took place with the soul. The Buddha was silent on the subject; was he refusing to say if the soul existed or not? If it was, or was not, immortal? The conclusion was that he was refusing its existence. On the political level there was the same confusion, the same sliding, but in a different place: indifferent to the hierarchy of castes, but refusing it only as regards salvation, the Buddhist path to deliverance was reputed to be revolutionary, subversive, egalitarian.

Into this process of negative transformation entered, paradoxically, nothingness itself. By definition, it was totally deprived of both existence and qualities. Instead of being nothing, and thenceforth considered for what it "is"—a neutral zero devoid of any attributes whatsoever—it became "lugubrious," somber, frozen. The worship the Buddhists celebrated was not really a nothing; it was an abyss of darkness, a place of terror, a pole of maleficence, an icy hell, an unnameable and terrible thing. This chasm of shadows was fascinating. Its gapingness was attractive. The abyss called us as much as it repulsed us. Studied first as a religion and as wisdom, Buddhism temporarily wandered over toward specters and secret initiations.

Why was a religion without a God so unnerving? Only because people saw a paradox in it? Simply because it constituted, timelessly, independent of any context, a difficulty for the mind? Or perhaps because such a religion began to resonate, in a manner that was both worrisome and unforeseen, with the decline in Christianity then in process: the already perceptible death of God, the recent vacuity of heaven, disillusioned longings for another religion, the worship of Reason or of the Supreme Being? In a Europe that had just seen atheism affirmed publicly, where quarrels about pantheism had been in the air for ages, the discovery of a religion devoid of any idea equivalent to that of the biblical God must have been leading to the conclusion that such a belief was denying that God. While Catholicism was endeavoring once again to impose its authority on the world, the figure of the Buddha—spiritual, even mystical, but purely human—was easily capable of transforming itself into a menacing presence. We should undoubtedly not be surprised if, in a time when the loss of God had its hold on a number of minds, a completely human religion was considered to be an accomplice of the enemies of the Church and an "objective ally," even before the adjective existed, of a materialism that was gaining in strength despite the Restorations.

Let us not think of this complicity and this alliance in the sense of support for atheists that some powerful foreign belief might have brought to spread around from outside. There was no outside. When the question of the Buddha's atheism arose, it was the atheism of the Europeans that was really in question. No one really believed, and almost no one ever said, that the beliefs of the Buddhists on the other side of the world were going to come and wreak havoc among the souls of the West. It was not a conversion, a corrosion, a "contamination" of any kind that was threatening, coming from the outside. It was in Europe itself that the enemy, and the danger, were to be found. The "fateful" example of Buddhism in Asia allowed us to understand what kind of "nihilization" of its beliefs was threatening Europe from within Europe itself, and what kind of destruction of Christianity was already undermining it.

This was indeed a case of destruction, at least in the fantasies of that vacillating Europe. The worship of nothingness, as we have seen, was considered to be neither an absence of worship nor the innocent veneration of a contentless void. It was implicitly imagined by most European interpreters as a rival of the true religion, sometimes relatively inoffensive because of its geographical and cultural distancing, sometimes menacing, the

164   worship of negation, the manifestation of the genius of the forces opposed to Christianity, a more or less satanic phenomenon. Once the calm returned, the Buddha finished the century, among certain theosophists, as a last and quite pitiful avatar of the Devil among the ignorant, as the confused and naïve hero of a distinguished little Lucifer.

It was for the same reason that, throughout the century, dreams of the Buddha were in relation to Christ. That their figures, depending on the author and the time, came into direct rivalry, into tacit complicity, or into pre-established symmetry, is another matter. What was constant was that their representations were connected, independent of the fact that their opposition might have been explicit or supposed, that their parallelism might have been displayed or present only in filigree. The same time period that saw historical studies extend to the life of Christ saw the biography of the Buddha become popular.

People of Little

A sign of the coming decline in Christianity, the worship of nothingness likewise bore the sign of democracy waiting in the wings. Nothingness was no longer, then, the absence of God, but rather anarchy. Of course, the Buddha welcomed into his monastic community all those who came in search of salvation with him, without distinction of caste or concern for origin. And of course, for his teaching, deliverance was disconnected from either birth or social position—contrary to Brahmanism's belief, where only Brahmans can attain deliverance. Of course, it is no longer out of the question for that antagonism between Brahmanism and Buddhism, in the history of ancient India, effectively to correspond to conflicts between castes (the Buddha was a *kshatriya*, a "warrior," not a Brahman). None of these elements, however, suffices to explain Buddhism being made into not only the sign of a world without God, but also that of a political revolution.

Here again, it is better to cease looking toward the East for an explanation. It was once again, and still, an issue concerning Europe. The cult of nothingness was clearly not an episode apart, isolated or isolatable from the ensemble of the historical and social movement of the nineteenth century. An imaginary construction of a given time, it echoed its principal tensions. It was between 1830 and 1848 that the Orientalists could discern the Buddha's traits, and it was between 1848 and 1871 that public opinion got worried and the rumor mill took hold of the worries. From the Three Glories to the Commune, the worship of nothingness made its way through Europe at the same time as the birth of the working class, aspirations

toward democracy, the specter of Communism, the awakening of the dangerous classes, and the "great fear" of the bourgeoisie. Why should we
be surprised that it managed to signify the negation of social hierarchies,
the challenging of the traditional order, the demands for egalitarianism,
the rebellion of the small, the destruction of the yoke, the refusal to be
dominated?

From this perspective, it was no longer God, as such, that this maleficent
cult was supposedly denying, but the realization of the divine will in an un-
changeably ordered social body. The nothingness of order corresponded to
the nothingness of being. Once again, this nothingness was not the equivalent of a pure and simple absence. It was supposed to undo and disorganize.
It was dangerous because it shattered, it leveled, it instigated anarchy. The
latter of these was not, as its etymology might lead us to think, a deprivation
of principles or political authority, a great vacancy of power. Suspending
domination means, first of all, destroying it. The worship of nothingness,
from the perspective of the struggle between classes, implies devastating
activity. This is dreaded or combated, but rarely desired or upheld.

There, too, the elsewhere was fictional. These egalitarian politics did not
shake up an extremist Orient. They did not take hold in the suburbs of the
great European cities, in the factories where labor unions were forming, in
the mines where the great strikes were taking place. The rebellion against
the hierarchy did not run wildly through India, in the past, in a form that
nineteenth-century men also imagined to be violent, engendering bloody
repression and prolonged wars. It was in Europe herself, during the time of
science and industry, that barricades were set up and the troops fired shots.
It was the people in the pretty neighborhoods who were frightened about
the subversion that was presently cooking up plots, who were imagining
that people with no class whatsoever, people of nothing, were once again off
in the shadows planning mischief. A few militants knew that war was already
taking place up in the attic or down in the cellar, deafly, dully; it was just
waiting for the chance to continue, some grand evening, out in the open.

Degenerates

Throughout this book, the issue has also been one of racial groups, of a
number of kinds of human beings, of superiors and inferiors. That century
long dreamed of the legend of a population of strong, vigorous individuals
full of appetites and plans, through whom run powerful tempers, animated
by the spirit of conquest and the virtues of war. These beings of generous
blood were regularly confronted by the gray existence of the weak, half-

166 dead "underbeings," listless from the time of their births, overcome with lassitude, incapable of carrying themselves about, inclined only—through some fateful penchant of their poor blood—to hope for the soon-to-come annulment of an existence that was already tenuous but still too weighty. Numerous were the strange questions that inhabited these modern myths: might this be a question of two different types of original humans? Of the result of a decline, of degeneration, of physical and psychic atrophy? Was this downslide toward annihilation engendered by climate, by the ill effects of the intermixing of racial groups, by the obscure necessities of a yellow soul?

Once again, if we allow that the worship of nothingness describes Europe and not Asia, that it reflects its time and not some ancient reality, it is normal to find in it this great image of degeneration. It runs through the century, continually inhabiting large sectors, and it undoubtedly constitutes one of its major keys, which has nevertheless remained insufficiently studied, given its breadth and its functions. Mixing psychology with physiology, pathology with what is cultural, the collective with the individual, the biological with the spiritual, medicine with history, the moral with the clinical, the considerable myth of degeneration could not but be found, again, in the worship of nothingness.

Where are these worn-down spirits, these irritable, unpredictable, "end-of-the-century" and "end-of-the-race" characters, these "exquisite"—as some pains are—sensibilities, these hysterical souls—these suicidal neurotics capable of developing a cult of nothingness—found? On the steppes of Mongolia? In the foothills of the Himalayas? In the heart of the warmth of Ceylon? How could we not see that Europe was still soliloquizing, that she was speaking only of herself? And yet the situation was different. The decline of Christianity was an attested reality of the French Revolution; struggles for political *and* social equality were in effect throughout the century. But racial groups? Degeneration? It was no longer her religious or social reality that Europe was projecting onto Buddhism, but her most enigmatic modern myth.

Projection, Yes

Which traits specifically do distinguish the worship of nothingness from other themes running through the same decades? If we find certain echoes of the death of God, or social revolution, or racist myths in speeches about the Buddha, they certainly are also seen elsewhere. It is the same banal situation. It is not sufficient to explain that Europe was speaking about her conflicts and crises. What did she say, about herself, that was truly particular, when she invented the cult of nothingness? The answer lies in the question: nothingness. Actually, what was singular and what was interesting about these speeches as a whole was not simply the echo or image projected from the historical situations of the time, but rather the specific way in which these themes crisscrossed in them, within the same preoccupations about destruction, the void, absence, and disappearance.

Europe was becoming "something without." Without what? No one yet knew. It was presumed that it would be, for example, without God, without classes, without a vital force. The time that was coming defined itself privately, at first. The world left behind was describable: divine, ordered, strong. Its reality could easily be something quite different, the manner in which people imagined their lives and their arrangements was seen through a lens of plenitude and affirmative points of reference. The world that was coming suspended this order of tradition, it undermined the pillars, profaning the host, killing the king, laughing about blue blood. The recent constructions of Reason, erected as a scaffold to replace these ancient foundations, did not have a comparable density. They still ran the risk of looking fragile, insufficient, ephemeral, even if they called themselves universal and coherent, even when they donned signs of power and surrounded themselves with the decorum that was appropriate for celebrations. Hollowness, frail and presumptuous human inventions, uncertain attempts . . . nothingness.

In inventing the cult of nothingness, the European consciousness was expressing that it was permeated by negative forces. Not, as always, inhabited by doubts, but this time traversed by abysses, the entire expanse or the greatest fascination of which European consciousness still was not aware. The analyses of nihilism were born in this crisis of foundations. Now Buddhism, considered as the worship of nothingness, was still closely associated with this development. From Hegel to Nietzsche, passing through Schopenhauer, of course, it was always in reference to this imaginary Buddhism that the different strata of nihilism were approached: the identity of pure Being with nothingness, the negation of the will to live, the existence of a world of values. In this sense, the cult of nothingness served as sort of a hidden laboratory for the theoretical development of European nihilism. Not a development site forgotten today, covered by other tracks, but a place of retreat, apart, partially masked, where European words were able to worry about themselves and about the nothingness that came to mind, all the while discoursing on distant elsewheres and ancient sages. Under the cover of understanding a newly discovered and passably disconcerting

168   Eastern religion, Europe composed an image of the Buddha made of what she feared in herself: collapse, the abyss, the void, annihilation.

Anticipation, No

The story of the "cult of nothingness" has been confused with that of a century that was leading to the time of world wars and totalitarian barbarity. It is difficult not to compare the two. But it would be illusory, dangerous, and false to think of them as simply similar. Between the speeches that the nineteenth century engendered and saw grow by scaring itself with an imaginary Buddha and the acts that the twentieth century perpetuated by piling up cadavers, by shattering hopes and dehumanizing humanity, there exist relationships of contiguity and strong resonances. But no causal connection can be made with certainty. Rather, we must be wary of the history "of a previous future," attributing to the individuals of one century the impossible knowledge of the actions of those in the following century. We can finally observe that anticipatory visions existed which prophesied, in the descriptions of the nineteenth century, the massacres of the twentieth— without the possibility of drawing clear consequences. So what can we do?

Let us accept that these forgotten texts take on a specific meaning for those of us who know how the story ends, who know that the twentieth century was one of tragedy, of annihilation by massacres, of the triumph of active nihilism, of the negation of the human. How could we, without thinking about it, read pages composed a few decades earlier, where we are told that man should become nothingness, that there remains nothing more before us other than nothingness, that a specter of nothingness is threatening us? Are we going to decree that there is no relationship between the fears, the anathemas, and the insinuations of so many volumes, so many faded brochures about annihilation, and disappearance, and the lost faces of those who were annihilated by the twentieth century? Can we consider only as objects of erudition those old speeches that used the Buddha as a pretext, when we see the fascination for destruction grow, when we see racial hatred surface, when we see an unrestrained taste for order and scorn for others assert itself?

It is undoubtedly for us—now, and after the fact—that the cult of nothingness, a forgotten episode in the history of ideas, can take on these characteristics. Despite everything, we could not act as if they did not exist.

Notes

INTRODUCTION

1. *Abhayarâjakumarâsutta, Majjhima-Nikâya*, no. 58, pp. 60–61, in *Pali Text Society Translation Series*, trans. I. B. Horner (London: Pali Text Society, 1975), 1:392–96.

2. These comparisons come from Vasubhandu, a Buddhist doctor who lived in India around the fifth century A.D.

3. On this point, see Guy Bugault, *La Notion de "prajnâ" ou de sapience selon les perspectives du "Mahâyâna"* (Paris: Publ. de l'Institut de civilisation indienne, 1968; re-ed. 1982), pp. 175–86, 202–3.

4. *L'Oubli de l'Inde: Une amnésie philosophique* (Paris: PUF, 1989; new ed., Paris: Le Livre de Poche, collection "Biblio-Essais," 1992).

5. There are very few studies on the specific aspects of the discovery of Buddhism. An early picture was painted by Henri de Lubac, *La Rencontre du bouddhisme et de l'Occident* (Paris: Aubier, 1952). But Orientalists had little concern about that aspect of the story where a number of their disciplines crossed paths with one another, with the notable exception of J. W. de Jong's study ("A Brief History of Buddhist Studies in Europe and America," *Eastern Buddhist* 7, nos. 1, 2 [1974]). Likewise, works relating to the many debates aroused in different European cultures by the sudden discovery of the last great spiritual tradition to be recognized in the West remain rare, despite a certain resurgence of interest in this question, mainly among Anglo-Saxon researchers who are more often historians than philosophers (e.g., G. R. Welbon, *The Buddhist Nirvana and Its Western Interpreters* [Chicago: University of Chicago Press, 1968], or Philip C. Almond, *The British Discovery of Buddhism* [London: Cambridge University Press, 1988]).

6. This expression appears as the title of a chapter in Edgar Quinet's work *Le Génie des religions* (Paris, 1842), as well as that of the important book by Raymond Schwab, *La Renaissance orientale* (Paris: Payot, 1950), the latter of which was responsible for the rediscovery of that moment in the history of ideas. The idea that European thought would be reinvigorated by Sanskrit works in the same way, *mutatis mutandis*, that it was via the rediscovery of Greek works by the humanists of "the" Renaissance is found in the writings of a number of quite different authors (Friedrich Schlegel, Schelling, Schopenhauer, Pierre Leroux, among others). See *L'Oubli de l'Inde*, chaps. 7–10, for a brief introduction to this subject.

7. *Le Génie des religions*, 2nd ed. (Paris: Chamerot, 1851), p. 71: "En même temps que l'Asie pénètre dans la poésie, dans la politique de l'Occident, elle s'insinue aussi dans ses doctrines: la métaphysique scelle à son tour l'alliance de deux mondes."

8. The most frequently cited sources are Strabon 15, Diodorus 2:35–42, Arrien's *Indica*, Ctesias, and Clement, *Stromates* 1:15.

9. Fo is the Chinese name for the Buddha, and Xaca is his name in Japanese, derived from Shakyamuni.

10. E. A. Schwambeck, *Megasthenis Indica*, "Fragmenta collegit, commentationem et indices addidit E. A. Schwambeck" (Bonn, 1846).

170   11. Michel-Jean-François Ozeray, *Recherches sur Buddou ou Bouddou, Instituteur religieux de l'Asie orientale: Précédées de considérations générales sur les premiers hommages rendus au Créateur, sur la corruption de la religion, l'établissement des cultes du soleil, de la lune, des planètes, du ciel, de la terre, des montagnes, des eaux, des forêts, des hommes et des animaux* (Paris: "Brunot-Labb," 1817). See chap. 2 of this book.

12. See Benjamin Constant, *De la religion considérée dans sa source, ses formes et ses développements*, 3 vols. (Paris: Béchet Aîné, 1827).

13. Eugène Burnouf and Christian Lassen, *Essai sur le Pali, ou Langue sacrée de la presqu'île au-delà du Gange* (Paris: Dondey-Dupré, 1826). It might be mentioned in passing that the *Robert* dictionary was mistaken in giving 1830 as the date of the appearance of the word "bouddhisme" in French.

14. Brian Houghton Hodgson, *Sketch of Buddhism: Derived from the Bauddha Scriptures of Nepal* (London: J. L. Cox, 1828); Edward Upham, *The History and Doctrine of Buddhism, Popularly Illustrated: With Notices of the Kappooism or Demon Worship and of the Bali or Planetary Incantations of Ceylon, embellished with 43 lithographic prints from original Singalese designs* (London: R. Ackermann, 1829).

15. Sylvain Lévi, "Le bouddhisme et les Grecs," *RHR* 28 (1891): 36—49: "Malgré les relations ininterrompues du monde hellénique avec l'Inde puis l'expédition d'Alexandre jusqu'aux derniers temps de l'Empire romain, la littérature grecque a presque ignoré l'existence du bouddhisme ou du moins l'a fort mal connu." This sentence appears on p. 36. See also, on a related subject, my study on India and the Greeks entitled "L'Inde des Grecs au XIXe siècle," in *Chercheurs de sagesse: Hommage à Jean Pépin*, Institut d'études augustiniennes (1992), p. 691—703.

16. "*Hoc igitur est quaestionis caput, Sarmanae qui sint*," asks the philologist Schwambeck; *Megasthenis Indica*, p. 45.

17. "*Quos alii Buddhaicos esse dixerunt, negaverunt alii*," wrote Schwambeck; ibid.

18. Peter von Bohlen, *Das Alte Indien, mit besonderer Rücksicht auf Ägypten dargestellt* (Königsberg: Bornträger, 1830).

19. Chr. Lassen, "De nominibus quibus a Veteribus appellantur Indorum philosophi," *Rheinisches Museum* (1833) 1:171—90 (on the *Sarmanai*, p. 180ff.).

20. For example, *Dighanikaya* 1, 2, 24ff., 31ff., etc. This point is emphasized by Helmut von Glasenapp, *La Philosophie indienne*, trans. A.-M. Esnoul (Paris: Payot, 1951), p. 14.

21. Cf. Jean Filliozat, "La doctrine des brahmanes d'après saint Hippolyte," *RHR* 130 (1945): 75.

22. Cf. Sylvain Lévi, "Le bouddhisme et les Grecs"; the text was cited again in *Mémorial Sylvain Lévi* (Paris, 1937).

23. Jules Barthélemy Saint-Hilaire, *Du Bouddhisme* (Paris: Benjamin Duprat, 1855), p. 17. This text, which originated in a series of articles published in 1854 and 1855 in the *Journal des Savants*, was to be widely read. Published under this title by Benjamin Duprat, in 1855, it was even reedited, with most of the notes left out, but enlarged with new chapters in 1860, then again in 1862 and 1866; its new title in these editions, published by Didier et Cie, was *Le Bouddha et sa religion*. See chap. 8 of the present work.

24. For the bibliographical references regarding these texts, see Henri de Lubac, *La Rencontre du bouddhisme et de l'Occident*.

25. Edward C. Sachau, *Alberuni's India*, 2 vols. (London, 1888). A partial French translation was published in 1961. Abû-Rayhân Al-Bîrûnî, *Le Livre de l'Inde* (Paris: Sindbad, UNESCO). For an overview of Arabic commentators on Indian teachings, see F. Mujtabai, *Aspects of Hindu-Muslims Cultural Relations* (New Delhi, 1978).

26. The *Asiatick Researches* series, the first modern scholarly publication, comprised

twenty-one volumes spread out over a period of time between 1788 and 1839. It was first
published in Calcutta, but was often reedited in London, beginning in 1800; partial translations had also been done in German, starting in 1795, with the first volume, published in Calcutta in 1788, translated into German by J. F. Kleucker and Johannes Fick (Riga, 1795) and into French in 1805.

27. See also Buchanan's study on the Burmese (1799), cited in chap. 3.

28. See the *Documenta Indica,* edited by Josephus Wicki, S. J., 2 vols. (Rome, 1948, 1950). See also the work by C. Wessels, *Early Jesuit Travellers in Central Asia, 1603–1721* (1924); there is a recent Indian edition of this work (New Delhi-Madras: Asian Educational Services, 1992).

29. Guillaume Postel, *Des merveilles du monde* (Paris, 1552), p. 10.

30. "Xaca n'est aultre qu'une nuée obscure, extraicte de l'histoire Evangélike," ibid., p. 22. The original French spelling is respected here.

31. Ibid., p. 31. At this point, the copy in the Bibliothèque Nationale has a cross clearly calligraphed in the margin. This annotation was probably by Guillaume Postel's own hand.

32. A recent fine-tuning of this subject, with important documentation and a bibliography, may be found in *Les Portugais au Tibet: Les premières relations jésuites (1624–1635),* translated and presented by Hugues Didier (Paris: Chandeigne, 1996).

33. Letter, 29 January 1552. The original translation is from Léon Paques, *Lettres de saint François-Xavier de la Compagnie de Jésus, apôtre des Indes et du Japon: Traduites sur l'édition latine de Bologne* (Paris, 1855), 2:209: "Si leur folle et arrogante prétention est convaincue de mensonge, l'occasion principale de leur gain cessera d'exister. Si leurs crimes honteux, si les désordres exécrables qui ne sont à leurs yeux qu'une chose légère, presque même un titre de gloire, sont flétris par une juste et vive réprobation, on les verra, ces sangliers furieux, se sentant percés de l'épieu dans leur fange immonde, se précipiter avec rage et vouloir déchirer ceux qui leur auront présenté des perles."

34. Ibid., p. 215.

35. Athanase Kircher, *China, monumentis qua sacris qua profanis, nec non variis naturae et artis spectaculis, aliarumque rerum memorabilium argumentis illustrata* (Amsterdam, 1667).

36. For example, Father Roberto de Nobili's remarkable *Information de quibusdam moribus nationis indicae,* which contains, in its fourth chapter, specific information entitled "De Buddheris sive Atheis," was written in 1613, although it remained practically unknown until 1972, due to its never having been published!

37. *Lettres édifiantes et curieuses écrites des Missions étrangères, par quelques Missionnaires de la Compagnie de Jésus,* Rec. 26 (Paris: Nicolas Leclerc, 1743), p. 220–59.

38. Alexander Dow, *History of Hindostan* (London, 1768) (with translations later, in French, in 1780, and in German in 1782). Dow explains, for example, that the Buddhists are atheists who believe in the universe, but not in God: "By reason, continues Goutam, men perceive the existence of God; which the Boada or atheists deny, because his existence does not come within the comprehension of the senses. These atheists, says he, maintain that there is no God but the universe."

39. John Zephaniah Holwell, *Interesting Events Relative to the Provinces of Bengal and the Empire of Indostan* (London, 1767) (French translation, 1768; German translation by Kleucker, 1778).

40. A. H. Anquetil-Duperron, "Réflexions sur l'utilité que l'on peut retirer de la lecture des écrivains orientaux," *Mémoires de l'Académie des Inscriptions et Belles-Lettres* (Paris: Imprimerie Royale, 1770) 35:150–70. On the figure of Anquetil-Duperron, see the now quite old and almost hagiographical work by Raymond Schwab, *Vie d'Anquetil-Duperron,* with a preface by Sylvain Lévi (Paris: Ernest Leroux, 1935). For a more recent look and a different analysis by the same author, see Lucette Valensi's study, "Eloge de l'Orient, éloge de

l'orientalisme: Le jeu d'échecs d'Anquetil-Duperron," *RHR* (Oct.–Dec. 1955). 212: fasc. 4, p. 419–52.

41. Most of these sources have been collected and analyzed in the works of Sylvia Murr: "Les conditions d'émergence du discours sur l'Inde au siècle des Lumières," *Purûsârtha 7* (1983): 233–84, and *L'Inde philosophique entre Bossuet et Voltaire* 2 vols. (Paris: Ecole française d'Extrême-Orient, 1987).

42. Cited by Guy Deleury in *Les Indes florissantes: Anthologie des voyageurs français (1750–1820)* (Paris: Robert Laffont, 1991), p. 1033: "Il y avait autrefois à la côte de Coromandel et à Ceylan un culte dont on ignore absolument les dogmes: le dieu Baouth, dont on ne connaît aujourd'hui en Inde que le nom, était l'objet de ce culte."

43. The references for the works of all these individuals may be found in chap. 3.

44. From p. 107 of the Nicolin and Pöggeler edition (Hamburg, 1969).

45. *Lessons on the Philosophy of Religion*, 2:1. From the Lasson edition (Leipzig, 1927), 13, 2, p. 133–34.

46. The expression *fanatisme du néant* first came from the pen of Jules Barthélemy Saint-Hilaire, in *Le Bouddha et sa religion* (1862).

47. This term (*Grand Christ du vide*) comes from Edgar Quinet, in *Le Génie des religions*.

48. See Ernest Renan, "Premiers travaux sur le bouddhisme," a work written in 1851 but published in 1884 in the *Nouvelles Etudes d'histoire religieuse*. The original expressions were "qu'assigne à la vie pour but suprême le néant," "machine à faire le vide dans l'âme," and "Eglise du nihilisme."

49. Letter number 381 to von Doss, 27 February 1856 (Hübscher, pp. 383–84; Jaedicke, pp. 509–10). For a detailed study of this point, see my article "Schopenhauer et le bouddhisme: une 'admirable concordance'?" in *Schopenhauer: New Essays in Honor of his 200th Birthday*, ed. Eric von de Luft (New York: Edwin Mellen Press, 1988), pp. 123–38.

50. See Nietzsche, *Oeuvres philosophiques complètes* (Paris: Gallimard), 11:303.

51. Ibid., 11:219.

52. Ibid., 1, 1:439.

CHAPTER ONE

1. See George Stanley Faber, *The Origin of Pagan Idolatry Ascertained from Historical Testimony and Circumstantial Evidence* 3 vols. (London, 1816). The passages cited are from vol. 2, book 3, chap. 2, VII, 3, pp. 42–44.

2. Jean-Sylvain Bailly, *Histoire de l'Astronomie ancienne depuis son origine jusqu'à l'établissement de l'école d'Alexandrie*, 2nd ed. (Paris, 1781), p. 84.

3. A. Court de Gébelin, *Le Monde primitif analysé et comparé avec le monde moderne*, 9 vols. (Paris, 1773–82).

4. Frédéric de Rougemont, *Le Peuple primitif, sa religion, son histoire et sa civilisation*, 2 vols. (Paris, Cherbuliez, 1855).

5. M. de la Loubère, *Du Royaume de Siam*, 2 vols. (Paris [Amsterdam], 1691). The sentence quoted is from 1:536.

6. For example, it is mentioned in Nathaniel Brassey Halhed's preface to the famous *A Code of Gentoo Laws* (London, 1776). This preface was reproduced in P. J. Marshall, *The British Discovery of Hinduism in the Eighteenth Century* (Cambridge, 1970), pp. 140–183. The list of Sanskrit denominations for the days is found on p. 160, no. 1.

7. Antoine Augustin Giorgi, *Alphabetum Tibetanum missionum apostolicarum commodo editum. Praemissa est disquisitio, qua de vario litterarum ac regionis nomine, gentis origine, moribus, superstitione,*

ac manichaeismo fuse desseritur. Beausobrii Calumniae in S. Augustinum, aliosque Ecclesiae patres 173
refutantur (Rome, 1762), 820 pp.

8. J. S. Bailly, *Histoire de l'astronomie ancienne . . .* , p. 79. It might be noted in passing that the old representation of an Egyptian origin of wisdom, which runs through the history of the West from Plato to modern times, begins here to move toward Asia.

9. A French version of this book, reworked and augmented, was published by Guigniaut in 1825.

10. Paulin de Saint Barthélemy, *Musei Borgiani Velitris Codices manuscripti Avenses Peguani Siamici Malabarici Indostani Animadversionibus Historicocriticis castigati et illustrati accedunt Monumenta inedita, et Cosmogonia Indico-Tibetana* (Rome, 1793).

11. For example, p. 50: *"Iterum arguitur, Fouhi, Godamam, Budham, seu Mercurium non esse hominem, sed genium Mercurii planetae rectorem, atque adastra referri debere, cum Phoenices & Indi astra sine geniorum ministerio moveri haud posse crederent."*

12. Notably, p. 67: *"Ex igitur omnibus iam omnino perspicuum est, ab omnibus gentibus Mercurium ut satorem rerum naturalium & terrestrium, atque ut auctorem rerum moralium, denique ut artium et scientiarum institutorem exhiberi."*

13. Thus p. 73: *"Vocabulum itaque Indicum* Budh *seu Budha, & cultus ipse hujus dei ad Aegyptios per Indos Aethiopes perlatus fuit, atque dictio Indica* Budh *seu Budha ibi corrupta, in* Toth, *Touth, Teut, Toith transiit, ut apud Sinenses in* Fo, *apud Tibetanos in* Pout *vel Put, apud Scythas in* Bogh, *apud Scandinavianos in* Oden *vel* Wod, *& apud Suidam in* Thont.*"*

14. Pp. 14 and 192, respectively.

15. Jacob Brucker, *Historia critica Philosophiae* (1742), vol. 1, 1st part, book 2, chap. 4, "De Philosophia Indorum," p. 202–4. Let us bear in mind that this monumental history of philosophy had some influence on the century of the Enlightenment.

16. Vol. 15.

17. *Recherches asiatiques*, French trans. by Labaume, 2 vols. (Paris: Impr. impériale, 1805). In a note regarding the translation of Goverdhan Kaûl's article on "La Littérature des Hindous" (1:391, n. 6), for example, Langlès underscores that the Indian Buddha was "absolutely the same as Mercury." See also 1:112–14, 218, 267, 283, and 2:179, 425.

18. Edward Upham, *The History and Doctrine of Buddhism, Popularly Illustrated, with notices of the Kappooism, or Demon Worship and of the Bali or Planetary Incantations of Ceylon, embellished with 43 lithographic prints from original singalese designs* (London: R. Ackermann, 1829).

19. *"The worshippers of Brahma were delighted to honour the bright star of Budha in the planet Mercury."* Cited by Philip C. Almond, *The British Discovery of Buddhism* (London: Cambridge University Press, 1988), p. 14.

20. Note by Langlès in the French translation of *Recherches asiatiques*, 2:564–65.

21. William Francklin, *Researches on the Tenets and Doctrines of the Jeynes and Buddhists conjectured to be the Brahmans of Ancient India, with discussion on Serpent Worship* (London, 1827), 213 pp.

22. Thus, the Buddha was a Jew: first, Noah, then Moses, and then a symbol of the kabbalah. It has even been wondered if the Essenes were not Buddhists. The Buddha was likewise connected with the Greeks. Orpheus has been seen in him, and even Plato, but more frequently Pythagorus.

23. See, for example, Friedrich Schlegel, *Über die Sprache und Weisheit der Indier* (Heidelberg, 1808), book 3, chapter 2 (contemporary critical edition by Ernst Behler in the *Kritische Ausgabe* of Schlegel's works, vol. 8-1, p. 106–433 (Paderborn, 1975).

24. Petrus Benjamin Sköldberg et al., *De Buddha et Wodan* (Uppsala, 1822). August Wilhelm Schlegel, "Wodan and Buddha" (Bonn, *Indische Bibliothek*, 1823), vol. 1, 5 pp.

174

25. Christian Andreas Holmboe, *Traces du Buddhisme en Norvège avant l'introduction du Christianisme* (Paris: S. Raçon, 1857), 74 pp.

26. Ragendrala Mitra, "Buddhism and Odinism, their Similitude. Illus. by Extracts from Pr. Holmboe's dissertation on the *Traces de Buddhisme en Norvège*," *Journal of the Royal Asiatic Society of Bengal* 27 (1858): 46–69.

27. See the introduction to the present book.

28. 1:30. This conviction led de Guignes to compose a "thesis in which it is proved that the Chinese are an Egyptian colony," which he read on 14 November 1758 at the Académie Royale des Inscriptions et Belles-lettres.

29. Ibid., 1:233.

30. See Introduction.

31. William Jones, "On the Hindus: The third anniversary discourse, delivered 2 February 1786," *Asiatic Researches* 1 (1788): 422ff.

32. Francis Wilford, "On Egypt and Other Countries, Adjacent to the Ca'li' River, or Nile of Ethiopia, from the Ancient Books of the Hindus," *Asiatic Researches* 3 (1792): 295–462; quote from pp. 414–15.

33. Robert Percival, *An Account of the Island of Ceylon: Containing its history, geography, natural history, with the manners and customs of its various inhabitants to which is added the journal of an embassy to the Court of Candy* (London, 1803), p. 145.

34. Jean-Pierre Abel-Rémusat, "Notes sur quelques épithètes descriptives de Bouddha," *Journal des Savants* (1819): 625–33.

35. See Philip C. Almond, *The British Discovery of Buddhism*, pp. 20–21.

36. *Le Lotus de la Bonne Loi*, trans. by Eugène Burnouf (Paris: Impr. nationale, 1852), Appendix 8, p. 554 (reprint, Paris: Adrien Maisonneuve, 1973).

37. Ibid., p. 561.

38. See chap. 4 for the texts and their references.

CHAPTER TWO

1. Michel-Jean-François Ozeray, *Recherches sur Buddou ou Bouddou, Instituteur religieux de l'Asie orientale: Précédées de considérations générales sur les premiers hommages rendus au Créateur, sur la corruption de la religion, l'établissement des cultes du soleil, de la lune, des planètes, du ciel, de la terre, des montagnes, des eaux, des forêts, des hommes et des animaux* (Paris: Brunot-Labbé, 1817). The sentence quoted is from p. 40.

2. Ibid., "Avis sur les considérations générales," p. xxxvi.

3. Born in Chartres in 1764, Ozeray was fifty-three when he published the work.

4. M.-J.-F. Ozeray, *Recherches*, p. 111.

5. Ibid., p. 31.

6. Ibid., p. 40.

7. Ibid., p. 36.

8. Ibid., p. xxxiii.

9. Ibid., p. 111.

10. Ibid., p. 113.

11. Ibid., p. xxxiv.

12. Ibid., p. 55.

13. Ibid., p. xxxv.

14. Ibid., p. 78.

15. Ibid., p. xxxiii.

16. Ibid., p. 46.

17. Ibid., p. 51.

18. André Bareau, *Recherches sur la biographie du Buddha dans les Sutrapitaka et les Vina-yapitaka anciens* (Paris: Ecole française d'Extrême-Orient, 1963), I; 1970, II-1; 1971, II-2.

19. This is a clearly paradoxical term, given the problematic status of any equivalent for the individual in Buddhist thought.

20. M.-J.-F. Ozeray, *Recherches*, p. xxxiii.

CHAPTER THREE

1. Calcutta, 1799, p. 163–308.

2. P. W., probably Guillaume (William) Pauthier, the Sinologue who was especially known for the publication of *La Chine, ou Description historique, géographique et littéraire de ce vaste empire d'après les documents chinois* (Paris, 1837), with 72 pl.

3. *Indische Bibliothek* (Bonn, 1833), 1, 4:414.

4. H. de Valroger, "Doctrines hindoues examinées, discutées et mises en rapport avec les traditions bibliques," sixth article: "Histoire du bouddhisme," *Annales de philosophie chrétienne* (1839): 91–92.

5. Father Coeurdoux's manuscript had actually been greatly plagiarized by Abbot Jean-Antoine Dubois's famous work, *Moeurs, Institutions et Cérémonies des peuples de l'Inde*, 2 vols. (Paris, 1825). See Sylvia Murr, *L'Inde philosophique entre Bossuet et Voltaire*, 2 vols. (Paris: École française d'Extrême-Orient, 1987).

6. F. Buchanan, "On the Religion and Literature of the Burma," *Asiatic Researches* 6 (1799): 166: "However idle and ridiculous the legends and notions of the worshippers of Buddha may be, they have been in a great measure adopted by the Brahmens, but with all their defects monstruously aggraved [*sic*]."

7. *Recherches asiatiques* (Paris: Impr. Impériale, 1805), 1:102.

8. Cited by Philip C. Almond, *The British Discovery of Buddhism* (London: Cambridge University Press, 1988), p. 29.

9. Ibid., p. 31.

10. "Observations on the Jains," *Transactions of the Royal Asiatic Society* (1827), vol. 1. The five studies by Henry Thomas Colebrooke constituted the first monographs that truly offered an overview of the systems of thought in India. In reading the work, Hegel himself recognized its specifically philosophical nature (see chap. 4, pp. 106–7). These five monographs were the object of communications to the Royal Asiatic Society on 21 June 1825 (I—"*Sâmkhya*," published in vol. 1 of *Transactions of the Royal Asiatic Society*, pp. 19–43), 21 February 1824 (II—"*Nyâya—Vaisésika*," published in ibid., pp. 92–118), 4 March 1826 (III—"*Mîmâmsî*," published in ibid., vol. 1, pp. 439–61), 7 April 1827 (IV—"*Vedânta*," published in ibid., vol. 2, pp. 1–39), 3 February 1827 (V—"Sectes hétérodoxes [Bouddhistes et Jaïna]," published in ibid., pp. 549–79). The work as a whole was included in the two-volume edition of *Essays on the Religion and Philosophy of the Hindus* (London: Trübner, 1837), 1:227–419), and then in the three-volume work titled *Miscellaneous Essays*, ed. E. B. Cowell (London: Trübner, 1873). Let us point out that a reprint of the English edition was done recently in India, by Chandigarh (Galav Publications, 1982).

11. "The *Jainas* and *Bauddhas* I consider to have been originally Hindus"; "Observations," p. 549.

12. *Réflexions sur l'étude des langues asiatiques adressées à Sir James Mackintosh, suivies d'une lettre à M. Horace Hayman Wilson, ancien secrétaire de la Société asiatique à Calcutta, "élu professeur à Oxford,"* by A. W. Schlegel (Bonn: Weber; Paris: Maze, 1832). The copy in the Bibliothèque Nationale is autographed by A. W. Schlegel, to Julius von Klaproth.

13. The article in question is by William Hugh Erskine, "Account of the Cave-Temple of Elephanta," Bombay, *Transactions of the Literary Society of Bombay* (1819), 1, 198−250; cit. p. 106. August Wilhelm Schlegel's mockery of the "Bouddhomanes" was probably directed at Baron von Eckstein, an influential and relatively enigmatic individual whom Heinrich Heine had nicknamed "Baron Buddha"; he is mentioned by Hegel in a note in the *Encyclopedia*.

14. See chap. 2.

15. William Jones, "On the Chronology of the Hindus," *Asiatic Researches* 2 (1790): 111−47.

16. Ibid., p. 123. (R.-P. Droit includes this text, in English, as a footnote in the French edition.)

17. Benjamin Constant, *De la religion considérée dans sa source, ses formes et ses développements*, 3 vols. (Paris: Béchet Aîné, 1827).

18. Ibid., 3:110−11.

19. In 1836, in the posthumous edition of his translation of his *Foé Koué Ki*, Charles Landresse wrote: "Twenty years ago, when M. Rémusat began to work on Buddhism, there was no model to follow." See Jean-Pierre Abel-Rémusat, *Foé Koué Ki, ou Relation des royaumes bouddhiques. Voyage dans la Tartarie, dans l'Afghanistan et dans l'Inde, exécuté à la fin du IVe siècle par Chy Fa Hian. Ouvrage posthume revu, complété et augmenté d'éclaircissements nouveaux par Klaproth et Landresse. Traduit du chinois et commenté par Abel-Rémusat* (Paris: Impr. Royale, 1836), p. 3.

20. See chapter 6.

21. See Isaac Jacob Schmidt: *Forschungen im Gebiete der älteren religiösen, politischen und literarischen Bildungsgeschichte der Völker Mittel-Asiens, vorzüglich der Mongolen und Tibeter* (Saint Petersburg: Karl Kray; Leipzig: Karl Knobloch, 1824); *Über die Verwandtschaft der gnostisch-theosophischen Lehren mit den Religions-Systemen des Orients, vorzüglich dem Buddhaismus* (Leipzig: Karl Knobloch, 1828), 25 pp.; "Über einige Grundlehren des Buddhaismus," *Mém. De l'Acad. impér. D. Sc. De St.-Pétersbourg* (1832), series 6: *Sc. polit. hist. et philol.*, 1:90−120, 222−62.

22. Isaac Jacob Schmidt, *Über das Mahâjâna und Pradschnâ-Pâramita der Bauddhen* (Berlin, 1836), 106 pp.

23. Paris, *Journal asiatique* (1824), ser. 1, vol. 4, pp. 9−23, 65−79.

24. Alexandre Csoma de Körös, "Analysis of the *Kah-gyur*," *Asiatic Researches* 20 (1820).

25. On Eugène Burnouf, see chap. 5.

26. Buchanan, "On the Religion and Literature of the Burma," 6:163−308; the text cited is from p. 180.

27. "Observations on the Jains," p. 578.

28. Ibid., p. 579.

29. Brian Houghton Hodgson, "Notice of the Language, Literature and Religion of the Bauddhas of Nepal and Tibet," in *Illustrations of the Literature and Religion of the Buddhists* (Serampore: 1841), p. 26 (first published in *Asiatic Researches* 16 [1828]).

CHAPTER FOUR

1. "*Des Nichts, das die Buddhisten zum Prinzip von allem, wie zum letzten Endzweck und Ziel von allem machen, ist dieselbe Abstraktion.*" *Enzyklopädie der philosophischen Wissenschaften*, Nicolin and Pöggeler edition (1830; Hamburg: Felix Meiner, 1969), p. 107. The addition of a reference to Buddhists in this paragraph dates from the 1827 edition. It is repeated, unchanged, in the 1830 edition.

2. An enumeration of the principal Hegelian sources on the subject of Orientalism can be found in Michel Hulin, *Hegel et l'Orient* (Paris: Vrin, 1979), pp. 218−21.

3. "*In Indien est Buddha eine historische Person*": *Vorlesungen über die Philosophie der Religion*, ed.

Walter Jaeschke (Hamburg: Felix Meiner, 1985), vol. 2a, p. 460. The text used in this chapter 177 is from this edition, which has carefully established the exact state of notes and manuscripts. While waiting for the French translation by P. Garniron, in progress, the correspondence with the translation by J. Gibelin (*Leçons sur la philosophie de la religion*, 5 vols. [Paris: Vrin, 1959], vol. 2–1, *La Religion déterminée: La Religion de la nature*) is indicated to the extent possible. In the references that follow, the page numbers of the German and French texts are indicated respectively by "J." and by "G.," followed by the page number.

4. Primarily Michel Hulin, *Hegel et l'Orient*, pp. 122–24, and Wilhelm Halbfass, *Indien und Europa: Perspektiven ihrer geistigen Begegnung* (Stuttgart: Schwabe, 1981), and the American edition of the same work, revised and expanded, *India and Europe: An Essay in Understanding* (Albany: State University of New York Press, 1988), pp. 92–93.

5. See especially J., p. 623. The details of these shifts and their effects on meanings would go beyond the scope of the present work.

6. J., p. 461; G., p. 99.

7. "*Der Mensch hat aus sich Nichts zu machen*": J., p. 463; G., p. 109.

8. "*Aus Nichts, heißt es, sei alles hervorgangen, in Nichts gehe alles zurück*": J., p. 461; G., p. 101.

9. J., pp. 462–63; G., pp. 108–9.

10. See chap. 3.

11. Joseph de Guignes, *Histoire générale des Huns, des Turcs, des Mongols et des autres Tartares occidentaux: Avant et depuis Jésus Christ jusqu'à présent; précédée d'une introduction contenant des tables chronologiques et historiques des princes qui ont régné dans l'Asie*, 4 vols. (Paris: 1756–58). The quote is from 1:277 § 2.

12. See the introduction to the present work.

13. De Guignes, *Histoire générale*, p. 226.

14. See chap. 1, including note 28.

15. De Guignes, *Histoire générale*, p. 224.

16. Louis Moreri, *Grand Dictionnaire historique ou Mélange curieux de l'histoire sacrée et profane* (Paris, 1725).

17. Ibid., vol. 5, first part.

18. Ibid., vol. 5, p. 360ff.

19. The *Histoire générale de la Chine* by Abbot Jean Baptiste Gabriel Grosier, originally edited by J. A. M. de Moyriac de Mailla in Paris from 1777 to 1785, was reedited about the time of Hegel's courses, under the title *De la Chine, ou Description générale de cet Empire, rédigée d'après les Mémoires de la Mission de Pé-kin par l'abbé J. B. A. Grosier*, 7 vols. (Paris, 1828–30). Cf. *Weltgeschichte* (Hamburg: Felix Meiner), 2:283.

20. Abbot Grosier, *De la Chine* (Paris: 1829), vol. 4, book 9, pp. 446–48.

21. Ibid., pp. 450–52.

22. "Immortality" translates the German *Unterblichkeit*.

23. *Encyclopédie des sciences philosophiques en abrégé*, French translation by Maurice de Gandillac of the text established by F. Nicolin and O. Pöggeler (Paris: Gallimard, 1970), p. 144.

24. J., pp. 464–65; G., p. 102.

25. This statement and the preceding ones are found in the section dedicated by Hegel to India in his *Leçons sur la philosophie de l'histoire*, French translation by J. Gibelin (Paris: Vrin, 1970), pp. 109–127.

26. *Einleitung in die Geschichte der Philosophie*, ed. J. Hoffmeister (Hamburg: Felix Meiner, 1962), p. 4.

27. I must emphasize this point even more clearly since I contributed to spreading this idea in *L'Oubli de l'Inde* (see in particular pp. 185–96 in the re-edition by Livre de Poche). Since I discovered sections of text where Hegel offers completely different opinions that,

178   without negating the preceding one, moderate it greatly, setting the record straight has seemed necessary to me. I began to do so in "Hegel entre les Indes occidentales et les Indes orientales" (commentary of the intervention of Pierre-Jean Labarrière, "Hegel et l'Amérique"), in *Penser la rencontre de deux mondes*, under the direction of Alfredo Gomez-Müller (Paris: PUF, 1993), pp. 29–33.

28. "*Wirklich philosophische Systeme der Inder*": *Vorlesungen über die Geschichte der Philosophie*, ed. Hoffmeister (Leipzig: 1940), p. 294.

29. "*Sehr wohl den Namen der Philosophie verdient*": *Berliner Schriften*, in *Werke*, vol. 11 (Frankfurt: 1970), p. 144.

CHAPTER FIVE

1. Eugène Burnouf, "De la langue et de la littérature sanskrites: Discours d'ouverture, prononcé au Collège de France" ("On the Sanskrit Language and Literature: Opening speech, delivered at the Collège de France"), *Revue des Deux Mondes* 1 (1833): 264–78.

2. E. Burnouf and Chr. Lassen, *Essai sur le Pali, ou Langue sacrée de la presqu'île au-delà du Gange, avec six planches lithographiées, et la notice des manuscrits palis de la Bibliothèque du Roi* (Paris, 1826), 222 pp. See chap. 3.

3. Among the numerous works of Isaac Jacob Schmidt, see *Forschungen im Gebiete der älteren religiösen, politischen und literarischen Bildungsgeschichte der Völker Mittel-Asiens* (Saint Petersburg-Leipzig: 1824), and his correspondence published by the *Mémoires de l'Académie impériale des Sciences* in Saint Petersburg, especially "Über einige Grundlehren des Buddhismus" (1832), ser. 6, vol. 1, pp. 90–120 and 222–62. This was one of Schopenhauer's primary sources.

4. Jean-Pierre Abel-Rémusat, *Mélanges asiatiques*, 2 vols. (Paris: 1825–26), and *Foé Koué Ki ou Relation des royaumes bouddhiques* (Paris: Impr. royale, 1836).

5. "Analysis of the *Kah-gyur*," Calcutta, *Asiatic Researches* 20 (1820): 41–66.

6. Eugène Burnouf, *Introduction à l'histoire du Buddhisme indien* (Paris: Impr. royale, 1844). The second edition (Paris: Maisonneuve et Cie, 1876) is preceded by a list of Burnouf's posthumous manuscripts by J. Barthélemy Saint-Hilaire, pp. xxiii–xxvi.

7. The text of the "Notice sur la vie et les travaux de M. Burnouf et sur le progrès qu'il a fait aux études orientales" was reproduced in the *Annales de philosophie chrétienne*, no. 33 (September 1852), p. 217ff.

8. Friedrich Wilhelm Schelling, "Jugement sur la philosophie de M. Cousins et sur l'état de la philosophie française et de la philosophie allemande en général," *Nouvelle revue germanique* (May 1834).

9. *Vendidad Sadé, l'un des livres de Zoroastre, lithographié d'après le manuscrit zend de la Bibliothèque royale* (Paris: 1829), 562 pp. (the publication, in ten fascicles, at the expense of the author, extended to 1842).

10. Eugène Burnouf, *Introduction*, 2nd ed. (1876), p. 97.

11. That was especially the case for Ernest Renan and Jules Barthélemy Saint-Hilaire: see chap. 8, p. 177ff.

12. Eugène Burnouf, *Introduction*, 2nd ed. (1876), pp. 463–64.

13. See chap. 8.

14. Ozanam, "Essai sur le bouddhisme," p. 226.

15. Ibid.

16. Ibid.

17. The expression is obscure. Ozanam probably meant the existence of polyandry

implied that the sense of decency (the last feeling) was extinguished in its last refuge (the hearts of women).

18. Ozanam, "Essai sur le bouddhisme," p. 226.

19. Ibid., p. 227.

20. Ibid., p. 228.

21. Ibid., p. 229

22. Ibid.

23. This expression and the preceding ones are from ibid., p. 232.

24. Ibid., p. 233.

25. Abbot Bigandet later became the author of works that reached a sizable audience and that were widely translated; in particular his biography of the Buddha, *The Life, or Legend of Gaudama, the Buddha of the Burmese, with Annotations: The Ways to Neibban* [The Paths of Nirvana], *and Notice on the Phongytes or Burmese Monks* (Rangoon: 1866); French translation by V. Vauvain, *Vie ou Légende de Gaudama, le Bouddha des Birmans, et notice sur les Phongytes ou moines birmans* (Paris: Ernest Leroux, 1878).

26. "Principaux points du système boudhiste [*sic*]," *Ann. de philos. chrét.*, no. 44 (August 1843), pp. 86–87.

27. "I consulted, questioned the Burmese of all classes," noted the missionary in a second article published in the same revue, "all unanimously answered that *Neiban* is deliverance from the vicissitudes of existence, from the influence of good and bad works, exemption of pleasure and pain, disappearance, the end of the being, etc., expressions that tend to lead to the understanding that *Neiban* is the destruction of being." *Ann. de philos. chrét.*, no. 46 (October 1843), p. 272.

28. Félix Nève, *De l'état présent des études sur le Bouddhisme et de leur application* (Gand, 1846), 63 pp. (the text had previously been published by the *Revue de Flandre*, vol. 1). The sentence cited is found on p. 63.

29. Ibid., p. 53.

30. Ibid., p. 63.

31. Ibid.

32. Ibid., p. 48.

33. Ibid., p. 45.

34. Ibid., p. 27.

35. Ibid., p. 42.

36. Ibid., p. 50.

37. See chaps. 7 and 8.

38. On Cousin, see the book by Patrice Vermeren, *Victor Cousin, le jeu de la philosophie et de l'Etat* (Paris: L'Harmattan, 1995). (Translator's note: Rendering of Cousin's expression, *culte du néant*, has been divided, in this English translation, between "worship of nothingness" and "cult of nothingness." The French word *culte* refers primarily to the visible, "practical" aspect of religion, and thus has a meaning that is slightly narrower than "religion" per se, and at the same time it lacks some of the emotionality that the word "cult" does in English, where it often refers to extremist or "extraordinary" sects. The fear that Buddhism aroused in the West, and its deviance from what was considered to be the religious norm, makes some of Droit's text quite appropriately translated by "cult." In other cases the author is referring primarily to the fact that the Buddha was worshiped, or that Buddhist beliefs existed as a religion.)

39. The idea was admittedly found in Hegel's works (see chap. 4) with a different meaning from the one given by Victor Cousin, but the expression did not exist in the writings of the Berlin philosopher.

180   40. Victor Cousin, *Cours de philosophie, introduction à l'histoire de la philosophie* (Paris: Pichon et Didier, 1828), Première leçon, 19 April 1828, p. 32. In the notes that follow, we will designate references to these lessons by "1828," followed by the page.

41. Let us remember that Hegel devoted an essay published in 1827 to the *Bhagavad-Gîtâ*, in numbers 7 and 8 of the *Jahrbücher für wissenschaftliche Kritik* (see the Hoffmeister edition of the *Berliner Schriften*, pp. 85–154, and the French translation of this text by Michel Hulin in *Hegel et l'Orient* [Paris: Vrin, 1979], pp. 145–206).

42. 1828, Deuxième leçon, 24 April 1828, p. 13.

43. Ibid., p. 14.

44. Ibid., p. 18.

45. Victor Cousin, *Cours de l'histoire de la philosophie* (Paris: Pichon et Didier, 1829). Our work is based on the text of Victor Cousin's *Œuvres complètes* (Brussels: Société belge de librairie Ahuman et Cie, 1841), vol. 1. In the notes that follow, we will designate references to these lessons by "1829 (1841)," followed by the page and the column (a = left or b = right). The sentence cited is from p. 153a.

46. 1829 (1841, p. 155b).

47. See chaps. 3 and 4.

48. Victor Cousin, *Histoire générale de la philosophie depuis les temps les plus anciens jusqu'au XIXe siècle* (Paris: Didier, 1863). Here the references refer to the tenth edition (Paris: Didier, 1873). In the following notes, we will designate these lessons by "1863 (1873)," followed by the page.

49. 1863 (1873, p. 89).

50. 1829 (1841, p. 155b).

51. It is difficult to know if Cousin had attentively read Colebrooke, or—especially regarding the fifth and last dissertation, *On Indian Sectaries*, about the Buddhists—if he made do with Abel-Rémusat's recension for the *Journal des Savants* in July 1828, which he cited several times.

52. 1829 (1841, p. 155a).

53. *Journal des Savants*, July 1828, p. 289. Cited by Cousin 1829 (1841, p. 155b, n. 3).

54. Cousin spoke this way about a "perfectly literal Latin translation," referring to the translation of the *Gîtâ* by A. W. Schlegel. Shortly thereafter, he affirmed, commenting on the Latin text of Schlegel in his own way: "I do not invent, I translate." These phrases appear in 1829 (1841, pp. 162b and 164a, respectively).

55. See in particular Jules Barthélemy Saint-Hilaire, *Eugène Burnouf, ses travaux et sa correspondance* (Paris: 1891).

56. "Mémoire sur la philosophie sanskrite, le Nyâya," published in the *Journal des Savants* (1840), pp. 147–240.

57. See chap. 8.

58. Jules Barthélemy Saint-Hilaire, in accord with his wishes, lies next to Victor Cousin in Père-Lachaise cemetery, in Paris.

59. *L'Inde anglaise, son état actuel, son avenir* (Paris: Perrin, 1887), p. 320.

60. See Jules Barthélemy Saint-Hilaire, "Rapport sur le tome I de l'*Introduction à l'histoire du Buddhisme indien* par M. E. Burnouf: Suivi d'observations par M. Cousin," *Séances et Travaux de l'Acad. des Sc. morales et politiques* (Paris: 1847), series 2, vol. 1.

61. 1863 (1873, pp. 90–95). The cited sentence is on p. 93.

62. Ibid., p. 91.

63. Ibid., p. 94.

64. Ibid., p. 90.

65. Ibid.
66. Ibid.
67. Ibid.
68. Ibid., p. 94.
69. Ibid., p. 95.

CHAPTER SIX

1. In the pages that follow we are translating from *Le Monde comme Volonté et comme Représentation* (MVR) in the French translation by A. Burdeau (new edition, reviewed and corrected by Richard Roos [Paris: PUF, 1966]). The other texts cited are from *De la Volonté dans la nature* (VDN), French translation by Édouard Sans (Paris: PUF, 1969), and *Correspondance Complète*, French translation by Christian Jaedicke (Paris: Alive, 1996) (J.). Here, VDN, pp. 187–88.

2. MVR, p. 861.

3. VDN, pp. 187–88.

4. MVR, p. 512.

5. This negation has nothing to do with destruction. A rigorous philosopher, Schopenhauer observed that nothing can be said of that which is "completely otherwise."

6. For a detailed discussion of the similarities and differences between Schopenhauer's thought and the main lines of Buddhist thought, see my study "Schopenhauer et le bouddhisme: une 'admirable concordance'?" in *Schopenhauer: New Essays in Honor of His 200th Birthday*, a trilingual collective volume published under the direction of Eric von der Luft (New York: Edwin Mellen Press Studies in German Thought and History, 1988), 10:123–38, and the summary of this study, entitled "Une statuette tibétaine sur la cheminée," in *Présence de Schopenhauer*, under the direction of Roger-Pol Droit (Paris: Grasset, 1989), pp. 220–38; 2nd edition (Paris: Le Livre de Poche, 1991), pp. 210–17; collection "Biblio-Essais" (1991), pp. 210–17.

7. "Übereinstimmung" was the German word Schopenhauer used in both his letter to von Doss (no. 381, 27 February 1856) and MVR (pp. 861–62).

8. "Damn": the word was in French [rather than German] in Schopenhauer's original text.

9. Letter no. 388, to Julius Frauenstädt, 7 April 1856; J., p. 518.

10. J., p. 519.

11. Edward Crüger had been, for a number of years during the decade from 1850 to 1860, one of Schopenhauer's companions at the Hôtel d'Angleterre's table d'hôte. The philosopher was indebted to him for two important gifts: an autographed copy of *The Critique of Practical Reason* and the Tibetan Buddha in question here.

12. Letter no. 378, 31 January 1856; J., p. 506.

13. The "sacred places" to which Schopenhauer was referring are the same as those in Mozart's *Magic Flute*.

14. Letter no. 389, to Carl Grimm; J., p. 519.

15. Cf. J., p. 520.

16. Letter no. 391, to Julius Frauenstädt, 6 June 1856; J., p. 525.

17. Letter no. 393, to Julius Frauenstädt, 11 July 1856; J., p. 529. See also a letter to von Doss, 19 March of the following year; J., p. 551.

18. Letter no. 402, to Edward Crüger, 29 November 1956; J., p. 542.

19. Letter no. 409, to Adam von Doss, 19 March 1857; J., p. 551.

182   20. Letter no. 410, to Christian Karl Josias Bunsen, 28 March 1857; J., p. 530.

21. Arthur Schopenhauer, *Journal du voyage*, French trans. Didier Raymond (Paris: Mercure de France, 1988), p. 30.

22. *Der handschriftliche Nachlass*, ed. A. Hübscher, 5 vols. (Frankfurt-am-Main: Waldemar Kzamer, 1966–75); 4, 1, p. 96.

23. In MVR, the main references to Buddhism are all in book 4 (pp. 449, 479, 481, 483, 516) and in the Supplements to book 4 (pp. 861–63, 1183, 1204, 1252–54,1258–59, 1343, 1349, 1376, 1378, 1383, 1393, 1400, 1406).

24. Schopenhauer was here referring to the first edition of *The World as Will and as Representation*; the 1844 *Supplements* formed the second volume.

25. Letter no. 381, to Adam von Doss (27 February 1856); J., pp. 509–12. This letter has a special importance for understanding Schopenhauer's connection with Buddhism.

26. MVR, pp. 861–62.

27. The chapter entitled "Sinology" of this latter work ends with a long bibliographical note in which Schopenhauer comments on the works on Buddhism.

28. VDN, pp. 187–88.

29. MVR, pp. 449.

30. Ibid., p. 861.

31. Ibid., p. 1253.

32. Ibid., p. 1376.

33. VDN, p. 190.

34. MVR, pp. 485, 862 et al.

35. Ibid., p. 1376.

36. Ibid., p. 515.

37. Ibid., p. 516

38. Ibid.

39. André Lalande, *Vocabulaire technique et critique de la philosophie*, article "nirvâna" (Paris: PUF, 1962), p. 682.

40. MVR, p. 516.

41. Ibid.

42. On the pertinence of a translation of the Sanskrit *prajna* by the word wisdom (Fr. *sapience*), see Guy Bugault, *La Notion de "prajnâ" ou de sapience selon les perspectives du "Mahâyâna"* (The idea of "prajna" or wisdom according to Mahayana perspectives) (Paris: Publ. de l'Institut de civilisation indienne, 1968, 1982).

43. I.e., the work by Isaac Jacob Schmidt, *Über das Mahâjâna und Pradschnâ-Pâramita der Baudden* (Berlin: 1836), p. 106. A specialist in Mongolian texts, I. J. Schmidt authored a number of works on Buddhism (primarily in St. Petersburg, where he taught) whose publication dates stretched from 1824 to 1847.

44. MVR, p. 265.

45. The 1862 *Études et Réflexions d'un pessimiste*, published in 1901, have been re-edited, followed by the article "Un bouddhiste contemporain en Allemagne" (A Contemporary Buddhist in Germany), in the *Corpus des Oeuvres de philosophie en langue française* (Paris: Fayard, 1993).

46. Ibid., p. 49.

47. "Un bouddhiste contemporain en Allemagne," *Revue des Deux Mondes*, 15 March 1970. The article made a considerable stir and was reedited a number of times thereafter. In *Études et Réflexions d'un pessimiste*, p. 232.

48. Ibid., p. 233.

49. Ibid.

50. Alexandre Foucher de Careil, *Hegel et Schopenhauer. Études sur la philosophie allemande moderne* (Paris: Hachette, 1862), p. 306.

51. Ibid.

52. Ibid., p. 371.

53. Ibid., p. 306.

54. Ibid., p. 306–7.

55. In France, the idea had already been seen, in a number of different ways, among authors as diverse as Benjamin Constant, Madame de Staël, Guigniaut (translator and adaptor of Görres), Victor Jacquemont, and Edgar Quinet. It was developed further in the last quarter of the century, with the reception of Schopenhauer's thought in France, the vogue of pessimism, and so on. In Germany, it was clearly a commonplace of Indo-Germanism and of Aryan myth.

56. A. Foucher de Careil, *Hegel et Schopenhauer*, pp. 307–8.

57. *Paralipomena*, cited by Etienne Osier, in Schopenhauer, *Sur la religion* (Paris: Garnier-Flammarion, 1996), p. 163 n. 113.

58. On this expression and its meaning in Schopenhauer, see Elisabeth de Fontenay's article "La pitié dangereuse," in R.-P. Droit, *Présences de Schopenhauer.*

59. "De l'éthique," in *Le Sens du destin*, excerpts from *Parerga* and *Paralipomena*, French trans. Marie-José Pernin (Paris: Vrin, 1988), p. 105.

CHAPTER SEVEN

1. See chap. 5.

2. Author, with Eugène Burnouf, of the *Essai sur le Pali (Essay on Pali)*, published in 1826, the Danish scholar of Indian studies Christian Lassen was composing one of the primary Indian *summae* of the nineteenth century when he wrote *Indische Altertumskunde* (Liepzig: L. A. Kittler; London: Williams & Norgate, 1847–61).

3. *Essai sur l'inégalité des races humaines*, p. 543. (All references to this text refer to the critical edition by Jean Gaulmier and Jean Boissel [Paris: Gallimard, 1983]).

4. Ibid.

5. Ibid., p. 294.

6. Ibid., p. 316.

7. Ibid., p. 285.

8. Ibid.

9. Ibid., p. 286.

10. Ibid., p. 312.

11. Ibid., pp. 338–39.

12. Ibid., p. 1163.

13. Ibid., p. 342.

14. Ibid., p. 282.

15. Ibid., p. 1163

16. Ibid., p. 1164.

17. Ibid., p. 345.

18. Ibid., p. 1166.

19. Ibid.

20. Ibid., pp. 541–58.

21. Ibid., p. 549.

22. Ibid., p. 543.

23. Ibid.

24. This "naturally" is a gem.

25. Ibid., p. 545.

26. Ibid., p. 548.

27. Ibid., p. 549.

28. Ibid., p. 546.

29. Ibid.

30. Ibid., p. 548.

31. Ibid., p. 549.

32. Ibid., p. 550.

33. Friedrich Schlegel, *Über die Sprache und Weisheit der Indier* (On the Language and Wisdom of the Indians) (Heidelberg: 1808). The references to this work from this point on will refer to the pages in the French translation by M. A. Mazure, *Essai sur la langue et la philosophie des Indiens* (Paris: Parent-Desbarres, 1837) (M.), and of the contemporary critical edition by Ernst Behler in the *Kritische Ausgabe* of the *Works* of Friedrich Schlegel, vol. 8-1, *Studien zur Philosophie und Theologie* (Paderborn/Zurich: F. Schöning/Thomas-Verlag, 1975), pp. 106–433 (B.).

34. On this point, see especially René Gérard, *L'Orient et la Pensée romantique allemande* (Paris: Didier, 1963); A. Leslie Willson, *A Mythical Image: The Ideal of India in German Romanticism* (Durham, N.C.: Duke University Press, 1964).

35. *Über die Sprache, op. cit.*

36. M., p. 1; B., p. 107.

37. M., pp. 74–90; B., pp. 173–90.

38. M., pp. 70–71; B., p. 171.

39. M., p. 72; B., p. 171.

40. M., p. 74; B., p. 173.

41. See M. Olender, *Les Langues du paradis: Aryens et Sémites: un couple providentiel* (Paris: Gallimard-Éd. du Seuil, 1989), coll. "Hautes études" (reedited in the collection "Points Essais," 1994), chap. 1, "Archives du Paradis."

42. M., p. 72; B., p. 171.

43. M., p. 71; B., p. 171.

44. M., p. 70; B., p. 169.

45. M., pp. 71–72; B., p. 171.

46. M., p. 72; B., p. 171.

47. M., p. 79; B., p. 179.

48. Ibid.

49. M., p. 81; B., p. 181.

50. M., p. 140; B., p. 241.

51. M., p. 117; B., p. 217.

52. See chap. 4.

53. M., p. 142; B., p. 243.

54. M., p. 152; B., p. 253.

55. M., p. 142; B., p. 243.

56. M., p. 142; B., p. 243.

57. These expressions are all found in M., p. 182; B., p. 283.

58. M., p. 182; B., p. 283.

59. M., p. 185, B., p. 285.

60. M., pp. 197–98; B., p. 229.

1. Ernest Renan, "Premiers travaux sur le bouddhisme," reprinted in *Nouvelles Études d'histoire religieuse* (1884) (Paris: Gallimard, 1992), pp. 348–49.

2. Ibid., p. 353.

3. Ibid., p. 364.

4. Ibid., p. 365.

5. Ibid., p. 379.

6. Ibid., p. 380.

7. Ibid., p. 384.

8. Ibid., pp. 386–87.

9. Ibid., p. 386.

10. Ibid., p. 387.

11. Ibid., p. 400.

12. *Le Bouddha et sa religion* (Paris: Didier et Cie., 1860) (reedited in 1862 and 1866).

13. Ibid., p. 180. Shortly thereafter, J. Barthélemy Saint-Hilaire mentioned "those peoples who, after all, are our brothers, even if they are not completely like us" (p. 182).

14. *Séances et travaux*, pp. 321–22.

15. Cited by Patrice Vermeren, *Victor Cousin: Le jeu de la philosophie et de l'État* (Paris: L'Harmattan, 1995), p. 323.

16. Letter to Adam von Doss, 19 March 1857, in *Correspondance complète* (Paris: Alive, 1996), p. 550.

17. Let us bear in mind that this is the way Schopenhauer referred to his earliest followers.

18. French trans. Edouard Sans (Paris: PUF, 1969), p. 48: "Il faut faire comprendre à ces messieurs, français ou allemands, que la philosophie n'est pas faite pour apporter de l'eau au moulin de la prêtraille."

19. Jean-Baptiste-François Obry, *Du Nirvâna indien, ou De l'affranchissement de l'âme après la mort, selon les Brahmanes et els Bouddhistes* (Amiens: 1856).

20. Letter to Adam von Doss, 19 March 1857, in *Correspondance*, p. 550.

21. J. Barthélemy Saint-Hilaire, "Le néo-bouddhisme" (Paris: Mém. De l'Acad. des Sciences morales et politiques, 1896), 19:416.

22. *Séances et Travaux*, p. 326.

23. See chap. 5.

24. Although it spanned a number of years and takes up several volumes when the texts are placed end to end, the quarrel is relatively poor from the point of view of theoretical content. Only the symptom that it constitutes is worthy of consideration.

25. *Séances et Travaux*, p. 326.

26. Ibid., p. 327.

27. See chap. 6.

28. *Séances et Travaux*, p. 330.

29. Ibid., p. 331.

30. Ibid., p. 344.

31. Ibid., p. 346.

32. See especially Burnouf's *The Lotus of the Good Law* (Paris: Imp. Nationale, 1852), and Foucaux's *Lalitavistara*, 2 vols. (Paris: Imp. Royale, 1847–48).

33. *Du Nirvana indien*.

34. *Séances et Travaux*, p. 334.

35. Ibid., p. 5.

186   36. *Du Nirvana bouddhique.*

37. Ibid., p. 5.

38. Ibid., p. 20.

39. Ibid., p. 31.

40. Ibid.

41. Ibid.

42. Ibid., p. 65.

43. Ibid., p. 66.

44. Ibid., p. 138.

45. See chap. 4.

46. *Du Nirvana bouddhique*, p. 101.

47. Ibid.

48. Ibid., p. 6.

49. Ibid., p. 101.

50. *Séances et Travaux*, p. 335.

51. Ibid.

52. Ibid., p. 336.

53. Ibid., p. 339.

54. Reprinted in *Chips from a German Workshop* (London: Longmans, Green, 1867), vol. 1, *Essays on the Science of Religion.*

55. Ibid., p. 223.

56. D. F. García Ayuso, *El Nirvâna buddhista en sus relaciones con otros sistemas filosóficos* (Madrid: 1885), 41 p.

57. Ibid., p. 31.

58. Ibid., p. 28.

59. "Un Mémoire espagnol sur le *Nirvana* bouddhique" (Paris: *Revue d'Histoire des religions*, 1885), 12:321–33.

CHAPTER NINE

1. Carl Friedrich Köppen, *Die Religion des Buddha.* The work was composed in two volumes, one two years after the other: vol. 1, *Die Religion des Buddha und Ihre Entstehung*; vol. 2, *Die Lamaische Hierarchie und Kirche* (Berlin: Ferdinand Schneider, 1857–59), 616, 408 pp.

2. Eugène Burnouf, *Introduction à l'histoire du Buddhisme indien* (Paris: Imprimerie Royale, 1844; re-ed. Paris: Maisonneuve et Cie, 1876).

3. J. W. de Jong, "A Brief History of Buddhist Studies in Europe and America," *Eastern Buddhist* 7-1 (1974): 55–106, and 7-2 (1974): 49–82; Wilhelm Halbfass, *India and Europe: An Essay in Understanding* (Albany: SUNY Press, 1988). ed. reviewed and expanded with *Indien und Europa: Perspektiven ihrer geistigen Begegnung* (Stuttgart: Schwabe, 1981).

4. Arthur Schopenhauer, *Gesammelte Briefe*, ed. Arthur Hübscher (Bonn: Bouvier, 1987). Letter no. 427, p. 425.

5. Arthur Schopenhauer, *Über den Willen in der Natur*, ed. Zürcher, in *Werke*, 10 vols. (Zurich: Diogenes Verlag, 1867), 5:327; French trans. Edouard Sans, *De la Volonté dans la nature* (Paris: PUF, 1969), p. 188.

6. Cited by Carl Suneson in *Richard Wagner und die Indische Geisteswelt* (Leiden: E. J. Brill, 1989), p. 24. See also in this work, regarding Wagner and Köppen, pp. 22–25, and regarding relations between Wagner and Buddhism, pp. 32–40.

7. See Charles Andler, *Nietzsche, sa vie et sa pensée* (Paris: Gallimard, 1958), 2:415, no. 1.

8. *Nouveaux Essais de critique et d'histoire* (Paris: Hachette, 1865), pp. 317–83 The ar-

ticle was reedited in *Philosophie, France, XIXe siècle. Écrits et opuscules*, presented by Stéphane
Douailler, Roger-Pol Droit, et Patrice Vermeren (Paris: Le Livre de Poche, 1994), 1024 pp.
In this re-edition, Taine's article is found on pp. 417–66. In the notes that follow, the
references refer only to this edition, with the mention "re-ed." and the page numbers.

9. Re-ed., p. 417.

10. See the end of the "Bibliographie chronologique abrégée des publications orien-
talistes consacrées au bouddhisme entre 1800 et 1890."

11. Re-ed., p. 418.

12. Ibid.

13. Re-ed., pp. 419–20.

14. Re-ed., p. 421.

15. Re-ed., pp. 422–23.

16. Re-ed., p. 424.

17. Re-ed., p. 426.

18. Re-ed., p. 425.

19. Re-ed., pp. 465–66.

20. Re-ed., pp. 428–29.

21. Re-ed., p. 434.

22. Re-ed., pp. 433–34.

23. Re-ed., p. 443.

24. Re-ed., p. 450.

25. Re-ed., p. 438.

26. Re-ed., pp. 436–37.

27. Re-ed., pp. 438–39.

28. Re-ed., p. 441.

29. Ibid.

30. Re-ed., pp. 450–51.

31. Re-ed., p. 460.

32. Re-ed., pp. 460–61.

33. Re-ed., p. 463.

34. Re-ed., p. 465.

35. Re-ed., p. 466.

36. Mervyn Sprung has shown that complete confidence in Nietzsche in this domain is
probably not appropriate, in a detailed, documented study: "Nietzsche's Trans-European
Eye," in a work under the direction of Graham Parkes, *Nietzsche and Asian Thought* (Chicago:
University of Chicago Press, 1991), pp. 76–90.

37. *Humain, trop humain*, in *Oeuvres philosophiques complètes* (Paris: Gallimard, 1968), vol. 3,
no. 1, p. 362. References to works by Nietzsche that follow refer to the edition by Gorgio
Colli and Massino Montinari, *Oeuvres philosophiques complètes* (Paris: Gallimard, 1968). The
titles are abbreviated as follows: *L'Antéchrist*, AC; *La Génealogie de la morale*, GM; *Le Gai
Savoir*, GS. Posthumous passages are noted according to volume and page in this edition.

38. Vol. 1, no. 1, p. 439.

39. Ibid., p. 441.

40. Ibid., p. 373.

41. Vol. 12, p. 300.

42. Vol. 13, p. 293.

43. AC, sect. 20, pp. 176–77.

44. Vol. 4, p. 116.

45. AC, sect. 20, p. 177.

188   46. Ibid.

47. Unpublished text from a lecture given by Michel Hulin on 7 March 1989 at the Collège International de Philosophie, for a program I was directing at the time. Some parts of this text, expanded and completed, may be found in Michel Hulin's study "Nietzsche and the Suffering of the Indian Ascetic," in Graham Parkes, dir., *Nietzsche and Asian Thought*, pp. 64–75. The deformation to which Nietzsche subjected Buddhist discipline is mentioned on pp. 71–72. On the other hand, it is appropriate to recall that, in this same program under my direction, Marcel Conche led a study of "Nietzsche and Buddhism." The remarks presented here are indebted to his text, published in the *Cahier du Collège international de philosophie*, no. 4 (Paris: Osiris, 1987, pp. 125–44.

48. AC, sect. 20, p. 177.

49. Ibid., pp. 177–78.

50. Vol. 11, p. 219.

51. Vol. 14, p. 93.

52. GM, I, sect. 6, p. 230.

53. Vol. 5, p. 17.

54. Vol. 14, p. 140.

55. Vol. 12, p. 140.

56. Vol. 13, p. 48.

57. Vol. 10, p. 86.

58. Vol. 13, p. 364.

59. *La Volonté de la Puissance*, French trans. Henry Albert, re-ed. (Paris: Le Livre de Poche, 1991), p. 40.

60. Vol. 12, p. 20.

61. Vol. 10, p. 45.

62. Vol. 11, p. 219.

63. Vol. 1, no. 1, p. 440.

64. GS, sect. 318, p. 202.

CHAPTER TEN

1. Henri-Frédéric Amiel, *Fragments du Journal intime*, 2 vols. (Geneva, October 1882), p. 48.

2. Charles Renouvier, "Philosophie de la réfléxion," *La Critique philosophique* 1 (1883): 140–41.

3. Amiel, *Fragments du Journal intime*, 31 August 1869.

4. Charles Renouvier, "Philosophie de la réfléxion," p. 180.

5. See, e.g., W. Sucker, "Buddha und Christus, Buddhismus und Christentum, nebst Bemerkungen zu dem Neubuddhismus Eduard von Hartmanns," *Beweis des Glaubens* 13 (July–Oct. 1877): 297–307, 362–74, 419–29, 471–86, 525–30.

6. Amiel, *Fragments du Journal intime*, 24 April 1869.

7. Published in Berlin in 1870 and translated to French in 1877, this work, which claims to be representative of Schopenhauer's thought, was an important influence on the thinking of both Nietzsche and Freud.

8. Amiel, *Fragments du Journal intime*, 8 December 1869.

9. Ibid.

10. Ibid., 9 September 1879.

11. Elmé Caro, *Le Pessimisme au XIXe siècle: Leopardi, Schopenhauer, Hartmann*, 2nd ed. (Paris: Hachette, 1880), p. 140.

12. Ibid., p. 237.

13. H. Fierens-Gevaert, *La Tristesse contemporaine* (Paris: Félix Alcan, 1908), 195 pp.; citation p. 82.

14. See *Au-delà du principe du plaisir* (*G. W.* 13:60; *S. E.* 18:51) and "Le problème économique du masochisme" (*G. W.* 13:373; *S. E.* 19:160).

15. Charles Renouvier, *Philosophie analytique de l'histoire* (Paris: Ernest Leroux, 1897), 4:420.

16. Eduard von Hartmann, *L'Autodestruction du christianisme et la Religion de l'avenir*, introduction, translation, and notes by Jean-Marie Paul (Nancy: Presses Universitaires de Nancy, 1989), 229 pp.; citation p. 160.

17. Ibid., p. 164.

18. Ibid.

19. See chap. 6.

20. Von Hartmann, *L'Autodestruction du christianisme*, p. 163.

21. J.-M. Guyau, *L'Irréligion de l'avenir* (Paris: Librairie Félix Alcan, 1887), 479 pp.

22. Ibid., p. 416.

23. Ibid.

24. Ibid., pp. 416–17.

25. Ibid., p. 417.

26. Ibid., pp. 417–19.

27. Charles Renouvier, "Difficultés proposées et résolues. Un point du problème sur l'immortalité de l'âme," *La Critique philosophique* 1 (1873): 373–74.

28. Sir Edwin Arnold, *The Light of Asia, or the Great Renunciation (Mahabhinishkramana): Being the Life and Teaching of Gautama, Prince of India and Founder of Buddhism, as Told in Verse by an Indian Buddhist, Based on the Lalitavistara* (Boston: Roberts Bros., 1879), 238 pp.

29. Ibid., p. xii.

30. Especially William Cleaver Wilkinson, *Edwin Arnold as Poetizer and as Paganizer: Containing an Examination of the "Light of Asia" for Its Literature and for Its Buddhism* (New York: Funk, 1885), 177 pp. Evidence of the expression's later destiny is seen, among other places, in the title by Samuel Henry Kellog, *The Light of Asia and the Light of the World: A Comparison of the Legend, the Doctrine and Ethics of the Buddha with the Story, the Doctrine and Ethics of Christ* (London: Macmillan, 1885), 390 pp. See also Edouard Schuré's recension in *Revue des Deux Mondes* 80 (1885): 589–622, on the occasion of the twenty-fifth edition of *The Light of Asia*: "Le Bouddha et sa légende: Une résurrection du Buddha." For a detailed summary, cf. Philip C. Almond, *The British Discovery of Buddhism* (London: Cambridge University Press, 1988).

31. Sir Edwin Arnold, *The Light of Asia*, p. xiii.

32. Léon de Rosny, *Le Bouddhisme éclectique* (Paris: E. Leroux, Bibliothèque orientale Elzévirienne, 1894), p. xxix.

33. As has been said by the theosophist Alfred Percy Sinnett, *Esoteric Buddhism* (London, Trübner, 1883), p. 215: "It should nevertheless be noted that the title Esoteric Buddhism offered by Mr. Sinnett for his last work does not mean that the teaching outlined should be identified with a particular religious belief; but *Buddhism* here refers to the teachings of the *Buddhas*, the sages, that is, the religion of Wisdom." This excerpt from the *Theosophist* is cited by Sinnett himself (!) in the new edition of his work (original French translation by Publications théosophiques [Paris: 1910], p. 12).

34. De Rosny, *Le Bouddhisme éclectique*, p. xxxi.

35. Ibid., p. xxxiii.

36. Jules Barthélemy Saint-Hilaire, "Le neo-bouddhisme," Paris, *Mém. De l'Acad. des Sc. Morales et politiques* 19 (1896), p. 415.

190

37. Ibid., p. 426.

38. Ibid., p. 434.

39. Ibid., pp. 426–27.

40. *La Vie de Vivekânanda et l'Evangile universel* (1930; re-ed. Paris: Stock, 1977); see esp. chap. 3, p. 38ff.

41. Ibid., p. 42.

42. *Entretiens et Causeries*, French trans. Jean Herbert (Paris: Albin Michel, 1955), "Mon Maître," p. 321.

43. Ibid.

44. A Sanskrit scholar and specialist in Vedanta, Deussen was also the project manager for an edition of Schopenhauer's works.

45. On this aberrant interpretation by Schopenhauer, see the work of Lakshmi Kapani, in *L'Inde inspiratrice*, under the direction of Michel Hulin and Christine Maillard (Strasbourg: Presses Universitaires de Strasbourg, 1996).

46. On this subject, the foundational work continues to be Léon Poliakov's *Le Mythe aryen: Essai sur les sources du racisme et des nationalismes* (Paris: Calmann-Lévy, 1971).

47. The primary passages are listed in the indices to the above-mentioned French works, as well as in those of Jean Herbert's translations of *Jnâna-Yoga* (Paris: Albin Michel, 1936, 1972) and *Les Yogas pratiques* (Paris: Albin Michel, 1936, 1970).

48. *Entretiens et Causeries*, "Entretiens de Thousand Islands Park," p. 92.

49. See esp. ibid., "Les Sages de l'Inde," pp. 280–81, as well as *Les Yogas pratiques*, "L'idéal du Karma-Yoga," p. 115.

50. See esp. *Entretiens et Causeries*, "Les Sages de l'Inde," p. 282ff., and *Jnâna Yoga*, p. 266ff.

51. *Entretiens et Causeries*, "Les Sages de l'Inde," p. 284.

52. Ibid., p. 283.

53. Amiel, *Fragments du Journal intime*, p. 129.

Bibliography

On the Origin of This Bibliography

In 1961 in Tokyo, Father Shinsho Hanayama's *Bibliography on Buddhism* was published by "The Hokuseido Press." An entire life's work was made available through the efforts of the scholar's students and friends. The work was an imposing 870 pages, listing 15,073 titles.

It was also extraordinarily unrecognized: in a few years of reading the most specialized publications, I have only seen it mentioned two or three times. I know of only two copies in Paris: at the Bibliothèque Nationale and at the Institut de Civilisation Indienne at the Collège de France. Perhaps there are others in France, but there cannot be many.

In any case, the volume is out of print in Tokyo, and is accessible only rarely in the Japanese used-book market; a friend of mine, an antique dealer in Orientalist publications, had the task of finding a copy for me at a rare book fair in Japan. Despite his unusual competence, he failed.

It was both unfortunate and unfair that the huge quantity of information assembled by Father Shinsho Hanayama and edited by his disciples and colleagues remained so inaccessible and so underused. Doubtless, the work was in part responsible for the disaffection of which it was the object: its inordinate ambition was to list, exhaustively, all the works in which Buddhism was studied. This task was practically destined for failure from the outset: it remained necessarily inaccessible without a network of international teams, the makeup of which one can scarcely imagine. Especially since the First World War, however, specialized bibliographies, regularly brought up to date by area, have surpassed this work in precision, despite how highly developed it already was. Father Hanayama's summa undoubtedly also suffered from its layout: the alphabetical order by author did not facilitate consultation by either discipline or theme, in spite of the presence of an index.

But, for the period the book concerns, this work remains, to my mind, the most complete and the most precise that has been composed. That is why I wanted a great part of the information contained in it to be republished through its appearance in the present bibliography. It seemed this was the least that could be done to pay tribute to the effort accomplished by the Japanese professor and to help researchers interested in pursuing new investigations, while allowing the reader who is simply curious to find another way to see, by reading the hundreds of references, how the discovery of Buddhism by European Orientalists took place.

In fact, this chronological bibliography can be looked upon as the last part of this book, and not as a specialized appendix. It is possible, in glancing through it, to notice repetitions, breaks, or the appearance or the disappearance of themes. It seems to me that in its own way, it allows one to learn and to understand something beyond the material in the preceding chapters.

Even though the majority of these entries come from the work of Hanayama, my intervention has taken three distinct forms.

The first is a *chronological* order. It includes Orientalist publications on the subject of

192 Buddhism arranged by years, beginning in 1800. This chronological arrangement allows us to see the changes in rhythm from decade to decade between 1800 and 1860, as well as to see the changes in theme from one decade to another, and so forth. This classification, all by itself, outlines a history of the discovery that cannot be seen otherwise.

The second is a choice made necessary by the imperatives of place and readability. Until 1860, the list of publications is nearly complete. From 1860 to 1880, we have listed only about half the titles mentioned by Hanayama (publications dealing with archeology, statuary, and numismatics have been omitted, as have the most specialized of the philological works). From 1880 to 1890, a decade in which publications began to number in the hundreds, only the most important titles regarding the main tendencies of the period have been preserved.

The third is the correction of a few rare errors in names or dates that persisted in the Japanese edition.

Despite the care put into the present work, there certainly will be imperfections of all kinds in it; where such is the case, I alone am responsible.

Abbreviations

PUBLICATIONS

Acad.	*The Academy* (Leyden)
AMG	*Annales du musée Guimet*
AR	*Asiatic(k) Researches*
BI	*Buddhist India* (London)
Bibl. I.	*Bibliotheca Indica* (Calcutta)
BOE	*Bibliothèque orientale Elzévirienne* (Paris, Ernest Leroux)
IA	*Indian Antiquary* (Bombay and London)
JA	*Journal asiatique* (Paris)
JAOS	*Journal of the American Oriental Society* (Boston, New York and New Haven)
JASB	*Journal of the (Royal) Asiatic Society of Bengal* (Calcutta)
JBB(R)AS	*Journal of the Bombay Branch of the (Royal) Asiatic Society* (Bombay and London)
JCBRAS	*Journal of the Ceylon Branch of the Royal Asiatic Society* (Colombo)
JIA	*Journal of the Indian Archipelago* (Singapore)
JNCB	*Journal of the North-China Branch of the Royal Asiatic Society* (Shanghai)
JPTS	*Journal of the Pâli Text Society* (London)
JRAS	*Journal of the Royal Asiatic Society of Great Britain* (and Ireland) (London)
JS	*Journal des Savants* (Paris)
JSS	*Journal of the Siam Society* (Bangkok)
RDM	*Revue des Deux Mondes*
RHR	*Revue de l'Histoire des religions* (Paris)
SBE	*Sacred Books of the East* (Oxford)
TASJ	*Transaction of the Asiatic Society of Japan* (Yokohama and Tokyo)
TBG	*Tijdschrift voor Indische Taal-, Land-, en Volkenkunde, uitgeg. door het Kon. Bataviaansche Genootschap voor Kunsten en Wetenschappen*
TOS	*Trübner's Oriental Series* (London)
WZKM	*Wiener Zeitschrift für die Kunde des Morgenlandes* (Vienna)
ZDMG	*Zeitschrift der Deutschen Morgenländischen Gesellschaft* (Leipzig)
ZMkR	*Zeitschrift für Missionskunde und Religionswissenschaft*

Abh.	*Abhandlungen*
Ann.	Annals, annual, *Annalen, année, annuaire*, etc.
Aufl.	*Auflage*
Ausg.	*Ausgabe, Ausgeber*
Bibl.	*Bibliotheca, Bibliothek, Bibliothèque*, etc.
Ed., éd.	Edition, *édition*, edited, *édité*, etc.
Einl.	*Einleitung*
Enl.	Enlarged
Hrsg.	*Herausgegeben*
Impr.	*Imprimerie*
Inst.	Institute, *Institut*, etc.
J.	Journal
Jb.	*Jahrbuch, Jahrbücher*, etc.
Libr.	Library, *librairie*
Mb.	*Monatsbericht, Monatsberichte*, etc.
Mh.	*Monatsheft, Monatshefte*, etc.
Mly.	Monthly
n.d.	No date
n.s.	New Series
OUP	Oxford University Press
PTS	Pali Text Society (London)
Publ.	Publication, published, etc.
R.	*Revue*, review, etc.
RAS	Royal Asiatic Society of Great Britain (and Ireland)
Rec.	Recension, *Rezension*
Relig.	Religion, *religieux, religiös*, religious, etc.
Rev., rév.	*Revu, révision, réviseur*, Revision, revised
Roy.	Royal
Sb.	*Sitzungsberichte*
s.d.	*Sans date*, no date
Ser., sér.	Series, *série*, etc.
SPCK	Society for Promoting Christian Knowledge
Taf.	*Tafel, Tafeln*, table
Tr.	*Traduit, traduction*, translation, translated, etc.
Transac.	Transaction(s)
Übers.	*Übersetzung, übersetzt*
Übertr.	*Übertragung, übertragen*
Verl.	*Verlag*
Vorw.	*Vorwort*
Wiss.	*Wissenschaft, wissenschaftlich*, etc.
Z.	*Zeitschrift*

Bibliographical Milestones of the Seventeenth and Eighteenth Centuries

1638

Herbert, (Sir) Thomas. *Travels into Asia and Afrique*. "A relation of some yeares travaile, begunne Anno 1626, into Afrique and the Greater Asia of their religion, language, habit, discent, ceremonies, and c. 1638."

194 **1663**
Caron, Fr., and Schouten, J. *Wahrhaftige Beschreibungen zweyer mächtigen Königreiche: Japan, Siam und Corea*. Nürnberg, 1663.

1667
Kircher, Athanasius. *China, monumentis qua sacris qua profanis, nec non variis naturae et artis spectaculis, aliarumque rerum memorabilium argumentis illustrata*. Amstelodami, 1667.

1681
Knox, Robert. *An Historical Relation of the Island Ceylon in the East Indies*. "Together with an account of the detaining in captivity, the author and divers other Englishmen, and of the author's miraculous escape. With a pref. by R. Hook." London, R. Criswell Fol., 1681 (1705), 189 pp.

1689
Knox, Robert. *Ceylanische Reise-Beschreibung*. Leipzig, 1689.

1691
Loubère, M. de la. *Du Royaume de Siam*. Paris (Amsterdam), 1691. 2 vols.

1692
Knox, Robert. *T'Eyland in sijn binnenste, of 't Koningrijck Candy*. "Vertaeld door S. de Vries." Utrecht, 1692. [Tr.]

1693
Knox, Robert. *Relation ou Voyage de l'Ile de Ceylon, dans les Indes Orientales*. Amsterdam, 1693. 2 vols. in 1.

1701
Ribeyro, J. *Histoire de l'Ile de Ceylan*. Trans. from Portuguese into French. Paris, 1701. [Tr.]

1727
Davy, John. *Negende Reys na Oost-Indien van Engelse Maatschappy door Capiteyn E. Marlow, van Bristol . . . gedaan in het jaar 1611 en vervolgens, door John Davy beschreven*. Leyden, 1727.

1728
Kämpfer Engelbert. *The History of Japan*, "giving an account of the ancient and present state and government of that kingdom . . . religions, customs, trade . . . with a description of the Kingdom of Siam. Tr. by J. G. Scheuchzer." 1728. 2 vols. [Tr.]

1730
Bayer, Theophili Sig. *Museum Sinicum, in quo Sinicae linguae et literaturae ratio explicatur*. "Auctore Theophili Sig. Bayer." Petropoli, 1730. 2 vols., 372 pp.

1731–39
Knox, Robert. *The Ceremonies and Religious Customs of the Idolatrous Nations*. "Together with historical annotations, etc., written originally in French (Amsterdam 1723–43)." London, 1731–39. 7 vols. [Tr.]

1735
Halde, P. Jean Baptiste du. *Description géographique, historique, chronologique, politique et physique de l'Empire de la Chine et de la Tartarie Chinoise, enrichie des cartes générales et particulières de ces pays, etc*. Paris, 1735. 4 vols., 592, 726, 567, 520 pp.

1738
Crasset, Joannes R. P. *Ausführliche Geschicht der in dem äussersten Welt-Theil gelegenen japonesischen Kirch*. Augsburg: In Verlag Frantz Antoni Ilger, Cathol. Buchhändlern, 1738. 2 vols., 534, 559 pp.

1740
Penna (di Billa), Francesco. *Orazio della Missio apostolica, thibetano-seraphica*. Munich, 1740. 2 vols., 128, 248 pp. [Tr.]

1741

Halde, P. Jean Baptiste du. *General History of China.* "Done from the French of (J. B.) du Halde by R. Knox." London, 1741. 4 vols. [Tr.]

1744

Freret, M. *Recherches sur les traditions religieuses des Indiens pour servir de préliminaires à l'examen de leur chronologie. Collection de l'Ancienne Académie des Inscriptions,* vol. 18. Paris, 1744.

Guyon. *Histoire des Indes Orientales, anciennes et modernes.* 1744. 2 vols.

1756–58

Guignes, Joseph de. *Histoire générale des Huns, des Turcs, des Mogols et des autres Tartares occidentaux.* "Avant et depuis Jésus-Christ jusqu'à présent; précédée d'une introduction contenant des tables chronologiques et historiques des princes qui ont régné dans l'Asie." Paris, 1756–58. 4 vols.

1759

Guignes, Joseph de. *Recherches sur les philosophes appelés Samanéens, Paris, Mém. de Litt. tirés des registres de l'Acad. des Inscript.,* vol. 26, pp. 770–804. 1759.

1762

Georgius, Augustinus Antonius. *Alphabetum Tibetanum missionum apostolicarum commodo editum. Praemissa est disquisitio, qua de vario litterarum ac regionis nomine, gentis origine, moribus, superstitione, ac Manichaeismo fuse disseritur. Beausobrii Calumniae in S. Augustinum, aliosque Ecclesiae Patres refutantur.* Rome, 1762, 820 pp.

1771

Swedenborg, E. *The True Christian Religion.* Amsterdam, 1771.

1771–76

Pallas, Peter Simon. *Reisen durch verschiedene Provinzen des Russ. Reiches in den Jahren 1768–74.* St. Petersburg, 1771–76. 3 vols.

1773

Guignes, Joseph de. *Recherches historiques sur la religion indienne et sur les livres fondamentaux de cette religion, qui ont été tr. de l'indien en chinois, Paris, Mém. de Litt. tirés des registres de l'Acad. des Inscript.,* vol. 40. 167 pp. 1773. See J.-P. Abel-Rémusat, JA, 1831.

1776

Carpani, Melchiore. *Alphabetum Barmanum seu Bomanum regni Avae finitimarumque regionum.* Romae, 1776.

Herbelot, B. d'. *Bibliothèque orientale, ou Dictionnaire universel, contenant généralement tout ce qui regarde la connaissance des peuples de l'Orient.* "Supplément par C. Visdelon et A. Galand." Maestricht, 1776.

1776–78

Pallas, Peter Simon. *Reise durch verschiedene Provinzen des Russischen Reiches in einem ausführlichen Auszuge.* Frankfurt and Leipzig, 1776–78. 3 vols., 384, 52; 464, 51; 488, 80 pp.

1776–1801

Pallas, Peter Simon. *Sammlungen historischer Nachrichten über die mongolischen Völkerschaften.* St. Petersburg, Kaiserl. Akad. der Wiss., 1776–1801. 2 vols., 232, 437 pp.

1776–1814

Batteux, C. *Mémoires concernant l'histoire, les sciences, les arts, les mœurs et les usages des Chinois par les missionnaires de Pékin (Amyot, Bourgeois, Gibot, Ko. Poirot, Gaubil).* "Publ. par C. Batteux, de Bréquigny, de Guignes et Sylvestre de Sacy." Paris, 1776–1814. 16 vols. [Ed.]

1777–78

Kämpfer, Engelbert. *Geschichte und Beschreibung von Japan.* "Aus den Originalhandschriften des Verfassers hrsg. von Chr. Wilh. Dohm." Lemgo, Meyer'schen Buchhandlung, 1777–78. 2 vols., 310, 478 pp.

196   **1777–85**
Grosier, Abbé Jean Baptiste Gabriel Alex. *Histoire générale de la Chine.* Tr. J. A. M. de Moyriac de Mailla. Paris, 1777–85. [Ed.] See J. B. G. Grosier, 1828.

1778
Hollwell. *Hollwell's merkwürdige und historische Nachrichten von Hindostan und Bengalen, nebst einer Beschreibung der Religionslehren, der Mythologie, etc.* "Mit Anmerkungen und einer Ab-handlung über die Religion und Philosophie der Inder. Aus dem Englischen von J. F. Kleucker." Leipzig, 1778. [Tr.]

Stewart, John. *Account of the Kingdom of Tibet.* "In a letter from John Stewart to Sir John Pringle." *Philos. Transac. of the Roy. Soc. of London*, vol. 47, 24 pp. London, 1778.

1780
Guignes, Joseph de. *Observations sur quelques points concernant la religion et la philosophie des Egyptiens et des Chinois, Mém. de Litt. tirés des registres de l'Acad. des Inscript.*, vol. 40, pp. 163–86. Paris, 1780.

1782
Pallas, Peter Simon. *Beschreibung der feierlichen Verbrennung eines Kalmückischen Lamas oder Ober-priesters.*, vol. 3, pp. 375–82. St. Petersburg and Leipzig, Neue Nordische Beiträge, 1782.

1783
Hakmann. *Nachricht betreffend Erdbeschreibung, Geschichte und natürliche Beschaffenheit von Tybet.*, vol. 4, 38 pp. St. Petersburg and Leipzig, Neue Nordische Beiträge, 1783.

1785
Hunter. *A concise Account of the Kingdom of Pegu, its Climate, Produce, the Manners and Customs of its Inhabitants.* "With an appendix, to which is added a description of the caves at Ele-phanta, Ambola and Canara." Calcutta, 1785.

1787
Adler (Pr). *Kammuva.* "Einweihungsformular zum zweiten Grad der Bomanischen Mönche in Ava. Aus der heiligen Sprache der Bomanen. Übers. von Prof. Adler." Leipzig. *Egger's Deutsches Gemeinnütziges Mag.* 1, 16 pp. 1787. [Tr.]

Carpani, Melchiore. *Alphabetum Barmanorum seu regni Avensio.* Romae, Editio II.

Gladwin, F. *Dictionary of the Religious Ceremonies of the Eastern Nations.* "With historical and critical observations, some account of their learned men, and situations of the most remarkable places in Asia, to which is added a medical vocabulary." Calcutta, 1787.

1788
Chambers, William. *Some Account of the Sculptures and Ruins at Ma(ha)valipuram, a place a few miles north of Madras and known to seamen by the name of the Seven Pagodas. AR*, vol. 1, pp. 145–70. 1788.

Turner, Samuel. *An Account of a Journey to Tibet. AR*, vol. 1, 14 pp. 1788.

Wilkins, Charles. *Translation of a Sanscrit Inscription, copied from a stone at Boodha-Gaya by Mr Wilmot. AR*, vol. 1, pp. 284–87. 1788. [Tr.]

1790
Giuseppe (Father). *Account of the Kingdom of Nepal.* "Communicated by John Shore." *AR*, vol. 2, 16 pp. 1790.

1791
Guignes, Joseph de. *Das Buch des Fo aus der chinesischen Sprache.* "Ins Deutsche übersetzt (aus De Guignes' *Histoire des Huns*)." Zürich. *Sammlung Asiatischer Originalschriften*, vol. 1, 10 pp. 1791. [Tr.]

Loubère, M. de la. *Das Leben des Tewetats.* "Aus der balischen Sprache. Ins Deutsche übers. (Aus *Du Royaume de Siam*)." Zürich. *Sammlung Asiatischer Originalschr.*, vol. 1, 25 pp. 1791. [Tr.]

——. *Die vornehmsten Lebensregeln in Siam.* "Aus dem Siamischen übers. u. ins Deutsche 197 Übertr." *Sammlung Asiatischer Originalschr.*, vol. 1, 11 pp. Zürich, 1791. [Tr.]

——. *Erklärung des Patimuk oder der Winak.* "Aus der Bali-Sprache. Ins Deutsche übers." *Sammlung Asiatischer Originalschr.*, vol. 1, 2 pp. 1791. [Tr.]

1794

Ith, J. *Die Sittenlehre der Brahminen oder die Religion der Indianer.* Berne and Leipzig, Typographische Gesellschaft, 1794.

1795

Hüllmann, K. D. *Historisch-kritische Abhandlung über die Lamaische Religion.* Berlin, Carl Ludwig Hartmann, 1795. 54 pp.

Thunberg, Carl Peter. *Über die japanische Nation.* "Aus dem Schwedischen übers. von D. C. G. Gröning." Leipzig, Heinrich Gräff, 1795. 56 pp. [Tr.]

1796

Laxmann, Erich. *Sibirische Briefe von Erich Laxmann.* "Hrsg. von Schloezer and Jh. Beckmann." Göttingen, 1796.

1798

Duncan, Jonathan. *An Account of the Discovery of Two Urns in the vicinity of Benares. AR*, vol. 5, 2 pp. 1798.

Forster, J. R. *Des Fra Paolino da San Bartolomeo, Reise nach Ostindien.* Berlin, 1798. [Tr.]

Goldingham, C. *Some Account of the Sculptures at Mahabalipoorum usually called the Seven Pagodas. AR*, vol. 5, 12 pp. 1798.

Symes, Michael. *Of the City of Pegu and the Temple of Shoemadoo Praw. AR*, vol. 5, 12 pp. 1798.

1799

Buchanan, F. *On the Religion and Literature of the Burma. AR*, vol. 6, pp. 163–308. 1799.

Mackenzie, Colin. *Remarks on Some Antiquities on the West and South Coasts of Ceylon. Written in the year 1796. AR*, vol. 6, 33 pp. 1799.

1800

Turner, Samuel. *An Account of an Embassy to the Court of the Teshoo Lama in Tibet.* "Containing a narrative of a journey through Bootan, and part of Tibet." London, 1800. 473 pp.

1801

Mahony (Captain). *On Singhala, or Ceylon, and the Doctrines of Bhooddha, from the books of the Singhalais. AR*, vol. 7, pp. 32–56. 1801.

Städlin, C. F. *Über die Lamaische Religion, Hannover, Mag. f. Religions', Moral- u. Kirchengesch.*, vol. 1, 65, 120 pp. 1801.

Turner, Samuel. *Reisen nach Butan und Tibet.* "Aus dem Engl. in einem gedrängten Auszuge mitgeteilt von M. C. Sprengel." Weimar, Verl. des Industrie-Comptoirs, 1801. 151 pp. [Tr.]

1802

Peregrin, Felix. *Marco Polo.* "Reise in den Orient während der Jahre 1272 bis 1295. Nach den vorzüglichsten Originalausgaben verdeutscht und mit Kommentar begleitet von Felix Peregrin." Ronnernburg and Leipzig, 1802. 248 pp. [Tr.]

1803

Percival, (Captain) Robert. *An Account of the Island of Ceylon.* "Containing its history, geography, natural history, with the manners and customs of its various inhabitants to which is added the journal of an embassy to the Court of Candy." London, 1803.

1804

Bergmann, Benjamin. *Nomadische Streiferien mit den Kalmücken in den Jahren 1802 und 1803.* Riga, C. J. G. Hartmann, 1804–05. 4 vols., 352, 352, 302, 356 pp.

198 Langlès, L. *Rituel des Tartars-Mantchous rédigé par l'Ordre de l'Empereur Kien-long*. "Ouvrage tr. par extraits du Tartar-Mantchou et accompagné des textes originaux par L. Langlès." Paris, 1804. 74 pp. [Ed. and tr.]

Turner, Samuel. *Gesandtschaftsreise an den Hof des Teshoo Lama durch Bootan u. einen Theil von Tibet*. "Aus d. Engl. übers. Mit 1 Karte u. Kupfern." *Bibliothek der Neuesten und Interessantesten Reisesbeschreibungen*, vol. 7, 391 pp. Berlin, Hamburg, 1804. [Tr.]

1805

Wilford, (Captain) F. *An Essay on the Sacred Isles of the West*. AR, vol. 8, pp. 245–368. 1805.

Zimmermann, Ernst S. *Koreanische Kunst*. Hamburg, Carl Griese, 1805. 22 pp.

1806

Hager, Joseph. *Panthéon chinois, ou Parallèle entre le culte religieux des Grecs et celui des Chinois*. "Avec de nouvelles preuves que la Chine a été connue des Grecs, et que les Sérès des auteurs classiques ont été des Chinois." Paris, Didot l'aîné, 1806.

Maurice, Thomas. *Indian Antiquities, or Dissertations relative to the ancient geographical divisions, the pure system of primaeval theology, the grand code of civil laws, the original form of government, and the various and profound literature of Hindostan, etc*. London, 1806. 7 vols.

1807

Mackenzie, Colin. *Account of the Jains*. "Collected from a priest of this sect, at Mudgeri by Cavelly Boria, Brahman, for Colin Mackenzie." AR, vol. 9, pp. 244–85. 1807.

1808

Amiot. *Letter of the Emperor of China (Kien-long) to the Dalai-Lama*. Dalrymple's Or. Repertory. Vol. 2. London, 1808. 10 pp.

l'Etondac, M. *Account of the Lamas and Bonzes*. In French and English. London. Dalrymple's Or. Repertory. Vol. 2. London, 1808.

Frazer, Robert Watson. *A Literary History of India*. London, 1808. 470 pp.

Goosain, Poorun Geer. *Narrative of the Teshoo-Lâma's Journey to Pekin, in 1799 and 1780, and of his Death there*. London, Dalrymple's Or. Repertory. Vol. 2. 1808. 20 pp.

Leydenn. *On the Language and Literature of the Indo-Chinese Nations. Calcutta*. AR, vol. 10, 132 pp. 1808.

Reuilly. *Description du Thibet, d'après la description des Lamas Tangoutes*. Trans. from German by Reuilly. Paris, 1808. [Tr.]

Städlin, C. F. *De religione lamaice cum christiana cognatione*. Goettingoe, 1808.

1810

Moor, Edward. *The Hindu Pantheon*. London and Madras, 1810. 402 pp.

1811

Abel-Rémusat, Jean-Pierre. *Essai sur la langue et la littérature chinoises*. "Contenant des textes chinois accompagnés de traductions, de remarques et d'un commentaire littéraire et grammatical." Strasbourg, 1811. 16 pp. See G. de Humboldt, 1827.

Kirkpatrik, William. *Account of the Kingdom of Nepaul*. "Being the substance of observations made during a mission to that country in 1793." London, 1811.

1812

Klaproth, Julius Heinrich. *Voyages au Caucase et en Géorgie*. 1812. vols. 1–2.

1814

Klaproth, Julius Heinrich. *Reise in den Kaukasus und nach Georgien in den Jahren 1807 und 1808* "auf Veranstaltung der Kais. Akademie der Wissenschaften zu St. Petersburg." Halle and Berlin, 1814. 2 vols.

Städlin, C. F. *Über die Verwandtschaft der lamaischen Religion mit der christlichen*. Archiv. f. Alte u. Neuere Kirchengesch, vol. 1, 39 pp. Leipzig, 1814.

1815

Elphinstone, Mountstuart. *An Account of the Kingdom of Caubul, and Its Dependencies in Persia, Tartary and India, comprising a View of the Afghaun Nation and a History of the Dooraunee Monarchy*. London, 1815.

Fonvent, M. de. *Mythologie grecque, latine et slavonne, suivie d'un traité sur le Chamanisme, le Lamaïsme et l'ancienne religion des différents peuples soumis à la Russie*. Moscou, Vsevollojsky, 1815.

Francklin, William. *Inquiry Concerning the Site of Ancient Palibothra*. London, 1815–22, 4 vols., 90, 96, 60, 86 pp.

Ward, (Rev.) W. *A View of the History, Literature, and Mythology of the Hindoos*. Serampore, 1815.

1816

Carey, William. *An Account of the Funeral Ceremonies of a Burman Priest*. *AR*, reprint *As. J. and Mly. Reg.*, vol. 4, pp. 441–43; vol. 12, pp. 186–90. 1816–17.

1817

Abel-Rémusat, Jean-Pierre. *Mémoires sur les livres chinois de la Bibliothèque du Roi et sur le plan du nouveau catalogue dont la composition a été ordonnée par S. Ex. le Ministre de l'Intérieur*. "Avec des remarques critiques sur le catalogue publié par E. Fourmont, en 1742." *Ann. Encyclopédiques*. Paris, 1817, 1818.

Golownin, R. Y. *Begebenheiten in der Gefangenschaft bei den Japanern in den Jahren 1811, 1812 und 1813*. "Nebst seinen Bemerkungen über das japanische Reich und Volk, mit einem Anhange des Kapitäns Rikard. Aus dem Russischen übers. von Carl Johann Schultz." Leipzig, Gerhard Fleischer dem Jungeren, 1817–18. 2 vols. [Tr.]

Ozeray, Michel-Jean-François. *Recherches sur Buddou ou Bouddou, Instituteur religieux de l'Asie orientale*. "Précédées de considérations générales sur les premiers hommages rendus au Créateur, sur la corruption de la religion, l'établissement des cultes du soleil, de la lune, des planètes, du ciel, de la terre, des montagnes, des eaux, des forêts, des hommes et des animaux." Paris, Brunot-Labbé, 1817. 139 pp.

Philalethes (i.e. Robert Fellowes). *The History of Ceylon, from the Earliest Period to the Year 1815*. "With characteristic details of religion, laws and manners of the people and a collection of their moral maxims and ancient proverbs, to which is subjoined Robert Knox's *Historical Relation of the Island of Ceylon*." London, 1817.

Tytler, Robert. *Inquiry into the Origin and Principles of Budaic Sabism*. "Observations on the Worship of Buddha and Vishnu." Calcutta, 1817. 116 pp.

1818

Knox, Robert. *An Account of His Captivity in the Island of Ceylon*. "To which is prefixed a Sketch of the Geography, Civil and Natural History, etc., of Ceylon down to the year 1815." London, 1818.

Marsden, William. *The Travels of Marco Polo, a Venetian, in the Thirteenth Century*. "Being a description, by that early traveller, of remarkable places and things in the Eastern parts of the world. Tr. from the Italian with notes, by William Marsden." 1818. 781 pp., with a map. [Tr.]

Ward, (Rev.) W. *The Hindoos*. Serampore, 1818. 2 vols.

1819

Abel-Rémusat, Jean-Pierre. *Notes sur quelques épithètes descriptives de Bouddha*. *JS*, pp. 625–33. 1819.

Buchanan-Hamilton, F. *An Account of the Kingdom of Nepal and the Territories Annexed to this Dominion by the House of Gorkha*. Edinburgh, 1819.

Creuzer, G. F. *Symbolik und Mythologie der alten Völker, besonders der Griechen*. Von G. F. Creuzer.

200   Fortgesetzt von F. G. Mone. Leipzig, Darmstadt, 1819–23. 6 vols. See G. F. Creuzer, 1825.

Erskine, William Hugh. *Account of the Cave-Temple of Elephanta. Transac. of the Liter. Soc. of Bombay*, vol. 1, pp. 198–250. Bombay, 1819.

Golownin, R. Y. *Recollections of Japan*. "Religion, Language, Government, Laws and Manners of the People." 1819.

Wilson, Horace Hayman. *A Dictionary, Sanscrit and English*. Tr., amended and enl. from an original compilation prepared by learned natives. Calcutta, 1819.

1820

Abel-Rémusat, Jean-Pierre. *Histoire de la ville de Khotan*, 1820.

——. *Recherches sur les langues tartares, ou Mémoires sur différents points de la grammaire et de la littérature des Mantchous, des Mongols, des Oigours et des Tibétains*. Paris, 1820. 398 pp.

Crawfurd, John. *History of the Indian Archipelago*. "Containing an account of the manners, arts, languages, religions, institutions, and commerce of its inhabitants." Edinburgh, 1820. 3 vols.

——. *On the Ruins of Boro Budor in Java. Transac. of the Liter. Soc. of Bombay*, vol. 2, pp. 154–66. Bombay, 1820.

Erskine, William Hugh. *Note to F. Dangerfield's "Account of the Cave near Bang called the Panch Pandoo." Transac. of the Liter. Soc. of Bombay*, vol. 2, 11 pp. Bombay, 1820.

Körös, Alexander Csoma de. *Analysis of the Kah-gyur, etc. AR*, vol. 20, pp. 41–66. Bombay.

1821

Abel-Rémusat, Jean-Pierre. *Sur la succession des trente-trois premiers patriarches de la religion du Bouddha. JS*, Jan. 1821. 10 pp.

Cox, Hiram. *Journal of a Residence in the Burmham Empire and More Particularly at the Court of Amarapoorah*. London, 1821.

Davy, John. *An Account of the Interior of Ceylon and of Its Inhabitants. With Travels in That Island*. London, 1821.

Johnston, (Sir) Alexander. *Translation of the Cinghalese Book, Called Rajewaliye (Rajavali), History of Ceylon*. "Communicated by the Hon. Sir A. Johnston." *Ann. of Oriental Lit.*, part 3, 65 pp. London, 1821.

Knox, Robert. *An Historical Relation of the Island of Ceylon*. "With a Pref. by W. M. Harvard." 1821.

Langlès, L. *Monuments anciens et modernes de l'Hindoustan*. Paris, 1821. 2 vols.

1822

Sköldberg, Petrus Benjamin, et al. *De Buddha et Wodan*. Upsala, 1822. parts 1–4.

1823

Bergmann, D. *Exposé des principaux dogmes tibétains-mongols*. "Extrait de l'ouvrage de D. Bergmann et tr. par Morris." *JA*, vol. 3, pp. 193–204. 1823. [Tr.]

Erskine, William Hugh. *Observations on the Remains of the Bouddhists in India. Transac. of the Liter. Soc. of Bombay*, vol. 3, pp. 494–537. London, 1823.

Gauttier, E. *Ceylon ou Recherches sur les Chingalais*. Paris, 1823.

Klaproth, Julius Heinrich. *Asia Polyglotta, ou Classification des peuples de l'Asie d'après l'affinité de leurs langues, avec d'amples vocabulaires comparatifs de tous les idiomes asiatiques*. Paris (Atlas in Folio), 1823.

Schlegel, August Wilhelm. *Indische Bibliothek*. Bonn, 1823–27. 2 vols., 467, 474 pp.

Sykes, William Henry. *An Account of the Caves of Ellora. Transac. of the Liter. Soc. of Bombay*, vol. 3, pp. 265–323. London, 1823.

Abel-Rémusat, Jean-Pierre. *Aperçu d'un mémoire intitulé: "Recherches chronologiques sur l'origine de la hiérarchie lamaïque."* *JA*, vol. 4, pp. 257–74. 1824.

Clough, (Rev.) Benjamin. *Compendious Pali Grammar, with a copious vocabulary*, Colombo, 1824.

Klaproth, Julius Heinrich. *Beleuchtung und Widerlegung der Forschungen über die Geschichte der mittelasiatischen Völker des Herrn J. J. Schmidt.* "Mit einer Karte und zwei Schrifttaf." Paris, 1824. 108 pp. See I. J. Schmidt, 1826.

——. *Mémoires relatifs à l'Asie, contenant des recherches historiques, géographiques et philologiques sur les peuples de l'Asie.* Paris, 1824–28. 3 vols.

——. *Vie de Bouddha d'après les livres mongols. JA*, ser. 1, vol. 4, pp. 9–23, 65–79. 1824.

Schmidt, Isaac Jacob. *Forschungen im Gebiete der älteren religiösen, politischen und literarischen Bildungsgeschichte der Völker Mittel-Asiens, vorzüglich der Mongolen und Tibeter.* St. Petersburg, Karl Kray; Leipzig, Karl Knobloch, 1824. 287 pp.

1825

Abel-Rémusat, Jean-Pierre. *Mélanges asiatiques, ou Choix de morceaux de critiques et de Mémoires, relatifs aux religions, aux sciences, aux coutumes, à l'histoire et à la géographie des nations orientales*, 2 vols., 456, 428 pp. Paris, 1825–26. Including *Discours sur l'origine de la hiérarchie lamaïque*, vol. 1, pp. 129–45; *Sur l'étude de quelques-uns des livres sacrés de Bouddha*, vol. 1, pp. 146–52; *Sur quelques épithètes descriptives de Bouddha, qui font voir que Bouddha n'appartenait pas à la race nègre*, vol. 1, pp. 100–112.

Creuzer, G. F. *Les Religions de l'Antiquité, considérées principalement dans leurs formes symboliques et mythologiques.* "Ouvrage tr. de l'allemand de Creuzer et refondu et complété par J. G. Guigniaut." Paris, 1825. 960, 102 pp. [Tr.] See G. F. Creuzer, 1819.

Deshauterayes. *Recherches sur la religion de Fo, professée par les bonzes Hochang de la Chine. JA*, vol. 7; vol. 8, pp. 150–73, 228–43, 311–17; vol. 8, pp. 40–49, 74–88, 179–88, 219–23. 1825.

Dubois, Jean-Antoine, Mœurs. *Institutions et Cérémonies des peuples de l'Inde.* Paris, 1825. 2 vols.

Marryat (Capt.): Lieut. Joseph Moore and Capt. Marryat. *Views Taken at or near Rangoon.* "24 coloured aquatints, with leaf of dedication." 1825–26.

Schmidt, M. A.: J. E. G. von Timkowski. *Reise nach China in den Jahren 1820 und 1821.* Leipzig, 1825–26. 3 vols. [Tr.]

Tytler, Robert. *Illustrations of Ancient Geography and History.* "Referring to the sites of Ophir, Sheba, Taprobane, the Aurea Chersonesus, and other scriptural and classical cities and subjects; elucidating, also, the visit of the Queen of Sheba to Solomon, at Jerusalem, derived from recent investigations in the Eastern Indian Archipelago." London, 1825.

1826

Burnouf, Eugène (et Lassen, Christian). *Essai sur le Pali, ou Langue sacrée de la presqu'île au-delà du Gange*, "avec six planches lithographiées, et la notice des manuscrits palis de la Bibliothèque du Roi, par E. Burnouf et Chr. Lassen." Paris, Dondey-Dupré, 1826. 222 pp.

Finlayson, George. *The Mission to Siam and Hué, the Capital of Cochinchina, in the Years 1821–2.* "From the Journal of the late George Finlayson, with a memoir of the author by Sir T. Stamford Raffles." London, 1826.

Hodgson, Brian Houghton. *Notices of the Language, Literature and Religion of Nepal and Tibet.* *AR*, vol. 3. 1826.

Klaproth, Julius Heinrich. *Raja Tarangini*, tr. H. H. Wilson. Paris, 1826.

Malpière, D. B. de. *La Chine: mœurs, usages, coutumes, arts et métiers, peines civiles et militaires, cérémonies religieuses, etc.*, "avec des notes explicatives et une introd." Paris, 1826–39. 2 vols.

202   Othmar, Frank. *Vjâsa.* "Eine Zeitschrift über Philosophie, Mythologie, Literatur und Sprache der Hindu." Munich-Leipzig, Fried. Fleischer, 1826. vol. 1, fasc. 1, 52 pp.

Schmidt, Isaac Jacob. *Würdigung und Abfertigung der Klaproth'schen sogenannten "Beleuchtung und Widerlegung" seiner Forschungen.* Leipzig, 1826.

Symes, Michael. *An Account of an Embassy to the Kingdom of Ava sent by the Governor-General of India in 1795.* "To which is now added a narrative of the late military and political operations in the Burmese Empire, by H. G. Bell." 1826. 2 vols.

Wilson, Horace Hayman. *Raja Tarangini.* "Histoire du Kaschmir, tr. de l'original sanscrit par H. H. Wilson, extraite et communiquée par Klaproth." Paris, 1826. [Tr.]

1827

Bohlen, Petrus von. *De Buddhaismi origine et aetate definiendis tentamen.* "Auctore P. a Bohlen." Regiomonti, 1827. 40 pp.

Buchanan-Hamilton, F. *Description of Temples of the Jainas in South Bihar and Bhagalpur, Transac. RAS,* vol. 1, pp. 523–27. 1827.

——. On the Srawacs or Jains, Transac. *RAS,* vol. 1, pp. 531–38. 1827.

Burnouf, Eugène. *Observations grammaticales sur quelques passages de l'"Essai sur le pali." de MM. E. Burnouf et Ch. Lassen.* Paris, Dondey-Dupré, 1827. 30 pp.

——. Sur la littérature du Tibet. (Extr. du no. 7 du *Quarterly Oriental Magazine,* Calcutta, 1826.) *JA,* vol. 10, pp. 129–46. Calcutta, 1827.

Davis, (Sir) John Francis. *Memoir Concerning the Chinese, Transac. RAS,* vol. 1, 18 pp. 1827.

Francklin, Will. *Researches on the Tenets and Doctrines of the Jeynes and Buddhists conjectured to be the Brahmans of Ancient India, with discussion on Serpent Worship.* London, 1827. 213 pp., 6 pl.

Hodgson, Brian Houghton. *On the Extreme Resemblance between Buddhism and Sivaism. Qu. Or. Mag.,* vol. 7, pp. 218–22; vol. 8, pp. 252–56. Calcutta, 1827.

Humboldt, G. de. *Lettre à M. Abel-Rémusat sur la nature des formes grammaticales en général et sur le génie de la langue chinoise en particulier.* 1827.

Judson, H. *An Account of the American Baptist Mission to the Burmese Empire.* "In a series of letters by H. Judson." 2d ed. London, 1827.

Rhode, J. G. *Über religiöse Bildung, Mythologie und Philosophie der Hindus mit Rücksicht auf ihre älteste Geschichte.* Leipzig, F. A. Brockhaus, 1827. 2 vols., 456, 655 pp.

Timkowski, G. von. *Voyage à Péking, à travers la Mongolie, en 1820 et 1821, par G. Timkowski.* "Tr. du russe et revu par J. B. Eyriès. Publ. avec des notes et corrections par Klaproth." Paris, 1827. 2 vols. [Tr.]

Valantyn. *The Great Buddhoo.* "Tr. from the Dutch of Valentyn." *As. J. and Mly. Reg.,* vol. 23, 2 pp. London, 1827. [Tr.]

Windischmann, Carl Josef Hieron. *Die Philosophie im Fortgang der Weltgeschichte.* Bonn, Adolf Marcus, 1827–32. 2 vols. in 4 vols. See P. F. Stuhr, 1835.

1828

Bitschurin Iakynth (le père Hyacinthe). *Mémoire sur la Mongolie* (en russe). Saint-Pétersbourg, 1828. 2 vols.

Grosier, l'abbé Jean Baptiste Gabriel Alex. *De la Chine, ou Description générale de cet Empire,* "rédigée d'après les Mémoires de la Mission de Pé-kin par l'abbé J. B. A. Grosier." Paris, 1828–30. 3d ed. 7 vols.

Hodgson, Brian Houghton. *Notice of the Languages, Literature and Religion of the Bauddhas of Nepal and Bhot. AR,* vol. 16, pp. 409–49. 1828.

——. Sketch of Buddhism, Derived from the Bauddha Scriptures of Nepal. London, J. L. Cox, 1828. 37 pp. See B. H. Hodgson, 1835.

Hough, (Rev.) C. H. *Translation of an Inscription on the Great Bell of Rangoon.* "With notes and illus." *AR,* vol. 16, 13 pp. 1828.

Low, James. *A Grammar of the T'hai, or Siamese Language*. Calcutta, 1828.

Schmidt, Isaac Jacob. *Über die Verwandtschaft der gnostisch-theosophischen Lehren mit den Religionssystemen des Orients, vorzüglich dem Buddhaismus*. Leipzig, K. Knobloch, 1828. 25 pp.

Wilson, Horace Hayman. *Mackenzie Collection*. "A descriptive catalogue of the Oriental manuscripts, and other articles illustrative of the literature, history, statistics, and antiquities of the south of India, collected by Colin Mackenzie." Calcutta, 1828. 2 vols., 358; 150, 14 pp.

———. *Notice of Three Tracts received from Nepal*. *AR*, vol. 16, 25 pp. 1828.

1829

Abel-Rémusat, Jean-Pierre, *Nouveaux Mélanges asiatiques, ou Recueil de morceaux de critiques et de Mémoires relatifs aux religions, aux sciences, aux coutumes, à l'histoire et à la géographie des nations orientales*. Paris, 1829. 2 vols.

Alexander, James Edward, *Notice of a Visit to the Cave Temple of Adjunta in the East-Indies, Transac. RAS*, vol. 2, 9 pp. 1829.

Bitschurin Iakynth (le père Hyacinthe). *Description of Tibet*, "tr. du chinois en russe par le père Hyacinthe, et du russe en français par M. . . ; revue sur l'original chinois, et accompagnée de notes par M. Klaproth." *Nouv. JA*, vol. 4, pp. 81–160, 241–324. 1829. [Tr.]

Callaway, John. *Yakkun Nattannawa*. "A Cingalese poem, descriptive of the Ceylon system of demonology; to which is appended *The Practices of a Capua, or Devil Priest*, as described by a Buddhist; and *Kolan Nattannawa, a Cingalese Poem*, descriptive of the characters assumed by natives of Ceylon in a masquerade. Illus. with pl. from Cingalese designs. Tr. by J. Callaway." London, 1829. [Tr.]

Crawfurd, John. *Journal of an Embassy from the Governor-General of India to the Courts of Siam and Cochin China*. "Exhibiting a view of the actual state of those kingdoms." London, 1829.

Johnston, (Sir) Alexander. *An Account of an Inscription Found near Trincomalee in the Island of Ceylon. JRAS*, vol. 2, 4 pp. 1829.

Koester, Hans. *The Indian Religion of the Goddess Shakti. JSS*, vol. 23, pp. 1–18. July 1829.

Schmidt, Isaac Jacob. *Geschichte der Ost-Mongolen und ihres Fürstenhauses, verfasst von Ssanang Ssetsen Chungtaidschi der Ordus*. "Aus dem Mongolischen übers., und mit dem Originaltexte, nebst Anmerk., Erläut., und Zitaten aus andern unediten Originalwerken, hrsg. von I. J. Schmidt." St. Petersburg, N. Grestch; Leipzig, Karl Knobloch, 1829. 510 pp. [Ed. and tr.]

Upham, Edward. *The History and Doctrine of Buddhism, Popularly Illustrated*. "With Notices of the Kappooism or Demon Worship and of the Bali or Planetary Incantations of Ceylon, embellished with 43 lithographic prints from original singalese designs." London, R. Ackermann, 1829. 136 pp.

1830

Alexander, James Edward. *Cavern Temples of Ajanta. Transac. RAS*, p. 362. 1830.

Bitschurin Iakynth (le père Hyacinthe). *Description of Tibet*, "tr. du chinois en russe par le père Hyacinthe, et du russe en français par M . . . ; revue sur l'original chinois, et accompagnée de notes par M. Klaproth." *Nouv. JA*, vol. 6, pp. 161–246, 321–50, 1 map (du Tibet). 1830. [Tr.]

Bohlen, Petrus von. *Das Alte Indien, mit besonderer Rücksicht auf Ägypten dargestellt*. Königsberg, Verlag der Gebr. Bornträger, 1830. 2 vols., 392, 496 pp.

Buchanan-Hamilton, F. *Description of the Ruins of Buddha Gaya, Transac. RAS*, vol. 2, pp. 40–51. 1830.

Davis, Samuel. *Remarks on the Religious and Social Institutions of the Bouteas, or Inhabitants of Boutan*. "From the unpublished journal of the late S. Davis." *Transac. RAS*, vol. 2, pp. 491–517. 1830.

204   Hodgson, Brian Houghton. *Notice sur la langue, la littérature et la religion des Bouddhistes du Népal et du Bhot ou Tibet.* Communiquée à la Société Asiatique de Calcutta, JAS, ser. 2, vol. 6., 40, 23 pp. 1830.

1831

Abel-Rémusat, Jean-Pierre. *Essai sur la cosmographie et la cosmogonie des Bouddhistes d'après les auteurs chinois. JS,* 14, 7, 16 pp. Oct.–Dec. 1831.

——. *Observations sur quelques points de la doctrine samanéenne, et en particulier sur les noms de la triade suprême chez les différents peuples bouddhistes.* Paris, 1831. 67 pp.

——. *Observations sur trois Mémoires de M. de Guignes insérés dans le tome XL de la Collection de l'Académie des Inscriptions et Belles-Lettres, et relatifs à la religion samanéenne. Nouv. JA,* vol. 7, pp. 241–302. 1831.

Bochinger, Johann Jacob. *La Vie contemplative, ascétique et monastique chez les Indous et chez les peuples bouddhistes,* Strasbourg, F. G. Levrault, 1831. 244 pp.

Desideri, Ippolito (ou Hippolyte). *Notes sur le Tibet par le P. Hippolyte Desideri, recueillies par N. Delisle, Nouv. JA,* vol. 8, 4 pp. 1831.

Hodgson, Brian Houghton. *Disputation Respecting Caste by a Buddhist.* "In the form of a series of propositions supposed to be put by a Saiva and refuted by the disputant, communicated by B. H. Hodgson." *Transactions of the JRAS,* vol. 3, pp. 160–69. 1831.

Kennedy, C. P. *Hindu Mythology.* London, 1831.

Klaproth, Julius Heinrich. *Account of Japan, Extracted from Japanese Works.* London. *As. J. and Mly. Reg.,* n.s., vol. 6, 16 pp. 1831.

——. *Explication et Origine de la formule bouddhique "Om mani padmé hoûm." JA,* ser. 2, vol. 7, pp. 185–206. 1831.

——. *Fragments bouddhiques.* Paris, 1831.

——. *Notes sur le Tibet par Hippolyte Desideri, recueillies par N. Delisle, JA,* ser. 2, vol. 7, 12 pp. 1831.

——. *Origin and Meaning of the Buddhist Prayer.* London. *As. J. and Mly. Reg.* n.s., vol. 5, pp. 271–77. 1831.

——. *Table chronologique des plus célèbres patriarches et des événements remarquables de la religion bouddhique, rédigée en 1678,* "tr. du mongol et commentée." *JA,* n.s., vol. 7, pp. 161–85. 1831.

Law, (Capt.) J. *On Buddha and the Phrabat (or Divine Foot), from Siamese sources.* 1831.

Miles, Wm. *On the Jainas of Gujerat and Marwar, Transac. of RAS,* vol. 3, 37 pp. 1831.

Neumann, Carl Friedrich. *Choo Hung, The Catechism of the Shamans, or The Laws and Regulations of the Priesthood of Buddha in China.* "Tr. from the Chinese original, with notes and illus." London, 1831. 152 pp.

Wilson, Horace Hayman. *Note on the Literature of Thibet, Calcutta, Gleanings in Science,* vol. 3, pp. 243–48. 1831.

——. *Notice sur trois ouvrages bouddhiques reçus du Népal, JA,* ser. 2, vol. 7, pp. 97–138. 1831.

1832

Abel-Rémusat, Jean-Pierre. *Observations sur l'histoire des Mongols orientaux de Ssanang Ssetsen, Nouv. JA,* 88 pp. 1832.

——. *Voyage dans la Tartarie, dans l'Afghanistan et dans l'Inde. RDM,* vols. 5, 11 pp. Paris, 1832.

Adelung, Fr. *Historical Sketch of Sanskrit Literature.* "With copious bibliographical notices of Sanskrit works and translations. From the German, with additions." 1832. 234 pp. [Tr.]

Ampère, J. J. *De la Chine et des travaux de M. Rémusat. RDM,* vol. 8, ser. 2, vols. 4, 31, 27, 35 pp. Paris, 1832–33.

Coleman, Charles. *Buddha.* In *The Mythology of the Hindus,* pp. 184–219. London, 1832.

Körös, Alexander Csoma de. *Geographical Notice of Tibet. JASB,* vol. 1, pp. 121–27. 1832.

———. *Translation of a Tibetan Fragment.* "With remarks by H. H. Wilson." *JASB*, vol. 1, pp. 269– 205 76. 1832.

Lamiot. *Ta-T'ang-Hsi-Yu-Chi.* "Esquisse du Sy-yu, ou des pays à l'ouest de la Chine." Tr. from Chinese. Paris, 1832. 2 parts. [Tr.]

Schmidt, Isaac Jacob. *Über einige Grundlehren des Buddhismus, Mém. de l'Acad. impér. d. Sc. de St.- Pétersbourg,* ser. 6: *Sc. Polit. Hist. et Philol.,* vol. 1., pp. 90–120, 222–62. 1832.

Wilson, Horace Hayman. *Abstract of the Contents of the Dul-va, or First Portion of the Kah-gyur, from the analysis of Mr Alexander Csoma de Körös, JASB,* vol. 1, pp. 1–8. 1832.

———. *Analysis of the Kah-gyur, JASB,* vol. 1, pp. 375–92. 1832.

1833

Bitschurin Iakynth (le père Hyacinthe). *History of Tibet and Kukunora.* Tr. from Chinese (in Russian). 2 vols., 260 pp. Saint-Pétersbourg, 1833. [Tr.]

Gützlaff, Karl Friedrich Augustus. *On the Present State of Buddhism in China.* London, s.d.

———. *The Buddhism of Siam. Chinese Repository,* vol. 1, 3 pp. Canton, 1833.

Hodgson, Brian Houghton. *Remarks on an Inscription in the Ranja and Tibetan (U'chhên) Charac- ter, Taken from a Temple on the Confines of the Valley of Nepal. JASB,* vol. 1, 5 pp.; vol. 4, pp. 196–98. 1833–35.

Körös, Alexander Csoma de. *Note on the Origin of the Kala Chakra and Adi-Buddha Systems. JASB,* vol. 2, pp. 57–59. 1833.

———. *Origin of the Shakya Race.* "Tr. from the La or the 26th vol. of the Do Class in the Kagyur, commencing on the 161st leaf." *JASB,* vol. 2, pp. 385–92. 1833. [Tr.]

Neumann, Carl Friedrich. *Pilgerfahrten buddh. Priester von China nach Indien.* "Aus dem Chin. übers. mit einer Einl. und mit Anm. versehen." *Z. f. die Hist. Theol.,* vol. 3, pp. 114–77. 1833. [Tr.]

Prinsep, Henry Thoby, and Prinsep, J. *Bactrian and Indo-Scythian Coins. JASB,* vol. 2, 12 pp. 1833.

Sangermano (R. P.). *A Description of the Burmese Empire.* "Compiled chiefly from native documents, by the Rev. Father Sangermano, and tr. from his MSS. by William Tandy." Rome, 1833. 224 pp. [Tr.]

Sykes, William Henry. *Personal Ornaments on Figures at the Buddha Cave Temple at Carli. JRAS,* p. 451. 1833.

Turnour, (Hon.) George. *An Epitome of the History of Ceylon, from Pali and Singhalese Records.* "With Notes." *Ceylon Almanac for 1833.* Colombo, 1833. 69 pp.

Upham, Edward. *The Mahavansa, the Raja-ratnacari and the Raja-vali.* "Forming the sacred and historical books of Ceylon; also, a collection of tracts illustrative of the doctrines and literature of Buddhism. Tr. from the Singhalese. Ed. by Edward Upham." 3 vols., 358, 326, 370 pp. London, Parpury, Allen, 1833. [Tr.]

———. *The Miniature of Buddhism in a Description of the Objects Represented in the Buddhist Temple Imported from India, and Opened for Public Inspection, at Exeter Hall.* London, J. Stephens, 1833. 20 pp.

1834

Benevolens. *Burmah:* "Doctrines and practices of the Buddhists; their geography, astronomy, and upper regions; rewards and punishments; their periods (or ages); duties; ideas of death, worship and c." *Chinese Repository,* vol. 2, pp. 554–63. Canton, 1834.

Clough, (Rev.) Benjamin. *The Ritual of the Buddhist Priesthood.* "Tr. from the original Pali work, entitled *Karmawakya,* by the Rev. Benjamin Clough. (In his *Miscellaneous Translations from Oriental Language*)." *Or. Tr. Fund,* vol. 3, 30 pp. London, 1830. [Tr.]

Court, A. *Remarks on the Name and Origin of the Topes of Manikyala,* "corrected by A. Cun- ningham." *JASB,* vol. 3, pp. 556–57. 1834.

206   Forbes, J. *Matale Antiquities.* "Description of the principal temples and ancient buildings in the Matale District and Kellania near Colombo." *Ceylon Almanac* for 1834. 7 pp. Colombo, 1834.

Hodgson, Brian Houghton. *Classification of the Néwârs of Aborigines of Népal Proper, Preceded by the Most Authoritative Legend Relative to the Origin and Early List of Phrase. JASB*, vol. 3, 7 pp. 1834.

———. *European Speculations on Buddhism. JASB*, vol. 3, pp. 382–88. 1834.

———. *Notice of Adi-Buddha and of the Seven Mortal Buddhas, JASB*, vol. 3, p. 215. 1834.

———. *On Bauddha Inscriptions. JASB*, vol. 3. 1834.

———. *Remarks on Remusat's Buddhism. JASB*, vol. 3, pp. 425–31, 499. 1834.

———. *Second Note on the Bhilsa Inscriptions. JASB*, vol. 3, 7 pp. 1834.

Kennedy, C. P., Alex. *Csoma Körösi. JRAS*, p. 128. 1834.

Körös, Alexander Csoma de. *A Dictionary, Tibetan and English.* Calcutta and London, 1834. 352 pp.

———. *Essay towards a Dictionary Tibetan and English.* "Bande Sangs-Rgyas Phun-Tshogs." Calcutta, 1834.

———. *Extracts from Tibetan Works.* "Tr. by M. Alexander Csoma de Körös." *JASB*, vol. 3, pp. 57–61. 1834. [Tr.]

———. *A Grammar of the Tibetan Language in English.* "Prepared under the patronage of the Government and the auspices of the Asiatic Soc. of Bengal." Calcutta, 1834. 2 parts, pp. 204–40.

Mill, W. H. *Restoration of the Inscription no. 2 on the Allahabad Column. JASB*, vol. 3, pp. 257–70, 339–44. 1834.

Neumann, Carl Friedrich. *Coup d'œil historique sur les peuples et la littérature de l'Orient. JA*, n.s., vol. 14, 35, 32 pp. 1834.

———. *Der Katechismus der Schamanen, oder Die Kloster-regel der untersten Klasse der buddhistischen Priesterschaft.* "Aus dem Chin. übers. und mit erlaüt. Anm. versehen." *Z. f. die Hist. Theol.*, vol. 4, pp. 1–70. 1834. [Tr.]

O'Brien, Henry. *The Round Towers of Ireland, or The Mysteries of Freemasonry, Sabaism and of Buddhism, for the First Time Unveiled.* London, 1834.

Philosinensis (pseud.). *Remarks on Buddhism.* "Together with brief notices of the Island of Poo-to, and the numerous priests who inhabit it." *Chinese Repository*, vol. 2, pp. 214–25. Canton, 1834.

Prinsep, Henry Thoby, and Prinsep, J. *Note on the Bauddha Image from Kabul. JASB*, vol. 3. 1834.

———. *Note on the Coins Discovered by M. Court. JASB*, vol. 3, pp. 562–66. 1834.

———. *On the Coins and Relics Discovered in the Topes of Manikyala. JASB*, vol. 3, pp. 318–436. 1834.

Ritter, Carl. *Die Entstehung der lamaischen Hierarchie und der westlichen Suprematie der Chinesen über das Volk der Tübete, Ritter's Erdkunde von Asien*, vol. 3, pp. 274–87. Berlin, 1834.

Schmidt, Isaac Jacob. *Über die sogenannte dritte Welt der Buddhisten.* "Als Forsetzung der Ab-handl. über die Lehren des Buddhismus." *Mém. de l'Acad. impér. d. Sc. de St.-Pétersbourg*, ser. 6. *Sc. polit. hist. et philol.*, vol. 2, pp. 1–39. 1834.

———. *Über die Tausend Buddhas einer Weltperiode oder gleichmässiger Dauer., Mém. de l'Acad. impér. d. Sc. de St.-Pétersbourg*, ser. 6: *Sc. polit. hist. et philol.*, vol. 2, pp. 41–86. 1834.

Schmitt, Joseph Hermann. *Uroffenbarung oder Die grossen Lehren des Christentums*, "nachgew. i. d. Sagen u. Urkunden der ältest. Völker, vorzügl. i. d. kan. Büchern der Chinesen." Landshut, Vienna; G. Joseph Manz, Karl Gerold, 1834.

Stevenson, (Rev.) John. *Restoration and Translation of Some Inscriptions at the Cave of Carli. JASB*, vol. 3, 4 pp. 1834.

Sykes, William Henry. *Remarks on the Identity of the Personal Ornaments Sculptured on Some Figures*   207
    in the Buddha Cave Temples at Carli with Those Worn by the Brinjaris. Transac. of the RAS, vol. 3,
    1 pp. 1834.

Troyer, A. *Remarks upon the Second Inscription of the Allahabad Pillar. JASB*, vol. 3, pp. 118–23.
    1834.

Turnour, (Hon.) George. *A Revised Chronological Table of the Sovereigns of Ceylon, Colombo, Ceylon*
    Almanac for 1834, 10 pp. 1834.

———. *Translations of Inscriptions to Serve as an Appendix to the "Epitome of the History of Ceylon with*
    an Introduction." Ceylon Almanac for 1834. 22 pp. Colombo, 1834. [Tr.]

Walter, H. *Translation of an Inscription in the Pali and Burmese Languages on a Stone Slap from*
    Ramavati (Ramree Island) in Arracan, "presented to the Asiatic Society by H. Walter, as
    explained by Ratna Paula." *JASB*, vol. 3, 5 pp. 1834. [Tr.]

1835

Armour, J. *Essay on Buddhism.* Ceylon Almanac for 1835. Colombo, 1835. 22 pp. [Tr.]

Blagdon, F. W. *A Brief History of India, Ancient and Modern: From the Earliest Periods of Antiquity to*
    the Termination of the Mahratta War. Calcutta, 1835.

Burney, H. *Notice of Pugan, the Ancient Capital of the Burmese Empire. JASB*, vol. 4, 5 pp. 1835.

Chapman, I. J. *Some Remarks upon the Ancient City of Anarajapura or Anaradhepura, and the Hill*
    Temple of Mehentélé, in the Island of Ceylon. Transac. RAS, vol. 3, pp. 463–95. 1835.

Forbes, J. *The Dangistra Dalada, or Right Canine Tooth of Gautama Buddha. Ceylon Almanac for*
    1835. 1835. 6 pp.

Gützlaff, Karl Friedrich Augustus. *Missionar Gützlaffs zweite u. dritte Reise nach China*, pp. 179–
    328. 1835.

Hardy, (Rev.) R. Spence. *Notices of the Holy Land and Other Places Mentioned in the Scriptures,*
    Visited in 1832–3. London, 1835. See R. S. Hardy, 1836.

Hodgson, Brian Houghton. *Account of a Visit to the Ruins of Simroun, Once the Capital of the*
    Mithila Province. JASB, vol. 4, pp. 121–24. 1835.

———. *Further Note on the Inscriptions from Sarnath. JASB*, vol. 4, pp. 196–99. 1835.

———. *Quotations from Original Sanskrit Authorities in Proof and Illustration of His "Sketch of Bud-*
    dhism." JRAS, vol. 2, pp. 288–323. 1835. See B. H. Hodgson, 1828.

Knox, George William. *The Ceremonial of the Ordination of a Burmese Priest of Buddha.* "With
    notes. Communicated by G. Knox." *JRAS*, vol. 3, pp. 271–84. 1835.

Körös, Alexander Csoma de. *Analysis of a Tibetan Medical Work. JASB*, vol. 4, pp. 1–20. 1835.

Low, James. *On Buddha and the Phrabât (or Divine Foot). JRAS*, vol. 3, pp. 57–127. 1835.

Neumann, Carl Friedrich. *Buddhism and Shamanism. As. J. and Mly. Reg.*, vol. 16, pp. 124–26.
    1835.

Palma, G. *Discorso in difesa degli ordini religiosi. Ann. delle Scienze Religiose*, ser. 1. 1835.

Penna (di Billa), Francesco. *Orazio della Breve notizia del Regno de Thibet 1730.* "Ouvrage publ.
    d'après le manuscrit autographe de l'auteur (Fra Francesco Orazio della Penna di Billa)
    et accompagné de notes par M. Klaproth." *JA*, 79 pp. 1835.

Prinsep, Henry Thoby, and Prinsep, J. *Further Particulars of the Sarum and Tirhut Laths and*
    Account of Two Buddhist Inscriptions Found, the One at Bakh (Tirhut) and the Other at Sarnath
    near Benares. JASB, vol. 4, pp. 124–28. 1835.

Schmidt, Isaac Jacob. *Mongolisch-Deutsch-Russisches Wörterbuch.* St. Petersburg, 1835.

Stevenson, (Rev.) John. *Excursion to the Ruins and Site of an Ancient City near Bakhra.* "Extract
    from the Journal of J. Stevenson." *JASB*, vol. 4, 10 pp. 1835.

Stuhr, P. F. *Die chinesische Reichsreligion und die Systeme der indischen Philosophie in ihrem Verhältnis*
    zu Offenbarungslehren. "Mit Rücksicht auf die Ansichten von Windischmann, Schmitt
    und Ritter." Berlin, Veit, 1835. 109 pp.

208   1836

[Abeel, David]. *Reise des nordamerikanischen Missionars*, "Herrn David Abeel, in den Ländern Hinterindiens in den Jahren 1830 bis 1833." *Mag. f. d. Neueste Gesch. d. Evangel. Missions- u. Bibelgesell*, pp. 155–344. 1836.

Abel-Rémusat, Jean-Pierre. *Foé Koué Ki, ou Relation des royaumes bouddhiques. Voyage dans la Tartarie, dans l'Afghanistan et dans l'Inde, exécuté à la fin du iv⁵ siècle par Chy Fa Hian.* "Ouvrage posthume revu, complété et augmenté d'éclaircissements nouveaux par Klaproth et Landresse. Tr. du chinois et commenté par Abel-Rémusat." Paris, Impr. roy., 1836. 424 pp. [Tr.] See Landresse, *infra.*

Burney, H. *Discovery of Buddhist Images with Deva-nagari Inscription at Tagoung, the Ancient Capital of the Burman Empire. JASB*, vol. 5, pp. 157–64. 1836.

——. *Translation of an Inscription in the Burmese Language, discovered at Buddha-Gaya in 1833. AR*, vol. 20, pp. 161–89. 1836.

Colebrooke, W. M. G. *Account of a Ceremonial Exhibition of the relic termed "the Tooth of Buddha," at Kandy, in Ceylon, in May 1828.* "Tr. and abridged from the original Singhalese, drawn up by a Native Eyewitness. (Communicated by Lieut.-Col. W. M. G. Colebrooke)." *JRAS*, vol. 3, pp. 161–64. 1836.

Davis, Sir John Francis. *The Chinese.* "A general description of the Empire of China and its inhabitants." London, Charles Knight, 1836. 2 vols., 420, 480 pp.

Eckstein, Baron d'. *Narasinha Oupanichat.* "Analyse de cet ouvrage par le baron d'Eckstein." *JA*, ser. 3, vol. 2, pp. 466–90. 1836.

Forbes, J. *Notes on the Buddhas from Ceylonese Authorities.* "With an attempt to fix the dates of the appearance of the last four, being those of the Maha Bhadra Kalpa." *JASB*, vol. 5, pp. 321–30. 1836.

Grindlay, Robert Melville. *An Account of Some Sculptures in the Cave-Temples of Ellora. JRAS*, vol. 2, pp. 326, 487. 1836.

Hardy, (Rev.) R. Spence. *Travels in the Holy Land and Other Places Mentioned in the Scriptures, in 1832–3. Christian Library*, vol. 5, 86 pp. 1836. [New ed.] See R. S. Hardy, 1835.

Hodgson, Brian Houghton. *Letter about Buddhist and Sanskrit MSS. from Nepal. JRAS*, p. vii. 1836.

——. *Note on the Inscription from Sarnath. JASB*, vol. 5, pp. 29, 71. 1836.

——. *Quotations re Buddhism. JRAS*, p. 391. 1836.

Jacquet, Eugène. *Notice of the Vallabhi Dynasty of Saurashta, Extracted from the Buddhist Records of the Chinese. JASB*, vol. 5, pp. 685–88. 1836.

Körös, Alexander Csoma de. *Abstract of the Contents of the Bstan-gyur. AR*, vol. 20, pp. 553–85. 1836.

——. *Analysis of the Dulva, a Portion of the Tibetan Work Entitled the Kah-gyur. AR*, vol. 20, pp. 41–93. 1836.

——. *Analysis of the Sher-chin, Phal-chhen, Dkon-seks, Do-de, Nyang-das and Gyut.* "Being divisions 2 to 7 of the Tibetan work entitled Kah-gyur." *AR*, vol. 20, pp. 393–552. 1836.

——. *Interpretation of the Tibetan Inscription of a Bhotian Banner taken in Assam. JASB*, vol. 5, pp. 264–66. 1836.

——. *Notices of the Life of Shakya, extracted from Tibetan Authorities. AR*, vol. 20, pp. 285–317. 1836.

——. *Translation of a Tibetan Sloka. JASB*, vol. 5, p. 384. 1836.

Kowalewsky. *Chrestomathie mongole* (en russe). Kazan, 1836–37. 2 vols., 592, 600 pp.

Landresse. *Aperçu des travaux de M. Rémusat sur le Bouddhisme, ou Introduction à son commentaire sur le Foé Koué Ki*. Paris, 1836.

Lenz, R. *Analyse du Lalita-vistara-pourana, l'un des principaux ouvrages sacrés des Bouddhistes de*

l'Asie centrale, contenant la vie de leur prophète, et écrit en Sanscrit. Bull. scient. de l'Acad. de St.-
Pétersbourg, vol. 1. St. Petersburg, 1836.

Lloyd, Major T. H. A. *Note on the White Satin Embroidered Scarf of the Tibetan Priest.* "With a translation of the motto by Csoma de Körös." *JASB*, vol. 5, 2 pp. 1836.

Schmidt, Isaac Jacob. *Über das Mahâjâna und Pradschnâ-Pâramita der Bauddhen.* Berlin, 1836. 106 pp.

——. *Über die Begründung des tibetischen Sprachstudiums in Russland und die Herausgabe der dazu nötigen Hilfswerke. Bull. scient. de l'Acad. de St.-Pétersbourg*, vol. 1, pp. 11–13. 1836.

——. *Über Lamaismus und die Bedeutungslosigkeit dieses Namens, Bull. scient. de l'Acad. de St.-Pétersbourg*, vol. 1, no. 2. 1836.

Stuhr, P. F. *Die Religionssysteme der heidnischen Völker des Orients*, vol. 12, 478 pp. Berlin, Veit, 1836.

Turnour, (Hon.) George. *Examination of Some Points of Buddhist Chronology. JASB*, vol. 5, pp. 521–36. 1836.

——. *The First Twenty Chapters of the Mahawanso, and a Prefatory Essay on Pali Buddhistical Literature.* "Originally publ. as an introduction to the above-mentioned portion of the *Mahawanso.*" Colombo, 1836. 140 pp.

1837

[Academia Albertina]. *De Buddhaismi origine et aetate definiendis, testamen quod auctoritate illustris philosophorum, in Academia Albertina ordinis pro dignitate professoris extraordinarii in eodem obtinenda.* Königsberg, 1837. 40 pp.

Adelung, Fr. *Literatur der Sanskrit Sprache.* St. Petersburg, Bibl. Sanskrita, 1837.

Ampère, J. J. *Histoire du Bouddhisme: Relation des royaumes bouddhiques,* "tr. du chinois par Abel-Rémusat." *RDM*, Paris, 15 June 1837. 2 pp.

Davis, Sir John Francis. *La Chine, ou Description générale des mœurs et des coutumes, du gouvernement, des lois, des religions, des sciences, de la littérature, des productions naturelles, des arts, des manufactures et du commerce de l'Empire Chinois.* "Ouvrage tr. de l'anglais par A. Pichard. Revu et augmenté d'un appendice par Bazin aîné . . ." Paris, Libr. de Paulin, 1837. 2 vols., 397, 418 pp. [Tr.]

Gogerly, (Rev.) Daniel John. *The Pansiya-panas-Jataka-pota. The Friend*, vol. 1; 2, 4, 1, 9 pp. Colombo, 1837–38. [Tr.]

Hodgson, Brian Houghton. *Note on the Primary Language of the Buddhist Writings. JASB*, vol. 6, pp. 682–89. 1837.

Jaquet, E. *Notice sur les d'écouvertes archéologiques faites par Königsberger pendant son séjour dans l'Afghanistan. JA*, p. 234. 1836; p. 401. 1837.

Köppen, Carl Friedrich. *Literarische Einleitung in die Nordische Mythologie.* Berlin, 1837.

Kowalewsky. *Cosmologie bouddhiste* (en russe). *Transac. of the Kasan Univ.*, part 1. Kazan, 1837.

Mill, W. H. *Restoration and Translation of the Inscription on the Bhutari lat.* "With critical and historical remarks." *JASB*, vol. 6, pp. 1–17. 1837.

Neumann, Carl Friedrich. *Japan.* In *Allgemeine Enzyklopaedia der Wissenschaften und Künste*, ed. J. S. Ersch and J. G. Gruber, sect. 2, vol. 14, pp. 366–78. Leipzig, 1837.

Newbold, T. J. *Notes on the Code and Historical MSS. of the Siamese and on the Progress of Buddhism to the Eastward. J. of Lit. and Sc.*, vol. 4, pp. 1–16. Madras, 1837.

Pauthier, G. *La Chine, ou Description historique, géographique et littéraire de ce vaste empire d'après les documents chinois.* Paris, 1837.

Prinsep, Henry Thoby, and Prinsep, J. *Note on Inscription no. 1 of the Allahabad Column, and on the Facsimiles of Various Inscriptions. JASB*, vol. 5, 17 pp. 1837.

——. *Note on Inscriptions at Udayagiri and Khandgiri, in Cuttack, in the Lat Characters. JASB*, vol. 6, pp. 1072–90. 1837.

210 ——. *Note on the Facsimiles of Inscriptions from Sanchi near Bhilsa, Taken for the Society by Captain Ed. Smith, Engineers; and on the Drawings of the Buddhist Monument Presented by Capt. Murray, at the Meeting of 7th June.* JASB, vol. 6, pp. 451–79. 1837.

——. *Note on the Facsimiles of the Various Inscriptions on the Ancient Column at Allahabad retaken by Edw. Smith.* JASB, vol. 3, pp. 114f.; vol. 4, pp. 963–80. 1837.

——. *Note on W. H. Sykes' Inscriptions.* JASB, vol. 6, 7 pp. 1837.

——. *Specimens of Hindu Coins descended from the Parthian Type and of the Ancient Coins of Ceylon.* JASB, vol. 6, 14 pp. 1837.

Schmid, B. *Traditions Concerning the Migration of Buddhists into Europe. Madras J. of Lit. and Sc.*, vol. 5, pp. 229–31. Madras, 1837.

Schmidt, Isaac Jacob. *Über die Heroen des vorgeschichtlichen Alterthums, Bull. scient. de l'Acad. de St.-Pétersbourg*, vol. 2, 4 pp. 1837.

Sykes, William Henry. *Inscriptions from the Boodh Caves, near Joonur.* "Communicated in a letter to Sir John Malcolm by H. W. Sykes." JRAS, vol. 4, pp. 287–91. 1837.

——. *Specimens of Buddhist Inscriptions, with Symbols, from the West of India.* JASB, vol. 6, part 2, pp. 1038–49. 1837.

Turnour, (Hon.) George. *An Examination of the Pali Buddhistical Annals.* JASB, vol. 6, pp. 501–28, 713–37; vol. 8, pp. 686–701, 789–817, 919–33, 991–1014. 1837–38.

——. *Further Notes on the Inscriptions on the Column at Delhi, Allahabad, Betial, etc.* JASB, vol. 6, pp. 1049–64. 1837.

——. *The Mahawanso, in Roman Characters, with the Translation Subjoined, and an Introd. Essay on Pali Buddhistical Literature*, vol. 1, "Containing the first 38 chapters," 30, 262 pp. Colombo, 1837. [Ed. and tr.]

Wroughton, R. *Account and Drawing of Two Burmese Bells Now Placed in a Hindu Temple in Upper India.* JASB, vol. 6, 8 pp. 1837.

1838

Abel-Rémusat, Jean-Pierre. *Mémoires sur un voyage dans l'Asie centrale, dans le pays des Afghans et des Béloutches et dans l'Inde, exécuté à la fin du ivᵉ siècle de notre ère par plusieurs samanéens de a Chine, Mém. de l'Inst. royal de France. Acad. des Inscript.*, p. 343. 1838.

Bailey, H. V. *Dorje-Ling.* Calcutta, 1838.

Brown, William. *Account of an Ancient Temple at Hissar, and of the Shop Model at that Place.* JASB, vol. 7, 2 pp. 1838.

Buddhism in China taken from Gützlaff's "China Opened" and Medhurst's "China: Its state, etc." The Friend, vol. 3, 8 pp. Colombo, 1838–39.

Burt, Capt. T. S. *Lithographs and Translations of Inscriptions taken by Capt. T. S. Burt and of one from Ghosi taken by A. Cunningham.* JASB, vol. 7, 8 pp. 1838.

Gogerly, (Rev.) Daniel John. *On Buddhism.* The Friend, vol. 2, 3. Colombo, 1838–39.

——. *On Transmigration.* The Friend, vol. 2; 8, 9, 10 pp. Colombo, 1838.

Gützlaff, Karl Friedrich Augustus. *China Opened.* "Display of the topography, history, customs, arts, literature, religion, etc., of the Chinese Empire. Rev. by Dr Reed." London, 1838. 2 vols. See *Buddhism in China, supra.*

Körös, Alexander Csoma de. *Enumeration of Historical and Grammatical Works to be met with in Tibet.* JASB, vol. 7, part 1, pp. 147–51. 1838.

——. *Notices on the Different Systems of Buddhism, extracted from the Tibetan Authorities.* JASB, vol. 7, part 1, pp. 142–47. 1838.

Medhurst, W. H. *China: Its State and Prospects.* London, 1838. See *Buddhism in China, supra.*

Postans, W. *An Account of the Jain Temple at Badrasir, and the Ruins of Badranagri in the province of Cutch.* JASB, vol. 7, 4 pp. 1838.

Prinsep, Henry Thoby, and Prinsep, J. *Discovery of the Name of Antiochus the Great, in Two of the*   211
     Edicts of Asoka, King of India. JASB, vol. 7, pp. 156–67. 1838.
——. *Examination of the Inscriptions from Girnar in Gujerat, and Dhauli in Cuttack. JASB*, vol. 7,
     pp. 334–56. 1838.
——. *Examination of the Separate Edicts of the Aswastama Inscription at Dhauli in Cuttack. JASB*,
     vol. 7, 21 pp. 1838.
——. *More Danams from the Sanchi Tope near Bhilsa*. "Taken in impression by Capt. T. S. Burt.
     Translated by J. Prinsep." *JASB*, vol. 7, pp. 562–66. 1838. [Tr.]
——. *On the Edicts of Piyadasi, or Asoka the Buddhist Monarch of India, Preserved on the Girnar Rock*
     in the Gujerat Peninsula and on the Dhauli Rock in Cuttack. JASB, vol. 7, pp. 219–82. 1838.
Ravenshaw. *Notice of Inscriptions in Behar*, "communicated by Mr Ravenshaw." *JASB*, vol. 8, 8
     pp. 1838; vol. 9, 2 pp. 1840.
Ritter, Carl. *Die Stupas (Topes), oder Die architektonischen Denkmale an der Indo-Baktrischen Königs-*
     trasse und die Kolosse von Bamiyan. "Eine Abh. zur Altertumskunde des Orients, vorgetr. in
     der Königl. Akad. der Wiss. am 6 Feb. 1837." Berlin, Nikolai'sche Buchhandlung, 1838.
     272 pp.
Wroughton, R. *Restoration and Translation of the Inscription on the Large Arracan Bell, now at*
     Nadrohighat, Zillah Alligarh, "described by R. Wroughton." *JASB*, vol. 7, 13 pp. 1838.
1839
Bridgnell, William. *The Buddhistical Doctrine of Sin and Suffering and their Opposites. The Friend*, vol.
     3, 2 pp. Colombo, 1839.
Gogerly, (Rev.) Daniel John. *On Buddhism. Laws of the Priesthood. The Friend*, vol. 3. Colombo,
     1839.
Gogerly, (Rev.) Daniel John, and Beal, S. *The Patimokkha, Ceylon Friend*. 1839. [Tr.]
Hodgson, Brian Houghton. *The Literature and Religion of the Buddhists*. s.d. *The Phoenix*, vol. 1.
——. *The Vajra-Soochi, or Refutation of the Argument upon Which the Brahmanical Institution of Caste*
     Is Founded, by the Learned Boodhist Ashwa Ghosha. "Also the *Tunku* by Soobajee Bupoo,
     being a Reply to the *Vajra-Soochi*. In Sanskrit with a Tr. by B. H. Hodgson and a Preface
     by L. Wilkinson." 1839. [Ed and tr.]
Pauthier, G. *Examen méthodique des faits qui concernent le Thien-tchu ou Inde*, "traduit du chinois
     par G. Pauthier." *JA*, ser. 3, vol. 8, pp. 38, 40, 48. 1839.
Schmidt, Isaac Jacob. *Die Taten Bogda Gesser Chan's, des Vertilgers der Wurzel der zehn Übel in den*
     zehn Gegenden. "Eine ostasiatische Heldensage. Aus dem Mongolischen übers." St. Pe-
     tersburg, W. Gräff; Leipzig, Leopold Voss, 1839. 287 pp. [Tr.]
——. *Grammatik der tibetischen Sprache*. St. Petersburg, Academia Scientiarium Imperialis,
     1839.
Sykes, William Henry. *Siva in the Cave Temples of Elephanta and Ellora. JRAS*, p. 81. 1839.
Wilson, Horace Hayman. *Account of the Foe Koue Ki, or Travels of Fa Hian in India*, "translated
     from the Chinese by J.-P. Abel-Rémusat. (Read 9th March and 7th April, 1838)." *JRAS*,
     vol. 5, pp. 108–40. 1839.
1840
Benfey, Theodor. *Indien*. In *Allgemeine Enzyklopaedia der Wissenschaften und Künste*, ed. J. S.
     Ersch and J. G. Gruber, sect. 2, vol. 17, pp. 1–356. Leipzig, 1840.
Bridgnell, William. *On Resentment. Extract from Buddha's Sermons. The Friend*, vol. 4, 3 pp.
     Colombo, 1840.
Burt, Capt. T. S. *Inscription Found near Bhahra on the Road to Delhi. JASB*, vol. 9, 4 pp. 1840.
Carte, W. E. *Notice on Amulets in Use by the Transhymalayan Boodhists*. "With notes by Csoma de
     Körös." *JASB*, vol. 9, pp. 904–7. 1840.

212 Forbes, J. *Eleven Years in Ceylon, Its History and Antiquities*. London, 1840. 2 vols.

Gogerly, (Rev.) Daniel John. *Buddhism: Damapadan. The Friend*, vol. 4, 26 pp. Colombo, 1840.

Hügel, Carl Frhr. von. *Kaschmir und das Reich der Siek*. Stuttgart, Hallberger'sche Verlags-buchhandlung, 1840–42. 4 vols.

Lassen, Christian. *Points in the History of the Greek and Indo-Scythian Kings in Bactria, Cabul and India, as Illustrated by Decyphering the Ancient Legends on their Coins. JASB*, vol. 9, pp. 251, 339, 449, 627, 733. 1840.

Schmidt, Isaac Jacob. *Kritischer Versuch zur Feststellung der Aera und der ersten geschichtlichen Momente des Buddhaismus. Bull. scient. de l'Acad. de St.-Pétersbourg*, vol. 6, pp. 353–68. 1840.

Troyer, A. *Raja Tarangini*. "Histoire des Rois du Kachmir, publ. en sanscrit et tr. en français par A. Troyer." 3 vols., 584, 640, 724 pp. Paris, 1840–52. [Ed. and tr.]

1841

Barthélemy Saint-Hilaire, Jules. *Le Nyaya*. "(Authenticité du *Nyaya*. Analyse du Nyaya. Appréciation de la doctrine du *Nyaya*)." *Mém. de l'Acad. roy. d. Sc. morales*, vol. 3, 86 pp. Paris, 1841.

——. *Traductions des Soutras du Nyaya composé par Gotama*. Paris. *Mém. de l'Acad. roy. d. Sc. morales*, vol. 3, 10 pp. Paris, 1841.

Bird, James. *Opening of the Topes at Kanari near Bombay and the Relics Found in them. JASB*, vol. 10, part 1, pp. 94–97. 1841.

Chitty, Simon Cassie. *Remarks on the Site and Ruins of Tammana and Nuwera. JRAS*, vol. 6, pp. 242–45. 1841.

Davis, Sir John Francis. *China en de Chinezen*. "Naar de laatste Uitgave, waarin de Geschie-denis van het Handelsverkeer met de Engelschen tot op dit Oogenblik toe behandeld wordt. Uit het Engelsch vertaald door Mr C. J. Zweerts. Met Houtsnedeplaaten." Amsterdam, G. J. A. Beijerinck, 1841. 3 vols., 378, 335, 327 pp. [Tr.]

Foucaux, Philippe Edouard. *Spécimen du Gya-tcher-rol-pa (Lalita Vistara)*. "Partie du chap. vii, contenant la naissance de Çakya-Mouni. Texte tibétain tr. en français et accompagné de notes par Ph. Ed. Foucaux." Paris, Benjamin Duprat, 1841. 27, 33 pp. (Tibetan text) [Ed. and tr.]

Gerard, Alex. *Account of Koonawur*, Ed. G. Lloyd. 1841.

Hardy, (Rev.) R. Spence. *The British Government and the Idolatry of Ceylon*. London, 1841.

Hodgson, Brian Houghton. *Illustrations of the Literature and Religion of the Buddhists*. Serampore, 1841.

Masson, Charles. *A Memoir on the Buildings called Topes*. In *Ariana antiqua*, ed. H. H. Wilson, pp. 55–118. London, 1841.

——. *Memoir on the Topes and Sepulchral Monuments of Afghanistan*. London, 1841. 60 pp.

Moorcroft, W., and Trebeck, G. *Travels in the Himalaya Provinces of Hindustan and the Panjab, in Ladakh and Kashmir, Kabul, etc., from the 1819 to 1825*, ed. H. H. Wilson. London, 1841. 2 vols.

Pigou, Lieut. *On the Topes of Darounta, and Caves of Bahrabad. JASB*, vol. 10, part I, pp. 381–86. 1841.

Schmidt, Isaac Jacob. *Neue Erläuterungen über den Ursprung des Namens Mandschu. Bull. scient. de l'Acad. de St.-Pétersbourg*, vol. 8, 4 pp. 1841.

——. *Tibetisch-Deutsches Wörterbuch nebst deutschem Wortregister, etc*. St. Petersburg, Vienna, 1841. 784 pp.

Spiegel, Friedrich von. *Kammavakya*. "Liber de officiis sacerdotum Buddhicorum. Palice et Latine primus edidit atque adnotationes adiecit F. Spiegel." Bonnae ad Rhenum, H. B. Koenig, 1841. 30 pp. [Ed. and tr.]

Sykes, William Henry. *Notes on the Religions, Moral, and Political State of India, before the Ma-*

homedan Invasion. "Chiefly founded on the travels of the Chinese Buddhist priest Fai Han in India AD 399, and on Commentaries of Messrs. Rémusat, Klaproth, Burnouf and Landresse." *JRAS*, vol. 6, pp. 248–484. 1841.

Tivarekar Ganpatreo, Krishna. *Index to the Transactions of the Library Society of Bombay*, vols. 1–3, *and to the Journals of the Bombay Branch, Royal Asiatic Society*, vols. 1–17. "With a historical sketch of the Society." 1841–86. 17 pp.

Wilson, Horace Hayman. *Ariana antiqua*. "A descriptive account of the antiquities and coins of Afghanistan. With a memoir on the buildings called Topes, by Ch. Masson, Esq." London, 1841. 452 pp.

——. *Introduction to the Grammar of the Sanskrit Language*. London, 1841.

1842

Campbell, A. *Report of the Death of Csoma de Körös*, "made to G. A. Bushby, Esq., and communicated to the Society." *JASB*, vol. 11, p. 303. 1842.

Cunningham, Sir Alexander. *An Account of the Discovery of the Ruins of the Buddhist City of Samkassa*. "By Lieut. Alex. Cunningham, in a letter to Col. Sykes, FRS." *JRAS*, vol. 7, pp. 241–49. 1842–43.

Foucaux, Philippe Edouard. *Le sage et le Fou*. "Extrait du Kanjur, revu sur l'éd. originale et accompagné d'un glossaire par Ph. Ed. Foucaux." Paris, 1842. 74 pp.

Kennedy, C. P. *Brahmanism versus Buddhism. As. J. and Mly. Reg.*, n.s., vols. 37–39. London, 1842.

Kröger, J. C. *Abriss vergleichenden Darstellung der indisch- persisch- und chinesischen Religionssysteme*. "Mit steter Rücksichtnahme auf die späteren Religionsformen und den Ursprung religiöser Ideen." Eisleben, Georg Reichardt, 1842. 358 pp.

Langdon, Williams B. *Ten Thousand Things Relating to China and Chinese*. "An epitome of the genius government, history, literature, agriculture, arts, trade, manners, customs and social life of the people of the Celestial Empire together with a synopsis of the Chinese collection." London, 1842.

Lassen, Christian. *Über eine Inschrift des königl. Satrapen von Surashtra, worin Kandragupta und sein Enkel Asoka erwähnt werden. Z. f. d. Kunde d. Morgenl.*, vol. 4, p. 56. Bonn, 1842.

Maupied (Abbé) F. L. M. *Prodrome d'ethnographie, ou Essai sur l'origine des principaux peuples anciens, contenant l'histoire neuve et détaillée du Bouddhisme et du Brahmanisme*. Paris, 1842.

Schott, Wilhelm. *Über den Doppelsinn des Wortes Schamane und über den tungusischen Schamanen-Cultus am Hofe der Mandju-Kaiser. Abh. d. Akad. d. Wiss. zu Berlin*. 1842. 8 pp.

Vigne, G. T. *Travels in Kashmir, Ladak, Iskardo, the Countries adjoining the Moutain Course of the Indus and the Himalaya, North of Punjab*. London, 1842. 2 vols.

1843

Abel-Rémusat, Jean-Pierre. *Mélanges posthumes d'histoire et de littérature orientales*, "publ. par F. Lajard, sous les auspices du Ministre de l'Instruction publique." Paris, 1843. 470 pp.

Bennett, T. W. *Ceylon and its Capabilities*. London, 1843.

Halbertsma, J. H. *Het Buddhisme en zijin stichter. Overrijsselsche Almanak*. Deventer, 1843. 75 pp.

Hodgson, Brian Houghton. *Translation of the Naipalïya Devata Kalyana*. "With notes." *JASB*, vol. 12, part 1, pp. 400–409. 1843.

Morton, W. *Vajra Suchi*. "In Bengali, with an English translation by W. Morton." Calcutta, 1843. [Tr.]

Nork, F. *Etymologisch, symbolisch, mythologisches Real-Wörterbuch. Zum Handgebrauche für Bibelforscher, Archäologen und bildende Künstler*. Stuttgart, J. F. Castsche Buchhdlg., 1843.

Ozeray, Michel-Jean-François. *Histoires des doctrines religieuses, ou Recherches philosophiques et morales sur la théologie naturelle, etc*. Paris, 1843.

Schmidt, Isaac Jacob. *Der Weise und der Tor*. "Aus dem Tibetischen übers, und mit dem

214   Originaltexte hrsg." St. Petersburg, W. Graff's Erben; Leipzig, Leopold Voss, 1843. 2 vols., 328, 404 pp. [Ed and tr.].

Stevenson, (Rev.) John. *An Account of the Bauddho-Vaishnavas, or Vitthal-Bhaktas of the Dekkan. JRAS*, vol. 7, pp. 64–73. 1843.

——. *On the Intermixture of Buddhism with Brahmanism in the Religion of the Hindus of the Dekkan. JRAS*, vol. 7, pp. 1–8. 1843.

Sykes, William Henry. *Buddhism versus Brahmanism. As. J.* 1843.

1844

Bird, James. *Historical Researches on the Origin and Principles of the Bauddha and Jaina Religions.* "Embracing the leading tenets of their system, as found prevailing in various countries; illus. by descriptive accounts of the sculptures in the caves of Western India, with tr. of the cave inscriptions from Kanari, Ajanta, Ellora, Nasik, and c., indicating the connexion of these caves with the topes and caves of the Punjab and Afghanistan." *JBBRAS*, vol. 2, no. 8, pp. 71–108. 1844.

Burnouf, Eugène. *Introduction à l'histoire du Buddhisme indien*, "tr. du sanscrit." Impr. roy., vol. 1, 647 pp. Paris, 1844.

Cauchy, A. L. *Considérations sur les ordres religieux*. Paris, 1844.

Fergusson, James. *On the Rock-cut Temples of India. JRAS*, vol. 8, pp. 30–92. 1844–45.

Jacob, L. G., and Westergaard, N. L. *Copy of the Asoka Inscription at Girnar. JBBRAS*, vol. 1, pp. 257–58. 1844.

Latter, Thomas. *A Note on Boodhism and the Cave Temples of India*. Calcutta, 1844. 21 pp.

——. *Remarks on Boodhist Coin or Medal. JASB*, vol. 13, part 2, pp. 571–86. 1844.

MacGovan, D. J. *An Inscription from a Tablet in a Buddhist Monastery at Ningpo in China. JASB*, vol. 13, part 1, pp. 113–14. 1844.

Murray, Hugh. *The Travels of Marco Polo.* "Greatly amended and enlarged from valuable early MSS. recently publ. by the French Soc. of Geogr. and in Italy by Count Baldelli Boni." 4th ed., 368 pp. Edinburgh, Oliver and Boyd, 1844.

Prinsep, Henry Thoby, and Prinsep, J. *Note on the Historical Results Deducible from Recent Discoveries in Afghanistan*. London, 1844.

Schott, Wilhelm. *Über den Buddhaismus in Hochasien und in China. Abh. d. Königl. Preuss. Akad. d. Wiss., Philos.-Hist. Kl*, pp. 161–288. Berlin, 1844.

Westergaard, Niels Ludwig. *A Brief Account of the Minor Bauddha Caves of Beira and Bajah, in the Neighbourhood of Karli.* "Communicated in a letter, from Mr N. L. Westergaard, to James Bird, Esq. With tr., by the latter, of inscriptions found at both." *JBBRAS*, vol. 1, no. 7, pp. 438–43. 1844.

1845

Canstadt, baron Schilling von. *Bibliothèque bouddhique, ou Index du Gandjour de Narthang, composé sous la direction du Baron Schilling de Canstadt.* "Avant-propos." *Bull. de la Cl. hist.-philol. de l'Acad. d. Sc. de St.-Pétersbourg*, vol. 4, pp. 321–31. 1845.

——. *Das ehrwürdige Mahajanasutra mit Namen: "Das unermessliche Lebensalter und die unermessliche Erkenntnis."* "Lithographischer Abdrück, besorgt durch den verstorbenen Baron Schilling von Canstadt. Hrsg. von der Kaiserl. Akad. der Wiss." St. Petersburg, 1845. 25 pp.

Fergusson, James. *Illustrations of the Rock-cut Temples of India: Selected from the Best Examples of the Different Series of Caves at Ellora, Ajunta, Cuttack, Salsette, Karli, and Mahavellopore.* "Drawn on stone by Mr T. C. Dibdin, fr. sketches carefully made on the spot, with the assistance of the Canera-Lucida, in the years 1838–9, by J. Fergusson. Text to accompany the folio-volume of pl. by James Fergusson." London, John Weale Esq., 1845.

Gogerly, (Rev.) Daniel John. *On Buddhism. JCBRAS*, nos. 1–4, 23, 49, 38, 14 pp. Colombo, 1845–48.

——. *On Buddhism.* "Paper read before the Ceylon Br. of the RAS, first nov. 1845." *JCBRAS,*   215
no. 2, 27 pp. Colombo, 1845.

Knighton, William. *History of Ceylon, from the Earliest Period of the Present Time.* "With an account of its present condition." Calcutta, London and Edinburgh, 1845. 399 pp.

Latter, Thomas. *A Grammar of the Language of Burmah.* Calcutta, 1845.

——. *On the Buddhist Emblem of Architecture. JASB,* vol. 14, part 2, pp. 623–40. 1845.

Müller, Samuel. *De Tand van Boedhha, een Indisch mirakel.* "Geschreven door Dr Samuel Müller." Leiden, 1845. 16 pp.

Neumann, Carl Friedrich. *Die Reisen des Venezianers Marco Polo im dreizehnten Jahrhundert.* "Deutsch von August Burck." Leipzig, 1845.

Nève, Félix. *De l'antériorité du Brahmanisme sur le Bouddhisme. R. catholique.* Louvain, 1845. 14 pp.

——. *Histoire du Bouddhisme indien. Correspondant,* vols. 11, 12. Paris, 1845.

Pavie, Théodore. *Les Trois Religions de la Chine, leur antagonisme, leur développement et leur influence. RDM,* n.s., vol. 9, 26 pp. 1845.

Schmidt, Isaac Jacob. *Bkah-hgyur-gui-dkar-chag, oder Der Index des Kandjur.* "Hrsg. von der Kaiserlichen Akademie der Wissenschaften, und bevorwortet von I. J. Schmidt, ordentlichem Mitgliede der Akademie u.s.w." St. Petersburg (and Leipzig, Leopod Voss), 215 pp. 1845. [Av.-pr.]

Silva, A. D. *Buddhism. The Friend,* vol. 8; 3, 3 pp. Colombo, 1845.

Spiegel, Friedrich von. *Anecdota Pâlica.* "Nach den Handschr. d. K. Bibl. in Kopenhagen im Grundtexte hrsg., übers. u. erklärt." Leipzig, Wilh. Engelmann, 1845. 92 pp. [Ed. and tr.]

——. *Geschichte des Buddhismus. Jb. f. Wissenschaft. Kritik.* Berlin, 1845. 14 pp. See E. Burnouf, 1844.

Tand, de. *Van Boeddha. Een Indisch Mirakel.* Leiden, 1845. 16 pp.

1846

Barthélemy Saint-Hilaire. *Jules, E. Burnouf: "Introduction à l'histoire du Buddhisme indien." R. encycl.* 1846. 26 pp. [Rec.]. See E. Burnouf, 1844.

Chitty, Simon Cassie. *The Sixth Chapter of the Tiruvathavur Purana entitled "The Vanquishing of the Buddhists in Disputation."* "Tr. with notes by Simon Cassie Chitty." *JCBRAS,* no. 2, 21 pp. 1846.

Gogerly, (Rev.) Daniel John. *Singalo Wada.* "Tr. by the Rev. D. J. Gogerly." *JCBRAS,* no. 2, 8 pp. 1846.

——. *The Discourse on the Minor Results of Conduct, or The Discourse addressed to Subha.* "Tr. by the Rev. D. J. Gogerly." *JCBRAS,* no. 2, 7 pp. 1846.

Hardy, (Rev.) R. Spence. *On the Language and Literature of the Singhalese. JCBRAS,* no. 2, 6 pp. 1846.

Latter, Thomas. *The Coins of Arakan. The Symbolical Coins. JASB,* vol. 15, 3 pp. 1846.

Marshall, W. H. *Ceylon.* "A general description of the Island and its Inhabitants, with an historical sketch of the conquest of the colony by the English." London, 1846.

Neumann, Carl Friedrich. *Tübet. Ausland,* vol. 19, 10 pp. Stüttgart, 1846.

Nève, Félix. *De l'état présent des études sur le Bouddhisme et de leur application. R. de Flandre,* vol. 1, 63 pp. Ghent, 1846.

Norris, Edwin. *On the Kapur-di-Giri Rock Inscription. JRAS,* vol. 8, pp. 303–14. 1846.

Postans, T. *A Few Observations on the Temple of Somnath. JRAS,* vol. 8, pp. 172–75. 1846.

Schwambeck, E. A. *Megasthenis Indica.* "Fragmenta collegit, commentationem et indices addidit E. A. Schwambeck." Bonn, 1846. [Ed.]

Spiegel, Friedrich von. *Ceylon. Ausland,* vol. 19. Stüttgart, 1846.

——. *Über den einheimischen Bearbeiter der Palisprache. Höfer's Z. f. die Wiss. d. Sprache,* vol. 1, 14 pp. Berlin, 1846.

216 ——. *Zur Geschichte des Buddhismus. Ausland*, vol. 19. Berlin, 1846.

Stevenson, (Rev.) John. *Analysis of the Ganesa Purana, with Special Reference to the History of Buddhism. JRAS*, vol. 8, pp. 319–29. 1846.

——. *The Ante-Brahmanical Religion of the Hindus. JRAS*, vol. 8, pp. 330–39. 1846.

Wilson, Horace Hayman. *Kapurdigiri Inscription. JRAS*, p. 308. 1846.

Yates, (Rev) W. *A Dictionary in Sanscrit and English.* "Designed for the use of private students and of Indian colleges and schools." Calcutta, 1846.

Yvan, Dr. *Die Insel der Bonzen. Ausland*, 3 pp. Stüttgart, 1846.

1847

Anderson, W. *An Attempt to Identify Some of the Places Mentioned in the Itinerary of Hiuan-Thsang. JASB*, vol. 16, pp. 1183–1211. 1847.

Barthélemy Saint-Hilaire, Jules. *Rapport sur le tome I. de l'"Introduction à l'histoire du Buddhisme indien" par M. E. Burnouf. Suivi d'observations par M. Cousin. Séances et Travaux de l'Acad. d. Sc. morales et politiques*, ser. 2, vol. 1, 25 pp. Paris, 1847.

Böhtlingk, Otto von, in I. J. Schmidt et O. von Böhtlingk. *Verzeichnis der tibetanischen Handschriften und Holzdrücke im Asiatischen Museum der Kais. Akad. d. Wissenschaften. Bull. de la Cl. hist.-philol. de l'Acad. impér. d. Sc. de St.-Pétersbourg*, vol. 4, cols. 81–125. 1847.

Cunningham, Sir Alexander. *Notes on the Antiquities of the District with the Bhopal Agency. JASB*, vol. 16, 24 pp. 1847.

Fortune, Robert. *Three Years' Wanderings in the Northern Provinces of China.* "Including a visit to the Tea, Silk and Cotton Countries. With an account of the agriculture and horticulture of the Chinese, new plants, etc." 2d ed. London, John Murray, 1847. 420 pp.

Foucaux, Philippe Edouard. *Rgya tch'er rop pa, ou Développement des Jeux, contenant l'histoire du Bouddha Cakya Mouni.* "Tr. sur la version tibétaine du *Bkah hgyour*, et revu sur l'original sanscrit (*Lalitavistara*), par Ph. Ed. Foucaux." Paris, Impr. roy., 1847–48. 2 parts in 2 vols., 388, 425 pp. [Ed. and tr.]

Gogerly, (Rev.) Daniel John. *The Discourse Respecting Rattapala.* Tr. Rev. D. J. Gogerly. *JCBRAS*, no. 3, 15 pp. 1847.

Hardy, (Rev.) R. Spence. *List of Books in the Pali and Singhalese Languages. JCBRAS*, no. 3, 12 pp. 1847.

Huc, (Abbé) Evariste-Régis. In *Notice sur la prière bouddhique "OM mani padmé houm,"* ed. E.-R. Huc and J. Gabet. *JA*, n.s., vol. 9, pp. 462–64. 1847.

Julien, Stanislas. *Renseignements bibliographiques sur les relations des voyages dans l'Inde et les descriptions du Si-yu, qui ont été composées en chinois entre le 1ᵉ et le xviiᵉ siècle de notre ère. JA*, ser. 4, vol. 10, pp. 265–69. 1847.

Kittoe, M. *Note on an Image of Buddha Found at Sherghatti. JASB*, vol. 16, part 1, pp. 78–80. 1847.

——. *Note on the Sculptures of Bôdh Gyah. JASB*, vol. 16, part 1, pp. 334–39. 1847.

——. *Notes on Places in the Province of Behar, Supposed to Be Those Described by Chy-Fa-Hian, the Chinese Buddhist Priest, Who Made a Pilgrimage to India, at the Close of the Fourth Century AD. JASB*, vol. 16, part 2, pp. 953–70. 1847.

——. *Notes on the Caves of Burabu. JASB*, vol. 16, 15 pp. 1847.

——. *Notes on the Viharas and Caityas of Behar. JASB*, vol. 16, 7 pp. 1847.

Knighton, William. *On the Ruins of Anuradha Pura, Formerly the Capital of Ceylon. JASB*, vol. 16, 13 pp. 1847.

——. *The Rock-Temples of Dambool. JASB*, vol. 16, 11 pp. Ceylon, 1847.

Lassen, Christian. *Indische Alterthumskunde.* Leipzig, Verl. v. L. A. Kittler; London, Williams and Norgate, 1847–61. 4 vols., 862, 1092, 1199, 988, 86 (Ann. to 2 and 3) pp.

Liebrecht, Felix. *Des heiligen Johannes von Damascus Barlaam und Josaphat.* "Aus dem Griechischen übertr. Mit einem Vorw. von Ludolph von Beckedorff." Münster, Theissing'sche Buchhandl., 1847. 304 pp.

Pasini, Lodovico. *I Viaggi di Marco Polo Veneziano tradotti per la prima volta dall'originale Francese di Rusticiano di Pisa et corredati d'illustrazioni e di documenti,* "Vincenzo Lazari pubblicati per cura di Lodovico Pasini, membro eff. e segretario del R. Istitute Veneto." Venezia, 1847. 484 pp. [Ed.]

Pavie, Théodore. *Le Thibet et les Etudes tibétaines, RDM,* n.s., vol. 19, 22 pp. 1847.

Peters, John R. *Miscellaneous Remarks upon the Government, History, Religions, Literature, Agriculture, Arts, Trades, Manners, and Customs of the Chinese, as Suggested by an Examination of the Articles Comprising the Chinese Museum.* Philadelphia, 1847.

Roth, R. *Zur Geschichte der Religionen. 2: Die Buddha-Religion, Tübingen, Theol. Jb.,* vol. 6, pp. 175–90. 1847.

Stevenson, (Rev.) John. *Some Remarks on the Relation that Subsists between the Jains- and Brahmanical-systems of Geography. JBBAS,* vol. 2, 4 pp. 1847.

1848

Abel-Rémusat, Jean-Pierre. *The Pilgrimage of Fa Hian;* "from the French edition of the *Foé Koué Ki* of MM. Rémusat, Klaproth, and Landresse with additional Notes and Illustrations. By J. W. Laidlay, Esq., Vice-President and Joint-Secretary of the Asiatic Society. Printed by J. Thomas, Baptist Mission Press." Calcutta, 1848. 373 pp. See J.-P. Abel-Rémusat, 1836.

Bitschurin Iakynth (le père Hyacinthe). *La Chine et sa situation civile et morale* (in Russian). Saint Petersburg, 1848. 4 vols.

Cunningham, Sir Alexander. *Verification of the Itinerary of the Chinese Pilgrim, Hwan Thsang, through Afghanistan and India during the First Half of the Seventh Century of the Christian Era. JASB,* vol. 17, pp. 13–60. 1848.

Cunningham, J. D. *On the Ruins of Putharee. JASB,* vol. 17, 8 pp. 1848.

Gabet, J. *Les Quarante-deux Points d'enseignement proférés par Bouddha,* "tr. du mongol par MM. Gabet et Huc." *JA,* ser. 4, vol. 11, pp. 535–57. 1848.

Hoffmeister, Werner. *Travels in Ceylon and Continental India, Nepal, Himalayas, Tibet, etc.* "Tr. from the German, with a Pref. by Carl Ritter." Edinburgh, 1848. [Tr.]

Klaproth, Julius Heinrich. *Fa-Hian.* (Pèlerinage de). "Tiré de l'édition française du *Foé Koué Ki* de MM. Rémusat, Klaproth et Landresse. Avec notes additionnelles et explicatives" (anon.; Cunningham attributes authorship to Laidley). Calcutta, 1848.

Low, James. *A Few Gleanings in Buddhism. JASB,* vol. 17, part 2, pp. 591–619. 1848.

——. *Gleanings in Buddhism, or Translations of passages from a Siamese version of a Pali work, termed in Siamese "Phrâ Pat'hom." with passing observations on Buddhism and Brahmanism. JASB,* vol. 17, part 2, pp. 72–98. 1848.

Selkirk, J. *Recollections from Ceylon.* London, 1848.

Stevenson, (Rev.) John. *Kalpa Sutra and Nava Tatva.* "Two Works Illus. of the Jain Religion and Philosophy. Tr. from the Maghadi, with an appendix, containing remarks on the language of the original, by the Rev. J. Stevenson." London, 1848. 144 pp. [Tr.]

Sykes, William Henry. *On a Catalogue of Chinese Buddhistical Works. JRAS,* vol. 9, pp. 199–213. 1848.

Wuttke, Carl Friedrich Adolf. *De Buddhaustarum Disciplina.* Vratislaviae, 1848. 42 pp.

1849

Campbell, A. *Journal of a Trip to Sikim, in December 1848.* "With sketch map." *JASB,* vol. 18, part 1, pp. 482–541. 1849.

Davis, Sir John Francis. *The Chinese.* "A general description of the Empire of China and its inhabitants." 2d ed. London, M. A. Nattali, 1849. 2 vols., 395, 459 pp.

218 Friederich, R. *A Preliminary Account of the Island of Bali. JIA*, vol. 3, 21 pp. 1849.

———. *Voorloopig verslag van het eiland Bali. Verhandelingen van het Bataviaasch Genootschap van Kunst en Wetensch*, vol. 22, 63, 57 pp. Batavia, 1849.

Impey, E. *Description of a Colossal Jain Figure nearly 80 feet high, cut in Relief, discovered on a Spur of the Satpoorah Range, in the district of Burwanie, on the Nirbuddha. JASB*, vol. 18, part 2, pp. 918–51. 1849.

Julien, Stanislas. *Concordance sino-sanscrite d'un nombre considérable de titres d'ouvrages bouddhiques, recueillis dans un catalogue chinois de l'an 1306, et publiée, après le déchiffrement et la restitution des mots indiens. JA*, ser. 4, vol. 14, pp. 353–446. 1849.

Low, James. *General Observations on the Contending Claims to Antiquity of Brahmans and Buddhists. JASB*, vol. 18, part 1, pp. 89–131. 1849.

———. *On an Inscription from Keddah. JASB*, vol. 18, 2 pp. 1849.

Pridham, Ch. *An Historical, Statistical and Political Account of Ceylon and Its Dependencies*. London, 1849. 2 vols.

Salisbury, Edward E. *Memoir on the History of Buddhism*. "Read before the Americ. Or. Soc. at their ann. meeting in Boston, 1844." *JAOS*, vol. 1, no. 11, pp. 79–135. 1849.

Sirr, Henry Charles. *China and the Chinese. Their Religion, Character, Customs and Manufactures, etc.* 1849. 2 vols.

1850

Bigandet, (Right Rev.) P. *Some Account of the Order of Buddhist Monks or Talapoins. JIA*, vol. 4, 25 pp. 1850.

Frere, Sir Henry Bartle Edward. *Memorandum on Some Buddhist Excavations near Karadh. JBBRAS*, vol. 3, part 2, no. 13, pp. 108–18. 1850.

Hammer-Purgstall. *Über einen halbbuddhistischen, halbmoslimischen Talisman. Denkschr. d. Kais. Akad. d. Wiss. in Wien*, vol. 1, pp. 327–30. Wien, 1850.

Hardy, (Rev.) R. Spence. *Eastern Monachism*. "An account of the origin, laws, discipline, sacred writings, mysterious rites, religious ceremonies, and present circumstances of the order of mendicants founded by Gotama Buddha, compiled from Singhalese MSS. and other original sources of information." London, Partridge and Oakay, 1850. 443 pp.

Latter, Thomas. *Selection from the Vernacular Buddhist Literature of Burmah*. Maulmain, 1850. 200 pp.

Pallegoix, D. J. B. *Grammatica Linguae Thaï*. Bangkok, 1850. 246 pp.

Sirr, Henry Charles. *Ceylon and the Cinghalese*. "Their History, Government and Religion, the Antiquities, Institutions, Produce, etc. With anecdotes illustrating the manners and customs of the people." London, 1850. 2 vols.

Tennent, (Sir) James Emerson. *Christianity in Ceylon*. "Its introd. and progress under the Portuguese, the Dutch, the British, and American Missions. With an historical sketch of the Brahmanical and Buddhist superstitions." London, J. Murray, 1850. 348 pp.

Veuillot, Eugène. *Le Thibet et les Missions françaises dans la Haute-Asie. RDM*, vol. 6, 42 pp. Nouv. Période, 1850.

Wilson, Horace Hayman. *On the Rock-Inscription of Kapur-di-Giri, Dhauli and Girnar. JRAS*, vol. 12, pp. 153–251. 1850.

Wilson, John. *Memoir on the Cave-Temples and Monasteries, and Other Ancient Buddhist, Brahmanical, and Jaina Remains of Western India. JBBRAS*, vol. 3, part 2, no. 13, pp. 36–107. 1850.

1851

Hoffmann, Johann Joseph. *Das Buddha-Pantheon von Nippon (Buts-zo dsu i)*. "Aus dem japanischen Originale übers. und mit erläut. Anm. versehen." *Nippon Archiv*, vol. 5, 41 pl. Leiden, P. F. Siebold, 1851. [Tr.]

Jones, (Rev.) J. Taylor. *Some Account of the Trai Phum. JIA*, vol. 5, pp. 538–42. 1851.

Low, James. *On the Ancient Connection between Kedah and Siam. JIA*, vol. 5, 30 pp. 1851.

Mason (Rev.) Francis. *Hints on the Introduction of Buddhism into Burmah. JAOS*, vol. 2, pp. 334–37. 1851.

Morton, W. *Vajra Suchi. The Needle of Adamant, or The Original Divine Institution of Caste.* "Examined and refuted by the Buddhist Pundit Ashwaghosha. English and Tamil versions of the Sanskrit original." Joffna, 1851. 42 pp. [Tr.]

Perry, (Sir) Erskine. *Account of the Great Hindu Monarch Asoka.* "Chiefly from the *Indische Alterthumskunde* of Pr Christian Lassen." *JBBRAS*, vol. 3, part 2, pp. 149–78. 1853.

Prinsep, Henry Thoby, and Prinsep, J. *Tibet, Tartary and Mongolia.* "Their social and political condition, and the Religion of Boodh, as there existing." London, 1851. 168 pp.

Schiefner, Anton (von). *Eine tibetische Lebensbeschreibung Cakjamuni's, des Begründers des Buddhatums. (Im Auszug mitgeteilt), Mém. présentés à l'Acad. impér. d. Sc. de St.-Pétersbourg*, vol. 6, pp. 231–332. 1851.

Taylor, W. C. *Ancient and Modern India.* "Rev. and continued to the present time by P. J. Mackenna." London, 1851.

1852

Alwis, James (d'). *The Sidath Sangawara.* "A grammar of the Singhalese language. Tr. into Engl., with Introd., Notes, and App." Colombo, 1852. 248 pp. [Tr.]

Barthélemy Saint-Hilaire, Jules. *Sur les travaux de M. Eugène Burnouf. JS*, pp. 473–87, 561–75. 1852.

Bennett, (Rev.) Chester. *Life of Gaudama.* "A tr. from the Burmese book entitled *Ma-la-len-ga-ra Wottoo* by Rev. Chester Bennet." *JAOS*, vol. 3, pp. 1–163. 1852. [Tr.]

Böhtlingk, Otto von. *Sanskrit-Wörterbuch.* "Hrsg. von der Kaiserlichen Akademie der Wissenschaften, bearbeitet von Otto Böhtlingk und Rudolph Roth." *Buchdr. d. Kais. Akad. d. Wiss.* 7 vols., 1142, 1100, 1016, 1214, 1678, 1506, 1822 pp. St. Petersburg, (1852)–1855–75.

Burnouf, Eugène. *Le Lotus de la Bonne Loi*, "tr. du sanscrit, accompagné d'un commentaire et de vingt et un Mémoires relatifs au Buddhisme, par M. E. Burnouf. (Ed., avec avertissement, par Jules Mohl)." Paris, printed with Government authorization at the Imprimerie nationale, 1852. 897 pp.

Campbell, A. *Diary of a Journey through Sikim to the Frontiers of Tibet.* "With a map. (Communicated by Sir James Colvile, Kt.)." *JASB*, vol. 21, pp. 407–28, 477–501, 563–75. 1852. See Ph. Ed. Foucaux, 1856.

Chapman, I. J. *Some Additional Remarks upon the Ancient City of Anarajapura or Anuradhapura, and the Hill Temple of Mehentélé, in the Island of Ceylon. JRAS*, vol. 13, pp. 164–78. 1852.

Cunningham, Sir Alexander. *Opening of the Topes or Buddhist Monuments of Central-India. JRAS*, vol. 13, pp. 108–14. 1852.

Drugulin, W. In J. F. Davis, *China und die Chinese.* Stuttgart, 1852. [Tr.]

Huc, (Abbé) Evariste-Régis. *Recollections of a Journey through Tartary, Thibet and China, 1844–6.* New York, Appleton, 1852. 2 vols. [Tr.] See J. Gabet and E.-R. Huc, 1853.

Köppen, Carl Friedrich. *Einige Worte über den Buddhismus. Archiv. f. Wissenschaftliche Kunde v. Russland*, vol. 11, pp. 51–81, 250–78, 450–75. Berlin, 1852.

Pococke, Edward. *India in Greece, or Truth in Mythology.* "Containing the sources of the Hellenic race, the wars of the Grand Lhama and the Buddhistic propaganda in Greece." 1852. 406 pp.

Schiefner, Anton (von). *Bericht über die neueste Büchersendung aus Peking. Mélanges asiatiques*, vol. 1, 25 pp. St. Petersburg, 1852.

220 ——. *Das buddhistiche Sûtra der zwei und vierzig Sätze*. "Aus dem Tibetischen übers. von A. Schiefner." *Mélanges asiatiques*, vol. 1, 18 pp. St. Petersburg, 1852.

——. *Ergänzungen und Berichtigungen zu Schmidt's Ausgabe des Dsanglun*. Buchdr. d. Kais. d. Wiss., 94 pp. St. Petersburg, 1852.

——. *Tibetische Studien*. *Mélanges asiatiques*, vol. 1, 70 pp. St. Petersburg, 1852.

——. *Über die Verschlechterungsperioden der Menschheit nach buddhistischer Anschauungsweise*. *Mélanges asiatiques*, 1, 10 pp. St. Petersburg, 1852.

Smith, T. *Five Years' Residence at Nepaul, 1841–5*. 1852.

Spiegel, Friedrich von. *Buddhismus*. *Allg. Msch. f. Wiss. u. Liter.*, 15 pp. Halle, 1852.

Tennent, (Sir) James Emerson. *Das Christentum in Ceylon, Mag. f. d. Neueste Gesch. d. Evangel. Missions- und Bibelgesell*, pp. 1–176. 1852.

Thomson, T. D. *Western Himalaya and Tibet*. "A narrative of a journey through the mountains of North India during the years' 1847–8." London, 1852.

Wade, J. *A Dictionary of Boodhism and Burman Literature*. "Compiled by J. Wade." Maulmain, 1852.

Weber, Albrecht Friedrich. *Akademische Vorlesungen über indische Literaturgeschichte*. Berlin, 1852. 285 pp.

Wuttke, Carl Friedrich Adolf. *Geschichte des Heidenthums in Beziehung auf Religion*. "Wissen, Kunst, Sittlichkeit und Staatsleben." Breslau, Josef Max u. Komp, 1852–53. 2 vols., 356, 598 pp.

1853

Bayley, E. Cliva. *Note on Some Sculptures Found in the District of Peshawur*. *JASB*, vol. 21, pp. 602–21. 1853.

Bradley, W. H. *Buddhist Cave-Temples in the Circars of Baitalbari and Dowlatabad, in H. H. the Nizam's Dominions*. *JBBRAS*, vol. 5, pp. 117–24. 1853.

Duncker, Max W. *Geschichte des Alterthums*. Berlin, 1853–63. 4 vols., 934, 698, 635, 907 pp.

Friederich, R. *Untersuchungen über die Kawisprache und über die Sanskrit- und Kawiliteratur auf der Insel Java*. *Weber's Indische Studien*, vol. 2, 26 pp. Berlin, 1853.

Gabet, J., and Huc, E.-R. *Souvenirs d'un voyage dans la Tartarie, le Tibet et la Chine, pendant les années 1844, 1845, 1846*. Paris, 1853 (3d ed., 1857; 4th ed., 1860). 2 vols., 430, 524 pp.

Gogerly, (Rev.) Daniel John. *Buddhism. Chariya-Pitaka*, *JCBRAS*, no. 6, 11 pp. 1853.

——. *The Laws of the Buddhist Priesthood*. *JCBRAS*, nums. 6, 8, 11, 14, 26, 9 pp. 1853–55.

Hardy, (Rev.) R. Spence. *Manual of Buddhism in Its Modern Development*. "Tr. from Singhalese MSS." London, Williams and Norgate, 1853. 533 pp.

Julien, Stanislas. *Voyages des pèlerins bouddhistes* (t. I: *Histoire de la vie de Hiouen-Thsang et de ses voyages dans l'Inde*; vol. 2–3: *Mémoires sur les contrées occidentales*). "Tr. . . . du chinois par M. Stanislas Julien." Paris, Impr. impér., 1853–58. 3 vols., 472, 493, 576 pp. [Tr.] See F. M. Müller, 1857; H. H. Wilson, 1860.

Knighton, William. *Forest Life in Ceylon*. "With four dialogues between a Buddhist and a Christian." London, Hurst and Blackett, 1853–54. 2 vols.

Nève, Félix. *Le Bouddhisme, son fondateur et ses écritures*. Paris, C. Douniol, 1853. 55 pp.

Schönberg, Erich von. *Blick auf die Felsentempel Indiens*. *ZDMG*, vol. 7, pp. 101–3. 1853.

Stevenson, (Rev.) John. *Names and Facts Connected in the Kanheri (Kenery) Inscriptions*. "With Tr. and appended by the Rev. J. Stevenson." *JBBRAS*, vol. 5, 34 pp. 1853.

Weber, Albrecht Friedrich. *Die Verbindungen Indiens mit den Ländern im Westen*. *Mschr. f. Wiss. u. Litt.* August and September, 1853.

Wilsen, F. C. *Boro Boedoer*. *TBG*, vol. 1, pp. 235–303. 1853. See R. Friederich, *TBG*, 1854.

Wilson, John. *Second Memoir on the Cave-Temples and Monasteries, and Other Ancient Buddhist, Brahmanical and Jaina Remains of Western India*. *JBBRAS*, vol. 4, no. 17, pp. 340–79. 1853.

1854

Barthélemy Saint-Hilaire, Jules. *De la morale et de la métaphysique du Boudddhisme.* "9 articles au sujet de *Le Lotus de la Bonne Loi de Burnouf.*" *JS*, May–Oct. 1854; Jan., Feb., and Apr. 1855. 153 pp.

——. *Mémoire sur le Bouddhisme. Séances et Travaux de l'Acad. d. Sc. morales et politiques*, ser. 3, vols. 9–12, 82, 68, 56, 21 pp. Paris, 1854.

Cunningham, Sir Alexander. *The Bhilsa Topes, or Buddhist Monuments of Central India.* "Comprising a brief historical sketch of the rise, progress and decline of Buddhism (with an account of the opening and examination of the various groups of topes around Bhilsa)." London, Smith, Elder, 1854. 370 pp.

——. *Coins of Indian Buddhist Satraps with Greek Inscriptions. JASB*, vol. 23, pp. 679–714. 1854.

——. *Ladak, physical, statistical and historical.* "With notices of the surrounding countries." London, 1854.

Fortune, Robert. *Wanderungen in China.* "Aus dem Englischen übers. von Julius Theodor Zenker." Leipzig, Dyk'sche Buchhandlung, 1854. 413 pp. [Tr.]

Foucaux, Philippe Edouard. *Parabole de l'enfant égaré, formant le chapitre iv du "Lotus de la Bonne Loi."* "Publ. pour la première fois en sanscrit et en tibétain, lithographiée à la manière des livres du Tibet, et accompagnée d'une tr. française d'après la version tibétaine du *Kanjour.*" Paris, Benjamin Duprat, 1854. 100 pp. [Ed. and tr.]

Frere, Sir Henry Bartle Edward. *Descriptive Notices of Antiquities in Scinde.* "Communicated." *JBBRAS*, vol. 5, no. 19, pp. 349–62. 1854.

Friederich, R. *Eenige aanteekeningen op het stuk over Boro-Boedoer, door F. C. Wilsen. TBG*, vol. 2, pp. 1–10. Batavia, 1854.

——. *Over inscription van Java, en Sumatra.* "Bijdrage van R. Friederich." *Verhandelingen van het Bataviaasch Genootschap van Kunst en Wetensch*, vol. 26, 100 pp. Batavia, 1854.

Graul, K. *Die tamulische Bibliothek der evangelisch-lutherischen Missionsanstalt zu Leipzig*, 2: *Widerlegung des buddhistischen Systems vom Standpunkte des Sivaismus. ZDMG*, vol. 8, pp. 720–38. 1854.

——. *Reise in Ostindien* (von Dez. 1849 bis Okt. 1852). Leipzig, Dörffling and Franke, 1854–56.

Hooker, J. D. *Himalayan Journals.* "Notes of a Naturalist in Bengal, the Sikkim and Nepal Himalayas, the Khasia Mountains, etc." London, 1854. 2 vols.

Impey, E. *Description of the Caves of Koolvee in Malwa. JBBRAS*, vol. 5, no. 19, pp. 336–49. 1854.

Krick (Abbé). *Relation d'un voyage au Thibet en 1852 et d'un voyage chez les Abors en 1853 suivie de quelques documents de Renou et Latry.* Paris, 1854.

Mason, (Rev.) Francis. *Mulamuli, or the Buddhist Genesis of Eastern India, from the Shan, through the Talaing and Burmah. JAOS*, vol. 4, pp. 103–16. 1854.

Milne, (Rev.) William Charles. *Pagodas in China.* "A general description of the pagodas in China. Read to the Society, 9th. May, 1854." *JNCB*, part 5, art. 2. 1854.

Neumann, Carl Friedrich. *Der indische Archipelagus und die Engländer. Historisches Taschenbuch*, 3, Folge, 5, pp. 1–74. 1854.

Pallegoix, D. J. B. *Description du royaume Thaï ou Siam.* "Comprenant la topographie, histoire naturelle, mœurs et coutumes, législation, commerce, industrie, langue, littérature, religion, annales des Thaï, etc." 2 vols., 488, 426 pp. Paris, 1854.

Stevenson, (Rev.) John. *On the Nasik Cave-inscriptions. JBBRAS*, vol. 5, 28 pp. 1854.

——. *Sahyadri Inscriptions. JBBRAS*, vol. 5, 28 pp. 1854.

——. *The Tithyas or Tirthakas of the Buddhists and the Gymnosophists of the Greeks, Digambar Jains. JBBRAS*, vol. 5, no. 20, pp. 401–7. 1854.

Tennent, (Sir) James Emerson. *Das Christenthum in Ceylon.* "Dessen Einführung und Fort-

222   schritt unter den Portugiesen, Hollandern, den britischen und amerikanischen Missionen nebst einer geschichtlichen Übersicht über den brahmanischen und buddhistischen Aberglauben. Übers. von J. Th. Zenker." Leipzig, 1854. [Tr.]

Thomas, Edward. *Note on the Present State of the Excavations of Sarnath. JASB*, vol. 23, pp. 469–76. 1854.

Thorton, Edward. *A Gazetteer of Territories under the East India Co. and of Native States*. London, 1854.

Weber, Albrecht Friedrich. *Die neuern Forschungen über das alte Indien*. "Ein Vortrag, im Berliner Wissenschaftl. Verein am 4. März 1854 gehalten." Halle, 1854. 46 pp.

Wendt, Richard. *Die Insel Ceylon bis in das erste Jahrhundert nach Christi Geburt*. Dorpat, Heinr. Laakmann, 1854. 121 pp.

1855
Barthélemy Saint-Hilaire, Jules. *Du Bouddhisme*. Paris, B. Duprat, 1855. 248 pp. See J. Barthélemy Saint-Hilaire, 1860.

———. *Le Néo-Bouddhisme. Mém. de l'Acad. d. Sc. morales*, vol. 19, p. 415. 1855.

Dalton, E. T. *Notes on Assam Temple Ruins. JASB*, vol. 24, 24 pp., 10 pl. 1855.

Edkins, (Rev.) Joseph. *Notices of Buddhism in China, Shanghai Almanac and Miscellany*. 1855. 39 pp.

———. *Notices of the Chinese Buddhism. N.C. Herald*, no. 196f. Shanghai, 1855.

Fausböll, Michael Viggo. *Dhammapadam*. "Ex tribus codicibus Havniensibus Palice edidit, Latine vertit, excerptis ex Commentario Palico notisque illustravit V. Fausböll." Havniae, 1855. 470 pp. [Ed. and Tr.]

Gabet, J., in J. Gabet and E.-R. Huc. *Wanderungen durch die Mongolei nach Tibet zur Hauptstadt des Tale Lama. Hausbibliothek für Länder- und Völkerkunde*, vol. 7, 360 pp. Leipzig, Carl B. Forck, 1855.

Hardwick, Charles. *Christ and Other Masters*. "An historical inquiry into some of the chief parallelisms and contrasts between Christianity and the religious systems of the ancient world." London, 1855. 2 vols.

Huc, (Abbé) Evariste-Régis. *The Chinese Empire*. London, Longmans, 1855.

Körös, Alexander Csoma de. *A Brief Notice of the Subhashita Ratna Nidhi of Saskya Pandita*. "With Extracts and Translation by M. Alexander Csoma de Körös." *JASB*, vol. 24, pp. 141–65; vol. 15, pp. 257–94. 1855–56. [Tr.]

Mason, (Rev.) Francis. *Note on Buddhism in Burmah. JAOS*, vol. 5. 1855.

Mitra, Rajendrala. *Notes on Ancient Inscriptions from the Chusan Archipelago and the Hazara Country. JASB*, vol. 24, 5 pp. 1855.

Roth, R. In R. Roth and O. Böhtlingk, *Sanskrit-Wörterbuch*. St. Petersburg, 1855–75.

Stevenson, (Rev.) John. *Buddhist Antiquities in China. JBBRAS*, vol. 5, no. 20, pp. 408–12. 1855.

Thomas, Edward. *On the Epoch of the Gupta Dynasty. JASB*, vol. 24, 26, 36 pp. 1855.

Troup, James. *A Paper on the Shin Sect*. "Read before the Asiatic Society of Japan." 1855.

Wuttke, Carl Friedrich Adolf. *China's religiöse, sittliche und gesellschaftliche Zustände*. Berlin, Evangelischer Verein, 1855.

1856
Allen, David. *India Ancient and Modern, Geographical, Historical, Political, Social and Religious*. Boston, 1856. 618 pp.

Baudry, F. J. B. F. Obry: "Du Nirvana indien." *R. de l'Instruction publique*. 6 Nov. 1856. [Rec.]

Bazin, M. *Recherches sur l'origine, l'histoire et la constitution des ordres religieux dans l'Empire chinois. JA*, ser. 5, vol. 8, 70 pp. 1856.

Eisenhart, Hugo. *Die gegenwärtige Staatenwelt in ihrer natürlichen Gliederung und ihren leitenden*

Grossmächten. vol. 1: *Die morgenländische Staattenwelt: Buddhistisches und muhammedanisches*   223
Staatensystem. Leipzig, F. Fleischer, 1856.

Foucaux, Philippe Edouard. *Le Tibet Oriental.* "(From a study by A. Campbell, in *JASB*)."
Extr. de la Revue de l'Orient et de l'Algérie. Paris, Aug. 1856.

Gützlaff, Karl Friedrich Augustus. *Remarks on the Present State of Buddhism in China.* "Communicated by Lieut.-Col. W. H. Sykes." *JRAS,* vol. 16, pp. 73–92. 1856.

Heine, Wilhelm. *Reise um die Erde nach Japan.* "In den Jahren 1853, 1854 u. 1855 unternommen im Auftrage der Regierung der vereinigt. Staaten. Deutsche Originalausgabe."
Leipzig, Hermann Costenoble; New York, Carl F. Günther, 1856. 2 vols., 321, 375 pp.

Huc, (Abbé) Evariste-Régis. *Das chinesische Reich.* "Deutsche Ausg." Leipzig, Dyk'sche Buchhdlg., 1856. 2 vols., 243, 276 pp. [Tr.]

Impey, E. *Description of the Caves of Bagh in Rath. JBBRAS,* 1856. vol. 5, 29 pp.

Julien, Stanislas. *Extrait du Livre IV (Royaume de Tsekia) des Mémoires de Hiouen-Thsang,* "tr. par M. Julien." *JRAS,* vol. 16, pp. 340–45. 1856. [Tr.]

——. *Notice sur le royaume de Tse-Kia (Tchêka) par Hiouen-Thsang,* "tr. du chinois par S. Julien." *R. de l'Or. et de l'Algérie,* vol. 20, pp. 209–16. 1856. [Tr.]

Kruse, Theodor. *Indiens alte Geschichte.* "Nach den ausländischen Quellen, im Vergleich mit den inländischen, dargestellt und besonders hinsichtlich des Handels und der Industrie mit Rücksicht auf die neuesten Zeiten zuerst bearbeitet." Leipzig, Dyk'sche Buchhandlung, 1856. 438 pp.

Macclatchie, (Rev.) T. M. *The Chinese on the Plain of China or a Connection Established between the Chinese and All Other Nations through Their Theology. JRAS,* vol. 16, 48 pp. 1856.

Mac Farlane, Charles. *Japan.* "An account, geographical and historical, from the earliest period at which the islands composing this Empire were known to Europeans, down to the present time, and the expedition fitted out in the United States, etc." Hartford, 1856.

Malan, Salomon Caesar. *A Letter on the Pantheistic and on the Buddhistic Tendency of the Chinese and of the Mongolian Versions of the Bible.* London, 1856. 38 pp.

Mitra, Rajendrala. *Index by Rajendrala Mitra to vol. 19–20 of the Asiatic Researches and vol. 1–22 of the Journal of the Asiatic Society of Bengal.* Calcutta, 1856.

Mohl, Jules. *Progrès du Bouddhisme dans l'Inde. Ann. de Philos. chrét.,* ser. 4, vol. 13, 3 pp. Paris, 1856.

Nève, Félix. *La Société bouddhique. Correspondant,* n.s., vol. 3, 4. Paris, 1856–57.

Obry, Jean Baptiste François. *Du Nirvâna indien, ou De l'affranchissement de l'âme après la mort, selon les Brahmanes et les Bouddhistes.* Amiens, 1856. 130 pp.

Oldfield, R. C. *Correspondence relating to the Exploration of the Ruins of Sarnath.* "Communicated by the Government of the N.W.P. to R. C. Oldfield." *JASB,* vol. 25, 10 pp. 1856.

Oldham, H. *Reports of the Mission to Ava in 1855.* "General Reports by H. Yule; Geological Reports by H. Oldham." Calcutta, 1856. 316, 70 pp.

Palladius (Palladji), O. (i.e. Piotr Ivanovicth Kafarov). *Historische Skizzen des alten Buddhismus,* Berlin, Archiv. f. Wissenschaftliche Kunde v. Russland,* vol. 15, pp. 206–36. 1856.

——. *Lebensbeschreibung des Buddha Sakjamuni. Berlin, Archiv. f. Wissenschaftliche Kunde v. Russland,* vol. 15, pp. 1–41. 1856.

Phayre, (Sir) Arthur Purves. *Original Text and Translation of a Scroll of Silver in the Burmese Language, found in a Buddhist Pagoda at Prome. JASB,* vol. 25, pp. 173–78. 1856.

Schiefner, Anton (von). *Bericht über Herrn Prof. Wassiljew's Werk "Über den Buddhismus, seine Dogmen-Geschichte und Literatur." Mélanges asiatiques,* vol. 2, 5 pp. 1856. See W. Wassiljew, 1857.

——. *Bericht über wissenschaftliche Thätigkeit des Herrn Prof. Wassiljew. Mélanges asiatiques,* vol. 2, 2 pp. 1856.

224   ——. *Ph. Ed. Foucaux: "Rgya-tch'er-rol-pa ou Développement des Jeux." Mélanges asiatiques*, vol. 1, 26 pp. 1856. [Rec.]

Schoebel, Charles. *Le Bouddha et le Bouddhisme. Ann. de philos. chrét.* 1856–57.

Speir, (Mrs.) C. *Life in Ancient India.* "With a map and illus. drawn on wood by George Scharf." London, Bombay, 1856. 464 pp.

Stevenson, (Rev.) John. *Parting Visit to the Sahyadri Caves. JBBRAS*, vol. 5, 4 pp. 1856.

Sykes, William, Henry. *On the Miniature Chaityas and Inscriptions of the Buddhist Religious Dogma, Found in the Ruins of the Temple of Sarnath, near Benares. JRAS*, vol. 16, pp. 37–53, 227–28. 1856.

Weber, Albrecht Friedrich. *Über den Buddhismus.* "Ein Vortrag." *Ausland*, vol. 29, pp. 289–93, 321–25. Stüttgart, 1856.

Wilson, Horace Hayman. *Buddhist Inscription of King Priyadarsi.* "Translation and observations." *JRAS*, vol. 16, pp. 357–67. 1856.

——. *Notes of a Correspondence with Sir John Bowring on Buddhist Literature in China.* "With notices of Chinese Buddhist works translated from the Sanskrit, by J. Edkins." *JRAS*, vol. 16, pp. 316–39. 1856.

——. *On Buddha and Buddhism. JRAS*, vol. 16, pp. 229–65. 1856.

—— [Theodor Goldstücker]. *Dictionary, Sanskrit and English.* "Extended and improved from the second edition of the dictionary of Pr H. H. Wilson, with his Sanction and Concurrence." Berlin and London, 1856.

Yule, Sir Henry. *Reports of the Mission to Ava in 1855.* Calcutta, 1856.

1857

Davis, Sir John Francis. *China.* "A general description of that empire and its inhabitants; with the history of foreign intercourse down to the events which produced the dissolution of 1857. A new ed. rev. and enl." London, John Murray, 1857. 2 vols., 480, 428 pp.

Eckstein, Baron d'. *Mémoires sur les contrées occidentales*, "tr. par S. Julien." *JA*, ser. 5, vol. 10, pp. 475–552. 1857. [Rec.]

Fonseca, Willheim da. *Altindische Mythologie.* Berlin, Gustav Hempel, 1857. 225 pp.

Friederich, R. *Over inscription van Java en Sumatra, voor het eerst ontcijferd.* Batavia, 1857.m

Holmboe, Christian Andreas. *Traces de Buddhisme en Norvège avant l'introduction du Christianisme.* Paris, S. Raçon, 1857. 74 pp. See R. Mitra, 1858.

Huc, (Abbé) Evariste-Régis. *Le Christianisme en Chine, en Tartarie et au Thibet.* Paris, 1857–58. 4 vols.

Köppen, Carl Friedrich. *Die Religion des Buddha.* Vol. 1. *Die Religion des Buddha und ihre Entstehung.* Berlin, F. Schneider, 1857. 616 pp. See C. F. Köppen, 1859.

Lavollée, Charles. *Le Royaume de Siam et une ambassade anglaise à Bangkok. RDM*, vol. 12, 32 pp. Paris, 1857.

Major, R. H. *India in the Fifteenth Century.* "Being a collection of narratives of voyages to India, tr. from Latin, Persian, Russian, and Italian sources." London, Hakluyt Soc., 1857.

Müller, Friedrich Max. *Buddhism and Buddhist Pilgrims.* "A review of S. Julien's *Voyages des pèlerins bouddhistes." The Times*, 17 and 20 April 1857.

——. *Buddhism and Buddhist Pilgrims.* "A review of M. Stanislas Julien's *Voyages des pèlerins bouddhistes*, reprinted with additions, together with a Letter on the Original *Meaning of Nirvana."* London, Williams and Norgate, 1857. 54 pp. See S. Julien, 1853.

——. *The Meaning of Nirvana.* London, 1857.

Pavie, Théodore. *Etude sur le Sy-yéou-tchin-tsuen, roman bouddhique chinois. JA*, ser. 5, vol. 9, pp. 357–92; vol. 10, pp. 308–74. 1857.

Scherr, Johannes. *Geschichte der Religion.* Leipzig, Otto Wigand, 1857. 2 vols.

Urquhart, D. *The Sraddha.* "The keystone of the Brahmanical, Buddhistic, and Arian religions, as illustrative of the dogma and duty of adoption among the princes and people 225 of India." London, 1857. 44 pp.

Wassiljew, W. *Bouddhisme. Sa doctrine, son histoire et sa littérature* (in Russian). 1857.

Weber, Albrecht Friedrich. *Buddhismus, in Bluntschli's Staatswörterbuch*. Vol. 2, pp. 279–83. Stüttgart, 1857.

———. *Indische Skizzen*. "Vier bisher in Zeitschriften zerstreute Vorträge und Abhandlungen. Mit 1 Schrifttaf." Berlin, Ferdinand Dümmler, 1857. 150 pp.

Williams, S. Wells. *The Middle Kingdom, or Survey of the Geography, Government, Education, Social Life, Arts, Language, Religion, etc., of the Chinese Empire and its Inhabitants*. New York, 1857. 2 vols., 590, 617 pp.

Yule, Sir Henry. *An Account of the Ancient Buddhist Remains at Pagan on the Irawadi. JASB*, vol. 26, pp. 1–51, 4 pl. 1857.

1858

Abel, Karl. *Arbeiten der Kaiserlich Russischen Gesandschaft zu Peking über China, sein Volk, seine Religion, seine Institutionen, sozialen Verhältnisse, etc.* "Aus dem Rüssischen nach dem in St. Petersburg 1852–57 veröffentlichen Original von Karl Abel u. F. A. Mecklenburg." Berlin, F. Heinicke, 1858. [Tr.]

Alger, W. R. *The Brahmanic and Buddhist Doctrine of a Future Life. North Amer. R.*, vol. 86. Boston, 1858. 29 pp.

Benfey, Theodor. *Nachweisung einer buddhistischen Recension und mongolischen Bearbeitung der indischen Sammlung von Erzählungen, welche unter dem Namen Vetâlapancavimçati bekannt ist, Bull. de la Cl. hist.-philol. de l'Acad. impér. d. Sc. de St.-Pétersbourg*, vol. 15. 1858.

Edkins, (Rev.) Joseph. *A Buddhist Shastra*. "Read before the Society, November 17th, 1857. Tr. from the Chinese, with an analysis and notes." *JNCB*, no. 1, pp. 107–28. 1858. [Tr.]

———. *Notice of the Wu-Wei-Kian, a Reformed Buddhist Sect*. "Read before the Society, January 13th, 1858." *Transac. NCB*, part. 6, art. 4. 1858.

Foucaux, Philippe Edouard. *Grammaire de la langue tibétaine*. Original book by Benjamin Duprat (printed with permisson of the emperor, at the Imprimerie impériale). Paris, 1858. 231 pp.

———. *Le Trésor des Belles Paroles*. "Choix de Sentences composées en tibétain par le Lama Saskya Pandita, suivies d'une élégie tirée du Kanjour tr. pour la première fois en français, par Ph.Ed. Foucaux, et texte tibétain." Paris, B. Duprat, 1858. 46 pp. [Ed. and tr.]

Gurius, O. *Die Gelübde der Buddhisten und die Zeremonie ihrer Ablegung bei den Chinesen*. In K. Abel et F. A. Mecklenburg, *Arbeiten der Kaiserlich Russischen Gesandtschaft zu Peking*, vol. 2, pp. 315–419. Berlin, F. Heinicke, 1858.

"Indian missionary." *The Indian Religions, or Results of the Mysterious Buddhism*. "By an Indian Missionary." London, 1858. 172 pp.

Kaüffer, J. Ernst Rudolf. *Geschichte von Ost-Asien*. "Für Freunde der Geschichte der Menschheit dargestellt." Leipzig, F. A. Brockhaus, 1858–60. 3 vols., 465, 814, 727 pp.

Logan, J. R. *The West-himalaic or Tibetan Tribes of Assam, Birma and Pegu. JIA*, n.s., vol. 2, pp. 68–114, 230–33. 1858.

Milne, (Rev.) William Charles. *Life in China*. 1858.

Mitra, Rajendrala. *Buddhism and Odinism, Their Similitude*. "Illus. by Extracts from Pr Holmboe's memoir on the Traces de Buddhisme en Norvège." *JASB*, vol. 27, pp. 46–69. 1858.

Muir, John. *Original Sanskrit Texts on the Origin and History of the People of India; Their Religion and Institutions*. "Collected, tr. and illus. by notes." London, Trübner, 1858–70. 5 vols. [Ed. and tr.]

Müller, Friedrich Max. *Dagobas aus Ceylon. ZDMG*, vol. 12, pp. 514–17. 1858.

Nil, archevêque de Iaroslav. *Le Buddhisme en Sibérie* (in Russian). St. Petersburg, 1858. 386 pp.

226   Palladius, O. (Piotr Ivanovicth Kafarov). *Das Leben Buddhas*. In K. Abel and F. A. Mecklenburg, *Arb. d. Kais. Russ. Gesandt. zu Peking*, etc., vol. 2, pp. 197–265. Berlin, 1858. [Tr.]

Pavie, Théodore. *Cakia-mouni*. "La société hindoue pendant la période bouddhique et l'invasion musulmane." *RDM*, Period 2, vol. 13, p. 26. 1858.

Prinsep, Henry Thoby, and Prinsep, J. *Essays on Indian Antiquities, Historic, Numismatic and Paleographic, of the late James Prinsep*. "To which are added his useful tables, illus. on Indian history, chronology, modern coinages, weights, measures, etc. Ed. with note and addit. matter, by Edward Thomas." London, 1858. 3 vols., 436, 224, 336 pp.

Saint-Martin, Louis Vivien de. *Mémoire analytique sur la carte de l'Asie centrale et de l'Inde, construite d'après le Si-yu-ki (Mémoires sur les contrées occidentales) et les autres relations chinoises des premiers siècles de notre ère, pour les voyages de Hiuoen-Thsang dans l'Inde, depuis l'année 629 jusqu'en 645*. Paris, Impr. impér., 1858. 178 pp. See H. H. Wilson, 1860.

Schiefner, Anton (von). *Buddhistische Triglotte, d.h. Sanskrit-tibetisch-mongolisches Wörterverzeichniss*. "Gedrückt mit den aus dem Nachlass des Barons Schilling von Canstadt stammenden Holztafeln u. mit einem kurzen Vorwort vorsehen von A. Schiefner." St. Petersburg, 1858. 80 pp. [Ed.]

———. *Über die unter dem Namen "Geschichte des Ardshi Bordshi Chan" bekannte mongolische Märchensammlung. Mélanges asiatiques*, vol. 3, 14 pp. 1858.

Schlagintweit. *Tibetische Handschriften*. "Gesammelt v. A., H. und R. Schlagintweit. Hektographiertes Manuskript, Zwibrücken, Ersch. nach 1858." 7 pp. [Ed.]

Sykes, William Henry. *Account of Some Golden Relics Discovered at Rangoon, and Exhibited at a Meeting of the Society on the 6th June 1857 by Permission of the Court of Directors of the East India Company. JRAS*, vol. 17, pp. 298–308. 1858.

Vidyasagara, Iswarachandra. *Sarvadarsana Sangraha, or Epitome of the Different Systems of Indian Philosophy, by Madhavacharya*. Bibl. I., ed. Iswarachandra Vidyasagara. Calcutta, 1858. 180 pp. [Ed.]

Weber, Albrecht Friedrich. *Derniers Résultats des travaux sur l'Inde antique*. "Tr. par F. Baudry." *R. germanique*, vol. 1, 29 pp. Paris, 1858. [Tr.]

———. *Über das Catrunjaya Mahatmya*. "Ein Beitrag zur Gesch. der Jaina." Leipzig, 1858. 118 pp.

———. *Über das Makasajâtakam, Mb. d. Königl. Akad. d. Wiss. zu Berlin*, pp. 265–70. 15 Apr. 1858.

Yule, Sir Henry. *A Narrative of the Mission Sent by the Governor-General of India to the Court of Ava in 1855*. "With notices of the country, government, and people." London, Smith Elder, 1858. 391 pp.

1859

Bigandet, (Right Rev.) P. *The Life of Gaudama, the Buddha of the Burmese*. "With annotations. Notice of the Phongies or Buddhist religions and the ways to Niban." Rangoon, 1859. 328 pp.

Bonneau, A. *Les Stoupas, monuments religieux du Bouddhisme. R. orientale et américaine*, vol. 2, 8 pp. Paris, 1859.

Brumond. *Über Altertümer des Ostindischen Archipels, insbesondere die Hindu-Altertümer und Tempelruinen auf Java, Madura und Bali von Brumond und Hoevell*. "Aus dem Holländischen, hrsg. von Joh. Müller." Berlin, 1859 (1865). [Tr.]

Edkins, (Rev.) Joseph. *The Religious Condition of the Chinese*. "With observations on the prospects of Christian conversion amongst that people." London, 1859. 288 pp.

Galsan-Gombojew. *Über alte und neue Gebräuche der Mongolen*. "Mit Beziehung auf Plano Carpini's Beschreibungen." *Erman's Archiv f. Wissenschaftliche Kunde v. Russland*, vol. 19, pp. 93–108. 1859.

Hall, Fitz-Edward. *An Index to the Bibliography of the Indian Philosophical System*. Calcutta, 1859.

Julien, Stanislas. *Les Avadanas*. "Contes et apologues indiens, inconnus jusqu'à ce jour, suivis   227
de fables, de poésies et de nouvelles chinoises, tr. par S. Julien." Paris, 1859. 3 vols., 240,
252, 272 pp. [Tr.]
——. *Listes diverses des noms des dix-huit écoles schismatiques qui sont sorties du Bouddhisme. JA*, ser. 5,
vol. 14, pp. 327–64. 1859.
Köppen, Carl Friedrich. *Die Religion des Buddha*. Vol. 2. *Die Lamaische Hierarchie und Kirche*.
Berlin, F. Schneider, 1859. 408 pp. See C. F. Köppen, 1857.
Laffitte, Pierre. *Cours philosophique sur l'histoire générale de l'humanité*. "Discours d'ouverture."
Paris, 1859.
Latham, R. G. *Ethnology of India*. London, 1859. 376 pp.
Mason, (Rev.) Francis. *A Sketch of Toungoo History. JASB*, vol. 28, 8 pp. 1859.
Phayre, (Sir) Arthur Purves. *On the History of the Shwe Dagon Pagoda at Rangoon. JASB*, vol. 28, 8
pp. 1859.
Schiefner, Anton (von). *Carminis indici "Vimalaprasnottaearatnamala."* "Versio Tibetica ab
A. Schiefner, Petropoli." *Gratulationsschr. d. Kais. Ak. zum Jubiläum d. Univ. Jena*. 1859.
26 pp.
Steinmetz, Andrew. *Japan and Her People*. London, 1859.
Tennent, (Sir) James Emerson. *Ceylon*. "An account of the island, physical, historical and
topographical. With notices of its natural history, antiquities and productions." London, 1859. 3d ed. 2 vols.
Weber, Albrecht Friedrich. *Die Pâli-Legende von der Entstehung des Sâkya (Cakya)—und Koliya-
Geschlechtes, Mb. d. Königl. Akad. d. Wiss. zu Berlin*, pp. 328–46. 31 March 1859.
——. *Die Vajrasûci des Açvaghosha*. "Eine buddhistische Streitschrift über die Irrigkeit der
Ansprüche der Brâhmana-Kaste. (Gelesen in d. Akad. d. Wiss. am 26. Mai 1859)." *Abh.
d. Königl. Akad. d. Wiss. zu Berlin*, pp. 227–54. 1859.
——. *Histoire de la littérature indienne*. "Tr. par A. Sadous." Paris, 1859. [Tr.]
——. *Le Bouddhisme*. "Discours, tr. par F. Baudry." *R. germanique*, vol. 4, 19 pp. Paris, 1859.
[Tr.]
Weber, Albrecht Friedrich, and Schiefner, Anton (von). *Über ein indisches Würfelorakel. Mb. d.
K. Preuss. Akad. d. Wiss.* 1859.
Whitney, William Dwight. *On the Vedic Doctrine of a Future Life. Bibl. Sacra*, vol. 16, 17 pp.
Andover, 1859.

1860

Barthélemy Saint-Hilaire, Jules. *Le Bouddha et sa religion*. Paris, Didier et Cie, 1860 (re-ed. 1862
and 1866). 441 pp. See J. Barthélemy Saint-Hilaire, 1855; F. M. Müller, *Buddhism*, 1867.
Deschamps (Abbé). *Le Bouddhisme et l'Apologétique chrétienne*. Paris, 1860. 40 pp. See J. Bar-
thélemy Saint-Hilaire, 1880.
Fowle, E. *Translation of a Burmese Version of the Nidikyam, a Code of Ethics in Pali. JRAS*, vol. 17,
pp. 252–66. 1860.
Heine, Wilhelm. *Japan und seine Bewohner*. "Geschichtliche Rückblicke und ethnographische
Schilderungen von Land und Leuten." Leipzig, Hermann Costenoble, 1860. 383 pp.
Jacobs, Alfred. *Le Bouddhisme, son législateur et son influence sur le monde. RDM*, vol. 26, 125 pp.
Période 2. Paris, 1860.
Latham, R. G. *On the Date and Personality of Priyadarsi. JRAS*, vol. 17, 13 pp. 1860.
Lavollée, Charles. *Légendes et Paysages de l'Inde. L'Ile de Ceylan. RDM*, vol. 29, 30 pp. Période 2.
Paris, 1860.
Marshall, W. H. *Four Years in Burmah*. 2 vols. London, 1860.
Nicolas, Michel. *Le Lamaïsme. R. germanique*, vol. 12, 32, 46 pp. Paris, 1860. See C. F. Köppen,
1857, 1859.

228   Phayre, (Sir) Arthur Purves. *Remarks upon an Ancient Buddhist Monastery at Pu-gân, on the Irrawaddy*. *JASB*, vol. 29, pp. 346–51. 1860.

Rosenhahn, P. von. *Ceylon*. *Westermann's Mh.*, no. 43, 38 pp. Braunschweig, 1860.

Scherzer, Karl von. *Über einige auf der Insel Ceylon erworbene singhalesische Manuskripte*. *Westermann's Mh.*, no. 51, 4 pp. Braunschweig, 1860.

Schiefner, Anton (von). *Über die hohen Zahlen der Buddhisten*. *Mélanges asiatiques*, vol. 4, 20 pp. 1860–63.

——. *Über ein indisches Krähenorakel*. *Mélanges asiatiques*, vol. 4, 14 pp. 1860.

Wassiljew, W. *Der Buddhismus, seine Dogmen, Geschichte und Literatur*, vol. 1: *Allgemeine Übersicht*. "Aus dem Russischen übers. (von A. Schiefner)." St. Petersburg, Eggers; Riga, Samuel Schmidt; Leipzig, Leopold Voss, 1860. 380 pp. [Tr.]

Weber, Albrecht Friedrich. *Das Dhammapadam*. "Die älteste buddhistische Sittenlehre. Übersetzt." *ZDMG*, vol. 14, pp. 29–86. 1860. [Tr.]

——. *Über einige Lalenburger Streiche*. *Mb. d. Königl. Akad. d. Wiss. zu Berlin*, pp. 68–74. 1860.

Westergaard, Niels Ludwig. *Om den aeldste Tidsrum i den indiske Histoire med Hensyn til Literaturen*. "Buddhas Dödsaarog nougle andre Tidspunkter i Indiens aeldre Histoire." Copenhagen, 1860.

Wilson, Horace Hayman. *Summary Review of the Travels of Hiouen Thsang, from the Translation of the Si-yu-ki by M. Julien, and the Mémoire analytique of M. Vivien de St.-Martin*. *JRAS*, vol. 17, pp. 106–37. 1860.

1861

Bohlen, Petrus von. *Aus Cochinchina, Über Land und Meer*, vol. 6, pp. 687–90. 1861.

Böttger Karl. *Kulturgeschichte Indiens, in Indien u. seine Regierung*. Vol. 2. "Hrsg. von Leop. v. Orlich." Leipzig, Gustav Mayer, 1861. 394 pp.

Brockett, L. P. *Buddhism. Its Origin and Results*. *Methodist Quarterly R.*, vol. 43, 8 pp. New York, 1861.

Carrière, Moritz. *Nirvana*. *Z. f. Philos.*, n.s., vol. 39, 15 pp. Halle, 1861.

Carter, C. *Buddhistical Atheism, and How to Meet It*. 1861.

Deschamps (Abbé). *Les Origines du bouddhisme*. "Vues pour servir aux travaux de l'apologétique chrétienne." Paris, 1861. 32 pp.

Fausböll, Michael Viggo. *Five Jatakas*. "Containing a fairy tale, a comical story and three fables. In the original Pali text, accompanied with translations and notes. By V. Fausböll." Copenhagen, 1861. 72 pp. [Ed. and tr.]

Foucaux, Philippe Edouard. *Kanjur*. "Trois sections d'après les manuscrits tibétains de la Bibliothèque nationale." Paris, 1861.

Gogerly, (Rev.) Daniel John. *Buddhism*. "A lecture delivered before the Colombo Young Men's Christian Association by the Rev. D. J. Gogerly." *Colombo Observer*, Suppl. Colombo, 15 Apr. 1861. 8 pp.

Hall, Fitz-Edward. *Letter on Some Recent Statements Touching Certain of the Gupta Kings and Others*. *JASB*, vol. 30, 5 pp. 1861.

——. *Note on Budhagupta*. *JASB*, vol. 30, pp. 139–50. 1861.

Hodgson, Brian Houghton. *Notice on Buddhist Symbols*. *JRAS*, vol. 18, pp. 393–99. 1861.

Land, J. P. N. *Over den oorsprong en het wezen van het Buddhisme*, vol. 35, 34 pp. Amsterdam, Godgeleerde Bijdragen, 1861.

Liesching, Louis F. *A Brief Account of Ceylon*. Jaffna, 1861.

Moore, George. *The Lost Tribes and the Saxons of the East and of the West*. "With new views of Buddhism, and translation of rock records in India." London, 1861. 423 pp.

Patterson, Arthur John. *Caste Considered under its Moral, Social and Religious Aspects*. 1861. 122 pp.

S(cherb), S. E. A. *The Buddha and His Religion. The Golden Verses of the Buddha.* "Tr. from the   229
    Dhammapadam." *Chr. Register,* 1861. [Tr.]

Schmarda, Ludwig K. *Die Bewohner Ceylons. Westermann's Mh.,* no. 62. Braunschweig, 1861. 18
    pp.

——. *Reise um die Erde in den Jahren 1853 bis 1857.* Braunschweig, 1861. 3 vols.

Scudder, (Rev.) David C. *A Sketch of Hindu Philosophy. Bibl. Sacra,* vol. 18, 61, 50 pp. Andover,
    1861.

1862

Barthélemy Saint-Hilaire, Jules. *Le Nirvana bouddhique, Séances et Travaux de l'Acad. d. Sc. morales
    et politiques,* ser. 4, vol. 10, 30 pp. Paris, 1862. See J. B. Obry, 1863.

Beal, (Rev.) Samuel. *Comparative Arrangement of Two Translations of the Buddhist Ritual for the
    Priesthood, Known as the Pratimoksha, or Patimokhan.* "By the Rev. S. Beal from the Chinese,
    and by the Rev. D. J. Gogerly from the Pali." *JRAS,* vol. 19, pp. 407–80. 1862. [Tr.]

——. *The Sutra of the Forty-Two Sections.* "From the Chinese, tr. by the Reverend S. Beal." *JRAS,*
    vol. 19, pp. 337–49. 1862.

Bianconi, G. Giuseppe. *Degli Scritti di Marco Polo et dell'Uccello Rue da lui menzionato.* "Memoria del
    Pr Cav. G. Giuseppe Bianconi, letta alla Accademia delle Scienze il 6 et 13 Marzo. (Estratta dalle
    Memorie dell'Accademia dell'Istituto delle Scienze di Bologna, ser. 2, vol. 2)." Bologna, Tipi
    Gamberini e Parmeggiani, 1862. 64 pp.

Deschamps (Abbé). *La Discipline bouddhique, ses développements et ses légendes.* "Etudes nouvelles
    pour servir aux travaux de l'apologétique chrétienne." Paris, 1862. 39 pp.

Dubois, Jean Antoine. *Description of the Character, Manners and Customs of the People of India, and
    of the Institutions, Religious and Civil.* 2d ed., with notes, by G. W. Pope. 1862.

Gilliot, A. *Etudes sur les religions comparées de l'Orient.* Colmar, 1862. 218 pp.

Huc, (Abbé) Evariste-Régis. *L'Empire chinois.* "Faisant suite à l'ouvrage intitulé: Souvenirs
    d'un voyage dans la Tartarie et le Thibet." Paris, 4th ed., 1862. 2 vols.

Lepsius, R. *Sur les rapports du chinois et du tibétain et sur l'écriture de ces deux langues. Abh. d. Berl.
    Acad.* Berlin, 1861.

Müller, Friedrich Max. *Buddhism.* Edinburg R., 1862.

Torrens (Lieut. Col.). *Travels in Ladak, Tartary and Kashmir.* London, 1862.

Weber, Albrecht Friedrich. *Die Pâli-Legende.* "Von Fausböll und dem Herausgeber." *Indische
    Studien,* vol. 5, pp. 412–37. Berlin, 1862.

Westergaard, Niels Ludwig. *Über den ältesten Zeitraum der indischen Geschichte mit Rücksicht auf die
    Literatur.* "Über Buddha's Todesjahr und einige andere Zeitpunkte in der älteren Ge-
    schichte Indiens. Zwei Abhandlungen aus dem Dänischen übers. mit einem Vorw. von
    A. F. Stenzler." Breslau, A. Gasohorsky's Buchhandl., 1862. 128 pp. [Tr.]

Wilson, Horace Hayman. *Essays and Lectures Chiefly on the Religion of the Hindus.* "By the late H.
    H. Wilson. Collected and ed. by Dr R. Rost." 2 vols., 400, 416 pp. London, Trübner,
    1862.

1863

Alwis, James d'. *An Introduction to Kachchâyana's Grammar of the Pâli Language.* "With an Introd.,
    App. and Notes." Colombo, 1863. 132, xvi pp.

Bartoli, Adolfo. *I Viaggi di Marco Polo secondo la lezione del codice Magiabechiano più antico reintegrati
    col testo Francese a stampa per cura di Adolfo Bartoli.* Firenze, Felice le Monnier, 1863. 83, 439
    pp. [Ed.]

Beal, (Rev.) Samuel. *Text and Commentary of the Memorial of Sakya Buddha Tathagata by Wong Puh.*
    "Tr. from the Chinese by the Rev. S. Beal. With prefatory notes by the Rev. Spence
    Hardy." *JRAS,* vol. 20, pp. 135–220. 1863. [Tr.]

Carrière, Moritz. *Die Kunst im Zusammmenhange mit der Kulturentwicklung und die Ideale der*

230   *Menschheit.* Vol. 1. *Die Anfänge der Kultur und das orientalische Altertum in Religion, Dichtung und Kunst.* Leipzig, F. A. Brockhaus, 1863. 569 pp.

Francken, J. J. C. *Godsdienst en Bijgeloof der Chinezen.* Vol. 14, 37 pp. *TBG,* 1863.

Hardy, (Rev.) R. Spence. *The Sacred Books of the Buddhists Compared with History and Science.* Colombo, 1863.

——. *Text and Commentary of the Memorial of Sakya Buddha Tathagata.* "Tr. by S. Beal." *JRAS,* pp. 135–220. 1863.

Obry, Jean Baptiste François. *Du Nirvâna bouddhique. En réponse à J. Barthélemy St.-Hilaire.* "Mémoire lu à l'Académie d'Amiens dans ses séances des 14 et 18 mars 1863." Paris, Librairie d'Auguste Durand, 1863. 240 pp. See P. E. Foucaux, *Doctine,* 1864.

Schiefner, Anton (von). *Bericht über die Reise nach England, Bull. de l'Acad. impér. d. Sc. de St.-Pétersbourg,* vol. 6, 3 pp. 1863.

Schlagintweit, Emil. *Buddhism in Tibet.* "Illus. by lit. documents and objects of relig. worship. With an account of the Buddh. systems preceding it in India. With a fo. atlas of 20 pl. and 20 tables of native print in the text." Leipzig, F. A. Brockhaus; London, Trübner, 1863. 403 pp. See P. E. Foucaux, *Le Bouddhisme,* 1864.

Ward, (Rev.) W. *A View of the History, Literature, and Religion of the Hindoos.* "Including a minute description of their manners and customs and translations from their principal works. 5th ed., carefully abridged and greatly improved, with a biographical sketch of the author, and an ample index, with coloured and other pl." Madras, 1863. 430 pp.

1864

Eden, Hon. A. *Report on the State of Bootan and of the Progress of the Mission of 1863–64.* Calcutta, 1864.

Feer, Henri Léon. *Le Tibet, le Buddhisme et la Langue tibétaine. R. orientale et américaine,* vol. 9, pp. 157–90. Paris, 1864.

——. *Tchandra-sûtra, Sûrya-sûtra, Tchatur Gâthâ.* Paris, Vve Duprat, 1864. 11 pp. (autogr.). [Ed.]

Foucaux, Philippe Edouard. *Doctrine des Bouddhistes sur le Nirvana.* Paris, 1864. 30 pp. See J. B. F. Obry, 1863.

——. *Le Bouddhisme au Tibet.* Paris, 1864. 20 pp. See E. Schlagintweit, 1863.

Fraissinet, Edouard. *Le Japon. Histoire et description; mœurs, coutumes et religion.* "Rapports avec les Européens. Expéditions américaines. Nouv. éd., augmentée de trois chapitres nouveaux, d'une introd. et d'une carte par V. A. Malte-Brun." Paris, 1864. 2 vols.

Jäschke, Heinrich August. *Brief des Missionars H. A. Jäschke an den Akademiker A. Schiefner. Bull. de l'Acad. de St.-Pétersburg,* St. Petersburg, 1864. 4 pp.

Phayre, (Sir) Arthur Purves. *On the History of the Burmah Race. JASB,* vol. 33, 30 pp. 1864.

Rost, Reinhold. *Fables of Beasts and Birds in Chinese.* "With a notice of Pr Julien's *Les Avadanas.*" *Summer's Chinese and Japanese Repository,* vol. 1, 4 pp. London, 1864.

Sargant, William Lucas. *Buddha and his Religion.* "A lecture delivered at the Midland Inst., Birmingham, 3 March 1860. avec front." Birmingham, 1864. 27 pp.

Schlagintweit, Emil. *Tibetische Inschrift aus dem Kloster Hemis in Ladak. Sb. d. K. Akad. d. Wiss,* vol. 2, pp. 305–18. 1864.

——. *Über den Gottesbegriff des Buddhismus. Sb. d. K. Akad. d. Wiss,* vol. 1, pp. 83–102. 1864.

Spiess, Gustav. *Die Preussische Expedition nach Ostasien.* Berlin; Leipzig, Otto Spamer, 1864. 428 pp.

1865

Ampère, J. J. *La Science et les Lettres en Orient.* "Avec une préf. par M. Barthélemy Saint-Hilaire." 1865. 489 pp.

Beal, (Rev.) Samuel. *The Paramita-hridaya Sutra, or, in Chinese, "Mo-ho-pô-ye-po-lo-mih-to-sin-king,"*

i.e. *"The Great Paramita Heart Sutra."* "Tr. from the Chinese by the Rev. S. Beal, Chaplain,   231
R.N." *JRAS*, n.s., vol. 1, pp. 25–28. 1865. [Tr.]

——. *Vajrachhekika, the "Kin Kong King." or Diamond Sutra.* "Tr. from the Chinese by the Rev. S.
Beal, Chaplain, R.N." *JRAS*, n.s., vol. 1, pp. 1–24. 1865. [Tr.]

Bigandet, (Right Rev.) P. *Mémoires sur les Phongies ou religieux bouddhistes, appelés aussi Talapoins.*
R. de l'Orient, ser. 4, 76 pp. Paris, 1865.

Eichthal, Gustave d'. *Etude sur les origines bouddhiques de la civilisation américaine. R. archéologique*,
part. 1, 86 pp. Paris, 1865.

Feer, Henri Léon. *Chandra-sûtra. R. de l'Orient*, ser. 4, 1. Paris, 1865. [Tr.]

——. *Composition des écritures bouddhiques.* Paris, Vᵛᵉ Duprat, 1865. 11 pp. (autogr.).

——. *Etudes bouddhiques. Des Vyakarana et de leur place dans la littérature des Bouddhistes. R.
orientale et américaine*, vol. 10, pp. 341–60. Paris, 1865.

——. *Exercice de langue tibétaine. Légende du roi Açoka.* Paris, Vᵛᵉ Duprat, 1865. 13 ff. (autogr.).

——. *Introduction du Bouddhisme au Kashmir. JA*, ser. 6, vol. 6, pp. 477–549. 1865.

——. *La Légende de Râhu chez les Brahmanes et les Bouddhistes. R. de l'Orient*, Jan.–Mar. 1865. 38
pp.

Gobineau, Comte A. de. *Les Religions et les Philosophes dans l'Asie centrale.* Paris, 1865.

Gogerly, (Rev.) Daniel John. *The First Discourse Delivered by Buddha. JCBRAS*, 1865–66. 5 pp.

Jamieson, R. A. *Remarks upon Exhibiting a To-lo Pall to the Society. JNCB*, vol. 2, p. 178. 1865.

Keightley, Thomas. *Geschichte von Indien.* "Deutschbearbeitet und bis auf die neueste Zeit
fortgeführt von J. Seybt." Leipzig, G. Senf's Buchhdlg., 2 vols., 294, 356 pp. 1865. [Tr.]

Kern, Jan Hendrik Caspar (ou: Johann Heinrich Kaspar). *Het Andeel van India.* "Redevoer-
ing, etc." Leiden, 1865.

Pauthier, G. *Le Livre de Marco Polo.* "Citoyen de Venise, Conseiller Privé et Commissaire
Impérial de Khoubilai-Khaan, rédigé en français sous sa dictée en 1298 par Rusticien de
Pise. Publié pour la première fois d'après trois manuscrits inédits de la Bibliothèque
impériale de Paris, présentant la rédaction primitive du Livre, revue par Marc Pol lui-
même et donnée par lui, en 1307, à Thiébault de Cepoy, accompagnée des variantes, de
l'explication des mots hors d'usage, et de Commentaires géographiques et historiques,
tirés des écrivains orientaux, principalement chinois, avec une Carte générale de l'Asie;
par M. G. Pauthier." Paris, 1865. 831 pp. [Ed.]

Silva, Dandris de. *On Demonology and Witchcraft in Ceylon. JCBRAS*, 1865–66. 117 pp.

Wassiljew, W. *Le Bouddhisme, ses dogmes, son histoire et sa littérature*, part 1, "Aperçu général." "Tr.
du russe par M. G. A. La Comte et précédé d'un discours préliminaire par E. La-
boulaye." Paris, A. Durand, 1865. 362 pp. [Tr.]

1866

Barthélemy Saint-Hilaire, Jules. *Du Bouddhisme et de sa littérature à Ceylan et en Birmanie.* "Collection de M. Grimblot." *JS*, 1866.

Bastian, Wilh. Adolf. *Die Völker des Östlichen Asien.* "Studien u. Reisen." 6 vols., 576, 522, 540,
436, 552, 664 pp. Leipzig and Iena, 1866–71.

——. *Ein Besuch bei burätischen Schamanen.* Ausland, 1866.

——. *Zur buddhistischen Psychologie. ZDMG*, vol. 20, pp. 419–26. 1866.

Beal, (Rev.) Samuel. *Brief Prefatory Remarks to the Translation of the Amitâbha Sutra from Chinese.*
JRAS, n.s., vol. 2, pp. 136–44. 1866.

——. *Confessional of Kwan Yin.* "An attempt to translate from the Chinese a work known as the
Confessional Service of the Great Compassionate Kwan-Yin, possessing 1000 Hands
and 1000 Eyes." *JRAS*, n.s., vol. 2, pp. 403–25. 1866.

Bigandet, (Right Rev.) P. *The Life, or Legend of Gaudama, the Buddha of the Burmese.* "With

232   annotations. The ways to neibban, and notice on the Phongyies or Burmese Monks."
Rangoon, 1866. 544 pp.

Bluntschli, J. C. *Alt-asiatische Gottes- und Welt-Ideen in ihren Wirkungen auf das Gemeinleben der Menschen*. Nördingen, 1866. 168 pp.

Elphinstone, Mountstuart. *The History of India*. "The Hindu and Mahometan Periods by Mountstuart Elphinstone." 5th ed., with notes and appendices by E. B. Cowell. London, 1866. 790 pp.

Feer, Henri Léon. *Brahmaçrî-Vyâkarana (Prédiction sur Brahmaçrî)*. Paris, 1866. 12 pp. (autogr.).

——. *Etudes bouddhiques. Des premiers essais de prédication du Buddha Cakyamuni. JA*, ser. 6, vol. 8, pp. 89–125. 1866.

——. *L'Ami de la Vertu (Kalyânamitra)*. "Sanskrit et tibétain." Paris, 1866. 13 pp. (autogr.).

——. *L'Essence de la Science Transcendante (Prajnâ-Pâramitâ-Hridaya-Sûtra)*. "En trois langues, tibétain, sanskrit, mongol." Paris, 1866. 7 pp. (autogr.). [Ed.]

——. *Le Sûtra des Quatre Préceptes. JA*, ser. 6, vol. 8, pp. 269–357. 1866.

——. *Prescriptions de la discipline bouddhique (Dul-va-Vinaya) relative aux coupables*. Paris, 1866. 13 pp. (autogr.).

——. *Sûtras des Quatre Préceptes*. Paris, Vve Duprat, 1866. 11 pp. (autogr.). [Ed.]

——. *Tableau de la grammaire mongole, suivi de l'élévation de Gengis Khan et de la lettre d'Arghoun Khan à Philippe le Bel*. Paris, 1866. 7 pp. (autogr.).

Hardy, (Rev.) R. Spence. *The Legends and Theories of the Buddhists, Compared with History and Science*. "With Intr. notices of the life and system of Gotama Buddha." London, Williams and Norgate, 1866. 244 pp.

Hunt, John. *Essay on Pantheism*. 1866. 384 pp.

Jülg, Bernhard. *Die Märchen des Siddhi-kür*. "Kalmükischer Text mit deutscher Übers. und einem kalmükisch-deutschen Wörterbuch." Leipzig, F. A. Brockhaus, 1866. 223 pp. [Ed. and tr.]

Müller, Friedrich Max. *A Sanskrit Grammar for Beginners*. London, 1866.

Schlagintweit, Emil. *Die Gottesurtheile der Indier*. "Rede gehalten in der Offentlichen Sitzung der Königl. Akad. der Wiss. am 28. Marz 1866 zur Erinnerung ihres einhundert und siebenten Stiftungstages." Munich, 1866.

——. *Die Könige von Tibet*. "Übers. des Gyelrap." *Abh. d. I. K. Bayr. Akad. d. Wiss.*, vol. 10, section 3, pp. 795–879. Munich, 1866.

——. *Über die Bon-pa-Sekte in Tibet. Sb. d. K. Akad. d. Wiss.*, vol. 1, pp. 1–12. 1866.

Thayer, (Rev.) T. B. *Demonology of the Hindoos, Buddhist and Chaldeans. Universalis Quarterly*, n.s., vol. 3, 13 pp. Boston, 1866.

Weber, Albrecht Friedrich. *Über ein Fragment der Bhagavatî*. "Ein Beitrag zur Kenntniss der heiligen Literatur und Sprache der Jaina." 2 vols., 78, 198 pp. Berlin, 1866–67.

Yule, Sir Henry. *Cathay and the Way Thither*. "Being a collection of mediaeval notices of China. Tr. and ed., with a preliminary essay on the intercourse between China and the Western Nations, etc." London, Haklyut Society, 1866. 2 vols.

1867

Courcy, Marquis de. *L'Empire du Milieu*. "Description géographique, précis historique, institutions sociales, religieuses, politiques, notions sur les sciences, les arts, l'industrie et le commerce." *Libr. académique*, Paris, 1867. 692 pp.

Feer, Henri Léon. *Des Vyâkaranas et de leur place dans la littérature des Bouddhistes. R. orientale*, Jun. 1867. 19 pp.

——. *Etudes bouddhiques. Sûtra des Quatre Perfections (Chatushka Nirhâra). JA*, ser. 6, vol. 9, pp. 269–330. 1867. [Tr. and ed.]

Foucaux, Philippe Edouard. *La Guirlande précieuse des demandes et des réponses*. "Publiée en

sanskrit et en tibétain, et traduite pour la première fois en français (*Praçnottararat-*   233
namâlikâ) par Ph. Ed. Foucaux." *Extr. des Mém. de l'Acad. de Stannislas*, 64 pp. Paris, 1867.
[Ed and tr.]

Gillera, Agatona. *Opisanie Zabajkalskiej krainy w Syberyi przez Agatona Gillera* ("Description of
Siberian districts beyond the Baïkal"). 3 vols., 294, 318, 340 pp. Lipsk, 1867.

Jülg, Bernhard. *Mongolische Märchen.* "Erzählung aus der Sammlung Ardschi-Bordschi. Mongolisch und Deutsch von B. Jülg." Innsbruck, 1867. 37 pp. [Ed. and tr.]

Kern, Jan Hendrik Caspar (ou: Johann Heinrich Kaspar). *Het Budhhisme in Indie, in Evan-
geliespiegel: Maandschrift tot bevordering der Kennis van Godsdienst, etc.* Amsterdam, 1867. 46 pp.

Müller, Friedrich Max. *Buddhism. A Critical Study of St.-Hilaire's "Le Bouddha et sa religion."* 1867.
Pp. 181–234. See J. Barthélemy St.-Hilaire, 1860.

———. *Chips from a German Workshop.* 4 vols., 1867–75. Vol 1. *Essays on the Science of Religion.*
London, Longmans, Green, 1867.

Spiegel, Friedrich von. *Grammatik der altbaktrischen Sprache.* "With Suppl. on the Gatha Dia-
lect." 1867. 410 pp.

Wheeler, James Talboys. *The History of India from the Earliest Ages.* London, Trübner, 1867–81.
4 vols. in 5, 576, 680, 500, 600 pp.

Wylie, Alexander. *Notes on Chinese Literature.* "With Introd. remarks on the progressive
advancement of the art, and a list of tr. from the Chinese into various European
languages." Shanghai, 1867. 260 pp.

1868

Bonhomme, Jean. *Le Frère aîné du Christ.* 1868.

Busch, Moritz. *Der Orient.* "Urgeschichte desselben bis zu den medischen Kriegen." Vol. 3,
388 pp. Leipzig, Ambroisus Abel, 1868.

Chine, G. W. *On Buddhism.* 1868.

Cowell, Edward Byles. *The Prakrita-Prakasa, or The Prakrit Grammar of Vararuchi, with the
Commentary (Manorama) of Bhamaha.* "The first complete ed. . . . with notes, an English
tr." 2d ed. London, Trübner, 1868. 204 pp. 1st ed., Hertford, 1854. [Ed. and tr.]

Feer, Henri Léon. *Le Sûtra en quarante-deux Articles.* "Textes chinois, tibétain et mongol,
autographiés par Léon Feer, d'après l'exemplaire polyglotte rapporté par l'abbé Huc."
Paris, Maisonneuve et Cie, 1868. 40 pp. (autogr.). [Ed.]

Godron, A. *Une mission bouddhiste en Amérique au 1ᶜ siècle de l'ère chrétienne. Ann. des voyages*, vol. 4,
pp. 6–20. Paris, 1868.

Jülg, Bernhard. *Mongolische Märchensammlung.* "Die neun Märchen des Siddhi-Kür nach der
ausführlichen Redaktion und die Geschichte des Ardschi-Bordschi Chan. Mongolisch
mit deutscher übers. und kritischen Anm. hrsg." Innsbruck, Wagner'sche Universitäts-
Buchhdlg., 1868. 256 pp. [Ed. tr.]

Mason, (Rev.) Francis. *Pali Grammar on the Basis of Kaccayana.* "With chrestomathy and vocabulary." Toungoo and London, 1868. 214 pp.

Müller, Friedrich Max. *Max Müller's Sanskrit Grammatik in Devanâgari und lateinischen Buchstaben.*
"Aus dem Englischen übers. von Dr F. Kielhorn and Dr G. Oppert." Leipzig, 1868. [Tr.]

Petermann. *Reisen und Aufnahmen zweier Punditen in Tibet, 1865–6. Petermanns Mitteilungen*, pp.
233–43. 1868.

Rosny, Léon de. *Variétés orientales.* Paris, 1868.

Schiefner, Anton (von). *Taranathae de doctrinae Buddhicae in India propagatione narratio.* "Con-
textum tibeticum e codicibus Petropolitanis edidit A. Schiefner." Petropoli, 1868. 220
pp. [Ed.]

Schiefner, Anton (von), and Weber, A. *Über ein indisches Würfelorakel. Mb. d. Königl. Preuss.
Akad. d. Wiss*, pp. 158–80. 1859. In A. Weber, *Indische Streifen*, vol. 1, pp. 274–307. 1868.

234 Sherring, (Rev.) Matthew Atmore. *The Sacred City of the Hindus*. "An account of Benares in ancient and modern times." London, Trübner, 1868. 388 pp.

Stenzler, Adolf Friedrich. *Elemantarbuch der Sanskrit-Sprache, Grammatik, Text, Wörterbuch*. Breslau, 1868.

Weber, Albrecht Friedrich. *Indische Streifen*. Berlin, Nicolaïsche Verlagsbuch (vols. 1 and 2); Leipzig, F. A. Brockhaus (vols. 3), 1868–79. 386, 495, 645 pp.

——. *Über die Praçnottararatnamâlâ, Juwelenkranz der Fragen und Antworten. Mb. d. Königl. Akad. d. Wiss zu Berlin*, pp. 92–117, 6 February 1868.

Wurm, Paul. *Der Buddhismus, Basel, Der Kirchenfreund*, no. 9–12. 1868.

1869

Beal, (Rev.) Samuel. *Travels of Fa-hian and Sung-yun*. "Buddhist pilgrims from China to India (400 AD and 518 AD). Tr. from the Chinese." London, Trübner and Co., 1869. 208 pp. [Tr.]

Clarke, James Freeman. *Buddhism, or the Protestantism of the East. Atlantic Monthly*, vol. 23, pp. 713–28. Boston, 1869.

Eitel, (Rev.) Ernest John. *The Fabulous Source of the Hoang-ho. JNCB*, n.s., vol. 6, pp. 45–51. 1869–70.

Elliot, Sir Henry M., KCB. *(Suppl. Gloss. of Terms Used in the North Western Provinces). Memoirs on the History, Folk-lore, and Distribution of the Races of the North Western Provinces of India*. "Being an amplified ed. of the original Suppl. Gloss. of Indian Terms. Ed., rev., and re-arranged John Beames, MRAS." London, Trübner, 1869. 2 vols., 369, 396 pp.

Feer, Henri Léon. *Le Prodige (Prâtihârya) de l'Avadâna Cataka, en tibétain et en sanskrit*. "Conversion de Nandopananda en tibétain et en pâli, précédés de l'alphabet pâli-siamois." Paris, Maisonneuve et Cie, 1869. 15 ff. (autogr.). [Ed.]

Hammer, Thor's. *The Svâstika of the Buddhists*. "Notes and Q. on CEJ, 3." *Shanghai News-Letter*, 20 August 1869.

Kistner, Otto. *Buddha and His Doctrines*. "A bibliographical essay." London, Trübner, 1869. 32 pp.

Manning, (Pr) C. *Ancient and Mediaeval India*. London, 1869. 2 vols.

Mayers, William Frederick. *Illustrations of the Lamaist System in Tibet, Drawn from Chinese Sources*. London, 1869. 24 pp.

Minayeff, Ivan Pavlovitch. *Prâtimoksa Sûtra*. "Texte sanskrit, transcription et commentaires en russe." St. Petersburg, 1869. [Ed.]

Müller, Friedrich Max. *Buddhist Pilgrims*. "A critical study of Julien's Voyages des pèlerins bouddhistes." In Vol. 2 of *Chips from a German Workshop*, pp. 235–78. London, 1869. See S. Julien, 1853; F. M. Müller, *Buddhism*, 1857.

——. *Chinesische Übersetzungen von Sanskrittexten*. In *Essays*. Vol. 1, pp. 253–63; Leipzig, 1869; vol. 2, 1879. [Tr.]

——. *Essays*. Vol. 1, *Beiträge zur vergleichenden Religionswissenschaft*. "Nach d. 2. engl. Ausg. mit Autorisation des Verfassers ins Deutsche übertr." Leipzig, Wilh. Engelmann, 1869. 342 pp. [Tr.] Including *Buddhistische Pilger*, pp. 205–41; *Die Bedeutung von Nirvana*, pp. 242–52; *Über den Buddhismus*, pp. 162–204.

——. *Lecture on Buddhist Nihilism*. "Deliv. before the General Meeting of the Assoc. of German Philologists at Kiel, 28th Sept. 1869. Tr. from the German." London, Trübner, 1869. 18 pp. [Tr.]

——. *Über den buddhistischen Nihilismus*. "Vortrag gehalten in der Allgemeinen Sitzung der Deutschen Philologen-Versammlung in Kiel am 28. September 1869, von Max Müller." Kiel, C. F. Mohr, 1869. 20 pp.

Nevius, John L. *China and the Chinese*. "A general description of the country and its in-

habitants, its civilization and form of government, its religious and social institutions, 235
its intercourse with other nations, and its present condition and prospects." London,
1869.

Schlagintweit-Sakünlünski, Hermann von. *Reisen in Indien und Hochasien*. Iena, Herm. Costenoble, 1869–80. 4 vols., 589, 468, 335, 553 pp.

Wassiljew, W. *Herrn Professor Wassiljew's Vorrede zu seiner russischen Übersetzung von Târanâtha's
Geschichte des Buddhismus in Indien*. "Deutsch mitgetheilt von A. Schiefner. Nachtrag zu
der deutschen Übers. Târanâtha's (von A. Schiefner)." Kommissionäre d. Kais. Akad. d.
Wiss., 32 pp. St. Petersburg, 1869. [Tr.]

Widmann, J. Viktor. *Buddha*. "Epische Dichtung in zwanzig Gesängen. Mit einer Einleitung
von Ferd. Vetter." Bern, A. Francke, 1869.

1870

Alabaster, Henry. *The Modern Buddhist*. "Being the views of a Siamese Minister of State on his
own and other religions. Tr. with remarks by H. Alabaster." London, 1870. 91 pp.

Alwis, James d'. *Descriptive Catalogue of Sanskrit, Pali and Sinhalese Literary Works of Ceylon*,
Colombo, 1870. 3 vols.

Bastian, Wilh. Adolf. *Die Weltauffassung der Buddhisten*. "Vortr. geh. im Wiss. Verein zu Berlin
von A. Bastian." Berlin, Wiegandt u. Hempel, 1870. 40 pp.

Child, Lydia Maria. *Resemblances between the Buddhist and the Roman Catholic Religions. Atlantic
Monthly*, vol. 26, pp. 660–65. Boston, 1870.

Childers, Robert Caesar. *Khuddaka-Pâtha*. "A Pâli text, with a translation and notes." *JRAS*,
n.s., vol. 4, pp. 309–89. 1870. [Ed. and tr.]

Eitel, (Rev.) Ernest John. *Hand-Book for the Student of Chinese Buddhism*. Hong Kong and
Shanghai, Lane, Crawford, 1870. 220, 3 pp. (errata and addenda).

———. *The Nirvana of Chinese Buddhists*. Chinese Recorder, vol. 3, pp. 1–6. 1870–71.

Feer, Henri Léon. *Le Dharmacakrapravartanam. Les Quatre Vérités*. "Textes tibétains, pâlis,
sanskrits." Paris, Maisonneuve, 1870. 47 ff. (autogr.). [Ed.]

———. *Les Quatre Vérités et la Prédication de Bénarès (Dharmacakra-pravartanam). JA*, ser. 6, vol. 15,
pp. 345–471. 1870.

Fergusson, James. *On Indian Chronology*. "Read Feb. 15th, 1869." *JRAS*, n.s., vol. 4, pp. 81–
137. 1870.

Foucaux, Philippe Edouard. *Etude sur le Lalita Vistara, pour une éd. critique du texte sanskrit*.
"Précédée d'un coup d'œil sur la publication des livres bouddhiques en Europe et dans
l'Inde; suivie du spécimen d'un glossaire des mots particuliers au sanskrit bouddhique."
Paris, Maisonneuve, 1870. 56 pp.

Kielhorn, Franz. *A Grammar of the Sanskrit Language*. Bombay, 1870.

Müller, Friedrich Max. *A Sanskrit Grammar for Beginners*. "In Devanâgarî and Roman letters
throughout 2 ed., rev. and accentuated." London, Longmans, Green, 1870. 300 pp.

Rogers, (Capt.) T. *Buddhaghosta's Parables*. "Tr. from Burmese by Capt. T. Rogers, RE. With an
Introd., containing Buddha's *Dhammapada*, or *Path of Virtue*, tr. from Pali by F. Max
Müller, MA." London, Trübner, 1870. 206 pp. See J. de Alwis, *Buddhist Nirvâna*, 1871.

Sewell, Robert. *Analytical History of India, from the Earliest Times to the Abolition of the Honourable
East India Company in 1858*. London, 1870.

Skeen, William. *Adam's Peak*. "Legendary, traditional, and historical notices of the Samanala
and Sri-Pada, with a descriptive account of the pilgrims' route from Colombo to the
Sacred Foot-Print." Colombo, 1870.

Summers, (Rev.) James. *The Buddhistic Literature of Tibet. The Phoenix*, vol. 1, pp. 9–11. 1870.

Taylor, W. M. *Handbook of Hindu Mythology and Philosophy*. "With biographical Notices."
Madras, 1870. 162 pp.

236 **1871**

Alabaster, Henry. *The Wheel of the Law.* "Buddhism illustrated from Siamese sources by the modern Buddhist, a life of Buddha and an account of the Phrabat." London, Trübner, 1871. 323 pp.

Alwis, James d'. *Buddhist Nirvâna.* "A review of Max Müller's *Dhammapada*, with an app. containing extracts from the Buddhist code in Pâli and English." Colombo (W. Skeen) and London, 1871. 140 pp.

———. *Pâli translations,* Part 1, *Metta Sutta, on Charity.* Colombo, W. Skeen, 1871. 24 pp.

Bastian, Wilh. Adolf. *Das Nirwana und die Buddhistische Moral. Z. f. Ethnol.,* vol. 3, pp. 236–53. Berlin, 1871.

Beal, (Rev.) Samuel. *A Catena of Buddhist Scriptures from the Chinese.* London, Trübner and Co., 1871. 436 pp. [Tr.]

Childers, Robert Caesar. *Notes on Dhammapada, with special reference to the question of Nirvâna. JRAS,* n.s., vol. 5, pp. 219–30. 1871.

Cunningham, Sir Alexander. *The Ancient Geography of India.* Vol. 1, *The Buddhist Period, Including the Campaigns of Alexander, and the Travels of Hwen-thsang.* London, Trübner, 1871. 590 pp.

Eitel, (Rev.) Ernest John. *Buddhism.* "Its historical, theoretical and popular aspects. In three lectures." Hong Kong, 1871. 149 pp.

Fausböll, Michael Viggo. *The Dasaratha-Jâtaka.* "Being the Buddhist story of King Râma. The original Pali text with a translation and notes." Copenhagen, Hagerup, 1871. 48 pp. [Ed. and tr.]

———. *Two Jâtakas.* "The original Pâli text, with an English translation and critical notes." *JRAS,* n.s., vol. 5, pp. 1–13. 1871. [Ed. and tr.]

Feer, Henri Léon. *Etude sur la tradition relative à la guerre de Prasenajit et d'Ajâçatru, Comptes-rendus de l'Académie des Inscriptions,* pp. 44–80. 1871.

———. *Une sentence du Buddha sur la guerre. Un Avadâna sanscrit, deux sûtras Pâlis, et un vers de Dhammapada.* Paris, 1871. 38 pp.

Foucaux, Philippe Edouard. *Iconographie bouddhique. Le Bouddha Sakya-Mouni. Extr. des Mém. de l'Athénée oriental,* vol. 1, 79, 86 pp. Paris, Maisonneuve, 1871.

Garrett, John. *A Classical Dictionary, Illustrative of the Mythology, Philosophy, Literature, Antiquities, Arts, Manners, Customs, etc., of the Hindus.* With supplement, 1871. 157 pp.

Grimblot, P. *Extraits du Paritta.* "Texte et commentaires en Pâli. Avec introd., tr. notes et notices par L. Feer." *JA,* Oct.–Dec. 1871. pp. 225–35.

Jäschke, Heinrich August. *Handwörterbuch der tibetischen Sprache.* 1871–76.

Leonowens, Anna H. *The English Governess at the Siamese Court.* "Being recollections of six years in the Royal Palace at Bangkok." Boston, Fields, 1870. 321 pp.

Philips, Richard. *The Story of Gautama Buddha and His Creed.* "An Epic by Richard Philips." London, Longmans, Green, 1871. 220 pp.

Sen, Ram Das. *A Lecture on the Modern Buddhistic Researches.* "Delivered at the Berhampore Literary Soc. on Monday 19th Sept 1870." Calcutta, Bose, 1871. 20 pp.

Senart, Emile. *Grammaire Pâlie de Kaccayana.* "Sûtras et commentaire, publ. avec une tr. et des notes." Paris, Ernest Leroux, 1871. 339 pp. [Ed. and tr.]

Steele, Thomas. *An Eastern Love Story (Kusa Jataka).* "A Buddhistic legend love story, tr. from the Sinhalese into English by Th. Steele." 1871. 296 pp. [Tr.]

Vijasinha, L. Comrilla. *On the Origin of the Buddhist Arthakathas.* "With an Introd. by R. C. Childers." *JRAS,* n.s., vol. 5, pp. 289–302. 1871.

Yule, Sir Henry. *The Book of Sir Marco Polo the Venetian concerning the Kingdoms and Marvels of the East.* "Newly tr. and ed., with notes, by Colonel Henry Yule." London, John Murray, 1871. 2 vols., 409, 525 pp.

1872

Boyd, Palmer. *Nagananda, or The Joy of the Snake World*. "A Buddhist drama in five acts, tr. into English prose from the Sanskrit of Sri-Harsha-Deva. With introd. by Professor E. B. Cowell." London, 1872. 100 pp. [Tr.]

Childers, Robert Caesar. *A Dictionary of the Pali Language*. London, Trübner, 1872–75. 624 pp.

Edkins, (Rev.) Joseph. *Buddhist Words and Phrases*. In Rev. Justus Doolittle. *A Vocabulary of the Chinese Language, etc.*, Vol. 2, part 3, no. 6. Foochow, 1872.

Fausböll, Michael Viggo. *Ten Jatakas*. "The original Pâli text, with translation and notes by Pr V. Fausböll." Copenhagen, 1872. 127 pp. [Ed. and tr.]

Foucaux, Philippe Edouard. *Le Religieux chassé de la communauté*. "Conte bouddhique tr. du tibétain pour la première fois, par Ph. Ed. Foucaux." *Mém. de l'Athénée oriental, session de 1872*, vol. 11, pp. 105–22. Paris, 1872. [Tr.]

Inman, Thomas. *Ancient faiths in Ancient Names*. "An attempt to trace the religious belief, sacred rites and holy emblems. With Index of Names, and Ancient Faith and Modern." 1872–76. 3 vols.

Minayeff, Ivan Pavlovitch. *Ocherk Phonetik i Morphologii Yazieka Pâli*. St. Petersburg, 1872.

Monier-Williams (Sir Monier). *A Sanskrit-English Dictionary*. "Etymologically and philologically arranged with special reference to Greek, Latin, Gothic, German, Anglo-Saxon and other cognate Indo-European languages." 1872.

Müller, Friedrich Max. *Lectures on the Science of Religion*. "With a paper on Buddhist nihilism, and a tr. of the *Dhammapada* or *Path of Virtue*." New York, C. Scribner, 1872. 300 pp. See E. Faber, 1879.

Seydel, Rudolf. *Die Religion und die Religionen*. Leipzig, J. G. Findel, 1872. 276 pp.

Twesten, Carl. *Die religiösen, politischen und sozialen Ideen der asiatischen Kulturvölker und der Ägypter in ihrer historischen Entwicklung dargestellt*. "Hrsg. von M. Lazarus." Berlin, Ferd. Dümmlers, 1872. 674 pp.

1873

Bastian, Wilh. Adolf. *Geographische und ethnologische Bilder*. Iena, Hermann Costenoble, 1873.

Beal, (Rev.) Samuel. *The Legend of Dipankara Buddha*. "Tr. from the Chinese (and intended to illustrate Plates 29 and L in Fergusson's *Tree and Serpent Worship*)." *JRAS*, n.s., vol. 6, pp. 377–95. 1873. [Tr.]

Capper, John. *A Full Account of the Buddhist Controversy, held at Pantura, in August 1873*. Colombo, 1873.

Eitel, (Rev.) Ernest John. *Feng-Shui, or the Rudiments of Natural Science in China*. Hong Kong, Lane, Crawford, 1873. 84 pp.

Feer, Henri Léon. *Etudes bouddhiques. L'Ami de la Vertu et l'Amitié de la Vertu (Kalyanamitra, Kalyânamitrata)*. *JA*, ser. 7, vol. 1, pp. 5–66. 1873.

Fergusson, James. *On Hiouen-Thsang's Journey from Patna to Ballabhi*. *JRAS*, n.s., vol. 6, pp. 213–74, 396. 1873.

Foucaux, Mme Charlotte (i.e. Mary Summer). *Les Religieuses bouddhistes, depuis Sakya-Mouni jusqu'à nos jours*, "par Mme Mary Summer. Avec une introd. par P. E. Foucaux." *BOE*, no. 1. Paris, E. Leroux, 1873. 70 pp.

Grimm, Eduard. *Descartes's Lehre von den angeborenen Ideen*. Iena, 1873.

Johnson, Samuel. *Oriental Religions and Their Relation to Universal Religion: India*. Boston, James R. Osgood, 1873. 802 pp.

Kern, Jan Hendrik Caspar (ou: Johann Heinrich Kaspar). *Over de jaartelling der Zuidelijke Buddhisten en de Gedenkstukken, van Açoka den Buddhist*. "Publ. par l'Académie royale d'Amsterdam." Amsterdam, C. G. der Post, 1873. 120 pp.

Klatt, J. *De trecentis Canakyae sententiis*. Berlin, 1873.

238   Muir, John. *Metrical Translations from the Hymns of the Veda and other Indian Writings.* "Publ. for private circulation." 1873. [Tr.]

Puini, Carlo. *Avalokiteçvara Sutra.* "Tr. italienne de la version chinoise avec introd. et notes par Carlo Puini. Texte chinois et transcription japonaise par François Turrettini." L'Atsume Gusa, 1873. [Tr.]

Schopenhauer, A. *Handschriftlicher Nachlass,* ed. by Julius Frauenstädt. Leipzig, 1873. [Ed.]

Schott, Wilhelm. *Zur Literatur des chinesischen Buddhismus. Abh. d. K. Akad. d. Wiss. z. Berlin, Philos.-Hist. Kl.,* pp. 37–65. 1873.

Selby, T. G. *Yan Kwo, Fuk Lik, or the Purgatories of Popular Buddhism. China R.,* vol. 1, pp. 301–11. Hong Kong, 1873.

Senart, Emile. *Essai sur la légende du Buddha, son caractère et ses origines. JA,* ser. 7, vol. 2, pp. 113–303; vol. 3, pp. 249–456; vol. 6, pp. 97–234. 1873–75.

Vincent, F. *The Land of the White Elephant.* "A record of travel in Siam, Burma, Cambodia and Cochin China." London, 1873, 335 pp.

Wassiljew, W. *Die Religion des Ostens. Konfuzianismus, Buddhismus und Taoismus.* 1873.

Yule, Sir Henry. *Northern Buddhism.* "Note from Col. H. Yule, addressed to the Secretary." *JRAS,* n.s., vol. 6, pp. 275–77. 1873.

1874

Adams, F. O. *The History of Japan from the Earliest Period to the Present Time, 1874–75.* 2 vols.

Claughton, Bishop Piers Calveley. *On Buddhism.* 1874. 36 pp.

Edgar, J. Ware. *Report on a Visit to Sikkim and the Tibetan Frontier.* Calcutta, 1874.

Feer, Henri Léon. *Entretien du Bouddha et de Brahma sur l'origine des choses.* "Premier chapitre du Lotus Blanc de la Grande Compassion. Tr. du tibétain." *Report of the first session of the Congr. intern. d. or., 1874–76,* pp. 463–96. Paris, 1874. [Tr.]

——. *Le 193ᵉ Jâtaka: Cula-Paduma-Jâtaka "sur la charité et contre les femmes."* "Tr. du sanscrit." *Report of the first session of the Congr. intern. d. or., 1874–76,* vol. 2, pp. 377–96. Paris, 1874. [Tr.]

——. *Le Sûtra de l'Enfant (Dahara-sûtra) et la conversion de Prasenajit. JA,* ser. 7, vol. 4, pp. 297–368. 1874.

Foucaux, Mme Charlotte (i.e. Mary Summer). *Histoire du Bouddha Sakya-Mouni, depuis sa naissance jusqu'à sa mort.* "Par Mme Mary Summer. Avec préf. et index par P. E. Foucaux." *BOE,* no. 2. Paris, E. Leroux, 1874. 247 pp.

Foucaux, Philippe Edouard. *La Confession auriculaire chez les Bouddhistes du Tibet. Report of the first session of the Congrès intern. d. or.,* vol. 1, pp. 458–59. Paris, 1874.

Hardy, (Rev.) R. Spence. *Christianity and Buddhism Compared.* Colombo, 1874. 136 pp.

Hodgson, Brian Houghton. *Essays on the Languages, Literature and Religion of Nepal and Tibet.* "Together with further papers on the geography, ethnology and commerce of those countries." London, Trübner, 1874. 124 pp.

Kudriaffsky, Eufemia von. *Japan.* "Vier Vorträge nebst einem Anhang. Drei japanische Original-Predigten." Vienna, Wilh. Braumüller, 1874. 202 pp.

Lafmann, Salomon. *Lalita Vistara.* "Erzählung von dem Leben und der Lehre des Cakya Simha. Aus dem Original des Sanskrit und des Gâthâdialekts zuerst ins Deutsche übers. und mit sachl. Erklärungen versehen." Berlin, Ferd. Dümmler's, 1874. 220 pp. [Tr.]

Lassen, Christian. *Indische Alterthumskunde,* vol. 2. *Geschichte von Buddha bis zum Ende der älteren Gupta-Dynastie.* "Nebst Umriss d. Kulturgesch. dieses Zeitraums. 2. verm. u. verb. Aufl. Mit einer Karte von Alt-Indien von Dr H. Kipert." Leipzig, Verl. v. L. A. Kittler; London, Williams and Norgate, 1874. 1238 pp.

Minayeff, Ivan Pavlovitch. *Grammaire Pâlie.* "Esquisse d'une phonétique et d'une morphologie de la langue Pâlie, tr. du russe par S. Guyard." Paris, E. Leroux, 1874. [Tr.]

Mitchell, John Murray. Abstract of a Lecture on Buddhism, historically considered. "Deliv.   239
before the Bethune Society, on the 17th Nov. 1870." *Proc. of the Bethune Society*. Calcutta,
1870. 13 pp.

Müller-(Hess), Eduard. *Der Dialekt der Gâthâs des Lalitavistara.* "Inauguraldissertation der
philosophischen Fakultät der Univ. Leipzig vorgel. von Eduard Müller." Weimar, Dr. d.
Hof-Buchdr., 1874. 36 pp.

Müller, Friedrich Max. *Einleitung in die vergleichende Religionswissenschaft.* 1874. See A. Gray,
1876.

Rosny, Léon de. *Les Religions et le Néobouddhisme au Japon. Compte-rendu de la 1re "Session du Congr.
Intern. d. or,"* vol. 1, pp. 142–48. Paris, 1874.

Rotermund, W. *Die Ethik Lao-tse's mit besonderer Bezugnahme auf die buddhistische Moral.* Gotha,
F. A. Pertes, 1874. 26 pp.

Schiefner, Anton (von). *Zur buddh. Apokalyptik. Bull. de l'Acad. impér. d. Sc. de St.-Pétersbourg,*
vol. 20, 1604, col. 379–87. 1874.

Schoebel, Charles. *Le Buddhisme, ses origines.* "Le Nirvana, accord de la morale avec le Nirvana." *Actes d. Soc. philol.,* vol. 4, no. 5, pp. 146–92. 1874.

Simpson, William. *Meeting the Sun.* "A journey all round the world through Egypt, China,
Japan and California." London, 1874.

Swâmy, Sir Mutu Coomâra. *The Dâthâvansa, or The History of the Tooth-relic of Gotama Buddha.*
"The Pali text, and its tr. into English, with notes by Mutu Coomâra Swâmy." London,
Trübner, 1874. 23–100 pp. [Ed. and tr.]

———. *Sutta Nipâta, or Dialogues and Discourses of Gotama Buddha.* "Tr. from the Pâli, with introd.
and notes, by Sir Coomâra Swâmy." London, Trübner, 1874. 160 pp. [Tr.]

Vollmer. *Wörterbuch der Mythologie aller Völker.* Stüttgart, Hoffmann, 1874. 456 pp.

Watters, Thomas. *Notes on the Miao-fa-lien-hua-ching, a Buddhist Sûtra in Chinese. JNCB,* n.s., no.
9, pp. 89–114. 1874.

Wurm, Paul. *Geschichte der indischen Religion.* "Im umriss dargestellt." Basel, Bahnmaier, 1874.
296 pp.

1875

Bastian, Wilh. Adolf. *Die Verkettungstheorien der Buddhisten.* ZDMG, vol. 29, pp. 53–75. 1875.

Beal, (Rev.) Samuel. *The Buddhist Work in Chinese in the India Office Library. IA,* vol. 4, pp. 90–
101. 1875.

———. *The Romantic Legend of Sâkya Buddha.* "From the Chinese-Sanscrit." London, Trübner
and Co., 1875. 395 pp. [Tr.]

Bretschneider, E. *Notices of the Mediaeval Geography and History of Central and Western Asia.*
"Drawn from Chinese and Mongol writings, and compared with the observations of
Western authors in the Middle Ages." *JNCB,* n.s., vol. 10, pp. 75–307. 1875 (publ.
1876).

Childers, Robert Caesar. *The Pali Text of the Mahâparinibbâna Sutta and Commentary.* "With a
translation." *JRAS,* n.s., vol. 7, pp. 49–80. 1875; vol. 8, pp. 219–61. 1876. [Ed. and tr.]

Davids, Thomas William Rhys. *Report on the Existing European Literature on Pâli and Singhalese.*
Transac. of the Philol. Soc., London, 1875–76.

Dickson, J. F. *The Upasampada-Kammavaca, being the Buddhist Manual of the Form and Manner of
Ordering of Priests and Deacons.* "The Pali Text, with a Tr. and Notes. By J. F. Dickson."
JRAS, n.s., vol. 7, pp. 1–16. 1875. [Ed. and tr.]

———. *Upasampada-Kammavaca.* "The Pâli MSS. written on papyrus, preserved in the library of
the Armenian Monastery, St.-Lazars. Tr. by J. F. Dickson." Venice, 1875. 36 pp.

Feer, Henri Léon. *Les Jâtakas. JA,* ser. 8, vol. 5, pp. 357–423; vol. 6, pp. 243–306. 1875.

Grimm, Eduard. *Ageuliux' Erkenntnistheorie und Occasionalismus.* Iena, 1875.

240   Heeley, W. L. *Târanâtha*. "Extracts from Taranatha's History of Buddhism in India." *IA*, vol. 4, pp. 101–4. 1875.

Kuhn, Ernst W. A. *Beiträge zur Pali-Grammatik*. Berlin, 1875. 120 pp.

Lafmann, Salomon. *Zum Gathadialekt*. *ZDMG*, vol. 29, pp. 212–34. 1875.

Leland, Charles Godfrey. *Fusang, or the Discovery of America by Chinese Buddhist Priests in the Fifth Century*. London, Trübner, 1875. 212 pp.

Monier-Williams (Sir Monier). *Indian Wisdom, or Examples of the Religious, Philosophical and Ethical Doctrines of the Hindûs*. "With a brief history of the chief departments of Sanskrit literature and some account of the past and present condition of India, moral and intellectual." London, Allen, 1875. 542 pp.

Montgomerie, T. G. *Journey to Shigatze, in Tibet, and Return by Dingri-Maidan into Nepaul in 1871 by the Native Explorer*. London, Roy. Geog. Soc., no. 9, vol. 45. 1875.

Satow, Sir Ernest Mason. *The Revival of Pure Shin-Tau*. *TASJ*, 1875.

Schiefner, Anton (von). *Bharatae responsa Tibetice cum versione Latina ab Antonio Schiefner edita*. Petropoli, 1875. [Ed]

——. *Mahâkâtjâjana und König Tschanda-Pradjota*. "Ein Zyklus buddh. Erzählungen. Mitgetheilt von A. Schiefner." *Mém. de l'Acad. impér. d. Sc. de St.-Pétersbourg*, ser. 7, vol. 22, no. 7, 67 pp. 1875. [Tr.]

Schott, Wilhelm. *Zur Uigûrenfrage*. *Abh. d. K. Akad. d. Wiss. z. Berlin, Philos.-Hist. Kl.*, div. 2, pp. 27–57. 1875.

Sherring, (Rev.) Mathew Atmore. *Handbook for Visitors to Benares*. "With four plans of the city and neighbourhood." Calcutta, W. Newman, 1875. 86 pp.

Warren, Sybrandus Johannes. *Over de godsdienstige en wijsgeerige Begrippen der Jaina's*. Zwolle, 1875.

Wassiljew, W. *Biographies of Açvaghosha, Nâgârjuna, Aryadeva and Vasubandhu*. "Tr. by Miss E. Lyall." *IA*, vol. 4, p. 141. 1875. [Tr.]

Westmacott, E. Vesey. *On Traces of Buddhism in Dinajpur and Bagura (Bogra)*. *JASB*, vol. 44, part 1, pp. 187–92. 1875.

Zoysa, Louis de. *Reports in the Inspection of Temple Libraries (in Ceylon)*, Colombo, G. J. A. Skeen, 1875. 17 pp.

1876

Adler, Felix. *A Prophet of the People*. Boston, Atlantic Monthly, 1876. Vol. 37, pp. 674–89.

Alwis, Cornelis. *A History of the Island Lanka, from the Earliest Period to the Present Time*. Chap. 1, "Visits of Buddhas to the Island, extracted from *Pujavaliya* and *Sarvajnagunalankaraya*, with a literal tr. into Engl." Colombo, 1876. 21 pp.

——. *Sinhalese History during the English Period*. Colombo, 1876. Vol. 1.

Balfour, Frederic Henry. *Waifs and Strays from the Far East*. "Being a series of disconnected essays on matters relating to China." London, 1876.

Beal, (Rev.) Samuel. *The Buddhist Tripitaka, as It Is Known in China and Japan*. "A catalogue and compendious report." Devonport, India Office, 1876. 117 pp.

——. *Results of an Examination of Chinese Buddhist Books in the Library of the India Office*. *Transac. of the 2. Sess. of the Intern. Congr. of Or.*, pp. 132–62. London, 1876.

Bousquet, G. *La Religion au Japon. La rivalité du Shinto et du Bouddhisme, le dogme chrétien devant les philosophes japonais*. *RDM*, Paris, 15 March 1876.

Burnouf, Eugène. *Introduction à l'histoire du Buddhisme indien*. 2d ed., "rigoureusement conforme à l'éd. originale et précédée d'une notice de M. Barthélemy Saint-Hilaire sur les travaux de M. Eugène Burnouf." Vol. 3, 587 pp. Paris, Bibl. or., Maisonneuve, 1876.

Childers, Robert Caesar. *The Whole Duty of the Buddhist Layman. A Sermon by the Buddha*. *Contemporary R.*, vol. 27, pp. 417–24. London, 1876. [Tr.]

Christlich, Th. *Eine alte Moralpredigt Buddha's und eine moderne buddhistische Glaubenspredigt.* 241
"Nach englischen Quellen mitgetheilt." *Allg. Missionschr.*, Oct.–Nov. 1876.

Cowell, Edward Byles, and Eggeling, J. *Catalogue of Buddhist Sanskrit MSS. in the possession of the Royal Asiatic Society (Hodgson Collection). JRAS*, pp. 1–52. 1876.

Dickson, J. F. *The Pâtimokkha, being the Buddhist Office of the Confession of Priests.* "The Pali Text, with a Tr., and Notes. By J. F. Dickson." *JRAS*, n.s., vol. 8, pp. 62–130. 1876. [Ed. and tr.]

Edkins, (Rev.) Joseph. *Visit to the Chan-T'an-Sï—Monastery of the Dandal-Wood Buddha. Chinese Recorder*, vol. 7, pp. 431–35. 1876.

Feer, Henri Léon. *Etudes sur les Jâtakas.* Paris, Maisonneuve, 1876. 144 pp.

——. *Sur les causes qui ont favorisé la propagation du Bouddhisme hors de l'Inde. Transac. of the II. Sess. of the Intern. Congr. of Or.*, pp. 405–16. London, 1876.

Foucaux, Philippe Edouard. *Rapport sur les études bouddhiques. Compte-rendu de la Ire Session du Congr. intern. d. or.*, vol. 2, pp. 409–23. Paris, 1876.

Giles, Herbert Allan. *Chinese Sketches.* London and Shanghai, 1876.

——. *Record of the Buddhistic Kingdoms.* "Tr. from the Chinese by Herbert A. Giles." London, Trübner; Shanghai, Kelly and Walsh, 1876. 120 pp. [Tr.]

Gray, A. *Max Müller and Buddhism. Acad.* 1876. 212 pp.

Grimblot, P. *Sept Suttas Pâlis tirés du Dîgha-Nikâya.* "Tr. diverses anglaises (par D. J. Gogerly) et françaises (par E. Burnouf). (Ed. par Mme Grimblot)." Paris, Impr. nationale, 1876. 350 pp.

Haas, Ernst. *Catalogue of Sanskrit and Pali Books in the British Museum.* London, 1876. 188 pp.

Hellwald, Friedrich von. *Hinterindische Länder und Völker.* "Reisen in den Flussgebieten des Irawaddy und Mekong, in Annam, Kambodscha und Siam." Leipzig, Otto Spamer, 1876. 358 pp.

Howorth, (Sir) Henry H. *History of the Mongols, from the 9th to the 19th Century.* London, 1876–1927. 4 vols. in 5.

Inman, Thomas. *Ancient Faith and Modern.* "A dissertation upon Worships, Legends and Divinities in Central and Western Asia, Europe, and elsewhere, before the Christian era. Showing their relations to religious customs as they now exist." New York, J. W. Bouton, 1876. 478, 45 pp.

Jacobi, Hermann. *Zwei Jaina-Stotra.* 1, *Das Bhaktâmarastotram*; 2, *Das Kalyânamandirastotram. Indische Studien.* 1876. 14, 2, 3 pp.

Laffitte, Pierre. *Les Grands Types de l'humanité.* Paris, Saint-Germain, 1876.

Markham, Clements R. *Narrative of the Mission of George Bogle to Tibet, and of the Journey of Thomas Manning to Lhasa.* "Ed., with notes, an introd., and lives of Mr G. Bogle and Mr T. Manning." London, 1876. 354 pp. [Ed.]

Mills, Charles D. B. *The Indian Saint, or Buddha and Buddhism.* "A sketch historical and critical." New York, Millan and Northampton, 1876. 192 pp.

Peschel, Oskar. *Völkerkunde.* Leipzig, Dunker and Humblot, 1876. 570 pp.

Pischel, Richard. *Zur Pâli-grammatik*, Z. f. Vergl. Sprach-forsch., n.s., 3, 4. 1876.

Rosny, Léon de. *Zitu-go-kyau. Dô-zi-kyau. L'Enseignement de la vérité, ouvrage du philosophe Kôbaudaisi, et l'Enseignement de la jeunesse.* "Publ. avec une transcription européenne du texte original et tr. pour la première fois du japonais." Paris, 1876. 160, 16 pp. [Ed. and tr.]

Ross, John. *L'Ilpon de Mah-lay (légende bouddhiste), by J. Ross (Fraser's Mag.), R. britannique*, n.s., vol. 5., pp. 171–82. 1876. [Tr.]

Senart, Emile. *Note sur quelques termes buddhiques. JA*, ser. 7, vol. 8, pp. 477–86. 1876.

Subhuti, Waskaduwe. *Namamala, or A Work on Pali Grammar.* "Prepared (in Singhalese character), with an Engl. introd." 1876. 104, 148, 70 pp. [Ed. and intr.]

Thomas, Edward. *Record of the Gupta Dynasty Illustrated by Inscriptions, Written History, Local*

242   *Tradition and Coins.* "To which is added a chapter on the Arabo in Sind." London, 1876. 64 pp.

Tiele, Cornelis Petrus. *Geschiedenis van den godsdienst tot aan de heerschappij der wereldgodsdiensten.* 1876.

Vaughan, (Rev.) J. *The Trident, the Crescent and the Cross.* "A view of the religious history of India, during the Hindu, Buddhist, Mohammedan and Christian periods." London, 1876. 344 pp.

Wesseloffsky, A. *Sagenstoffe aus dem Kandjur. Russ. R.*, vol. 5, 3. 1876.

Zoysa, Louis de. *Catalogue of Pali, Singhalese, and Sanskrit Manuscripts, in the Ceylon Government Oriental Library.* Ceylon, Henry Herbert, 1876. 26 pp.

1877

Batuwantudawa, Don Andris de Silva, and Sumangala, H. Mahânâma: *The Mahâwansa.* "Tr. into Singhalese (with Singhalese-English Glossary) and ed. under orders of the Ceylon Government, by H. Sumangala and Don Andris de Silva Batuwantudawa." Colombo, 1877–83. 2 vols. [Gloss.]

Blodget, (Rev.) Dr. *The Chinese Term for God.* "Statement by the Rev. Dr. Eitel and reply by the Rev. Dr. Blodget." London, 1877.

Chattopâdhyâya, Nisikânta (pseud.: "Ein Hindu"). *Buddhismus und Christenthum. Deutsche Wochenschrift*, vol. 2, 1, 2. 1877.

Clarke, James Freeman. *Ten Great Religions.* Part 1, *An Essay in Comparative Theology.* Boston, James R. Osgood, 1877. 528 pp.

Davids, Thomas William Rhys. *Buddhism.* "Being a sketch of the life and teachings of Gautama, the Buddha." *Non-Christian Religious Systems.* London, SPCK, 1877. 252 pp.

——. *On Nirvâna, and on the Buddhist Doctrines of the "Groups," the Sanskâras, Karma and the "Paths." Contemporary R.*, vol. 29, pp. 249–70. London, 1877.

Deussen, Paul. *Die Elemente der Metaphysik. Über das Wesen des Idealismus.* 1877.

Dods, Marcus. *Mohammed, Buddha, and Christ.* "Four lectures on natural and revealed religion." London, Hodder and Stoughton, 1877. 240 pp.

Doon, Moung Kyaw. *Essay on the Sources and Origin of Buddhist Law.* Rangoon, 1877. 19 pp.

Fausböll, Michael Viggo. *The Jataka, Together with its Commentary.* "Being tales of the anterior births of Gautama Buddha. For the first time ed. in the original Pâli by V. Fausböll." London, Kegan Paul; Trench, Trübner, 1877–97. 7 vols. (index volume by Dines Andersen), 511, 451, 543, 499, 511, 246, 246 pp. [Ed.]

Feer, Henri Léon. *Etudes cambodgiennes.* "La collection Hennecart de la Bibliothèque nationale." *JA*, ser. 7, vol. 9, pp. 161–234. 1877.

——. *Le Bikkuni-samyuttam, groupe de soutras sur les Bhixunis (religieuses). R. orientale et américaine*, n.s. vol. 1, pp. 50–71. 1877.

——. *Le Bouddhisme à Siam.* "Une soirée chez Prhra-Klang en 1863. Le dernier roi de Siam et ses projets de réformes religieuses." *Mém. de la Soc. indo-chinoise*, vol. 1, p. 146. 1877.

Foucaux, Philippe Edouard. *Note sur le Nirvana. E. de philol.*, vol. 1. 1877.

Griffis, William Elliot. *The Mikado's Empire.* New York, Harper, 1877. 2 vols.

Grimm, Eduard. *Die Lehre über Buddha und des Dogma von Jesus Christus*, Berlin. *Deutsche Zeit- und Streitfragen*, fasc. 90, pp. 343–74. C. Havel, 1877.

Hordern, P. *Buddhist Schools in Burmah. Living Age*, vol. 135, pp. 692–98. Boston, 1877.

Johnson, Samuel. *Oriental Religions and Their Relation to Universal Religion: China.* Boston, James R. Osgood, 1877. 975 pp.

Krishna, A. K. *Account of the Pandit's Journey in Great Thibet from Leh in Ladâkh to Lhâsa, and of His Return to India via Assam. J. Roy. Geogr. Soc.*, vol. 52. 1877.

Mitra, Rajendrala. *The Lalita Vistara, or Memoirs of the Early Life of Sâkhya Sinha. As. Soc. of Bengal, BI*, vol. 164, 575 pp. Calcutta, 1877. [Ed.]

Monier-Williams (Sir Monier). *Hinduism. Non-Chr. Relig. Systems*. London, SPCK; New York, Macmillan, 1877, 1887, 1897, 1906, 1919. 238 pp.

——. *A Practical Grammar of the Sanskrit Language*. "With special reference to the classical languages of Europe." Oxford, Henry Frowde (OUP), 1877. 410 pp.

Puini, Carlo. *Enciclopedia Sinica-Giapponese*. "Notizie estratte dal Wa-Kan San-Sai Tu-Ye intorno al Buddismo." Florence, 1877.

Rehatsek, Edward. *Christianity among the Mongols till Their Expulsion from China in 1368*. "Comprising the Eastern Grand Khans or Emperors, with the Western or Persian Khans." *JBBRAS*, vol. 13, no. 35, pp. 152–302. 1877.

Schuyler, E. *Turkistan*. London, 1877. 2 vols.

Shunker, Munshi Shew. *History of Nepal*. "Tr. of the Parvatiyâ by Munshi Shew Shunker and Shri Gunanand." Cambridge, 1877. 324 pp.

Spiess, Edmuns. *Entwicklungsgeschichte der Vorstellungen vom Zustande nach dem Tode auf Grund vergleichender Religionsforschung*. Iena, Hermann Costenoble, 1877. 615 pp.

Sucker, W. *Buddha und Christus, Buddhismus und Christentum*. "Nebst Bemerkungen zu dem Neubuddhismus Eduard von Hartmanns." *Beweis d. Glaubens*, vol. 13, pp. 297–307, 362–74, 419–29, 471–86, 525–30. July–October 1877.

Thomas, Edward. *The Early Faith of Asoka. JRAS*, n.s., vol. 9, pp. 155–234. 1877.

——. *Jainism, or the Early Faith of Asoka*. "With illustrations of the ancient religions of the East from the Pantheon of the Indo-Scythians." 1877. 82 pp.

Tiele, Cornelis Petrus. *Outlines of the History of Religion to the Spread of the Universal Religions*. "Tr. from the Dutch by J. Estlin Carpenter, MA." London, 1877. [Tr.]

Tietz. *Die indischen Religionssysteme und ihre Verhältnisse zum Christenthum, Z. f. Weibl. Bildung*, 8, 9. 1877.

Williams, Charles Reynolds. *Letters Written during a Trip to Southern India and Ceylon in 1876–7*. "With original illus. Pr. for private circulation." London, 1877. 159 pp.

Wilson, John. *Indian Caste*. Bombay, 1877. 2 vols.

Wordworth, W. *The Church of Thibet and the Historical Analogies of Buddhism and Christianity*. "A lecture delivered before the students of Literary and Scientific Society, in the Framji Cowasji Institution, Bombay." London, Trübner, 1877. 52 pp.

Wormann, J. H. *Nirvâna and Pass-Buddhas*. McClintock und Stroug's Cyclop., vol. 7. 1877.

Wright, Daniel. *History of Nepal*. "With an introductory sketch of the country and people. Tr. from the *Parbatuja* by Munshi S. Shunker and Pandit Gunanand." Cambridge, 1877. 324 pp. See H. L. Feer, 1878, *Notice*.

1878

Barthet, P. *Essai sur la chronologie indienne et sur les Bouddhas anciens et nouveaux. Ann. d. philos. chrét.*, Nov. 1878.

Beal, (Rev.) Samuel. *On a Chinese Version of the Sânkhya Kârikâ, etc., found among the Buddhist Books comprising the Tripitaka, and two other works. JRAS*, n.s., vol. 10., pp. 355–60. 1878.

——. *Texts from the Buddhist Canon, Commonly Known as the Dhammapada, with Accompanying Narratives*. "Tr. from the Chinese by S. Beal." TOS, no. 2. London, Trübner and Co. 1878. 176 pp. [Tr.]

Bigandet, (Right Rev.) P. *Vie ou légende de Gaudama le Bouddha des Birmans, et notice sur les phongyies ou moines birmans*. "Tr. en fr. par Victor Vauvain." Paris, E. Leroux, 1878. 540 pp. [Tr.]

[Brüger]. *Brüger's Account of the Religious Sects of the Japanese. Chinese Repository*, vol. 2, p. 318. Canton, 1878.

244   Chantre, E. *Notes anthropologiques. Relations entre les sistres bouddhiques et certains objets de l'âge de bronze européen*. Compte-rendu du Congr. d. or., 13 pp. Lyon, 1878.

Cordier, Henri. *Bibliotheca Sinica*. "Dictionnaire bibliographique des ouvrages relatifs à l'Empire chinois." *Publ. de l'Ec. d. Langues or. vivantes*. Paris, E. Leroux, 1878–95. 2 vols. and suppl., 2243 col. (in 8 and 3 installments), vol. 10, 11; ser. 3, vol. 15.

Cust, Robert Needham. *Ling. and Or. Essays*, ser. 1 (London, 1880): *The Languages of the East Indies* (1878), pp. 107–43; *The Religions of India* (1878), pp. 144–71.

Davids, Thomas William Rhys. *The Origin of Legend in the Lives of Buddha*. Theolog. R., Jan. 1878.

Edkins, (Rev.) Joseph. *Religion in China*. "A brief account of the three religions of the Chinese." London, Kegan Paul, 1878.

Feer, Henri Léon. *Etudes bouddhiques. Maitrakanyaka-Mittavindaka, La Piété Filiale*. JA, ser. 7, vol. 11., pp. 360–443. 1878.

——. *Le Bouddhisme à l'Exposition de 1878*. R. polit. et litt., Oct. 1878. 8 pp.

——. *Le Sûtra en quarante-deux articles*. "Tr. du tibétain avec introduction et notes par L. Feer." BOE, vol. 21. Paris, E. Leroux, 1878. 82 pp.

——. *Notice sur l'histoire du Népâl de Daniel Wright*. Paris, 1878, 32 pp.

Foulkes, (Rev.) Thomas. *Fah Hian's Kingdom of the Dakshina*. IA, vol. 7, pp. 1ff. 1878.

Fryer, George Edward. *Pâli Studies*. No. 2, *Vuttodaya (Exposition of Metre)*, by Sangharakkhita Thera. "Pâli Text, with English Tr. and Notes." JASB, vol. 46, part 1, no. 4, 44 pp. 1878.

Fytche, A. *Burma, Past and Present*. "With personal reminiscences of the country." 1878. 2 vols.

Ganzenmüller, Konrad. *Tibet*. "Nach den Resultaten geographischer Forschungen früherer und neuester Zeit." Stuttgart, Levy u. Müller, 1878. 132 pp.

Giles, Herbert Allan. *A Glossary of Reference on Subjects Connected with the Far East*. Shanghai, 1878.

Guimet, Emile. *Promenades japonaises*. "Texte par E. Guimet, dessins d'après nature par F. Regamey." 1878–80. 2 vols.

——. *Religions de l'Extrême-Orient*. "Notice explicative sur les objets exposés par M. E. Guimet et sur les peintures et dessins faits par M. F. Regamey, aux Galeries historiques du Trocadéro." Paris, Leroux, 1878.

Harlez, Charles Joseph de. *Grammaire pratique de la langue sanscrite*. Louvain, 1878. 150 pp.

Hartshorne, B. J. *A Chapter of Buddhist Folk-lore*. Fortnightly R., August 1878. 17 pp.

Hû, Fernand. *Le Dhammapada*. "Avec intr. et notes par Fernand Hû." BOE, vol. 21. Paris, E. Leroux, 1878. 100 pp. [Tr.]

Metchnikoff, L. *L'Empire japonais*. "Texte et dessins." 1878. 693 pp.

Mitra, Rajendrala. *Buddha Gayâ, the Hermitage of Sâkya Muni*. "Publ. under orders of the Government of Bengal." Calcutta, Bengal Secretariat Press, 1878. 257 pp.

Monier-Williams (Sir Monier). *Indian Rosaries*. London, Athenaeum, 9 February 1878.

——. *Progress of Indian Religious Thought*. Contemporary R. London, September–December 1878.

Muir, John. *Asia and Buddha, or the Indian Simeon*. IA, vol. 7, pp. 232–34. 1878.

Müller, Friedrich Max. *Lectures on the Origin and Growth of Religion, as illus. by the Religions of India*. "Deliv. in the Chapter House, Westminster Abbey, in April, May and June, 1878." London, Williams and Norgate, 1878. 408 pp.

Peebles, J. M. *Buddhism and Christianity Face to Face*. "On an oral discussion between the Rev. Migettuwatte . . . and the Rev. D. Silva . . . with an introd. and annotations." London, 1878.

Pfleiderer, Otto. *Die Religion, ihr Wesen und ihre Geschichte auf Grund des gegenwärtigen Standes der*

philosophischen und historischen Wissenschaft. Vol. 2, *Die Geschichte der Religion.* 2d ed. Leipzig,   **245**
Fues' Verlag, 1878. 495 pp.

Phayre, (Sir) Arthur Purves. *History of Burma, including Burma Proper, Pegu, Taungu, Tenasserim and Arakan, from the earliest time to the end of the First War with British India.* 1878. 311 pp.

Puini, Carlo. *Il Buddha, Confucio e Lao-tse.* "Notizie e studii intorno alle religioni dell'Asia Orientale." Florence, 1878.

St. Barbe, Henry Louis. *Burmese Transliteration. JRAS,* p. 228. 1878.

Schiefner, Anton (von). *Über Vasubandhu's Gâthâsangraha. Mélanges asiatiques,* vol. 8, Bk. 3; 4, 35 pp. 1878.

Schoebel, D. *Le Bouddhisme et son fondateur. Compte-rendu des Séances de l'Athénée orient.,* vol. 8, part 2. 1878.

Sherring, (Rev.) Mathew Atmore. *The Hindoo Pilgrims.* "A poem on the travels of the Buddhist pilgrims." London, 1878. 125 pp.

Weber, Albrecht Friedrich. *The History of Indian Literature.* "Tr. from the second german ed. by J. Mann and T. Zachariae." TOS, no. 3. London, Trübner, 1878. [Tr.]

Zimmer, Heinrich. *Zur Pâli-Grammatik. Z. f. Vergl. Sprachforsch.,* n.s., 4, 3. 1878.

1879
Arnold, Sir Edwin. *The Light of Asia, or the Great Renunciation (Mahabhinishkramana).* "Being the life and teaching of Gautama, prince of India and founder of Buddhism, as told in verse by an Indian Buddhist. Based on the *Lalitavistara.*" Boston, Roberts Bros, 1879. 238 pp.

Aynsley, H. G. *Visit to Ladakh.* London, 1879.

Barth, Auguste. *Les Religions de l'Inde. Religions védiques, Brahmanisme, Bouddhisme, Jainisme et Hindouisme. Enc. d. Sc. relig.* Paris, 1879. 175 pp.

Beal, (Rev.) Samuel. *The Fo-Sho-Hing-Tsan-King.* "A life of Buddha by Asvaghosha Bodhisattva. Tr. from Sanskrit into Chinese by Dharmaraksha, AD 420, and from Chinese into Engl. by S. Beal." *SBE,* vol. 19, 380 pp. Oxford, Clarendon Press, 1879. [Tr.]

——. *The Story of Faithful Deer. IA,* vol. 8, p. 253. 1879.

Bergaigne, P. A. *Nâgânanda: la joie des serpents.* "Drame bouddhique attribué au roi Crî-Harcha-Deva,* tr. pour la première fois du sanscrit et du prakrit en français." *BOE,* no. 27, 144 pp. Paris, E. Leroux, 1879. [Tr.]

Böhtlingk, Otto (von). *Sanskrit-Wörterbuch in kürzerer Fassung.* "Bearbeitet von Otto Böhtlingk." *Buchdr. d. Kais. Akad. d. Wiss,* 7 vols., 299, 301, 265, 302, 264, 306, 390 pp. St. Petersburg, 1879–89.

Childers, Robert Caesar. *On Sandhi in Pali.* "By the late R. C. Childers." *JRAS,* n.s., vol. 11, pp. 99–121. 1879.

Cowell, Edward Byles. *The Northern Buddhist Legend of Avalokiteswara's Descent into the Hell Avîchi. IA,* vol. 8, pp. 249–53. 1879.

Davids, Thomas William Rhys. *Buddha's First Sermon. Fortnightly R.,* vol. 32, pp. 899–910. London, 1879.

——. *Het Buddhisme en zijn Stichter.* "Uit het engelsch door J. P. van der Vegte." Amsterdam, J. H. de Bussy, 1879. 322 pp. [Tr.]

Dowson, John. *A Classical Dictionary of Hindu Mythology and Religion, Geography, History, and Literature. TOS,* no. 6. London, Trübner, 1879. 411 pp.

Dutt, Jogesh Chunder. *Kings of Kaskmira:* "Being a translation of the Sanskrita work Rajatarangini of Kahlana (sic) Pandita. By Jogesh Chunder Dutt." Calcutta, I. C. Bose, 1879. 303, xxiii pp. [Tr.]

Edkins, (Rev.) Joseph. *The Buddhist Doctrine of Future Punishment. Sunday at Home,* Jul. 1879.

246   Eitel, (Rev.) Ernest John. *Outlines of History of Chinese Philosophy. Travaux de la IIIe Sess. du Congr. d. or.*, vol. 2, 14 pp. St. Petersburg and Leyden, 1879.

Estrey, Comte de Meyners d'. *Manuscrits sanscrits au Japon. Ann. de l'Extrême-Orient*, vol. 2, no. 24, pp. 353–55. Paris, 1879–80.

Faber, Ernst. *Introduction to the Science of Chinese Religion.* "A critique of Max Müller and other authors." Hong Kong, Lane, Crawford, 1879. 154 pp.

Feer, Henri Léon. *Conférence sur le Bouddhisme à l'Exposition de 1878.* Paris, 1879. 22 pp.

——. *Etudes bouddhiques. Le Livre des Cent Légendes (Avadâna-Cataka). JA*, ser. 7, vol. 14, pp. 141–89, 273–307. 1879.

Forchhammere, Emile. *Report on the Pali Literature of Burma.* Government of India Publication, 1879.

Giles, Herbert Allan. *A Cremation on China. Cornhill Mag.*, 1879.

——. *Present State of Affairs in China. Fortnightly R.*, Sept. 1879.

Gray, James. *Pâli Primer.* "Adapted for schools in Burma." Maulmain, 1879.

Hillebrandt, Alfred. *Das altindische Neu- und Vollmondsopfer in seiner einfachsten Form.* "Mit Benützg. handschriftl. Quellen dargestellt." Iena, Fischer, 1879. 199 pp.

Jacobi, Hermann. *Bhadrabahu; The Kalpasutra.* "Ed. in transcription with Introd., Notes and a Prakrit-Sanskrit Glossary." *Abh. f. K. f. M.* Leipzig, 1879. [Ed.]

James, J. M. *A Discourse on Infinite Vision as Attained to by Buddha.* "A translation of a Discourse on Ten-Gan-Hiyau Shiyaku by Sata Kaiseki." *TASJ*, vol. 7, pp. 267–81. 1879.

Keene, H. G. *Religion in India. Calcutta R.*, avr. 1879.

Leydenn, (Major) T. H. *A Manual of Tibetan.* "Being a Guide to the Colloquial Speech of Tibet, in a Series of Progressive Exercises." Calcutta, 1879. 176 pp.

Monier-Williams (Sir Monier). *Buddhism and Jainism. Contemporary R.* London, Dec. 1879.

——. *Indian Religious Thought. Contemporary R.* London, August 1879.

——. *Modern India and Indians.* "A series of impressions, notes and essays." London, 1879. 365 pp.

Müller, Friedrich Max. *Origine et Développement de la religion étudiés à la lumière des religions de l'Inde.* "Leçons faites à Westminster-Abbey. Tr. de l'anglais par J. Darmesteter." Paris, Reinwald, 1879. 347 pp. [Tr.]

——. *The Sacred Books of the East.* "Tr. by various oriental scholars, and ed. by F. Max Müller." London, Macmillan (OUP), 1879–1910. 50 vols. [Ed.]

Nivedita, Sister (i.e. Margaret Elisabeth Noble). *The Dipavamsa.* "An Ancient Buddhist Historical Record." 1879. 227 pp. [Ed. and tr.]

Oldenberg, Hermann. *The Dipavamsa.* "An ancient Buddhist historical record. Ed. and tr. by Hermann Oldenberg." London and Edinburgh, Williams and Norgate, 1879. 227 pp.

Paske, (Col.) Edward. *Buddhism in the British Provinces of Little Tibet. J. of the Anthrop. Inst.*, vol. 8, pp. 195–210. London, 1879.

Root, E. D. *Sakya Buddha.* "A versified, annotated narrative of his life and teachings with an excursus containing citations from the Dhammapada, or Buddhist canon." New York, 1879. 171 pp.

Rosny, Léon de. *Le Bouddhisme dans l'Extrême-Orient.* "Cours de M. Léon de Rosny, Ecole des Langues orientales vivantes." *R. scient.*, pp. 581–85. 20 Dec. 1879.

Ross, John. *A History of Corea, Ancient and Modern.* Paisley, 1879. 404 pp.

Sachau, Edward C. *The Chronology of Ancient Nations.* "An English version of the Arabic text of the Athâr-ul-Bâkiya of Albîrûnî, or *Vestiges of the Past* (AD 1000). Tr. and ed." London, Allen, 1879. 464 pp. [Tr.]

St. Barbe, Henry Louis. *Pali Derivations in Burmese. JASB*, vol. 48, part 1, no. 4. 1879.

Schiefner, Anton (von). *Über eine tibetische Handschrift des India Office in London. Bull. de l'Acad.*   247
impér. d. Sc. de St.-Pétersbourg, vol. 25. July 1879.

Stokes, M. *Indian Fairy Tales*. Calcutta, 1879.

Whitney, William Dwight. *Indische Grammatik umfassend die klassische Sprache und die älteren Dialekte.* "Aus dem Engl. übers. von H. Zimmer." Leipzig, Bibl. Indogerman. Gramm., Breitkopf and Härtel, 1879. Vol. 2, 519 pp. [Tr.]

———. *A Sanskrit Grammar, including Both the Classical Language and the Older Dialects of Veda and Brahmana.* 1879.

1880

Alwis, Cornelis. *Visites des Bouddhas dans l'île de Lanka.* "Extraits du *Poujavaliya* et du *Sarvajnagounalankaraya* d'après la tr. anglaise du Révérend C. Alwis, tr. de l'anglais par M. L. de Milloué." *AMG*, vol. 1, pp. 117–38. 1880. [Tr.]

Barth, Auguste. *Bulletin des religions de l'Inde. RHR*, vols. 1–45. 1880–1902.

Barthélemy Saint-Hilaire, Jules. *Le Christianisme et le Bouddhisme.* "Trois lettres de M. Barthélemy St.-Hilaire à M. l'abbé Deschamps intitulées *Le Bouddhisme et l'apologétique chrétienne*, etc." Paris, E. Leroux, 1880. 11 pp.

Beal, (Rev.) Samuel. *The Eighteen Schools of Buddhism. IA*, vol. 9, pp. 299–302. 1880.

———. *Remarks on the Word Sramana. IA*, vol. 9, p. 122. 1880.

———. *Succession of Buddhist Patriarchs. IA*, vol. 9, pp. 148–49. 1880.

———. *The Sutra called Ngan-Shih-Niu, i.e. "Silver-White Women." IA*, vol. 9, p. 145. 1880.

———. *The Tooth-Seal of Asoka. IA*, vol. 9, p. 86. 1880.

Bendall, Cecil. *The Megha-Sûtra. JRAS*, pp. 286–311. 1880. [Ed. and Tr.]

Bunsen, Ernst von. *The Angel-Messiah of Buddhists, Essenes, and Christians.* London, Longmans, 1880. 395 pp.

Bushell, Stephen W. *The Early History of Tibet from Chinese Sources. JRAS*, p. 435. 1880.

Carpenter, Joseph Estlin. *The Obligations of the New Testament to Buddhism*, vol. 8, pp. 971–94. London, Nineteenth Century, 1880.

Cust, Robert Needham. *Les Religions et les Langues de l'Inde. BOE*, no. 29, 198 pp. Paris, Ernest Leroux, 1880.

Davids, Thomas William Rhys. *Buddhist Birth Stories, or Jataka Tales.* "The oldest collection of fokl-lore extant, being Jâtakattavannana, for the first time ed. in the original Pâli by V. Fausböll and tr. by T. W. Rhys Davids." *TOS*, vol. 1, 347 pp. London, Trübner, 1880. [Tr.]

———. *Is Life Worth Living?* "An answer from Buddha's first sermon to some questions of today. A lecture . . . 1880." *Sel. of the London Sunday Lect. Soc.*, vol. 4, 21 pp. 1880.

Doon, Moung Kyaw. *An Essay on Buddhist Law.* Rangoon, 1880. 19 pp.

Dutt, Shoshee Chunder. *India, Past and Present, with Minor Essays on Cognate Subjects.* 1880. 468 pp.

Edgar, J. Ware. *The Development of Buddhism in India. Fortnightly R.*, vol. 33, pp. 801–21. London, 1880.

Edkins, (Rev.) Joseph. *Chinese Buddhism.* "A volume of sketches, historical, descriptive, and critical." *TOS*, 453 pp. London, Trübner, 1880.

Eitel, (Rev.) Ernest John. *Feng-Shui, ou Principes de science naturelle en Chine.* "Tr. de l'anglais, par M. L. de Pilloué." *AMG*, vol. 1, pp. 203–53. 1880. [Tr.]

Feer, Henri Léon. *Bulletin critique du Bouddhisme extra-indien (Tibet et Indo-Chine). RHR*, vol. 2, pp. 363–76. 1880.

———. *Etudes bouddhiques.* Comment on devient Buddha. *JA*, ser. 7, vol. 16, pp. 486–514. 1880.

———. *Les Nouveaux Manuscrits Pâlis de la Bibliothèque nationale. Ann. de l'Extrême-Orient*, May 1880.

248   Fergusson, James. *On the Saka Samvat and Gupta Eras.* "A supplement to his paper of Indian Chronology." *JRAS,* n.s., vol. 12, pp. 259–85. 1880.

Frankfurter, Oscar. *Buddhist Nirvâna, and the Noble Eightfold Path. JRAS,* n.s., vol. 12, pp. 548–74. 1880.

Gill, William John. *The River of Golden Sand.* "The narrative of a journey through China and Eastern Tibet to Burmah. With an intr. essay by Col. H. Yule." London, Murray, 1880. 2 vols., 420, 453 pp.

Guimet, Emile. *Conférence dans le Hioun-Kakou entre la mission scientifique française et les prêtres de la secte Sin-Siou sur la religion bouddhique. AMG,* vol. 1, pp. 337–73. 1880.

Hodgson, Brian Houghton. *Miscellaneous Essays Relating to Indian Subjects.* London, Trübner, 1880. 2 vols., 407, 348 pp.

Kunte, M. M. *The Vicissitudes of Aryan Civilization in India.* "History of the Vedic and Buddhistic politics, explain. their origin, prosperity and decline." Bombay, 1880. 14 pp.

Mason, (Rev.) Francis. *Burma, Its People and Natural Productions.* Rangoon, 1880.

Morris, (Rev.) Richard. *Division of the Buddhist Scriptures. Acad.,* 21 August 1880.

——. *Report on Pali. Transac. Philol. Soc.,* part 1. 1880–81.

Müller, Friedrich Max. *Division of the Buddhist Scriptures. Acad.,* 28 August 1880.

——. *Sanskrit Texts Discovered in Japan. JRAS,* n.s., vol. 12, part 2, pp. 153–88. 1880.

——. *Vorlesungen über den Ursprung und die Entwicklung der Religion, mit besond. Rücksicht auf die Religionen des alten Indiens.* Strasbourg, 1880. 439 pp.

Nève, Félix. *Le Sacrifice personnel selon le Bouddhisme. R. catholique.* 1880.

Olcott, Henry Steele. *The Life of Buddha and Its Lessons.* Colombo, Adhyar Pamphlet, no. 15. 1880. 12 pp.

Oldenberg, Hermann. *Bemerkungen zur Pali-Grammatik. Z. f. Sprachforsch.,* n.s., vol. 5, 3. 1880.

——. *The Vinaya Pitakam.* "One of the principal Buddhist holy scriptures in the Pâli language. Ed. by Hermann Oldenberg." Vol. 2. *The Cullavagga.* "Publ. with the assistance of the Roy. Acad. of Berlin and of the Secretary of State of India in Council." London and Edinburgh, Williams and Norgate, 1880.

Oldfield, Henry Ambrose. *Sketches from Nipal, Historical and Descriptive.* "With anecdotes of the court life and wild sports of the country in the time of the Maharaja Jang Badadur GCB, to which is added an essay on Nipalese Buddhism, and illustrations of religious monuments, architecture and scenery." London, W. H. Allen, 1880. 2 vols.

Oppert, Ernst. *Ein verschlossenes Land. Reisen nach Korea.* Leipzig, F. A. Brockhaus, 1880. 313 pp.

Pischel, Richard. *The Assalâyanasuttam.* "Ed. and tr. by Richard Pischel." Chemnitz, Ernst Schmeitzner; London, Trübner, 1880. 42 pp. [Ed. and tr.]

Piton, Charles. *La Chine. Sa religion, ses mœurs, ses missions.* "Publ. par la Soc. des livres religieux de Toulouse." Toulouse, Lagarde, 1880.

Poor, Laura Elizabeth. *Sanskrit and Its Kindred Literatures. Studies in Comparative Mythology.* Boston, Robert Brothers, 1880. 468 pp.

Pornet, J. Alfred. *Le Bouddha et le Christ. Fatalité ou liberté.* Lausanne, 1880. 182 pp.

Reed, Sir Edward James. *Japan.* "Its History, Traditions and Religions. With the narrative of a visit in 1879–80." 2d ed. London, John Murray, 1880. 2 vols.

Regel, A. *Turfan. Peterm. Mitt.,* 6. 1880.

Rein, I. I. *Japan nach Reisen und Studien.* "Im Auftrage der K. Preuss. Regierung dargestellt." Leipzig, Wilh. Engelmann, 1880.

Remy, Jules. *Pèlerinage d'un curieux au monastère bouddhique de Pemmianti.* Châlons-sur-Marne, 1880. 59 pp.

Schiefner, Anton (von). *Über das Bonpo-Sûtra.* "Das weisse Nâga-Hundert-Tausend." *Mém. de*   249
   l'Acad. impér. d. Sc. de St.-Pétersbourg, ser. 7, vol. 28, no. 1, 86 pp. 1880.
Schlagintweit, Emil. *Indien in Wort und Bild.* "Eine Schilderung des indischen Kaiserreiches."
   Leipzig, Heinrich Schmidt u. Karl Günther, 1880–81. 2 vols., 202, 227 pp.
Scott, Sir James George (pseud.: Shway ou Shwe Yoe). *Buddhists and Buddhism in Burma.*
   Cornhill Mag., Nov.–Dec. 1880.
Sewell, Robert. *Note on Hiouen-Thsang's Dhanakacheka.* "With remarks by Mr Fergusson on
   this paper." *JRAS,* n.s., vol. 12, part 1, pp. 98–109. 1880.
Tagore, Sourindro Mohun. *The Ten Principal Avataras of the Hindus.* "With a short history of
   each incarnation and directions for the representation of the Murttis as tableaux vi-
   vants." Calcutta, I. C. Bose, 1880. 157 pp.
Thiessen, Jacob H. *Die Legende von Kisagotami.* "Eine literarhistor. Untersuchung." Breslau, W.
   Köbner, 1880. 70 pp.
Thomas, Edward. *Buddhist Symbols. IA,* vol. 9, pp. 135–40. May 1880.
Tomii. *Conférence entre la mission scientifique française et les prêtres de la secte Sin-siou.* "Tr. d'un livre
   japonais intitulé Notes abrégées sur les questions et les réponses. Tr. par Ymaïzoumi,
   Tomii et Yamata." *AMG,* vol. 1, pp. 335–64. 1880. [Tr.]
———. *Réponses sommaires sur les principes de la religion secte Sin-siou.* "Tr. fr. de M. Tomii." *AMG,*
   vol. 1, pp. 365–73. 1880. [Tr.]
Trenckner, V. *The Milindapanho.* "Being dialogues between King Milinda and the Buddhist
   sage Nâgasena. The Pali text ed. (with various readings and notes) by V. Trenckner."
   London, William and Norgate, 1880. 430 pp. [Ed.]
Wheeler, James Talboys. *A Short History of India and the Frontier States of Afghanistan, Nipal and*
   Burma. London, Macmillan, 1880. 730 pp.
Wurm, Paul. *Der Buddhismus, oder Der vorchristliche Versuch einer erlösenden Universal-religion. Allg.*
   Miss.-Z. Gütersloh, C. Bertelsmann, April–May–June 1880. 50 pp.
Ymaïz(o)umi (Imaïzumi), Y. *Shiddha.* "Résumé historique de la transmission des quatre
   explications données sur le Sanscrit. Tr. fr. de MM. Ymaïzoumi et Yamata." *AMG,* vol.
   1, pp. 321–33. 1880. [Tr.]

1881

Adamy, Rudolf. *Architektonik des orientalischen Altertums.* Hannover, Helwing'sche Verlags-
   buchhdl., 1881. 330 pp.
Bastian, Wilh. Adolf. *Über die Psychologie des Buddhismus. Abh. u. Vortr. d. V. Intern. Or. Kongr.,*
   vol. 2, 2, sect.4, pp. 10–12. Berlin, 1881.
Davids, Thomas William Rhys. *Buddhist Suttas,* 1: *The Mahâ-parinibbâna Suttanta;* 2: *The*
   Dhamma-kakkappavattana Sutta; 3: *Tevigga Suttanta;* 4: *The Akankeyya Sutta;* 5: *The Ketokhila*
   Sutta; 6: *The Mahâ-sudassana Suttanta;* 7: *The Sabbêsava Sutta.* "Tr. from Pâli by T. W. Rhys
   Davids." *SBE,* vol. 11, 320 pp. Oxford, Clarendon, 1881. [Tr.]
———. *Vinaya Texts.* "Tr. from the Pâli by T. W. Rhys Davids and Hermann Oldenberg." *SBE,*
   vols. 13, 17, 20; 360; 444; 444 pp. Oxford, Clarendon, 1881–85.
Fausböll, Michael Viggo. *The Sutta-Nipâta.* "A collection of discourses. Being one of the
   Canonical Books of Buddhists. Tr. from Pâli by V. Fausböll." *SBE,* vol. 10, part 2, 224
   pp. Oxford, Clarendon, 1881. [Tr.]
Jäschke, Heinrich August. *A Tibetan-English Dictionary.* "With special reference to the prevailing dialects. To which is added an English-Tibetan vocabulary. Printed and publ. by order of HM's Secretary of State for India in Council." London, Kegan Paul, 1881. 671 pp.
Lillie, Arthur. *Buddha and Early Buddhism. The World's Epochmakers.* London, Trübner, 1881.
   256 pp.

250   Müller, Friedrich Max. *Buddhist Nihilism*. "Selected Essays on Language, Mythology and Religion." Vol. 2, pp. 292–312. London, 1881.

——. *The Dhammapada*. "A collection of verses. Being one of the canonical books of the Buddhists. Tr. from Pâli by F. Max Müller." *SBE*, vol. 10, part 1, 99 pp. Oxford, Clarendon, 1881. [Tr.]

Olcott, Henry Steele. *Buddhist Catechism*. Adyar, 1881. [Tr.]

Oldenberg, Hermann. *Buddha; Sein Leben, seine Lehre, seine Gemeinde*. Berlin, W. Hertz, 1881. 459 pp.

Schlagintweit, Emil. *Le Bouddhisme au Tibet*. "Précédé d'un résumé des précédents systèmes bouddhiques dans l'Inde. Tr. de l'anglais par L. de Milloué." *AMG*, vol. 3, 292 pp., 41 pl. Lyon, 1881. [Tr.]

1882

Adams, W. H. D. *Curiosities of Superstition and Sketches of Unrevealed Religions. Incl. Buddhism, Hindu Mythology*. 1882. 328 pp.

Barth, Auguste. *The Religions of India*. "Author. tr. by Rev. J. Wood." *TOS*, 309 pp. London, Trübner, 1882. [Tr.]

Bastian, Wilh. Adolf. *Der Buddhismus in seiner Psychologie*. "Mit einer Karte des buddhistischen Weltsystems." Berlin, Ferd. Dümmlers Verlagsbuchhdl., 1882. 366 pp.

Carus, Paul. *Lieder eines Buddhisten*. Dresden, 1882. 59 pp.

Chattopâdhyayâya, Nisikânta (pseud.: "Ein Hindu"). *Buddhism and Christianity*. London, 1882. 24 pp. [Tr.]

——. *Buddhismus und Christentum. Mit einem Anhang über das Nirvana*. "Von einem Hindu." Zürich, Rudolphi u. Klemm, 1882. 32 pp.

Frankfurter, Oscar. *List of Pâli, Sinhalese and Sanskrit MSS. in the Colombo Museum, JPTS*, pp. 46–58. 1882.

Garnier, F. *De Paris au Tibet*. Paris, 1882. 422 pp.

Gough, Archibald Edward. *The Sarva-darsana-samgraha*. "Tr. by E. B. Cowell and A. E. Gough." London, 1882.

Gray, James. *First Lessons in Pali*. "Adapted for use in middle schools." 3d ed. Rangoon, 1882. 36 pp.

Humboldt (Baron). *Christ and Buddha Contrasted by an Oriental who Visited Europe*. "Extracted from a work entitled *Happiness*. With an introduction, a comparison of utterances, and a story of Christian missions by Baron Humboldt." *Leek Bijou Freethought Repr.*, no. 5. London, 1882. 114 pp. See Rydiny, *infra*.

Kellog, Samuel Henry. *The Legend of Buddha and the Life of the Christ. Bibl. Sacra*. July 1882.

Kuenen, Abraham. *Lectures on National Religions and Universal Religions*. "Hibbert Lectures for 1882." London, 1882. 339 pp.

Oldenberg, Hermann. *Buddha; His Life, His Doctrine, His Order*. "Tr. from the German by Hermann Hoey." London, William and Norgate, 1882. 455 pp. [Tr.]

Rydiny, Happiness. *A Detailed Comparison of Christianity and Buddhism*. "By a Buddhist." London, 1882. 96 pp.

Senart, Emile. *Le Mahâvastu*. "Texte sanscrit publ. pour la première fois et accompagné d'une introd. et d'un comment. par E. Senart." *Soc. As. Collection d'ouvr. or.*, Impr. nat., ser. 2. Paris, 1882. 3 vols., 633, 575, 588 pp. [Ed.]

Seydel, Rudolf. *Das Evangelium von Jesu in seinen Verhältnissen zur Buddha-Sage und Buddha-Lehre*. "Mit fortlaufender Rücksicht auf andere Religionskreise untersucht." Leipzig, Breitkopf and Härtel, 1882. 361 pp.

See Büchner, 1884.

1883   251

Bendall, Cecil. *Catalogue of the Buddhist Sanskrit Manuscripts in the University Library, Cambridge.* "With introductory notices and illustrations on the palaeography and chronology of Nepal and Bengal." Cambridge, Cambridge University Press, 1883, 225 pp.

Braunholtz, Eug. *Die erste nichtchristliche Parabel des Barlaam und Josaphat, ihre Herkunft und Verbreitung.* Diss. Berlin, Halle, Buchdr. v. Karrs, 1883. 33 pp.

Broglie, Abbé de. *Le Bouddhisme. Le Contemporain.* Sept. 1883.

———. *La Morale bouddhique. Ann. de philos. chrét.* Nov. 1883.

Clarke, James Freeman. *Affinities of Buddhism and Christianity. North American R.* May 1883.

———. *Ten Great Religions*, Part 2. *A Comparison of All Religions.* Boston, Houghton, 1883. 413 pp.

Cordier, Henri. *Essai d'une bibliographie des ouvrages publiés en Chine par les Européens au xviie et au xviiie siècle. Mél. or.*, pp. 493–546. Paris, 1883.

Cosquin, Emmanuel. *Bouddhisme et Christianisme.* Paris, Le Français, 1 Sept. 1883.

Feer, Henri Léon. *Fragments extraits du Kandjour.* "Tr. du tibétain." *AMG*, vol. 5. Paris, E. Leroux, 1883. 577 pp.

Frankfurter, Oscar. *Handbook of Pali.* "Being an elementary grammar, a chrestomathy and glossary." London, 1883. 179 pp., 4 tables of alphabets.

Happel, Julius. *Die Verwandtschaft des Buddhismus und des Christentums. Jb. f. Prot. Theol.*, vol. 9, pp. 353–421; vol. 10, pp. 49–70. 1883–84.

Hoerning. *List of Pâli MSS. in the British Museum acquired since 1883. JPTS*, pp. 133–44, 1883; pp. 108–11, 1888.

Jäschke, Heinrich August. *Tibetan Grammar.* "2 ed. Prepared by A. Wenzel." *Trübner's Coll. of Simplified Grammar*, no. 7. London, Trübner, 1883. 104 pp.

Lillie, Arthur. *The Popular Life of Buddha.* "Containing an answer to the Hibbert Lectures (by T. W. Rhys Davids) of 1881." London, Kegan Paul, 1883. 340 pp.

Monier-Williams (Sir Monier). *Religious Thought and Life in India.* "An account of the religions of the Indian peoples, based on a life's study of their literature and on personal investigations in their own country." London, 1883. 520 pp.

Olcott, Henry Steele. *Le Bouddhisme selon le canon de l'église du sud et sous forme de catéchisme.* "Tr. franç. de la 14e éd. par D.A.C." Paris, Ghio, 1883. 105 pp. [Tr.]

Prowe, Ad. *Der Buddhismus in Deutschland und England* In A. P. Sinnett, *Esoteric Buddhism*, 1883. *Mag. f. d. Lit. In- u. Ausl.*, pp. 145 ff. 8 March 1883.

Renan, Ernest. *Bouddhisme et Brahmanisme. R. polit. et litt.*, no. 214, vol. 32, pp. 57–58. July 1883.

———. *Essai sur la légende du Bouddha. JS*, p. 177. 1883.

Sinnett, Alfred Percy. *Esoteric Buddhism.* London, Trübner, 1883. 215 pp.

Treblin, Adolff. *Buddhismus und Christentum. Eine religionsgeschichtliche Studie*, Breslaw, Woywod, 1883. 24 pp.

1884

Alviella, Eugène Goblet d'. *Un catéchisme bouddhiste en français, R. de Belg.*, vol. 46, pp. 113–24. 1884. See H. S. Olcott, 1883.

Bastian, Wilh. Adolf. *Religionsphilosophische Probleme aus dem Forschunsfelde buddhistischer Psychologie und der vergleichenden Mythologie.* Berlin, A. Ascher u. Co. (ex-Behrend u. Co.), 1884. 2 div., 148 (42); 59 (52) pp.

Beal, (Rev.) Samuel. *Buddhism in China.* "Publ. under the direction of the Committee of General Literature and Education appointed by SPCK." London, *SPCK*; New York, E. and J. B. Young and Co. *Non-Christian Religious Systems.* 1884. 264 pp.

252 ———. *Si-yu-ki.* "Buddhist *Records of the Western World. Tr. from the Chinese of Hiuen-Tsiang.*" *TOS,* 2 vols., 242 pp. London, Trübner and Co., 1884.

Büchner, Ludwig. *Christus und Buddha.* In *Aus Natur und Wissenschaft,* vol. 2, pp. 409–17. Leipzig, 1884. See R. Seydel, 1882.

Feer, Henri Léon. *The Samyutta-Nikâya of the Sutta-Pitaka.* "Ed. by M. Léon Feer." London, Henry Frowde (OUP) (pour la PTS), 1884–98. Vols. 1–5 (2ff.: *Samyutta-Nikâya*), 258, 297, 291, 421, 505 pp. (Vol. 6: Index by Mrs. Rhys Davids.) [Ed.]

Foucaux, Philippe Edouard. *Le Lalita Vistara.* "*Développement des Jeux,* contenant l'histoire du Bouddha Cakya-Mouni; depuis sa naissance jusqu'à sa prédication. Tr. du sanskrit en français par Ph.Ed. Foucaux." *AMG,* vols. 6, 19; 406, 240 pp. Paris, Ernest Leroux, 1884–92. [Tr.]

Müller-(Hess), Eduard. *Simplified Grammar of the Pâli Language. Trübner's Coll. of Simplified Grammars,* no. 12. London, Trübner, 1884.

Pogor, V. *Buddhaismu, ce este si cum se capata Nirvana, Convortiri Literare.* Anul 18, no. 1, pp. 37–38. 1 Apr. 1884.

Renan, Ernest. *Nouvelles Etudes d'histoire religieuse.* Paris, 1884.

Rockhill, William Woodville. *Pratimoksha Sutra, ou le traité d'émancipation selon la version tibétaine avec notes et extraits du Dulva (Vinaya).* "Tr. par W. Woodville Rockhill." *RHR,* vol. 9, no. 1, pp. 3–26; no. 2, pp. 167–210. 1884. [Tr.]

Seydel, Rudolf. *Buddha und Christus,* Breslau. *Deutsche Bücherei,* no. 33. Schottländer, 1884. 24 pp.

———. *Die Buddha-Legende und das Leben Jesu nach den Evangelien. Erneuerte Prüfung ihres gegenseitigen Verhältnisses.* Leipzig, Otto Schultze. 1884. 83 pp.

1885

Andreozzi, Alfonso. *Il Dente di Buddha.* "Racconto estratto dalla Storia delle Spiagge (Shiu Hu Chuan) e letteralmente tradotto dal Chinese da A. Andreozzi." Milan, E. Sonzogno, 1885 (Florence, Dotti, 1883). 100 pp. [Tr.]

Ayuso, F. Garcia. *El Nirvâna buddhista en sus relaciones con otros sistemas filosoficos.* Madrid, 1885. 41 pp. (*La Ciencia cristiana,* Jan.–Feb. 1885).

Broglie, Abbé de. *Problèmes et Conclusions de l'histoire des religions.* Paris, Putois-Cretté, 1885. 420 pp.

Courtney, W. L. *Socrates, Buddha and Christ. North American R.,* vol. 140, pp. 63–77. New York, 1885.

Duka, Theodore (Tivadar). *The Life and Works of Alexander Csoma de Körös.* "A biography compiled chiefly from hitherto unpublished data; with a brief notice of each of his published works and essays, as well as of his still extant manuscripts." *TOS.* London, Trübner, 1885. 234 pp.

Foucaux, Philippe Edouard. *Un mémoire espagnol sur le Nirvana bouddhique.* "F. Garcia Ayuso. *El Nirvâna buddhista, etc.,* Madrid 1885." *RHR,* vol. 12, pp. 321–33. 1885. [Rec.]

Gogerly, (Rev.) Daniel John. *The Kristiyani Prajnapti, or Evidences and Doctrines of the Christian Religion.* "A sketch of Buddhist doctrine and its refutation." *Christ. Vernacular Education Soc.* Colombo, 1885. 105 pp.

Hartmann, Eduard von. *Philosophische Fragen der Gegenwart.* Leipzig, Wilh. Friedrich, 1885. 298 pp.

———. *Was ist Nirvana? Mag. f. d. Litt. d. In- u. Auslandes,* vol. L4, no. 1, pp. 4–6. 3 Jan. 1885.

Kellog, Samuel Henry. *The Light of Asia and the Light of the World.* "A comparison of the legend, the doctrine and ethics of the Buddha with the story, the doctrine and ethics of Christ." London, Macmillan, 1885. 390 pp.

Lee, Lionel. *The Bâlâvatârâ, a Pâli Grammar.* "With an English tr. and notes." *The Or.*, vol. 2,   253
part 3–4, pp. 71–73; part 5–6, pp. 97–98; vol. 3, part 9–10, pp. 198 *sq.*; part 11–12, pp.
210–12. 1885–90. [Ed. and tr.]

Macdonald, Frederika. *Buddhism and Mock Buddhism. Fortnightly R.*, vol. 43, pp. 701–16.
London, 1885.

Mayer, Julius. *Christliches Mönchtum und Buddhismus. Der Katholik*, vol. 65, pp. 630–41. Dec.
1885.

Mitra, Rajendrala. *Centenary Review of the As. Soc. of Bengal*, part I. *History of the Society.* 1885.

Schuré, Edouard. *Le Bouddha et sa légende. Une résurrection du Bouddha.* "E. Arnold. *The Light of
Asia*, 25th ed." *RDM*, vol. 80, pp. 589–622. 1885. [Rec.]

Sellin, A. W. *Der Buddhismus in Deutschland, Mag. f. d. Lit. d. In- u. Auslandes*, pp. 55f. 24 Jan.
1885.

Wilkinson, William Cleaver. *Edwin Arnold as Poetizer and as Paganizer.* "Containing an examination of the *Light of Asia* for its literature and for its Buddhism." New York, Funk,
1885. 177 pp.

1886

Allen, Herbert J. *Similarity between Buddhism and Early Taoism. China R.*, vol. 15, pp. 96–99.
Hong Kong, 1886.

Bartet, M. *Notice sur le Bouddha et sa doctrine à propos d'une grande statue bouddhique qui se trouve dans
les Collections de la Société de géographie de Rochefort, Bull. Soc. Géogr.*, vol. 8, pp. 266–83.
Rochefort, 1886–87.

Bose, Ram Chundra. *Buddha as a Man, Calcutta R.*, vol. 82, no. 163, pp. 65–84. Jan. 1886.

——. *Buddha as a Moralist, Calcutta R.*, vol. 83, no. 165, pp. 36–56. July 1886.

Colinet, Ph. *Ist der Buddhismus atheistisch? Allg. Osterr. Lztg.*, vol. 2, nums. 1 and 2, pp. 9–10. 1
Apr. 1886.

Elwell, L. H. *In translation, Nine Jâtakas.* "Pâli text, with vocabulary." Boston, Ginn, 1886. 118
pp. [Ed. and tr.]

Feer, Henri Léon. *E. B. Cowell and J. Eggeling.* "Catalogue of the Buddhist Skt. MSS. in the possession
of RAS"; W. W. Hunter, "Catalogue of the Skt. MSS. collected by B. H. Hodgson"; C. Bendall,
"Catalogue of the Buddhist Skt. MSS. in the Univ. Libr." JA*, ser. 8, vol. 7, pp. 88–95. 1886.
[Rec.]

Müller, Friedrich Max. *A Sanskrit Grammar for Beginners.* "New and abridged ed., accented
and transliterated throughout, with a chapter on syntax and an appendix on classical
metres, by A. A. Macdonell." London, Longmans, Green, 1886. 192 pp.

Renan, Ernest. *Studies in Religious History.* 1886. [Tr.]

Reynolds, Henry Robert. *Buddhism.* "A comparison and contrast between Buddhism and
Christianity." *Present Day Tracts*, vol. 8, ser. 2, no. 46. London, 1886. 64 pp.

1887

Ahles. *Buddhismus und Christentum, ZMkR*, vol. 2, pp. 1–20. 1887.

Alexander, Sidney Arthur, Sakya-Muni. *The Story of Buddha.* London, Newdigate Prize Poem,
Simpkin Marshall, 1887.

Benham, (Rev.) William. *The Dictionary of Religion.* "An encyclopedia of Christian and other
religious doctrines, denominations, sects, heresies, ecclesiastical terms, history, biography, etc. Ed. by the Rev. William Bentham." London, Paris, New York, and Melbourne,
Cassel and Co., 1887. 1148 pp.

Bose, Ram Chundra. *Buddha as a Philosopher, Calcuttay R.*, part 1–2, pp. 16–35, 362–80. 1887.

Bühler, Johann Georg. *Three New Edicts of Asoka. IA*, vol. 6, pp. 149–60; vol. 7, pp. 141–60.
1887, 1888.

254   Dasa, Philangri. *Swedenborg the Buddhist, or the Higher Swedenborgianism. Its Secret and Thibetan origin.* "Publ. by the Buddhistic-Swedenborgian Brotherhood." Los Angeles, 1887. 322 pp.

Dering, Edward H. *Esoteric Buddhism. The Month*, vol. 59, p. 219. London, 1887.

——. *Esoteristic Buddhism. The New Gospel of Atheism.* "Repr. and a little enl. from 2 articles in *The Month* (Febr.–Mar. 1887)." London, Washburn, 1887. 48 pp.

Forlong, James George Roche. *Through What Historical Channels Did Buddhism Influence Early Christianity? Open Court*, vol. 1, pp. 382–84, 416–18, 439–41. Chicago, 1887.

Lacaze, H. *Le Bouddhisme et le Christianisme, R. scient.*, vol. 39, pp. 272–76. 1887.

Liesching, Louis F. *Buddha and Christ, or the Light of Asia and the Light of the World.* "A lecture delivered at the National Club." Norwood, 1887. 22 pp.

Lillie, Arthur. *Buddhism in Christendom, or Jesus the Essence.* London, Kegan Paul, 1887. 410 pp.

Olcott, Henry Steele. *Ein buddhistischer Katechismus nach dem Kanon der Kirche des südlichen Indiens.* "Geprüft und zum Gebrauch f. buddh. Schulen empfohlen von H. Sumangala, dem Hohenpriester von Sripada und Galle (Ceylon). Mit den Anm. der amerik. Ausg. von E. Coues. Erste deutsche Ausg. (von Hübbe-Schleiden)." Berlin, Th. Grieben, 1887. 100 pp. [Tr.]

Sinnett, Alfred Percy. *The Buddha's Teaching. London Lodge Transac.*, no. 12. London, G. Redway, 1887.

1888

Blavatsky (ou Blavatzky), Helena Petrovna. *The Secret Doctrine.* "The synthesis of science, religion and philosophy." New York, Boston, 1888. ("2d ed., 2 vols. and separate index. Additional 3 vols. publ. by Theosophical Publ. House." London, 1897. 594 pp.)

Bühler. Johann Georg. *A New Asoka Inscription, Acad.*, 11 Feb. 1888. pp. 100ff.

Burnouf, Emile. *Le Bouddhisme en Occident. RDM*, vol. 48, pp. 340–72. 1888.

Burnouf, Emile. *The Science of Religions.* "Tr. by Jule Liebe. With a pref. by E. J. Rapson." London, Swan Sonnenschein, Lowrey, 1888. 275 pp. [Tr.]

Burrell, J. *The Religions of the World.* "An outline of the great religious systems." Philadelphia, 1888. 332 pp.

Koeber, Raph. *Buddhas Leben und Lehre, dem "Buddhistischen Katechismus" von Subhadra Bhikshu nacherzählt.* 1: *Das Leben*; 2: *Die Lehre. Sphinx*, vol. 6, pp. 320–24, 361–67. 1888.

Mitra, Rajendrala. *Ashtasâhasrikâ.* "A collection of discourses on the metaphysics of the *Mahâyâna* school of the Buddhists, now first ed. from Nepalese Sanskrit MSS." Calcutta, As. Soc., BI, 1888. 530 pp. [Ed.]

Preiss, Hermann. *Religionsgeschichte.* "Geschichte der religiösen Entwicklung des religiösen Bewusstseins in seinen einzelnen Erscheinungsformen, eine Geschichte des Menschengeistes." Leipzig, Maeder and Wahl, 1888. 548 pp.

Sinnett, Alfred Percy. *Esoteric Buddhism and the Secret Doctrine, Lucifer*, vol. 3, pp. 247–54. 1888–89.

Subhadra, Bhikschu (*i.e.* Heinrich Zimmermann). *Buddhistischer Katechisusmus.* "Zur Einführung in die Lehre des Buddha Gotamo. Nach den heil. Schr. der Südl. Buddhisten zum Gebrauche für Europäer zusammengestellt u. in Anmerk. versehen." Braunschweig, C. A. Schwetschke and Son, 1888. 88 pp. See R. Koeber, *supra*.

Trégard, L. *Le Parrain du Bouddhisme en France, M. Emile Burnouf. Lettre à un catholique, Etudes religieuses, philos., hist. et litt.*, pp. 377–95. Nov. 1888.

Trenckner, V. *The Majjhima-Nikâya.* "Ed. by V. Trenckner." Vol. 1. London, Humphrey Milford (for PTS), 1888. 573 pp. (Vols. 2–3, by R. Chalmers; index volume by Mrss Rhys Davids.) [Ed.]

Voigt, G. *Buddhismus und Christentum, Heilbronn, Zeitfragen des Christl. Volkslebens*, vol. 13. Gebr. Henninger, 1888. 45 pp.

1889

Carpenter, Joseph Esltin. *Dîgha Nikâya*. "Ed. by T. Rhys Davids and Carpenter" (vol. 3, by J. Estlin Carpenter). London, Henry Frowde (for PTS), 1889–1911. 3 vols., 261, 394, 327 pp. [Ed.]

Fausböll, Michael Viggo. *Das Sutta Nipâta*. "Eine Sammlung von Gesprächen, welche zu den kanonischen Büchern der Buddhisten gehört. Aus der engl. übers. von V. Fausböll ins Deutsche. Übertr. von Arthur Pfungst." Strasbourg, Karl J. Trübner, 1889. Vol. 1, 80 pp. [Tr.]

Fujishima, Ryauon (Ryoon). *Le Bouddhisme japonais, doctrine et histoires des douze grandes sectes bouddhiques du Japon*. Paris, Maisonneuve, 1889. 160 pp.

Glardon, Aug. *La Déconvenue de Mandalou*. "Scènes de mœurs bouddhistes." *Bibl. univ. et R. suisse*, vol. 43, 128, pp. 242–70. 1889.

Martin, (Rev.) William Alexander Parsons. *Is Buddhism a Preparation for Christianity? Chinese Recorder*, pp. 193–203. May 1889.

Monier-Williams (Sir Monier). *Buddhism, in Its Connexion with Brahmanism and Hinduism, and in Its Contrast with Christianity*. London, John Murray, 1889. 563 pp.

Subhadra, Bhikschu (i.e. Heinrich Zimmermann). *Catéchisme bouddhique, ou Introduction à la doctrine du Bouddha Gotama*. "Extrait à l'usage des Européens, des livres saints des bouddhistes du sud et annoté." *BOE*, no. 61. Paris, E. Leroux, 1889. 120 pp.

———. *De Leer van Boedhha*. "Naar de heilige Boeken van het zuidelijk Boeddhisme voor Europeanen bewerkt. Uit het Duitsch vertaald en met een Voorwoord voorzien door Mr S. van Houten." s'Gravenhage, Mouton, 1889. 101 pp. [Tr.]

1890

Arnold, Sir Edwin. *The Light of Asia*. "Tr. into Russian by A. Annenskoi, with an introd." St. Petersburg, 1890. 103, 239 pp. [Tr.]

Davids, Thomas William Rhys. *The Question of King Milinda*. "Tr. from Pâli by T. W. Rhys Davids." Oxford. *SBE*, Clarendon Pr., 1890. 2 vols., vols. 35–36, 320, 388 pp.

Green, R. F. *Christianity and Buddhism. Proc. Lit. and Philos. Soc. Liverpool*, vol. 44, pp. 299–322. 1890.

Macdonald, Kenneth Somerland. *Note on Buddha's Atheism and Nihilism*. Calcutta, 1890. 2 pp.

McKerlie, (Miss) Helen Graham. *Western Buddhism, As. Quarterly R.*, ser. 1, vol. 9, pp. 192–227. Jan.–Apr. 1890.

Mariano, Raffaele. *Buddismo e Cristianesimo: studio di religione comparata*. Napoli, Tip. d. Univ., 1890. 97 pp.

Milloué, Léon de. *Précis de l'histoire des religions. Part 1, Vol. 2. Religions de l'Inde*. AMG: Bibl. de vulgarisation. Paris, E. Leroux, 1890. 335 pp.

Minayeff, Ian Pavlovitch. *Cântideva: Bodhicaryâvatâra*. "Spasenie po uceniju pozdnejsich buddhistov." *Zap.*, vol. 4, pp. 153–228. 1890. [Ed.]

Petrenz, Otto. *Buddha und Christus (Eine Parallele), Die Kritik*, vol. 12, pp. 446–56. 1890.

Scott, Archibald. *Buddhism and Christianity. A Parallel and a Contrast. Croalle Lectures*, 1889–90. Edinburgh, Douglas, 1890. 391 pp.

Weber, Albrecht Friedrich. *Die Griechen in Indien. Sb. d. Pr. Akad. d. Wiss.*, philos.-hist. Kl., pp. 901–33. Berlin, 1890.

Primary Nineteenth-Century Philosophical Texts regarding Buddhism

A. Comte

Système de politique positive. Vol. 3, pp. 243–60. Paris, 1853.

256   **B. Constant**

De la religion considérée dans ses sources, ses formes et ses développements. Vol. 3, pp. 109–119. Paris, Béchet aîné, 1827.

V. Cousin

Cours de l'Histoire de la philosophie, p. 155. Paris, Pichon et Didier, 1829.

Histoire générale de la philosophie, depuis les temps les plus anciens jusqu'au xixe siècle, pp. 90–95. Paris, Didier, 1863.

G. W. F. Hegel

Vorlesungen über die Philosophie der Religion, 2, 1, 3, 1, ed. Lasson. Leipzig, 1927. S. W., vol. 13, 2. "Die Religion des Insichseins," pp. 119–37. New ed. Walter Jaeschke, vol. 2a. Hamburg, Felix Meiner, 1985.

Vorlesungen über die Philosophie der Weltgeschichte, Vol. 2, *Die Orientalische Welt*, ed. Lasson. "Der Buddhismus" (1822–23), pp. 411–13; "Das mongolische Prinzip" (1830), pp. 332–42. Hamburg, Felix Meiner, 1968.

F. Nietzsche

Der Antichrist, § 20–23.

Der Wille zur Macht, § 64, 220.

Die Fröhliche Wissenschaft, § 353.

Ecce Homo, § 6.

Jenseits von Gut und Böse, § 56, 262.

Zur Genealogie der Moral, 3, § 7.

Numerous occurrences in posthumous works, from the time of *Die Geburt der Tragödie* until the final pieces.

E. Quinet

Le Génie des religions, pp. 208–17. Paris, Chamerot, 1842.

E. Renan

Nouvelles Etudes d'histoire religieuse. Paris, Calmann-Lévy, 1884. "Premiers travaux sur le bouddhisme" (1851), pp. 41–130; "Nouveaux travaux sur le bouddhisme" (1862), pp. 131–66.

C. Renouvier

Philosophie analytique de l'histoire. Vol. 2, pp. 122–210; vol. 5, pp. 400–424. Paris, Ernest Leroux, 1897.

F. W. J. von Schelling

Sämtliche Werke. Vol. 12, *Philosophie der Mythologie*, chap. xx–xxii, pp. 431–520. Stüttgart, 1856–61.

A. Schopenhauer

Correspondance complète. French translation by Christian Jaedicke. Paris, Alive, 1996.

Correspondence with Adam von Doss (1856).

Die Welt als Wille und Vorstellung: numerous references scattered throughout book 4, especially § 68, as well as in the *Supplements* from 1844, revised and expanded in 1859, especially in regard to Buddhism.

Gesammelte Briefe. Ed. A. Hübscher. Bonn, Bouvier, 1987.

Parerga und Paralipomena, especially § 181–82, 189.

Über den Willen in der Natur. "Sinologie."

Posthumous manuscripts. *Der Handschriftliche Nachlass*, ed. A. Hübscher. 5 vols. Frankfort-sur-le-Main, Waldemar Kzamer, 1966–75.

H. Taine

Nouveaux Essais de critique et d'histoire, pp. 317–83. Paris, Hachette, 1865.

Other Works   257

Almond, Philip C. *The British Discovery of Buddhism*. Cambridge, Cambridge University Press, 1988.

Bareau, André. *Recherches sur la biographie du Bouddha dans les Sutrapitaka et les Vinayapitaka anciens: de la Quête de l'Eveil à la conversion de Sariputra et de Maudgalyana*. Paris, Ecole française d'Extrême-Orient, 1963.

Bear, Douglas, "Early Assumptions in Western Buddhist Studies." *Religion*, vol. 5, 2, pp. 136–59. 1975.

Benfey, Theodor. *Geschichte der Sprachwissenschaft und der orientalischen Philologie in Deutschland*. Munich, Gotta, 1861.

Bugault, Guy. *La Notion de "prajña" ou de sapience selon les perspectives du "Mahâyâna."* Paris, Institut de civilisation indienne, 1968.

——. *L'Inde pense-t-elle?*. Paris, PUF, 1994.

Cannon, Garland. *Sir William Jones: A Bibliography of Primary and Secundary Sources. Library and Information Sources in Linguistics, Amsterdam Studies in the Theory and History of Linguistic Science*. Amsterdam, John Benjamins, 1979.

Collins, Steven. *Selfless Persons: Imagery and Thought in Theravada Buddhism*. Cambridge, Cambridge University Press, 1982.

Conche, Marcel. "Nietzsche et le bouddhisme." *Cahier du Collège international de Philosophie*, no. 5. 1987.

Conze, Edward. *Thirty years of Buddhist Studies*. Oxford, Bruno Cassirer, 1967.

Das Gupta, R. K., "Schopenhauer and Indian Thought." *East and West*, n.s., vol. 13, 1, pp. 32–40. 1982.

Dharmasiri, G., "Principles and Justifications in Morals: The Buddha and Schopenhauer." *Schopenhauer Jahrbuch*, no. 53, pp. 88–92. 1972.

Frank, Bernard. *L'Intérêt pour les religions japonaises dans la France du dix-neuvième siècle et les collections d'Emile Guimet. Essais et conférences*. Collège de France. Paris, PUF, 1986.

Gérard, René. *L'Orient et la Pensée romantique allemande*. Paris, Didier, 1963.

Giard, Luce (dir.). *Les Jésuites à la Renaissance. Système éducatif et production du savoir*. Paris, PUF, 1995.

Glasenapp, Helmuth von. "Das Gottesproblem bei Schopenhauer und in den metaphysischen Systemen der Inder." *Schopenhauer Jahrbuch*, no. 28, pp. 151–98. 1941.

——. *Das Indienbild Deutscher Denker*. Stuttgart, Koeler Verlag, 1960.

Gusdorf, Georges. *Du néant à Dieu dans le savoir romantique*. Paris, Payot, 1983.

Hadot, Pierre. *Exercices spirituels et Philosophie antique*. Paris, Etudes augustiniennes, 1981. 2d ed. revised and expanded, 1987.

Halbfass, Wilhelm. *India and Europe. An Essay in Understanding*. Albany, SUNY Press, 1988. Revised and expanded version of *Indien und Europa. Perspektiven ihrer geistigen Begegnung*. Stuttgart, Schwabe, 1981.

Hecker, Max F. *Schopenhauer und die indische Philosophie*. Köln, Hübscher and Teuffel, 1897.

Hulin, Michel. *Hegel et l'Orient*. Followed by an annotated translation of an essay by Hegel on the *Bhagavad-Gîtâ*. Paris, Vrin, 1979.

——. Le Principe de l'ego dans la pensée indienne classique, la Notion d'ahamkâra. Paris, Institut de civilisation indienne, 1978.

Jong, J. W. de. "A Brief History of Buddhist Studies in Europe and America." *Eastern Buddhist*, vol. 7, 1, pp. 55–106; vol. 7, 2, pp. 49–82. 1974.

Kapani, Lakshmi. *La Notion de samskâra*. 2 vols. Paris, Publications de l'Institut de civilisation indienne, De Boccard, 1992, 1994.

258   Kishan, B. V. "Schopenhauer and Buddhism." *Schopenhauer Jahrbuch*, no. 53, pp. 185–89. 1972.

Kopf, David. *British Orientalism and the Bengal Renaissance. The Dynamics of Indian Modernization 1773–1835*. Calcutta, Mukhopadhyay, 1969.

Lacombe, Olivier. *Indianité. Etudes historiques et comparatives sur la pensée indienne*. Paris, Les Belles Lettres, 1979.

Lubac, Henri de. *La Rencontre du bouddhisme et de l'Occident*. Paris, Aubier, 1952.

Marshall, P. J. *The British Discovery of Hinduism in the Eighteenth Century*. Cambridge, Cambridge University Press, 1970.

Merkel, R. F. "Schopenhauers Indien-Lehrer." *Schopenhauer Jahrbuch*, no. 32, pp. 158–81. 1948.

Mockrauer, Franz. "Schopenhauer und Indien." *Schopenhauer Jahrbuch*, no. 15, pp. 3–26. 1928.

Murti, T. R. V. *The Central Philosophy of Buddhism. A Study of the Mâdhyamika System*. London, George Allen and Unwin, 1955.

Nichitani, Keiji. *The Self of a Coming of Nihilism*. Trans. Graham Parkes and Setsuko Aihara. Albany, SUNY Press, 1990.

Olender, Maurice. *Les Langues du Paradis. Aryens et Sémites: un couple providentiel*. Preface by Jean-Pierre Vernant. Paris, Gallimard-Le Seuil, 1989.

Peris, William. *The Western Contribution to Buddhism*. New Delhi, Motilalbanarsidass, 1973.

Poliakov, Léon. *Le Mythe aryen*. Paris, Calmann-Lévy, 1971.

Renou, Louis. *Les Maîtres de la philologie védique. Annales du Musée Guimet*, vol. 388. Paris, Librairie orientaliste Paul Geuthner, 1928.

Rhothermund, Dietmar. *The German Intellectual Quest for India*. New Delhi, Manohar, 1986.

Schwab, Raymond. *La Renaissance orientale*. Paris, Payot, 1950.

Silburn, Lilian. *Instant et Cause, le discontinu dans la pensée philosophique de l'Inde*. Paris, Vrin, 1955.

——. *Le Bouddhisme*. Paris, Fayard, 1977.

Société asiatique. *Le Livre du centenaire (1822–1922)*. Paris, Librairie orientaliste Paul Geuthner, 1922.

Stache-Rosen, Valentina. *German Indologists. Biographies of Scholars in Indian Studies Writings in German*. 2d ed., rev. Agnes Stache-Weiske. New Delhi, Max Müller Bhavan, 1990.

Vermeren, Patrice. *Victor Cousin. Le jeu de la philosophie et de l'Etat*. Paris, L'Harmattan, 1995.

Welbon, G. R. *The Buddhist Nirvâna and Its Western Interpreters*. Chicago, University of Chicago Press, 1968.

Wickremeratne, Ananda. *The Genesis of an Orientalist. Thomas William Davids Rhys, Davids and Buddhism in Sri-Lanka*. New Delhi, Motilalbanarsidass, 1984.

Willson, A. Leslie. *A Mythical Image: The Ideal of India in German Romanticism*. Durham, N.C., Duke University Press, 1964.

Windisch, E. *Geschichte des Indo-arischen Philologie und Altertumskunde*. Strasbourg, Trübner, 1917.

Young, Richard Fox. *Resistant Hinduism. Sanskrit Sources on Anti-Christian Apologetic in Early Nineteenth Century India*. Vienna, Publications of the De Nobili Research Library, vol. 8, 1981.

Zimmer, Heinrich. "Schopenhauer und Indien." *Schopenhauer Jahrbuch*, no. 25, pp. 266–73. 1938.

Material for some parts of this book first appeared in a number of different studies on related subjects already published, especially the following:

"Le bouddhisme et la philosophie du xixe siècle" [summary of a seminar held in 1986–87]. *Cahier du Collège international de Philosophie*, no. 4, pp. 182–85. Paris, Osiris, November 1987.

"Le bouddhisme et la philosophie du xixe siècle. Le cas Schopenhauer" [summary of a seminar held in 1986]. *Cahier du Collège international de Philosophie*, no. 5, pp. 152–57. Paris, Osiris, April 1988.

"Les philosophes d'hier face au bouddhisme." In *Atlas des religions*, pp. 60–61. Paris, Ed. de l'Encyclopaedia Universalis, 1988.

"Schopenhauer et le bouddhisme: une 'admirable concordance'?" In Schopenhauer, *New Essays in Honor of His 200th Birthday*, a trilingual collective volume published under the direction of M. Eric von der Luft. *Studies in German Thought and History*, vol. 10 pp. 123–38. Lewiston, Edwin Mellen Press, 1988,

"Victor Cousin, la *Bhagavad-Gîtâ* et l'ombre de Hegel." In *Purûsartha*, vol. 11, *L'Inde imaginaire*, pp. 175–95. Paris, Ed. de l'EHESS, 1988.

"Gobineau et la mort de l'humanité." *Lignes*, no. 12, pp. 82–95. December 1990.

"Cette déplorable idée de l'anéantissement. Cousin, l'Inde et le tournant bouddhique." In Victor Cousin, *Corpus*, special ed., no. 18–19, pp. 85–103. 1991.

"French Philologists and Philosophers: The Hopes of the 19th Century." In *Indo-French Relations: History and Perspectives*, pp. 137–47. Seminar Proceedings, Office of the Counsellor for Cultural, Scientific and Technical Cooperation, New Delhi, 17–19 April 1990. New Delhi, Ambassade de France, 1991.

"Une statuette tibétaine sur la cheminée." In *Présences de Schopenhauer*, under the direction of R.-P. Droit. Paris, Grasset, 1989.

"L'Inde des Grecs au xixe siècle." In *"Chercheurs de sagesse,"* pp. 691–703. *Hommage à Jean Pépin*, under the direction of Marie-Odile Goulet-Cazé. Paris, Institut d'études augustiniennes, 1992.

" 'Philosophie rapide' et longue durée." *Le Débat*, no. 72, pp. 242–48. Paris, Gallimard, November–December 1992.

"Hegel entre les Indes occidentales et les Indes orientales" [Commentaire de l'intervention de Pierre-Jean Labarrière, "Hegel et l'Amérique"]. In *Penser la rencontre de deux mondes*, under the direction of Alfredo Gomez-Müller, pp. 29–33. Paris, PUF, 1993.

"Vivekânanda entre l'Inde et l'Occident." In *Le Métis culturel*, pp. 38–54. Paris, Babel-Maison des cultures du monde, 1994.

"Comme des enfants à la poursuite des alouettes" (on the interpretation of the Buddha's silence). *Diogène*, no. 169, pp. 100–112. January–March 1995.

"Vérité et erreur dans la pensée indienne classique" [a reply to Navjyoti Singh]. In *Qu'est-ce qu'on ne sait pas?*, pp. 34–37. Paris, Gallimard, coll. "Découvertes," 1995.

"Taine et la faiblesse bouddhiste." In *L'Inde inspiratrice. Réception de l'Inde en France et en Allemagne (xixe-xxe siècle)*. Texts collected by Michel Hulin and Christine Maillard. Strasbourg, Presses universitaires de Strasbourg, 1996.

Index of Authors

Abel-Rémusat, Jean-Pierre, 19, 35, 47, 55, 85, 174 (n. 34), 176 (n. 19), 178 (n. 4), 180 (n. 51)
Al-Bîrûnî, Abû-Rayhân, 15
Almond, Philip C., 169 (n. 5), 189 (n. 30)
Amiel, Henri-Frédéric, 20, 149–51, 160
Anquetil-Duperron, A. H., 18, 171 (n. 40)
Aristotle, 48, 87
Arnold, Edwin, 157
Arrien, 169 (n. 8)

Bailly, Jean-Sylvain, 29, 31
Banier, Abbot, 64, 65
Bareau, André, 42
Barthélemy Saint-Hilaire, Jules, 14, 20, 75, 76, 87–88, 102, 119, 122–24, 125–27, 128–29, 157–58, 170 (n. 23), 172 (n. 46), 178 (n. 11), 185 (n. 13)
Beal, Samuel, 14
Bigandet, Abbot, 80–81, 179 (n. 25)
Bohlen, Peter von, 13
Brucker, Jacob, 32
Buchanan, Francis, 45–46, 47, 49, 57, 62
Bugault, Guy, 169 (n. 3)
Bulloz, 120
Burnouf, Eugène, 12, 19, 35, 56, 75–78, 81, 83, 87, 88–89, 102, 104, 122, 123, 125, 128, 134, 139
Burnouf, Jean-Louis, 76

Caro, Elmé, 151
Challemel-Lacour, Paul, 100–101
Chambers, 41
Chézy, Léonard de, 75
Childers, 14
Clément d'Alexandrie, 14
Coeurdoux, Father, 48–49, 175 (n. 5)
Colebrooke, Henry Thomas, 14, 50, 51, 57, 62, 70–71, 84, 85, 86, 127, 175 (n. 10), 180 (n. 51)
Comte, Auguste, 20

Conche, Marcel, 188 (n. 47)
Constant, Benjamin, 12, 53, 183 (n. 55)
Cora, Jean de, 15
Cosmes de Torres, Father, 17
Court de Gébelin, A., 29
Cousin, Victor, 5, 20, 76, 84–90, 122–23, 126, 179 (n. 38), 180 (nn. 51, 54, 58)
Creuzer, Friedrich, 31
Csoma de Körös, Alexandre, 19, 55, 76
Ctesias, 169 (n. 8)
Cunningham, 14
Cuvier, 49–50

Deleury, Guy, 172 (n. 42)
Deussen, Paul, 159, 190 (n. 44)
Diderot, 32, 35
Didier, Hugues, 171 (n. 32)
Diodorus of Sicily, 10–11, 169 (n. 8)
Dow, Alexander, 18
Dubois, Abbot Jean-Antoine, 175 (n. 5)
Du Halde, Father, 18

Eckstein, Baron von, 176 (n. 13)
Erigena, John Scotus, 80
Erskine, William Gugh, 51, 176 (n. 13)

Faber, George Stanley, 28, 29, 31
Faziz, Abul, 15
Feuerbach, 133
Fichte, 153
Fierens-Gevaert, H., 151–52
Filliozat, Jean, 21
Fontenay, Elisabeth de, 183 (n. 58)
Forlani, Nicolas, 14
Foucaux, Philippe Edouard, 125, 129
Foucher de Careil, Alexandre, 101–2
Franck, Adolphe, 124
Francklin, William, 32
François-Xavier, Saint, 79
Frauenstädt, 93, 94, 95, 134
Freud, 152, 188 (n. 7)